The Modernization of Inner Asia

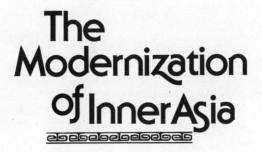

**Studies on Modernization
of the Center of International Studies
at Princeton University**

*The Modernization
of Japan and Russia* (1975)

The Modernization of China (1981)

The Modernization of Inner Asia (1991)

*The Modernization of the Ottoman Empire
and Its Afro-Asian Successors* (forthcoming)

The Modernization of Inner Asia

CYRIL E. BLACK
LOUIS DUPREE
ELIZABETH ENDICOTT-WEST
DANIEL C. MATUSZEWSKI
EDEN NABY
ARTHUR N. WALDRON

An East Gate Book

M. E. Sharpe, Inc.
Armonk, New York
London, England

An East Gate Book

Library of Congress Cataloging-in-Publication Data

The modernization of inner Asia / by Cyril E. Black . . . [et al.].
p.   cm.
Includes bibliographical references and index.
ISBN 0-87332-778-0 (c)   ISBN 0-87332-779-9 (p)
1. Asia, Central—Economic conditions.
2. Asia, Central—Social conditions.
3. Asia, Central—Politics and government.
I. Black, Cyril Edwin, 1915–
HC412.M58   1991
338.958—dc20
90-23385
CIP

Printed in the United States of America

∞

TS (c)   10   9   8   7   6   5   4   3   2   1
TS (p)   10   9   8   7   6   5   4   3   2   1

To the memory of

CYRIL EDWIN BLACK
September 10, 1915–July 19, 1989

and

LOUIS BENJAMIN DUPREE
August 23, 1925–March 21, 1989

Scholars   Coauthors   Friends

Contents

Part III   Patterns and Prospects: Inner Asia and the World

Maps

The Authors

CYRIL E. BLACK published widely in Russian and European history and was concerned as well with questions of comparative history and modernization. His *Dynamics of Modernization* (1966) stressed the pivotal role of applied science and technology in modernization and outlined the sequential transformations. Professor Black collaborated on *The Modernization of Japan and Russia* (1975) and *The Modernization of China* (1981), and as director of the Center of International Studies at Princeton University, furthered other studies on modernization. He pioneered this volume. At the time of his death in July 1989 he was professor of history and international relations emeritus at Princeton University.

LOUIS DUPREE was an anthropologist and archaeologist with a special interest in Afghanistan. After receiving a Ph.D. from Harvard University, he traveled throughout Afghanistan and conducted numerous excavations. He lectured at many universities in the United States and abroad and published extensively on the diverse disciplines of his interest; his volume *Afghanistan* (1973) is particularly well known. He will best be remembered for his commitment to the people of Afghanistan, especially during its recent period of turmoil. He died in 1989 shortly after returning from a visit to combat areas.

ELIZABETH ENDICOTT-WEST, a specialist in Yuan-dynasty history, works primarily with Chinese and Mongolian sources and has visited the Mongolian People's Republic four times, most recently to attend the Fifth International Congress of Mongolists in Ulan Bator in 1987. Her *Mongolian Rule in China: Local Administration in the Yuan Dynasty* was published in 1989. Professor Endicott-West teaches in the Department of East Asian Languages and Civilizations at Harvard University.

DANIEL C. MATUSZEWSKI is a historian and the author of studies on modernization and nationality trends in Inner Asia, as well as works on Soviet international affairs and policy in Asia. He received his Ph.D. in Russian and Turkic history from the University of Washington after extended research and travel in Moscow, Istanbul, and Central Asia. After having taught at Rutgers University, he directed the Soviet and Asian programs at the International Research and Exchanges Board for twenty years. He is currently executive director of the International Foundation in Moscow.

EDEN NABY is a specialist in the modern cultural history of the Muslim societies of Inner Asia, with particular interest in ethnic minorities, Muslim and non-Muslim, living in Soviet and Chinese Central Asia, Iran, and Afghanistan. She has traveled and worked in all these areas, beginning with Peace Corps service in Afghanistan. Her research includes extensive use of indigenous-language publications from Turkic and Iranian areas, and she has published articles about cultural and political patterns in scholarly journals. Professor Naby teaches at Harvard University.

ARTHUR N. WALDRON is a historian of China, with a special interest in comparative history, nationalism, and military questions. Trained at Harvard, he has studied in China, Japan, and the USSR, and has traveled extensively in Asia. His first book, *The Great Wall of China: From History to Myth* (1990), is published by Cambridge University Press. Professor Waldron teaches at Princeton University.

Preface

This study of the modernization of Inner Asia is the third in a series of collaborative studies of modernization conducted under the auspices of the Center of International Studies at Princeton University. The two earlier investigations resulted in two volumes: *The Modernization of Japan and Russia* (1975), by eight authors, and *The Modernization of China* (1981), by nine. A fourth volume on the modernization of the Middle East, also by nine authors, is in preparation. Support for this volume on Inner Asia came from the Ford Foundation.

The importance of Inner Asia as an example of the process of modernization lies in the way the distinctive premodern characteristics of the countries and territories of this region extend the comparative basis for understanding how diverse societies cope with the common problems of societal transformation. At the same time, however, these regions and territories are more diverse and resistant to generalization than those analyzed in the earlier volumes. Japan and Russia had powerful and effective central governments for centuries before the period of modernity. China was one of the world's oldest civilizations, and its unique political and cultural heritage played a crucial role in the modernizing transformation of the nineteenth and twentieth centuries. In all three of these major states, potent indigenous factors interacted with external influences.

Inner Asia had a far less cohesive political and cultural history, and much of its modernization was imposed from outside. Despite being the site of expansive nomadic empires for almost a millennium up until the sixteenth century, empires that had subjugated the agricultural states of Russia, China, and Persia along the periphery, Inner Asia entered the modern age in political and social disarray. Divided up among the newly dominant sedentary states they had earlier ruled, the diverse societies of the region have been subjected to comprehensive experiments of social transformation introduced from the Russian, Chinese, and British-influenced metropolises to the west, east, and south. The nexus of questions centering on the relations between nomadism, empire, nationalism, and modernization is the particular focus of this study. The intricate mix of outcomes resulting from the interaction between externally imposed programs and indigenous structures, talents, and aspirations gives Inner Asia its special place among variants of modernization.

This book is not a symposium of chapters produced by authors writing alone, but rather a collaborative product in which each of the authors contributed to all the chapters. Each author had primary responsibility for composing the initial text on specific geographic regions or themes, and all materials and drafts were discussed intensively by all the authors. Louis Dupree produced the essential materials and writing on Afghanistan; Elizabeth Endicott-West on Mongolia and Tibet; Daniel Matuszewski on the Turkic and Iranian regions of Russian and Soviet Central Asia; Eden Naby on modern Iran and on knowledge and education in Central Asia and modern Sinkiang, as well as the chronological table; and Arthur Waldron on Turkic Sinkiang and related issues and regions in China. Cyril Black drafted the introduction and conclusions as well as the interpretive sections while bearing responsibility for the overall shaping and editing of the text. Although consensus was reached on many points within the analysis, the reader will find divergence and differences of opinion among the authors, even to some extent on the validity of the presumably unifying concept of modernization itself. This is as it should be with such a complex and controversial subject. The authors offer their tentative conclusions in a pioneering spirit and trust that these differences will have a catalyzing effect on future studies.

One stylistic comment is in order. Specialists will note an eclectic quality in our choice of forms for transliterating and spelling foreign words. The unusual mix of languages and peoples across the geographic spectrum under consideration in this volume makes satisfactory transliteration of names, places, and terms extremely difficult and, ultimately, arbitrary. Our primary aim was not consistency but the readers' ease. We trust we have not offended those whose languages we are using.

This volume is quite properly dedicated to the memory of our two late colleagues, Cyril Black and Louis Dupree. Cyril Black, who died as the manuscript was in its final stages, considered our work on Inner Asia to be a crucial part of the spectrum of studies of modernization. He played an indispensable orchestrating role throughout. Without his driving commitment to the intelligent design and elaboration of this study, it would never have come into being. Louis Dupree completed his insightful work on Afghanistan before he died in March 1989. His energy, industry, and infectious enthusiasm infuse every page of this study.

We have received assistance from many sources in the course of our work.

Charles Issawi reviewed chapter 11 on economic growth, and Gilbert Rozman made detailed recommendations on chapter 12 on social integration. They as well as Carl Brown helped shape the conceptual core of our study through their frequent contact with the authors. We are indebted to V. R. Boscarino, who drew the maps for this volume, and to Richard Eisendorf and Christopher Gilman, who helped with the bibliography and glossary.

We are especially indebted to Corinne Black, who coordinated the completion of the project after her husband's death, and to our editor, Barbara Westergaard, whose remarkable editorial abilities and skillful handling of complex materials were invaluable. Nancy Dupree was of great assistance in the last months of the work, reviewing and amending final versions of the sections on Afghanistan, in spite of the complex pressures of preparation for an extended research stay in Pakistan.

We could not have produced the manuscript without the diligence of the staff of the Center of International Studies, headed by Gladys Starkey until April 30, 1989, and thereafter by Jerri Kavanagh. Particular thanks are due Patricia Zimmer for patiently guiding the manuscript through many drafts. We would also like to thank Jeffrey Perry, of the Princeton CIT Information Center, for making it possible for us to work with a diverse collection of computer files.

With the support of the Ford Foundation, the Kennan Institute for Advanced Russian Studies, and the Wilson Center, two conferences were held at the Wilson Center in Washington, D.C., in March 1987 and in April 1989, to review the structure and conclusions of the manuscript. Over sixty leading specialists from the United States and Europe participated in a constructive critique of the text at those stages. Their comments and suggestions have been invaluable in the reworking of our arguments. One name that cannot go unmentioned here is that of Paul Balaran of the Ford Foundation, whose constant encouragement and personal scholarly involvement in this field played an important role in moving the work along.

As this comparative study makes its appearance, we are aware of the extraordinary political and cultural volatility of the Inner Asian region. The Soviet reform experiments under Gorbachev, for all their positive features, have engaged a broad complex of ethnic and nationality aspirations across the entire span of Soviet republics. This has entailed a substantial degree of turmoil and unrest, in which the features of ethnicity, nationalism, and modernization have come to the fore, especially in Central Asia. China has recently undergone a major trauma after the June 1989 events in Tiananmen Square, events that are likely to have significant consequences for the elaboration of minority policy. With the death of Khomeini in Iran, the nature of the continuing Iranian revolution continues to change, with important shifts in alignment of the indigenous concepts of Islam, ethnicity, and state. The Soviet withdrawal from Afghanistan did not end the fractious civil war in that country, where patterns of tribalism and religious identity will continue to clash with notions of statehood and modernization.

In each of these areas, critical decisions are being formulated about the future shape of these societies, decisions attempting to achieve a precarious balance between the diverse indigenous traditions and aspirations of these peoples and the statist concerns of the dominant political centers at Moscow, Peking, Kabul, and Tehran. The future of these areas will be shaped by the deeper structural variables that have long been at work at the center of these societies.

The Modernization of Inner Asia

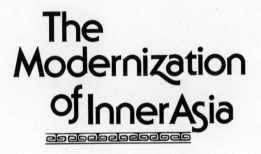

The Problem

Inner Asia and Modernization

The purpose of this study is to draw conclusions from the experience of Inner Asia as a contribution to the comparative study of modernization. Such comparative studies seek to gain a better understanding both of the common features of societal development in the modern era and of the problems faced by individual societies in adapting their diverse institutional heritages to the universal challenges of modernity. We interpret the adaptation to modern functions of the premodern heritages of institutions and values of Inner Asia on the basis of a framework that has been employed in studies of Japan and Russia, of China, and of the Middle East (C10, C11, C35). This framework includes chapters on the international context, political development, economic growth, social mobilization, and knowledge and education, for both the premodern era and the subsequent period of societal transformation. The 1920s are considered to be the dividing point between these two periods in Inner Asia, although it fell somewhat earlier in some cases and somewhat later in others. Where relevant, comparisons are made with Japan, Russia/USSR, China, and the Middle East, and with a variety of other countries as seems appropriate.

Inner Asia is defined to include the three independent states of Iran, Afghanistan, and Mongolia; the Kazakh, Kirgiz, Tajik, Turkmen, and Uzbek union republics in the Soviet Union; and the autonomous regions of Tibet and Sinkiang in China. Inner Asia so defined has an area of 4.9 million square miles and a population (in 1989) of some 135 million. A case could be made for including Inner Mongolia and Manchuria in Inner Asia, but in the course of the nineteenth and twentieth centuries these territories were almost completely settled by Chinese and became for all practical purposes an integral part of China. We make a few comparisons between the Mongols in Mongolia (formerly Outer Mongolia) and Inner Mongolia where it seems appropriate. The inclusion of Iran raises the question of whether it is sufficiently "inner" to be included with the other more isolated territories. Iran's contacts with the West have of course been continuous

3

over the centuries, and to this extent it resembles the Ottoman Empire much more than Sinkiang or Tibet. At the same time, both geographically and culturally, Iran tilts more toward the north and east than toward the south and west. The many Inner Asian empires based in Iran, and the Persian settlers who have formed an important part of the urban elites in Central Asia, have given it a major role in the history of this region. We have found Iran to be much more "in" than "out," and it serves as a useful benchmark for measuring the other societies of the region.

Despite the considerable diversity among these countries and territories, they share certain features that permit us to consider them as a distinct type of society. One way to view their commonalities is to compare them with countries at the other end of the scale of modernization. An interesting framework for such a comparison is offered by E. L. Jones's *European Miracle,* an interpretation of the preconditions of European modernization from 1400 to 1800 which has aroused much interest and received general approbation among scholars concerned with this subject. Stated very succinctly, the questions Jones seeks to answer are: "What was there about [Europe] that promoted *very* long-term economic change, as well as what thwarted change in the productive and initially promising lands of Asia?" (C22, p. 225). He is particularly impressed by the rich moist soil of Europe, suitable for agriculture; the tradition of relatively late marriage and small families, permitting more savings and investment per capita; diversified and nonoppressive political systems; and the openness of European societies, both geographically and politically, to outside influences. Jones's comparisons with Asia are limited to Islam and the Ottoman Empire, India and the Mughal empire, and China and the Ming and Manchu empires with a few remarks about Japan. The contrasts between Europe and Inner Asia, in the similarly long premodern period from the sixteenth to the twentieth century we deal with here, are even more striking than those he finds.

Environment

On a continent that has been the home of some of the world's most creative civilizations, the societies of Inner Asia have been remarkable for their limited interaction with the outside world in the period (16th to the 20th century) that we are defining as premodern.

The most obvious barriers to the outside world are represented by the series of mountain ranges that form the southern border of the region and that also divide it at various points. Starting in the west, most of Iran is a high plateau, and some four-fifths of its territory drains inland. The Elburz Mountains to the north represent a formidable barrier, and the Zagros Mountains along the southwest approach close to the Persian Gulf. The Iranian plateau continues eastward into Afghanistan, where it meets the massive Hindu Kush range that extends to the Pamirs and the Himalayas.

The southern barrier of Inner Asia continues eastward along the Himalayas, which separate Tibet from India. Eastern Tibet and Inner Mongolia are more open, and the Khingan Mountains form the natural border of Outer Mongolia on the east. These mountain ranges present a formidable obstacle to penetration from the outside, yet one should also note the important links to the south that geography has provided. Although only a fifth of Iran drains to the south, the Karun River, which flows into the Persian Gulf, forms an important link with the outside world. Much is made of Tibet's isolation, but it is important to note that the Indus, the Sutlej, and the Tsangko (the Brahmaputra in India) rivers all rise in southern Tibet; and the Salween, the Mekong, and the Yangtze rise in eastern Tibet. While Tibet's river links with India are of more geographical than historical significance, there are also important trade routes that cross the Himalayas from Shigatse and Lhasa to India.

Inner Asia is not lacking in other major rivers, but none of them provides communication with the outside world. The small rivers of northern Iran drain into the Caspian Sea, and the Amu Darya and Syr Darya flow into the Aral Sea; the Ili and numerous smaller rivers that rise in western Sinkiang flow into Lake Balkhash or into the Taklamakan desert in southern Sinkiang; and the Selenge and other rivers of northern Mongolia flow into Lake Baikal. Although these rivers can be used for navigation, the Caspian, Aral, Balkhash, and Baikal are landlocked and their waters evaporate, and the Tarim River is absorbed into the Taklamakan desert. Other rivers that rise in Russian Turkestan, such as the Ishim, the Irtysh, and the Yenisei, flow northward into the frozen lands of Siberia and are likewise without value as links to the outside world.

The relative inaccessibility of Inner Asia is not limited to these barriers. The Pamir and T'ien-shan mountains separate Russian Central Asia from Tibet and Sinkiang, and the T'ien-shan also divide Sinkiang between the Jungaria basin in the north and the Tarim basin in the south. Sinkiang is separated from Outer Mongolia by the Altai Mountains. Further obstacles to communication within the area are also represented by the major deserts characteristic of the region: the Lut and Kavir in Iran, Kyzyl Kum and Kara Kum in Soviet Central Asia, the Taklamakan in Sinkiang, and the Gobi in Mongolia.

Although these geographical features separate Inner Asia from the outside world and present obstacles to communication within the area, other geographical features have provided the basis for commercial routes and social systems that were influential far beyond the boundaries of the region in the centuries before the modern era.

The geographical attributes of Inner Asia affect the physical as well as the human environment. The southern barrier of mountains prevents moisture from reaching the region from the Indian Ocean, and the distance separating it from the Atlantic and the Pacific results in a relatively dry continental climate with limited rainfall. Moisture is provided as much by melting snows as by rain, and in many areas evaporation counterbalances precipitation.

6

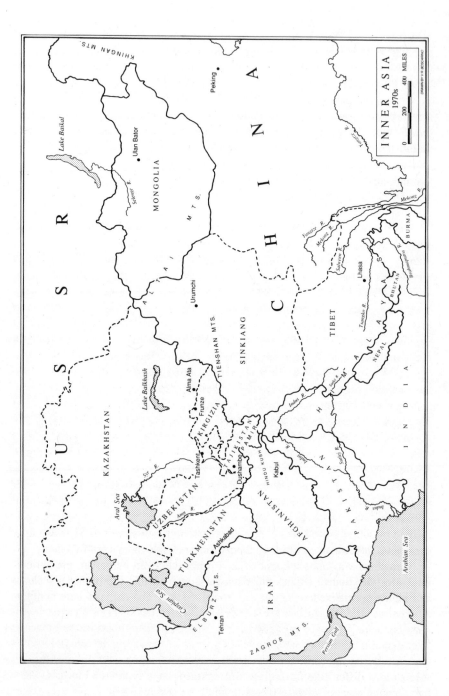

The continental climate that characterizes most of the region provides the environment for the steppe—the extensive grassland on the high plateaus from southern Russia to China. This environment is the setting for the symbiosis of pastoral nomads and settled peoples that has formed the basis of much of Inner Asian history. The settled peoples have been concerned with agriculture, and in the cities with trade, technology, and culture. The pastoral nomads have not only been preoccupied with herding and trade but have provided the political linkages that formed the great empires that from time to time unified the region and dominated neighboring territories as well.

Nomadism

Pastoral nomadism is a way of life based on the marginal areas between agricultural settlements and the deserts and mountains. Nomads live by herding, chiefly sheep and horses in Inner Asia, and move across the countryside in accordance with the seasonal availability of water and fresh grass for their livestock. This often involves migrating a thousand miles or more each year in a highly disciplined fashion. Their mobile way of life gives them little opportunity for handicrafts, and since they leave few written records our knowledge of them is derived principally from outside observers. Herding provides only part of the needs of the nomads. They drink the milk of their herds and hunt small animals. The herds are their capital, and they sell milk products, animals, and skins to the sedentary peoples on whom they depend for grain and vegetables as well as for tools and weapons.

Pastoral nomadism is thus a very specialized way of life, and one that could not function independently of the sedentary world. For much of the time this was a peaceful relationship. Pastoral nomads would normally stop and trade in settled areas in the course of their migrations. They were usually at the same cultural level as the sedentary people, and the latter likewise depended on the nomads for certain commodities. At the same time, pastoral nomads possessed a significant military potential. The males were trained from childhood to be archers and horsemen. Over the centuries their unusual mobility as mounted archers, supplemented by sabres and swords at close quarters, and their tactics of harassing their opponents rather than confronting them head-on, made them a fearful enemy.

Nomadism was once thought of as a primitive, even barbarian, pre-agricultural lifestyle. Recent studies have shown, however, that it is rather a separate and highly specialized economic and social system. The nomads were nonliterate, but they were learned in the skills required for their survival, such as veterinary medicine, biology, geography, and astronomy. They used the resources at their disposal quite efficiently, and their way of life has survived into the twentieth century. At the same time, theirs is a static existence, and the nomads one meets today differ little from those who roamed the grasslands a thousand years ago. Such new acquisitions as firearms and transistor radios may give the appear-

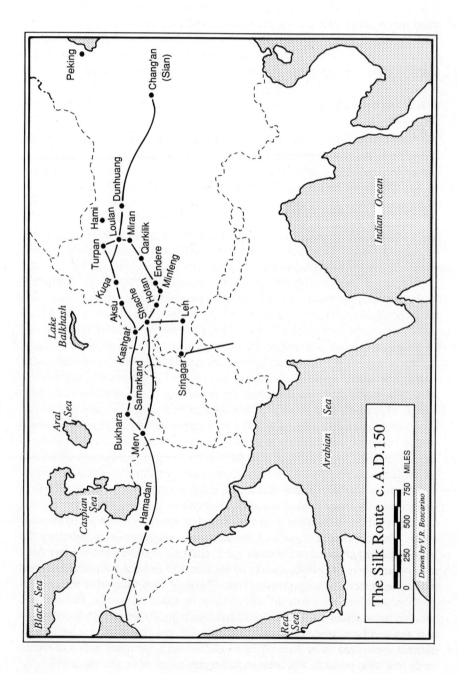

The Silk Route c. A.D.150

Drawn by V.R. Boscarino

0 250 500 750 MILES

ance of modernity, but they have not significantly changed their way of life. They are not susceptible to modernization, and they are gradually being transformed into seminomads and settlers. Yet today there are still some two million nomads or seminomads in Afghanistan, out of a population of some sixteen million, and an even larger proportion in Kazakhstan and Mongolia.

Trade and Urban Life

The isolation of Inner Asia from the more developed outside world from the sixteenth to the twentieth century was a phenomenon of its era of decline. In earlier centuries, the peoples of what we now call Inner Asia played a major role in the destinies of both Europe and East Asia, and their territories provided one of the main thoroughfares of world trade before the opening of the Atlantic sea routes in the sixteenth century. Inner Asia also played an important role as a transmitter—and at times originator—of several important technological and ideological innovations. Each successive wave or contact of culture, commerce, and conflict affected already existing political structures. Since early times this overland route had proved shorter and less exposed to pirates and brigandage than the maritime route through the Red Sea and across the Indian Ocean, and for some fifteen centuries it made Inner Asia one of the main centers of international commerce. It has been known to the modern West as the Silk Route, because of Rome's heavy demand for the highly valued Chinese fabric, but over the centuries gold and silver, woolen and linen textiles, frankincense, topaz, lapis lazuli, jade, coral, amber, and precious stones were also transported across this route. The commerce was conducted by camel and horse caravans working in relays, organized by Mongols at the eastern end and by Arabs and others in Central Asia and further west. The caravansaries were located some ten to twelve hours of travel apart, stretching across some five thousand miles. In the mid-thirteenth century Marco Polo took this route to Cathay, as China was then called, returning to Venice by sea some forty years later.

The influence of pastoral nomadism is so great that one is in danger of overlooking the more modest but significant role of the agriculture-based cities. The city-states of early Inner Asia were based on the control and use of land and water. The centralized control of the land and water resources necessary for large-scale irrigation led to a vicious cycle, still true in some parts of Inner Asia: massive numbers of people, mobilized by a central or local authority, built and maintained extensive irrigation systems. These, in turn, supported the concentrated populations who paid tribute or taxes to those in control. But the area suitable for irrigated crops was finite, and barely produced enough food to support the numbers needed to build and maintain the irrigation systems. These patterns dominated Inner Asia where available water combined with technology made irrigation possible, a process repeated generation after generation.

Always waiting in the wings—the mountains, steppes, and deserts—were the "barbarian" nomads and seminomads. These borderland peoples, usually in ferment, seized power from the city folk time after time, only to find themselves entrapped culturally and politically by those whom they had conquered. After an initial renewed vigor from the mixture of the nomad and settled, another cycle of conquest would descend from the hills to the plains.

Empires

Much of the political history of Inner Asia is a history of "empires." One is inclined to put this term in quotation marks, because these structures are so different from those that have gone by the same name in the eastern Mediterranean and in Europe. These empires were all initiated by pastoral nomads.

Nomads usually lack formal organization much above the herding group of a few families. Nomadic communities form states only occasionally, and when they do their states are weaker and shorter-lived than those in settled areas. When considering the nature of Inner Asian states, certain factors should be borne in mind.

First, the primacy of the military. Until the nineteenth century, even small numbers of nomads usually enjoyed military superiority over settled peoples. The skills fostered in nomads by their peacetime ways of life were also the keys to premodern warfare—nomads were masters of horsemanship and archery; peasant farmers were not—and the economic and political units fostered by their way of life were easily adaptable to military units.

Two sorts of processes led these skilled fighters to form states in the premodern period. One was based on religion. Tibetan Buddhism provided a cement of sorts to traditional Mongolian society; the Sufi orders performed a similar role among Inner Asian Turks. Tibetan Buddhism (unlike Indian or Chinese forms) had a clear ranking of spiritual leaders and provision for orderly succession to key positions, and as a hierarchical religion, lent itself to state-building.

The other process was based on military leadership. The nomadic economy is not self-sufficient, and nomadic peoples must trade with settled areas to obtain such necessities as grain and metals. In the settled world, indigenous leaders formed states in order to gather an indigenous surplus. In the nomadic world, military leaders, whether indigenous or not, helped bring into being states whose primary purpose was securing, usually by force or the threat of force, some share of the wealth of settled areas. These leaders founded dynasties. States formed by these means lack the kind of social cohesiveness characteristic of modern national states which draw ultimately on the deeply rooted sense of shared identity that settled agriculture produces. Stable proto-nation-states were largely absent.

The key to Inner Asian politics in traditional times was the empire builder. A repeated pattern saw an individual use military prowess to attain leadership of a tribe, and make his tribe the leading group in a confederation that would then conquer sedentary areas. Chinggis is perhaps the best example. The unity of such empires was always precarious. Succession struggles in which the leader's sons and brothers battled one another for his position typically split the families apart fairly fast. And once the ruling house was split, little remained.

In the western territories of Inner Asia, one can trace the succession of no-madic empires from the Cimmerians and the Scythians before the Christian era to the Durrani empire in the eighteenth century. Although the western and east-ern territories of Inner Asia were linked by trade throughout this period, their political development took a separate course. The central theme of the eastern territories was the interplay between the Chinese and the nomadic tribes pressing on their borders. The Hsiung-nu empire (200 B.C.–A.D. 370), formed by pastoral nomads and centered in what is now Mongolia, was the first major challenge to the Chinese. Later challenges came from the Juan-juans, the Turks, the Uighurs, the Kirgiz, and the Khitans in a constant ebb and flow of tribes and political systems. These successive nomadic conquerors limited their activity primarily to China's northwest boundary, which the Chinese defended behind the Great Wall.

The western and eastern territories of Inner Asia were politically united for the first and last time by the great Mongolian empire, the disintegration of which marked the end of nomadic empire building and commerce. The decline of Inner Asia coincided with, and was to a large extent caused by, the historic change from a continental to a maritime orientation in international commerce. The sea routes developed after the discoveries of Columbus soon drew commerce away from the age-old caravan routes from China to Europe, and Inner Asia gradually lost the basis for its former historic role.

The Mongolian empire was one of the greatest achievements of nomadic statehood and one of the last major efforts of the pastoral nomads to dominate the sedentary peoples. During its period of greatest influence Mongolian rule extended from Russia to China, and threatened Hungary in the West and Japan and Java in the East. This was an empire of a special type, however, for it lacked the unity that one normally associates with imperial rule. In the West, the Mongols did not seek direct rule over the Kievan principalities and Lithuania, but were satisfied with extracting tribute from them. Moscow in fact continued to pay tribute to Tatar heirs of the Mongols until 1480. But in the meantime war-ring Tatar factions sought alliances with the various Russian principalities among which Moscow was becoming predominant, and this soon diluted their influence.

In China, the Mongols founded the ruling Yuan dynasty (1260–1368), retain-ing many aspects of their Inner Asian culture up to the fall of the dynasty. In Central Asia, the Mongols retained their nomadic institutions and developed a symbiotic relationship with the Iranian urban peoples who contributed their ad-ministrative, technical, and commercial skills. Similarly from a cultural stand-point, the traditional shamanism of the Mongols gave way to Islam in the west and to Buddhism in the east.

An empire that was so loosely constructed was not very stable, and in the

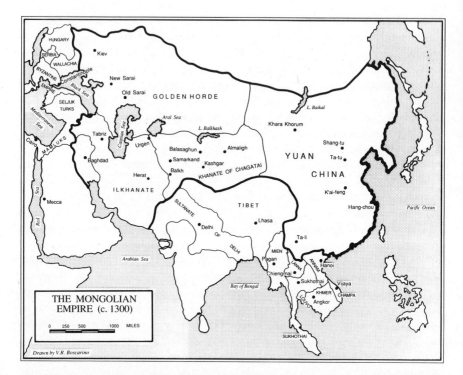

THE MONGOLIAN
EMPIRE (c. 1300)

0   250   500   1000   MILES

Drawn by V.R. Boscarino

course of the fourteenth and fifteenth centuries conflicts among Mongolian factions and the reassertion of local sovereignties contributed to the political disintegration of Inner Asia. Henceforth, until the intrusion of Russia, Britain, and
China in the nineteenth century, Inner Asia was in a state of inertia and even
decadence. It is with this period of four hundred years, from the sixteenth to the
twentieth century, that Part I of this study is concerned.

Ethnicity and Culture

The succession of empires in Inner Asia was accompanied by constant human
migration, which has led to an unusually complex mixture of peoples and faiths.
Multi-ethnicity throughout the region has provided for a rich and diversified
cultural heritage, at the same time complicating political development. Multi-
ethnicity exists not just in the region as a whole but within each of its political
subdivisions, continuing throughout the premodern and modern periods as it had
before. Just as in medieval Europe the chief reason for multi-ethnicity lay in the
movement of tribes and peoples, generally from the north and east toward the
south and west, so too in Inner Asia, Iranian, then Turkic migrations have reshaped ethnicity patterns. The exceptions in the premodern period to influence
from Turkic migrations are Mongolia and Tibet. Here as in other parts of Inner

Asia subjected to colonialism or neocolonialism, however, the immigration of representatives of colonial states, China and Russia, has contributed to multi-ethnicity.

The spread of the Turkic peoples, more fully documented than that of the earlier Iranian peoples, began in the sixth century. The last major impact of Turkic movement came with the migration of the Moghuls from Central Asia, through Afghanistan, into India during the sixteenth century. This spread of Turkic peoples resulted in an interlacing, but rarely assimilation, of Turkic groups with those already settled in the region.

Language preservation is the single most prominent feature of ethnicity in this area. Because of the necessity for interaction among the various ethnic groups, however, bilingualism and even multilingualism was common among urbanites, traders, and administrative officers. Use of several languages did not imply assimilation or loss of identity. Bilingualism was most common among Turkic and Iranian settled peoples, more often among men than women. Many men could converse in a dialect of both Persian and Turkic without being literate in either. The pattern was most often that the minority population spoke the language of the majority: thus Azeris in Persian-dominated Iran used Persian as well, while Tajiks in Uzbek-dominated Bukhara knew Turki. In much of the settled part of Inner Asia that lay in the Irano-Turkic sphere, Persian maintained additional status as the language of culture and trade. During the premodern period the Sarts represent that rare instance when a group identity was anchored not in language but in occupation or genealogical origin. The exclusive use of Persian by urban Turkic groups in Iran and urban Pushtuns in Afghanistan represents the modern manifestation of this phenomenon.

The geographical features of Inner Asia have contributed to the continuation of multi-ethnicity rather than to widespread assimilation and amalgamation. Mountains, deserts, and the oases settlement patterns together with pastoral economies have combined to foster separation of peoples who had few needs for integrative activities. Urban settlements were sparse and served as nominal seats of government and trade. Rural rather than urban settlement patterns predominated among sedentary peoples. The nomadic lifestyle, by its very nature, necessitated the preservation of kin relationships that precluded assimilation into other settings and groups. Colonial garrisons, railroad depots, and single-ethnic rural settlements continued the previous pattern of ethnic separation through to the modern period when urban centers gained in prominence. It is significant, however, that during the premodern period, urban settlements divided into ethnic quarters.

Alongside diverse ethnic identities there existed religious identities that often overcame ethnic heterogeneity. Islam, Buddhism, and shamanism compose the major religions of the area with minority pockets of Christianity, Judaism, Zoroastrianism, and Hinduism. The impact of religion on the peoples of this area can hardly be overstated, particularly in the premodern era. On the level of statecraft, law, education, commerce, and family life, the religions as practiced in the area exercised quantitative as well as qualitative authority.

In family life especially, the peoples of this region have clung to the agrarian tradition of having many children. In the Soviet Union today, for example, the birth rate of the Muslim population is four times that of the rest of the population. This custom, which has religious sanction, is usually attributed to considerations of social security. The more children, the better will the parents be taken care of in old age. But this practice also has economic consequences. A large number of children reduces a family's savings per capita, and impedes economic growth.

Islamic armies, which swept across Inner Asia in the seventh century, laid the basis for the spread of Islam. The most widely practiced religion of the area, it provides the framework for an individual's private and public life. Prior to the establishment of Shi'ite Islam as the state religion of Iran in 1502, Sunnite Islam had provided an umbrella of unity to the entire Muslim part of Inner Asia. In confrontation with Russia, with India, and with China, Muslim Inner Asia could and did rally around religion as a unifying force for defensive or offensive purposes. On the other hand, the divisions within Islam sometimes led to bloodshed on both the state and individual levels. In the sixteenth century Uzbek and Iranian competition for control of Transcaspia and Transoxiana was garbed in the hues of Sunnite-Shi'ite conflict; Pushtun enslavement of Hazaras was justified by the Sunnite perception of Shi'ite as heterodox. These examples may be seen replicated with some frequency in the premodern period.

As an integrative social factor, Islam served to bring together the diverse ethnic groups of the area. The effect of Islam on the formation of elites is particularly significant for understanding the modernization process. The Islamic system of education, consisting of *maktab* and *madrasa,* provided the primary institutions for literacy and intellectual achievement. The state bureaucracies came out of this system as did the judiciary, the poets, historians, scientists, educators, and religious leaders. By allowing accommodation to local custom when not in direct contradiction to traditional Islam, this religion coexisted with ethnic diversity among peoples as different as the nomadic Kazakhs and the Bukharan clerics. Sunni Islam in particular also accommodated mysticism better than Shi'ite Islam; and the Islamic mystic orders, the Sufi *tariqa* (pl. *turuq*) provided paths to cross-ethnic integration and mobilization that are especially important in the premodern period.

As the premodern period came to a close, unity under Islam, expressed in political terms such as pan-Islamism, came into conflict with politicized ethnicity expressed in terms such as pan-Turkism, pan-Turanism, pan-Iranianism. The onset of political ethnicity, or nationalism, led to the submergence of religion as a political factor, but it did not spell the end to the role of religion in shaping a response to modernization.

Similarly in Mongolia, where Buddhism had reigned strong since the late sixteenth century, pan-Buddhist and pan-Mongolian movements gained momentum in the 1920s and 1930s, mainly as reactions to the perceived threat posed by the Russian revolution and as a part of longstanding anti-Chinese nationalism. Because the pan-Buddhist movement was heavily supported by the Japanese in Inner Mongolia, the Buddhist church, already under attack by Soviet-backed antireligion campaigns in Outer Mongolia, was further damaged, since the motivation behind Japanese support was primarily territorial aggrandizement. Unlike Islam in Central Asia, Buddhism in Mongolia failed to recover from this period of tribulation, and played a far less significant role in the process of modernization in eastern Inner Asia.

Great Games

After some three centuries of relative isolation and stagnation, the countries and territories comprising Inner Asia became a central issue of world politics as a borderland between the competing security interests of the great powers. The reemergence of Inner Asia as a factor in world politics was in turn closely related to the processes of modernization initiated in this period.

The competition for western Asia—known to British policy makers as the "Great Game"—had its origin in the discussions Emperors Paul and Alexander I had with Napoleon about a possible Russian invasion of India. The perceived threat to British India, principally from Russia but also from Iran and Afghanistan, remained a continuing British concern throughout the nineteenth century. Concurrently, the rivalries of Japan, China, and Russia in eastern Asia—primarily over Manchuria and Korea—developed into another Great Game which became linked to the competition in western Asia.

The Anglo-Russian rivalry in western Asia became one of the central issues of European diplomacy in the nineteenth century. From the Russian point of view, the conquest of the peoples of Central Asia was essentially a defensive operation. Its major purpose was to protect Russian trade and economic development from the disruptions caused by the unruly Turkic tribes, but Russia was also under pressure from land-hungry peasants seeking to settle in this area. Despite occasional unofficial plans proposed by the Russian military for the invasion of British India, the ambitions of the Russian government were strictly limited. In discussions with the British, Gorchakov referred to Russia's "oeuvre civilisatrice" in Central Asia—the nineteenth-century term for technical assistance or "modernization"—and compared it with Britain's role in India. This begged the question of who was going to civilize whom, and the borderline peoples of Iran, Afghanistan, and peripherally Tibet became the main issues of controversy.

From the British point of view, defense of British India was the central issue, and the Russian conquest of Central Asia was seen as the major and compelling threat. Britain sought to stem the Russian tide chiefly through gaining control over Iran and Afghanistan, and keeping a sharp eye on the possibility of Russian influence in Tibet. In the latter part of the nineteenth century Britain gradually came to acknowledge the limited aims of the Russians, and moved from confrontation to compromise.

About the turn of the century, the Great Game began to be affected by the geographer Halford Mackinder's theory, enunciated in 1904, to the effect that "the geographical pivot of history was moving from sea power to land power." This theory, based on the view that men and machinery could be moved more rapidly and inexpensively by railroads than by ships, implied that the end of the British hegemony based on sea power was in sight, and that the advantage would henceforth be held by the "heartland"—Russia. There was considerable discussion of Mackinder's views among geographers and in the British press. It was noted by some that his article was published just six months after the first successful flight of the Wright brothers in North Carolina—although it was a decade before air power began to become a factor in the railroad-sea power equation. There is no evidence that the Russians paid any attention to Mackinder's views.

In eastern Asia the expansion of the Russians across Siberia was perceived to threaten Chinese as well as British interests, and the focus of the threat was in Manchuria. As a defensive measure, the Manchus heading the declining Ch'ing dynasty encouraged the migration of Han Chinese into Manchuria to the extent that today the population of one hundred million is overwhelmingly Chinese. The Manchus also ceded to Russia all territory beyond the Amur and Ussuri rivers (treaties of 1858 and on maps 1860). In addition, the Russians obtained the rights to build a railroad across Manchuria, a connecting line to the Liaotung Peninsula, and a naval base at Port Arthur. Japan, threatened by Russia's proximity, attacked Port Arthur in 1904 and destroyed the fleet sent to defend it. In the 1905 settlement, Japan gained Russia's rights to Manchuria. Two years later, Japan and Russia signed a treaty agreeing to separate spheres of influence in Manchuria and Korea—partly to counter threats of investments by American entrepreneurs.

This Japanese-Russian agreement of 1907 on spheres of influence was part of a general series of compromises, in the course of which Inner Asia ceased to become a major center of international conflict. The most important of these compromises was the Anglo-Russian agreement of 1907, which provided for the territorial integrity of Tibet as a buffer, under the suzerainty of China; Russian acceptance of Afghanistan as a British sphere of influence; and the division of Persia into three regions. To quote a leading authority (A8, p. 220):

> The northern and largest region, bordering on Russia and comprising the richest and most populous parts of Persia, was to be a Russian sphere of influence, in which Great Britain would not seek for itself, or any third Power, any concessions of a political or commercial nature. The southern region, largely barren desert but containing roads leading to India was in like manner

to be a British sphere, in which Russia would seek no concessions. Between these two lay a central neutral region, including the head of the Persian Gulf, in which neither was to seek concessions except in consultation with the other. In all this the Shah was not consulted in the least.

Related to these two major compromises were the Anglo-Afghan agreement of 1893 defining the frontier between Afghanistan and British India (the Durand Line); the Anglo-Japanese treaty of 1902; and the Franco-Japanese treaty of 1907.

By the turn of the century security problems in other parts of the world—the European developments leading to the First World War—had reduced the role of Inner Asia as a center of international conflict. The various compromises relating to Inner Asia at the turn of the century freed England, France, and Russia to cooperate against the main perceived threats to their security—Germany and Austria-Hungary.

The Great Game concept was revived after World War II in relation to the American-Soviet competition for influence in Afghanistan and the Chinese-Soviet rivalry in Sinkiang and Mongolia. Once again the competition ended in compromise, as China, the USSR, and the United States came to realize that domestic change and budgetary constraints limited their ability to wield influence in Inner Asia.

Inner Asia and Europe

To return briefly to the theme of "the European miracle," it seems clear that Inner Asia lacked all of the preconditions that account for Europe's prosperity and possessed all the factors that thwarted change in Asia. The soil was not conducive to agriculture, and required extensive artificial irrigation. The region was to a large extent cut off by geography from the more developed areas of the world. Savings per capita, the key to Jones's argument, were impeded not only by early marriage and large families, and in Tibet and Mongolia by the practice of encouraging many men to become priests; but also by the political oppression of empires more interested in plunder than in promoting growth; and by an inward-looking clergy who feared new ideas and was ignorant of the progressive role its faiths had played in earlier centuries. Despite these handicaps, Inner Asia enjoyed a degree of passive prosperity so long as the trade routes between China and Europe remained active. When these declined in competition with the newly discovered ocean trade routes, the peoples of Inner Asia gradually lost regular contact with the outside world until foreign settlers (and pilgrims) reintroduced it in the nineteenth century.

Modernization

Modernization studies as an approach to the comparative analysis of societal development are concerned with the process by which societies have been and are being transformed under the impact of the scientific and technological revolution.

The concept of "modernization" embraces a considerable range of interpretations of human development, but these views share certain assumptions that give the term a distinctive meaning and at the same time distinguish it from other conceptions. Three factors are particularly relevant to the concept of modernization: the role of the advancement of knowledge, as reflected mainly in the scientific and technological revolution, as the primary source of change that distinguishes the modern era from earlier eras; the capacity of a society in political, economic, and social terms to take advantage of the possibilities for development offered by the advancement of knowledge; and the utility of various policies that the political leaders of a society may follow in seeking both to convert its heritage of values and institutions to modern requirements and to borrow selectively from more modern societies.

This societal transformation is usually conceptualized in terms of a transition from traditional to modern ways of life. The "traditional" differs in each society, although it has many common features. The "modern" is more uniform in function, despite continuing structural differences based on the differing institutional heritages. The attributes of modernity have been succinctly described in the following terms (C36, pp. 3–4):

> "Modernity" assumes that local ties and parochial perspectives give way to universal commitments and cosmopolitan attitudes; that the truths of utility, calculation, and science take precedence over those of the emotions, the sacred, and the non-rational; that the individual rather than the group be the primary unit of society and politics; that the associations in which men live and work be based on choice not birth; that mastery rather than fatalism orient their attitude toward the material and human environment; that identity be chosen and achieved, not ascribed and affirmed; that work be separated from family, residence, and community in bureaucratic organizations; that manhood be delayed while youth prepares for its tasks and responsibilities; that age, even when it is prolonged, surrender much of its authority to youth and men some of theirs to women; that mankind cease to live as races apart by recognizing in society and politics its common humanity; that government cease to be a manifestation of powers beyond man and out of the reach of ordinary men by basing itself on participation, consent, and public accountability.

Most interpretations of the process of modernization stress the differences in the institutional heritage of the Western and other societies, and assume that the latter are likely to retain many distinctive characteristics long after they have undergone modernizing transformations. It would follow from this view that not just Western institutions but those of other societies as well can be adapted in varying degrees to the requirements of modernity. The problem of the later-developing societies is not to discard their institutions in favor of those borrowed from the West, but rather to evaluate their institutional heritage and decide to what extent it can be converted to the requirements of the modern era.

The diverse later-developing societies should be studied for their own interest, and not simply in terms of their relationship to the influence of more developed societies. To say this is not to say that such outside influences are not a significant force, but rather that they are secondary to the conversion that the native institutional heritage of these societies must undergo.

One important contribution of the concept of modernization to the interpretation of societal development—as compared with the approaches of liberalism, Marxism, or Marxism-Leninism—is that modernization studies place more emphasis on the behavioral and social sciences and less on Western or other models. Modernization studies are more concerned with process than with goals.

Seen in historical perspective, modernization is a transformation of the human condition no less fundamental than that which took place some eight or ten thousand years ago from hunting and gathering to agriculture and the formation of civilized societies. As with this earlier transformation, its motivating force is a heightened human understanding of the natural environment and a markedly increased ability to make use of it for human ends.

Modernization is a continuous process, reflecting the influences on all aspects of human activity of a rapidly increasing ability to harness nature for the furtherance of human goals. Any division of such a process into stages or periods is, of course, artificial, and numerous schemes of periodization can be developed that are valid for a variety of purposes. We employ here the simplest possible periodization, which stresses the difference between traditional societies before thoroughgoing modernization has been undertaken, and the process of transformation once the leaders of a society have decided to adapt their existing institutions and values to modern functions. The problems relating to the initial confrontation of tradition and modernity are the subject of Part I of this study, which is concerned with the period from the sixteenth to the twentieth century. The questions one usually asks about the capacity of a society to make this transition are set forth in chapter 1. Part II, in turn, is concerned with the problems of modernizing transformation in the twentieth century, and these are introduced in chapter 8. One can also envisage a stage of advanced modernization, when many of the processes of change reach a logical conclusion, and a related trend toward international integration. Many societies are concerned with these problems today, but it will be many decades before the societies of Inner Asia will be confronted by these challenges.

The study of the process of change in the modern era must be set in a framework that is both global and multidisciplinary. The comparative study of modernization starts with the observation that unprecedented changes have taken place in the modern era in the advancement of knowledge, political development, economic growth, social mobilization, and individual change. We seek to understand these changes, to evaluate the results of different policies of change in the various societies of the world, to study the assets and liabilities brought to the process of change by their differing institutional heritages. It is an approach that seeks to reduce ethnocentric bias through the application of the comparative method, and does not assume that any of the patterns of policy currently predominant in the advanced societies are necessarily applicable to other societies or are themselves immune to drastic change.

In this study we adopt a multidisciplinary approach to the special needs of later-modernizing societies, as set forth in chapters 2–6 and 9–13. We lead off with the international context, because these societies confronted the challenge of modern knowledge not through domestic developments but through contacts with more advanced societies. The chapters on the political, economic, and social dimensions, and on the advancement of knowledge, are intended together to embrace all aspects of societal transformation. The introduction to each chapter seeks to establish the significance of each particular aspect for the larger picture.

The one aspect not treated is individual change. The personalities of individuals result from the interaction of biological characteristics with the social environment—the family, the community, and the larger society with which the individual comes into contact. It is generally agreed that the personalities of individuals brought up in advanced societies differ significantly from those raised in traditional villages. There have regrettably been few studies of this aspect of modern change, certainly none dealing with the diverse personality types of Inner Asia, and it seems better to neglect the subject than to attempt to make general statements about it based on ignorance.

One further observation is in order before we leave this subject. "Modernization" should not be seen as synonymous with "progress." Certainly many features of modernity are progressive in the sense of improvements in per capita productivity, and in health and welfare. Individuals in advanced societies are better off in the conventional sense of the term than those in poor countries. It should not be forgotten, however, that the essence of modern change is the increased control of human beings over their environment. This increased control can be used as easily to destroy civilization as to improve the human lot. It remains to be seen how humankind will use its awesome power.

I

The Premodern Heritage

(to the 1920s)

1

Introduction

In Part I (chapters 1–7) of this study we are concerned with the bearing of the premodern heritage of the societies of Inner Asia on their capacity to modernize in the twentieth century. More specifically, we are asking which aspects of the traditional heritage were assets to future change and which were liabilities. Which traditional structures were readily convertible to modern functions? Which requisites of modernity were so lacking in the heritage that adoption of foreign institutions rather than the adaptation of traditional ones proved to be necessary?

A framework for answering questions such as these, supplementing the brief introduction to problems of comparative modernization set forth in the opening pages ("The Problem: Inner Asia and Modernization"), may be drawn from the studies of modernization of Japan, Russia, China, and the Ottoman Empire, which are forerunners of this study of Inner Asia, as well as from the general literature on the subject. In effect, we are setting forth the characteristic attributes of relatively modernized societies, and seeking to determine the extent to which the institutions and values of selected premodern societies are adaptable to these modern functions.

Since later-modernizing societies of necessity confront the problems of societal transformation in a context of more advanced societies, the first set of questions we ask deals with their capacity to operate in this environment. Do the societies of Inner Asia have a sense of national identity adequate to sustain their cohesion in a period of domestic and international strife? Have they experienced a reasonable stability of population and integrity of territory and boundaries? Have their political systems developed a capacity for social engineering such as is involved in regulating systems of land tenure and administering communications and public works?

The ultimate test of a society with a firm sense of national identity and an effective political system is its capacity to defend itself against colonization. Such a capacity depends on the recognition of the need to adapt traditional institutions to new functions and to borrow from more advanced societies without significant loss of national identity. Although many societies meet the initial challenge of the scientific and technological revolution by borrowing advanced institutions for the purpose of defending the traditional system—Peter the Great borrowed foreign military technology, but strengthened serfdom—this is as likely to impede as to further later efforts at modernization.

A second set of questions concerns the political structure of a traditional society. Do the dominant interest groups accept the leading role of the central political authorities? Does service to the state have a high priority for traditional elites? Does the government have the capacity to mobilize and allocate skills and resources on a regional and national basis? What experience does the bureaucracy have in administering political structures extending from the national to the local level? Do mechanisms exist for communication between the central government and the variety of local and regional corporate interest groups that characterize most societies?

As regards the economy of premodern societies, one wishes to know whether the political system had the capacity to mobilize resources for central purposes, and to pursue economic policies favorable to growth. Did agriculture produce a surplus? Were raw material resources exploited? Were handicrafts and manufacturing at a level sufficient to provide a basis for the development of modern industry? Had a groundwork been laid in such services as communications and transportation, local and regional markets, and financial institutions that might be adapted to modern needs?

A fourth set of questions concerns the premodern level of social integration— the interdependence of individuals and organizations welding families, villages, and regions into a functioning society. More specifically, was a significant share of the population located in towns and cities? Was occupational stratification developed to provide skills for management, manufacturing, and administration? Had the demographic cycle evolved beyond the typical premodern pattern of high birth and high death rates? To what extent did administrative, religious, and economic organizations provide a bridge between the primary family and kinship loyalties and the larger society?

Finally, in the realm of knowledge and education, we wish to understand the nature of premodern world views—the traditional interpretations of the physical and human environment—and the problems faced by premodern societies in adapting to modern knowledge as it has evolved since the revolution in science and technology. Is the premodern society inward looking, in the sense that its culture assumes that it has the ultimate truths and that all other views are by definition heretical? Or is it outward looking as a result of experiences in borrowing from and interaction with other cultures before the modern era? How does a premodern society become acquainted with modern knowledge? To what extent and in what ways is the traditional culture a barrier to the acceptance of modern knowledge? What efforts are made to translate foreign books? Were the elites introduced to modern knowledge from within through a reform of native education, or from without by colonizers or by missionaries? Did the traditional culture include libraries and the publication of books and periodicals? Did they have schools for commoners, and what did these schools teach?

2

International Context

Introduction

All societies face in due course the challenge of adapting traditional institutions and values to modern functions, and the process normally involves a struggle within each society between traditional and modernizing leaders. The nature of this struggle depends to a very significant degree on the international context of a given society: whether policies of modernization are undertaken relatively early or relatively late as compared with other societies; whether the process of change is essentially domestic, or takes place predominantly under foreign influence; and whether the society has a heritage of territorial and cultural continuity providing a strong sense of identity, or was formed from diverse peoples and territories during the modern era.

England and France adapted their societies to the new functions made possible by the revolution in science and technology over a period of many decades and in the absence of more advanced foreign models. For them the process was a natural one, and in a sense unconscious, insofar as it was gradual and pragmatic and did not involve threats to national identity or security from more advanced societies. To a considerable extent the offshoots of the early-modernizing societies in the New World benefited from a similar absence of outside pressure.

For the later modernizers, however, the international context plays a vital role in the aims and methods of their leaders. At the very least, the later modernizers are under the pressure of the example provided by more modern societies, which can be easily observed. Individuals going to more advanced countries for specialized training return with images of the reforms needed in their own society. More often than not, the example of more modern societies is imposed by military defeat and colonialism. Under these circumstances, the adaptation of traditional institutions and values to modern functions is marked not only by the normal domestic conflict but also by a struggle for national liberation.

In such relatively developed countries as Germany and Italy, for example, problems of national unification slowed the pace of political, economic, and social change substantially. To a much greater extent in less developed societies, the formation of nations from tribes and ethnic groups, with no common historical experience apart from subjection to colonial rule, presents almost insuperable obstacles to the efforts of their leaders to formulate common policies.

The influence of the international context on the process of societal transformation is explored here in terms of three factors: (1) the extent to which a society has developed a sense of identity before the modern era; (2) the nature of the foreign influences to which a society is exposed; and (3) the ways in which a society meets the challenges of modernity.

The capacity of a society to meet the challenges of the modern world depends significantly on the existence of a society-wide sense of identity—the loyalty of individuals and groups to institutions and values that facilitate the pursuit of common policies. The extent to which leaders can command the loyalty and altruism of its citizens is based largely on this sense of identity. In most premodern societies, identity is primarily related to kinship, and to a lesser degree to villages, regions, and religious associations. The great majority of people do not see their personal security as significantly related to larger linguistic or ethnic affiliations. The creation of society-wide, or "national," patterns of identity is a distinctly modern development, called for by the need to mobilize resources for a wide range of political, economic, and social undertakings.

Premodern societies vary considerably in the extent to which a significant degree of society-wide identity was developed before the modern era. In England and France, Japan and Russia, most citizens, even though they did not yet think of themselves as English, French, Japanese, or Russians, were aware of national institutions and society-wide languages that transcended their local customs and dialects. Even today significant localisms remain in these countries, but the heritage of common loyalties has been sufficient to provide a viable basis for the society-wide organizational efforts required by political development, economic growth, and social mobilization. Most countries have not had this degree of premodern social cohesion. There is no easy way to compare identity patterns, but one must do the best one can to evaluate the extent to which a society enters the modern world with a sense of loyalty and altruism that extends beyond the immediate local environment and kinship structures.

In all later-modernizing societies the struggle between traditional and modernizing leaders has taken place under the influence of foreign models. In the case of Inner Asia, and of most other parts of Asia and also Africa, the nature and degree of foreign influence were less the choice of political leaders than the result of the irresistible pressures of outside forces. Especially in the period of the imperial expansion of the European powers and the complementary assertion of Chinese influence in the nineteenth century, even the remote territories of Inner Asia became the object of imperial competition. The Great Game of British-Russian rivalry in

Inner Asia is the best known of these competitions, but France, Italy, and Japan also played a role. In its declining years, Ch'ing China likewise extended its influence to the north and west even as it surrendered to European influence in the east.

The purpose of this imperial activity was security rather than modernization, but the intrusion of outside military forces and political influences inexorably impressed the subject peoples with the levels of achievement that enabled the outside powers to exert their influence. In seeking to resist foreign influence, local leaders sought to adopt some of their practices. At the very least, they sought foreign assistance in strengthening their military forces by introducing modern weapons and principles of organization. This often led to a form of defensive modernization, the reform of military and political institutions for the purpose of preserving the traditional culture. As contacts with the outside world became more frequent, however, this in turn led to a more profound understanding of the multiple challenges of the modern era and of the need for undertaking thoroughgoing modernization.

The process of modernization is also affected by the way in which a society meets the initial challenge of the scientific and technological revolution. The leaders of some societies become aware of the challenge before they are directly confronted with it. They meet it by sending commissions to survey the institutions of more advanced countries, by establishing research and training institutions to translate and study foreign books, and by launching programs of defensive modernization designed to strengthen the state against foreign intrusion before they are ready to undertake a broader program of societal transformation. Japan and Russia, and to a lesser extent the Ottoman Empire, followed this pattern. In the case of most other societies, the traditional leaders failed to anticipate the necessity for modernizing reforms, and their countries underwent a prolonged period of turbulence as rival groups interacted with foreign influences in the search for appropriate policies.

In countries that were able to resist direct foreign intervention, either because they had developed reasonably effective central governments before the modern era, as in the case of Iran, or because they survived as a buffer zone between major powers, as in the case of Afghanistan and Outer Mongolia, native political leaders had the capacity to exercise considerable influence in deciding which foreign models seemed most suited to their needs. The societies that underwent one degree or another of colonial rule, more often than not because they lacked the capacity to resist foreign intrusion, came under more direct foreign influence and tended to adopt the institutions and sometimes even the languages of the colonial powers in their early efforts to modernize.

Identity Patterns

Despite many differences in historical experience, Iran and Afghanistan resemble each other in that they were composed of diverse tribal and ethnolinguistic

groups concerned primarily with local issues and lacking in a sense of what has come to be known as "national" identity. Although empires embracing these local entities rose and fell over the centuries, they had little influence on the predominance of locally centered identity patterns. Even the Islamic culture, shared by most of these peoples, was so fractured by sectarianism and ethnic diversity that it failed to provide a common basis for political action. The predominant concern of the peoples of these regions with local tribal and territorial conflicts was much too intense to be affected by the abstract precepts of a common religious heritage.

In the case of Iran (or Persia as it was known until 1935), the geographic distribution of ethnic groups has remained approximately the same since the Safavid period (1501–1736). Persian speakers dominate the central plateau and mountains and most of the eastern border with Afghanistan, while non-Persian speakers occupy the rimlands from Azerbaijan in the northwest down the Zagros

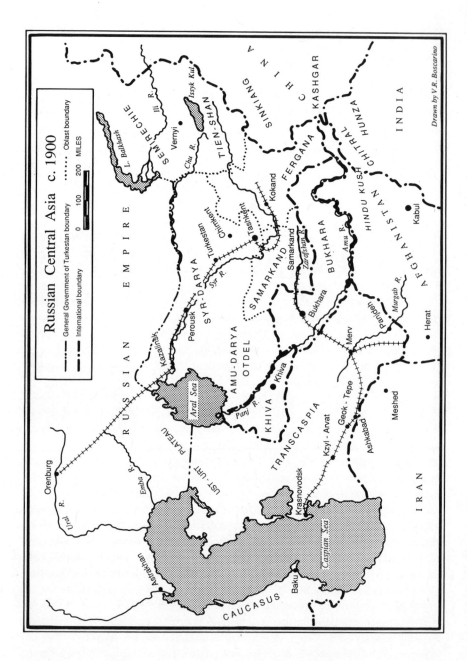

Russian Central Asia c. 1900

General Government of Turkestan boundary
International boundary
Oblast boundary

0   100   200   MILES

Drawn by V.R. Boscarino

Mountains and along the Persian-Arabian Gulf coast. Using Azerbaijan again as a pivot, and moving to the east to the shore of the Caspian Sea and across the Elburz Mountains to Turkestan, other non-Persian ethnic groups are found. Persian is not only the administrative language, however, it is also the lingua franca for most of the country.

Imami Shi'a Islam has been the state religion since the sixteenth century, and the instability of the royal inheritors led to an increase in the influence of the Shi'a religious leaders. With few exceptions, they have retained at least residual political power. The dominant Shi'a have also tended to persecute members of other Islamic sects, particularly Sunni, and also Zoroastrians (Parsees) and Bahais.

Afghan ethnolinguistic distribution has varied more widely from period to period than that of Iran. Mass shifting of dissident populations became the favorite outdoor sport of Afghan amirs in the nineteenth century, but reached a climax during the reign of Abdur Rahman (1880–1901). A Durrani Pushtun himself, Abdur Rahman first defeated rival Pushtun tribes (the population of modern Afghanistan is about one-half Pushtun) and then set about the conquest of non-Pushtun areas, a process of "internal imperialism." The amir forcibly moved various dissident Pushtun groups to north Afghanistan and resettled them among non-Pushtun elements: Tajik, Uzbek, Turkmen, Hazara, Aimaq. To non-Pushtun "Afghans," the term "Afghan" refers only to the Pushtun. This has proved to be a great barrier to the creation of a feeling of nationalism, a necessary corollary to modernization.

Hanafi Sunni Islam is the dominant sect in Afghanistan, with about one-fifth of the population Shi'a, mainly Imami Shi'a (Hazara) or Ismailiya (some Hazara, but mainly in parts of Badakhshan and Wakhan). Christian missionaries, partly successful in Persia, have never been permitted to proselytize openly in Afghanistan.

Russian Central Asia reflects a more complex pattern of ethnic and cultural interaction, dominated by the Turkic and Iranian populations who have inhabited the area for at least a millennium and a half. The Turkic peoples today by far outnumber the Iranian, but the Iranian population was initially both more numerous and administratively and culturally more significant. By the time of Cyrus the Great in the sixth century B.C., Iranian merchant groups and craftsmen had established a strong commercial and bureaucratic presence in the caravan cities and oases of Central Asia, adding a creative new element to the indigenous Soghdian, Khorezmian, and Baktrian peoples of the area. Their commercial, cultural, and administrative skills have been important in shaping the civilization of the area to this day. These have been essentially urban, settled groups whose influence on, and critical interaction with, the initially rougher and less polished Turkic nomadic peoples who migrated into the area later shaped the peculiarly symbiotic culture of the Inner Asian heartland.

The superior military power of the Turkic peoples allowed them to dominate the sedentary urban and oases complexes throughout these regions and gradually impose their political control over the Iranian peoples who inhabited the settled areas. It was the Turkic nomads who provided the ruling houses for the various oasis states that emerged in this fashion, with the Iranian urban groups supplying the essential administrative and bureaucratic skills and services that made up the infrastructure of those political formations. These Turkic ruling dynasties would often establish a nominal residence in some conquered urban capital, but maintain their essentially nomadic habits and move with their herds in traditional migratory patterns, assigning lieutenants to oversee the urban settlements.

Both economically and politically the Turkic nomadic tribes and the Iranian settled groups were dependent on each other, the relationship being one of classic symbiosis. The settled urban areas provided the nomads with critical manufactured goods, weaponry, and luxury items, as well as major items of sedentary agriculture, while the nomads afforded in return not only meat products, other foodstuffs, and leather goods, but, in the best of times, military protection, defense relationships, and the political structure of the state. The Turkic populations gradually settled down over the centuries, but a substantial percentage remained nomadic into the beginning of the twentieth century. The degree of that settlement differed from region to region across Central Asia.

These Turkic peoples also became differentiated into distinct ethnic groupings. The conventional dividing line for physical types is the Amu Darya, with tribes and groups to the west of the river displaying Irano-Caucasian features, and tribes to the east largely Mongoloid features. The earlier migrations of the Oghuz family of Turkic peoples to the southwest of this line split into the Seljuk, Ottoman, and Turkmen groups. The later Turkic migrations, which stopped short of the Amu-Darya line, were divided into the Kazakh nomads of the north, the Kirgiz mountain herders and nomads of the northeast, and the Uzbek cattle herders and semisettled groups of the southern valleys, oases, and urban areas. The interplay of Iranian and Turkic groups east of this line brought a striking mixture of ethnic types. Significant Iranian populations persisted in the urban areas east of the Amu Darya, producing a remarkable bilingual and bicultural amalgam with the Uzbeks who came into the cities. There was also a concentrated population of Iranian Tajiks inhabiting the valleys and foothills of the Pamirs to the north of Afghanistan.

The important Arab and Mongolian incursions left surprisingly few physical traces in the area since these were essentially military campaigns which did not involve the movement of large populations. The relatively small dynastic and military elites they left in their wake commanded mixed forces with substantial proportions of indigenous troops. These elites intermarried with the local populace, creating a kaleidoscopic ethnic patchwork. Such was the case, for example, under the Chagatai khanate which was the major political and cultural force in the area for almost a century: the Chinggissid dynasty was of Mongolian origin but became thoroughly Turkified through extensive intermarriage with local tribal aristocracies. By the end of the thirteenth century, this elite was Turkic speaking and closely linked with the indigenous Turco-Iranian peoples.

Although they may have left few physical traces on the anthropological map of Central Asia, the Arabs and Mongols left cultural and political markers in their wake, which became major features in the identity of the indigenous peoples for centuries to come: the powerful cultural phenomenon of Islam, and the political legacy of empire left by the Mongolian khan, Chinggis. Both of these phenomena have continued to shape society in Central Asia to the present day.

The linguistic pattern of the area reflected the basic ethnic mix, with some important distinctions in the use of these languages. To oversimplify somewhat the pattern that pertained for centuries, the language of religion and jurisprudence was Arabïc, the administrative and bureaucratic language of the towns and khanates was Persian (with the exception of Khorezm, where it was Turkic), and the language of the ruling dynasties was essentially Turkic. Written work in various genres was produced in all three languages, with Arabic the language for religion, science, and medicine; Persian the overwhelmingly dominant language for history, poetry, and prose fiction; and, starting in the thirteenth century, Chagatai Turkic an important new vehicle for literary creativity. An artificial language similar to Ottoman Turkish in the western empire of Istanbul, Chagatai blended grammatical and lexical elements of high literary Persian and Arabic into the primary base of the eastern Turki languages of Inner Asia. Whereas Persian was the dominant literary language of the area, Chagatai shared its distinction by being the only Turkic literary language in Central Asia from the fourteenth to the early twentieth century.

The several Turkic vernacular languages emerged much later, making their appearance in the nineteenth century, and developing into full literary vehicles only in the twentieth. Uzbek, Kazakh, Kirgiz, Turkmen, and the Iranian Tajik have their roots in the rich common traditions of the Central Asian cultural past, but find their separate and distinctive beginnings in the face of the Russian challenge and catalyst of the last two centuries.

The introduction of Islam into this region beginning in the seventh century brought what was to become its most powerful single cultural force, but that phenomenon was to be modified substantially by the diversity of its establishment in the several subregions such as Turkmenia, the Kazakh steppes to the north, the distant Kirgiz Mountains in the east, and the Uzbek River valleys to the south, as well as by the variety of its adaptation in those areas. Animist and shamanist traditions remained extremely powerful among the Kazakh and Kirgiz tribes, and Muslim missionaries there had to cater to and make substantial accommodations with such beliefs and practices. The result was a relaxed, undogmatic form of Islam somewhat carelessly devoid of ritual. The bellicose, mobile Turkmen nomads of the western deserts also adopted an unorthodox but intense form of Islamic piety, likewise unencumbered by formal ceremony and observance, but increasingly imbued with Sufi habits and principles from the thirteenth century on.

As far as orthodoxy was concerned, the Uzbek khanates to the south were an exception, and it was in the urban settings of Bukhara and Khiva that ultraconservative patterns of Islamic theology and ritual became entrenched over the centuries. The major impetus to this conservatism came from the isolation and defensiveness of the area after the Sheibanid Uzbek wars with the Safavids of Persia in the sixteenth and seventeenth centuries. Those wars effectively placed a long-term cultural barrier between the Shi'ite state of Persia and the Sunni khanates of the Uzbek areas. As that isolation grew after the seventeenth century, and was compounded by the virtually simultaneous decline in the east-west overland trading routes as the world sea lanes were opened, the theological schools of Bukhara became increasingly conservative. Once known as the jewel of Islam because of its important cultural and religious role in the great Islamic age, Bukhara and its *madrasas* gradually turned inward and grew increasingly rigid and distrustful of any outside influences and intellectual trends.

From the thirteenth century on, a powerful parallel current of Islam became entrenched in the Uzbek south: the several Sufi orders, which apparently drew strength from the troubled and destructive times of the Mongolian invasions. Given the physical and psychic dislocation of the invasion, with tremendous destruction and violence in the old cultural centers of Central Asia, much of the communal leadership shifted to the Sufi brotherhoods.

Together with the prestigious religious schools in the urban areas, these Islamic brotherhoods consolidated the pervasive and characteristic role of Islam throughout the region. It is a powerful and ubiquitous cultural phenomenon, which has strongly marked the everyday life and habits of these peoples. Yet those influences were of a broad cultural type, with little or no unifying force either of a political nature or even of a social nature beyond regional subdivisions. The divisions between the High Islam of the urban theological schools and the Low Islam of the Kazakh steppes; the divisions between the relaxed animist Islam of the Kirgiz Mountains and the more structured, intense beliefs of the various Sufi brotherhoods; indeed, the very divisions of style and ritual between those brotherhoods themselves—all of these made the ultimate influence of Islam a very special one: a powerful but very general cultural marker on the one hand, but an insufficient focus for political unity on the other, perhaps even playing a disjunctive political role.

By the late eighteenth and early nineteenth centuries, the residuum of significant Mongolian military and political power had clustered in the several khanates of Khiva, Bukhara, and Kokand. Each was headed by a Turkic ruling house sprung from steppe nomadic origins, asserting Mongolian imperial descent, professing an Arab Islamic religion, and supported by a traditional Iranian urban bureaucratic and commercial elite.

From the middle of the eighteenth century, each of these khanates was engaged in similar attempts to subdue and restrict the power of its local aristocracy. Individual notable families had retained substantial influence within the khanates, putting those lands and their resources beyond the power of the ruling families at the center. The khanates moved to curb the independence of these families and centralize control within their respective realms. That process was incomplete when the Russians began to move into Central Asia. Not only was there conflict among the khanates at the time, there was also substantial turmoil within them as the ruling dynasties were caught up in a confrontation with segments of their recalcitrant aristocracies. All of this made it much easier for the Russians to play off one group against the other and to manipulate the political scene to their own advantage.

Sinkiang, among the territories of Inner Asia that came under Chinese influence, lacked a clear identity in the premodern period. The name itself was the product of military conquest by the Ch'ing. Assigned in 1768, it meant simply "New Territory."

Although Sinkiang has come under Chinese rule in modern times, its historical links with China were intermittent, and its population, even today, is largely non-Chinese. The T'ien-shan Mountains, which run roughly east to west, divide Sinkiang into two parts: the northern called Jungaria, the southern called East Turkestan, Altishahr, or Kashgaria. Culturally Jungaria is part of the Mongolian world, while East Turkestan belongs to the Turco-Iranian civilization of Central Asia.

In the seventeenth century, the Mongol Galdan (1644–1697), khan of Jungaria, created an Inner Asian kingdom, including much of Sinkiang, with its capital at Ili. It was a formidable power, not least because of its eagerness to adopt new military technology, and even manufacture firearms. But it was conquered by the Ch'ien-lung emperor (1736–1796) in a series of wars, and a Manchu outpost was placed at Ili in 1755. Thus did Jungaria join the Manchu empire, and then eventually the Chinese world.

In traditional times the oasis towns of southern Sinkiang tended to be rather self-sufficient both politically and culturally. What regional unity there was came from Islam. Sunni Muslims and followers of the Hanafite school of law, most of the population of southern Sinkiang, or Altishahr, had been ruled by the Afaqi *khojas* of the Naqshbandiyya brotherhood, a Sufi order. These were descendants of the famous sixteenth-century Naqshbandiyya shaykh known as Makhdum-i 'Azam. The family divided into two rival lines of *khojas*, the Ishaqiyya and the Afaqiyya, and until the Chinese conquest the political history of the region was largely one of their rivalry. After the Ch'ing conquest, some of the *khojas* cooperated with the new rulers, were ennobled, and made to live in Peking. Others fled, and their descendants maintained communication with their old domain through the extensive overland trade.

Firm Ch'ing rule initially suppressed any political manifestation of the religious and ethnic identity of the scattered Sinkiang people, and some of their leaders were co-opted. But by the nineteenth century, Russian and British military competition, as well as new intellectual and political currents, began to stir the people up again, even as the Chinese grip weakened. The new ferment in Sinkiang had two sources. One was indigenous: the reaffirmation of Muslim

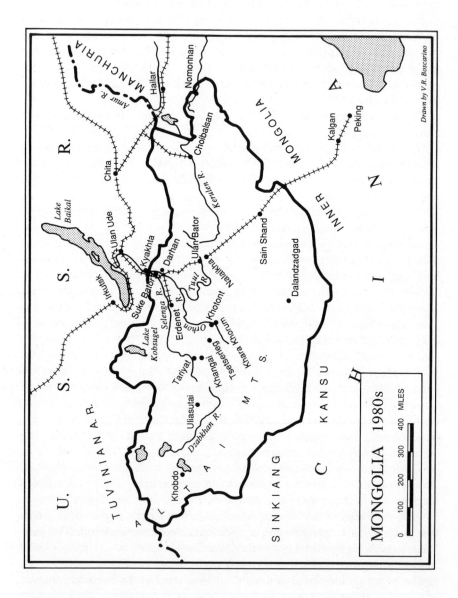

MONGOLIA 1980s

0 100 200 300 400 MILES

Drawn by V.R. Boscarino

ideas, spurred on by developments in the world of Islam beyond Sinkiang's borders. The other was externally imposed: the extension of Western influence, mostly Russian, in response to economic and strategic impulses.

Mongolia, despite the fact that it was situated between the Russian and Chinese empires, developed and retained through the centuries a remarkably consistent and strong self-identity. Culturally and economically, the contrast between the Mongols and their sedentary neighbors was significant, even when in the eighteenth and nineteenth centuries different groups of Mongols were absorbed into the Russian and Ch'ing Chinese empires.

The Mongolian language, which belongs to the Altaic language group, was partially responsible for maintaining that cultural identity. Unrelated to Chinese or Russian, the Mongolian language was used as the primary language of government documents in the Yuan dynasty when the Mongols ruled China. In 1204 the Turkic Uighur script (based ultimately on the Aramaic alphabet) was adapted to the spoken Mongolian language, and that script (or for a brief time the Tibetan 'Phags-pa script) continued to be used by the Mongols until very recent times.

The eastern Mongols' success in retaining their cultural "otherness" is borne out not only by their continued use of the Mongolian language (and not Chinese) but also by the failure of either Chinese Confucians or Tibetan Buddhists to convert the Mongols from their indigenous shamanism in the thirteenth and fourteenth centuries. While espousing tolerance for other religions and philosophies, the eastern Mongols who ruled China completely avoided sinicization or conversion to Buddhism (Tibetan or Chinese).

The Mongolian empire, which briefly stretched over Eurasia, had by the generation of Chinggis's grandsons dissolved into four separate geographical domains (Russia, Persia, Central Asia, and China-Mongolia). Linguistic and ethnic assimilation as well as conversion to Islam (and concurrent sedentarization) on the western end of the steppe (Persia, Russia, and parts of Central Asia) led to the weakening of the ethnic identity of the Western Mongols as early as the late thirteenth century. By contrast, the Eastern Mongols—those Mongols who ruled over and resided in China and Mongolia in the thirteenth and fourteenth centuries—preserved their cultural and ethnic integrity, as evidenced by the fact that the sixty thousand or so Mongols who fled the Yuan capital of Ta-tu (Peking) in 1368 as the troops of the Ming approached, returned north to the steppe where they reassimilated themselves to a traditional steppe environment. The post-Yuan eastern Mongols did not build Chinese-style cities on the grasslands of Mongolia, although the technology and know-how were available to them.

The legacy of the period of domination over most of the Eurasian continent remained alive and treasured by Mongols of later centuries. The Mongolian chronicles of the seventeenth and eighteenth centuries such as the *Altan tobci* (The Golden Summary) and the *Erdeni-yin tobci* (The Bejeweled Summary) attest to the vitality of the Mongols' historical memory. History and folklore interwoven together formed the basis for the heroic self-image that contributed to the survival of the Mongols as a nation even in the worst of times.

Tibet is unusual among Inner Asian societies both for its active, and for a considerable period successful, resistance to all outside influences, and for the degree to which, even today, while under relentless pressure to sinify, it continues to maintain the culture it originated.

Tibet was not traditionally a state that isolated itself. Its warlike people ranged as far as the T'ang capital on various occasions, and today the world of ethnic Tibet runs from Baltistan in the west to Szechwan in the east. In traditional times the Tibetan world was not fully unified politically. Only gradually did Lhasa and the Dalai Lama achieve direct control of a Tibetan state, and a looser preeminence with regard to Ladakh, Sikkim, Bhutan, and the districts of eastern Kham and Amdo.

The extensive and ill-defined network of Tibetan societies became vulnerable to outside pressure in the nineteenth century. Tales of Tibetan gold, and knowledge of the fine wools that were traded with north India, led the British to probe the outlying regions. Russia, too, was interested, and this led to British strategic concern. And of course the Manchus had no intention of seeing the dissolution of their empire, though for most of the nineteenth century they had little influence at Lhasa.

Tibet is a natural fortress. To the north the Kun Lun and Nan Shan protect it; to the west are the Karakoram and Ladakh ranges; to the south, the Himalayas. Much of Tibet lies at an altitude of roughly three miles, and outsiders easily become sick. Lhasa, at twelve thousand feet, is the world's highest capital. Only to the east is the approach relatively open, and thus not surprisingly China has been the state ultimately able to incorporate Tibet into its empire.

The Tibetan people and language derive from varied sources. Tibetans of the southern valleys may be related racially to Tai, Burmans, and Yunnanese in the east, and Greco-Indo-Scythians in the west. Northern Tibetans are most likely related to Turkic and Mongolian tribes (N34, p. 95). The Tibetan language is often classified as belonging to a Sino-Tibetan language family, though recent scholarship, which underscores the unique characteristics of Tibetan, has demonstrated the unlikelihood that Chinese and Tibetan are related at all. The linguistic connection with Burmese is most acceptable to these scholars (N3, pp. 4–5, notes 2 and 3; and N34, p. 96).

Tibetan culture is certainly unique. The culture is inextricably bound to that form of Indian Buddhism called "Lamaism" by Westerners. The term "Lamaism," which scholars of Buddhism and Tibetans themselves regard as unfortunate since it implies that the Tibetan form of Buddhism is somehow unorthodox, emphasizes the central place that the teacher or lama holds in this branch of Buddhism. This religion possesses a well-developed canon of scripture and exegesis, which in addition to encompassing religious and metaphysical questions, also incorporates much medical and protoscientific thought. Far from being threatened by other religions, Tibetan Buddhism has spread through Mongolia, and remains strong today. Some ethnic Tibetans, though, are Muslims: those in Baltistan, and the people called Salars of Ch'ing-hai, among whom the "New Teaching" of the Naqshbandiyya has been strong.

Foreign Influences

Iran came under active European influence during the Qajar period (1794–1925). Western interests in Iran were partly strategic, located as it was on the crossroads of French, British, and Russian influence; partly economic, as a market and a source of raw materials; and partly educational and cultural.

Early French influence included a military mission in 1807, which sought to reorganize the shah's army, but after Napoleon's defeat French influence in Iran was primarily educational and cultural. A British military incursion into Iran in 1810 led to a treaty in 1814 that provided for mutual assistance in case of an attack, a provision that Iran cancel all treaties with European powers hostile to British interests, and a substantial annual subsidy to the shah. At the same time, Iran was engaged in a series of wars with Russia which led to significant cessions of territories under the treaties of 1813 and 1828.

Economic competition between the Russians and the British accelerated after the shah signed a monopoly in 1872 with the British entrepreneur Baron de Reuter of news service fame. The concessions included building railways, establishing a bank, and developing mines. Although the concessions were soon canceled, the Russians demanded (and received) fishing rights in the Caspian Sea, and the right to establish a railroad and toll road in northwestern Iran. More important, in 1879 the Qajar shah, Nasiruddin (r. 1848–1896), engaged the Russians to create, train, and provide officers for the Persian Cossacks.

In 1889, another concession to Baron de Reuter enabled the British to establish the Imperial Bank of Iran, with the right to issue banknotes. The Russians also demanded banking rights, and established the Discount Bank (Banque d'Escompte) in 1891. The bank functioned as a political, not a commercial, enterprise. It became an instrument of coercion, primarily through loans. Foreign loans to the shah (and his successor, Muzaffaruddin, r. 1896–1907) and his court and sycophants began in 1892 and increased almost annually. The government bureaucrats were paid pittances, however, which only encouraged corruption at all levels.

Probably the most important episode in early twentieth-century Iran involved the D'Arcy oil concession of 1901, which the British co-opted during World War I as the Royal Navy gradually converted from coal to oil. By the 1920s the Anglo-Iranian Oil Company, as it was ultimately called, had great influence on Iran's modernization. Oil royalties contributed to the gradual expansion of industrialization in other sectors. The managerial skills taught to Iranians found their way into the bureaucratic network, and a whole new class of technocrats came into being.

Drawn by V.R. Boscarino

The final nail in the coffin of Iran's political autonomy was driven when the British and Russians, after decades of competition in the region, signed the Anglo-Russian Convention of 1907, which divided Iran, and also Afghanistan and Tibet, into zones of influence.

Similarly in Afghanistan, imperial rivalries between Russia in Central Asia and Britain in India led to frequent confrontations. Twice (1838–1842; 1878–1880) the British invaded the Afghan region in response to real or imagined Russian threats. In 1880, near the end of the second Anglo-Afghan war, Abdur Rahman rode into Kabul. For several years previously, he had lived in Central Asia as a refugee under Russian sponsorship. But the British gambled on his ethnic pride and personal charisma to keep Afghanistan out of the Russian sphere of influence and the gamble proved successful. At the same time, the British and Russians drew Afghanistan's frontiers without regard to ethnolinguistic boundaries and geographic entities.

Afghanistan, though never a European colony, was maintained as a buffer between the two great imperial powers. Abdur Rahman brought British and Indian technicians to establish small factories in and around Kabul. His son, Habibullah I (1901–1919), was entranced with photography and motor cars and imported such symbols of modernization for the exclusive use (and amusement) of his family and friends.

Three historical events in the early twentieth century greatly influenced the small Afghan intellectual cadre: the defeat of a great European nation (Russia) by an Asian nation (Japan) in 1904–1905; the abortive 1905 revolution in Russia (which also influenced Persian, Indian, and Chinese intellectuals); and the First World War (1914–1918), which drastically changed the face of the world.

In the territories of Central Asia that came under Russian influence, the intrusion of the outer world was both direct and indirect. As early as 1826 a Russian major-general submitted a memorandum to Tsar Nicholas I in which he called urgently for the occupation of Khiva and the establishment of Russian imperial control over Central Asia. He advanced two reasons for these steps: first, to ensure the security of Russia's trade routes because of the increasing volume and importance of commercial contacts with Central Asia; second, to forestall the continuing advance of the British into the area as they moved up from Persia and India in the south. He was almost thirty years ahead of his time, but he foreshadowed the eventual Russian conquest of those regions for exactly those reasons.

From the 1820s to the middle of the century, the value of Russian trade with Central Asia increased fourfold to four million rubles. Russia's cotton textile industry grew dramatically during this period, and its demand for sources of raw cotton expanded proportionately. Since St. Petersburg had lifted a ban on the export of metals to the khanates earlier in the century, the range, variety, and costs of materials and manufactures sold and traded had grown. The interest and dependence of Russian industrialists and merchants on the Inner Asian market became a major public issue by the 1850s.

While these concerns were mounting within the empire, a parallel set of stimuli was acting on Russia from the outside, compelling new attention to Central Asian issues. The so-called Eastern Question was being played out in the Balkans and the Middle East, with the European powers divided about the fate of the Ottoman Empire and the ultimate division of its sprawling and disparate remains. Differences of approach and geopolitical aims embroiled the powers in the Crimean War from 1853 to 1856, with Britain, France, Austria, and Turkey all aligned against Russia in what was to become a military and political debacle for the tsarist empire. The war and its aftermath were to have important consequences for both Russia and Central Asia.

The length and intensity of the war, and its concentration on the Crimean peninsula, put special pressure on the Tatar population of the area. Hundreds of thousands fled the peninsula for Anatolia and the Ottoman provinces, with large numbers of intellectuals and entrepreneurs concentrating in Istanbul at a critical time in the transformation of the Ottoman state. The next half-century saw an extraordinary flow and counterflow of people and information between the Muslim areas of tsarist Russia and the Ottoman realms. Ideas on the reform and renovation not only of the Ottoman state but of the Muslim East and Islam in general were engendered and elaborated in the Turkish cities and carried back to the Crimea, the Volga Tatar regions of Kazan, and the Muslim areas of Central Asia. The Crimean, and especially Kazan, Tatars were important intermediaries in this process, but the influences of these contacts in the formation of the *jadidist* ("new way") approaches spread throughout Muslim Russia.

The confrontation between Russia and Britain intensified after the Crimean War, and their intelligence and reconnaissance services engaged in an increasingly active global competition, as the two states maneuvered for position not only in the disintegrating areas of the Ottoman Empire, but in Persia, Afghanistan, Central Asia, Tibet, and western China. This was the Great Game, which was played for almost a century as the two states attempted to prevent each other from seizing control of critical areas in the Inner Asian heartland and its periphery. England, concerned about the security of its position on the Indian subcontinent, sought to exclude Russia from the Persian, Afghan, and Central Asian approaches to India, while Russia for its part developed a mirror interest in preventing English commercial and military influences in the Central Asian khanates and regions that were of increasing importance to its own economy. The game of thrust and counterthrust developed a momentum of its own, and heightened St. Petersburg's sense of urgency to dominate the region.

International circumstances created one other major incentive for Russia's move into Central Asia: European pressure on China after the Opium Wars and the opening of the treaty ports in China. The resulting deflection of trade and commercial patterns to the eastern littoral brought a corresponding substantial decline in Russia's overland trade with China through the city of Kyakhta. This decline came at a time when Russia could ill afford the disappearance of such a market. What was worse, China's weakness in the east engendered a restlessness and rebellion among the Muslim tribes of Sinkiang province in the west, attracting English attention and involvement in ways that were even less pleasing to tsarist officials. In the wake of the humiliating Crimean defeat, with the substantial decline of the China market, with new English pressures from Persia and the Indian subcontinent, and substantial Muslim unrest in Turkestan, the dwindling of raw cotton supplies as a result of the American Civil War was another serious blow to the Russian economy. The needs of Russia's growing cotton textile industry, which had expanded dramatically in the first half of the nineteenth century, were an additional impetus to the tsarist conquest of the area.

The outcome of the Crimean War had shaken the prestige of Russia in Central Asia. It inspired the several khanates to attempt to push Russian forces back in Kazakhstan and Turkestan, to attack Russian forts in the Kazakh steppes, and to lend assistance to Kazakh insurgencies such as that under Kenesary. The Russian popular press played on these fears of subversion and combined with commercial interests in calling for military subjugation of the area.

From the 1860s on, Russian imperial forces moved into Central Asia very gradually, playing one khanate, one faction, one set of notables, off against another, sometimes responding to the request of one faction to intervene, sometimes striking directly when the opportunity presented itself. Tashkent was a key strategic link in the area and was to become the command post for Russian dominance. Within the city itself there were intense debates between the Muslim religious establishment, which sought alliance with or the protection of Bukhara, and commercial groups, which preferred an expansion of trade contacts with Russia. The city was nominally within the orbit of the Khanate of Kokand, and military hostilities begun by Bukhara against Kokand gave the Russian General M. G. Cherniaev a pretext to intervene and take the city in June 1865. Similar patterns of manipulation and intervention brought almost all of the major cities of Central Asia under Russian control during the 1860s and 1870s: Bukhara, Samarkand, Kokand, and others. In virtually every case the Russians took advantage not only of indigenous arguments for commercial and diplomatic contacts with St. Petersburg, but of sharp internal divisions within the khanates and other major urban areas as well, where disparate groups sought to dispose of their immediate enemies, albeit their ethnic kin, by calling in the Russians for assistance. With Kazakhstan and the major Uzbek khanates subdued by the late 1870s, the Russians mounted a series of expeditions from 1877 to 1885 that resulted in the seizure and annexation of Turkmen areas to the south.

Although Bukhara and Khiva technically remained protectorates and separate, tsarist control was secured throughout Russian Turkestan. Tsarist strategy in both the khanates and the Russian-administered regions of Turkestan was essentially to leave existing administrative and social patterns and institutions in place. The Russians permitted former local judicial and political institutions of the villages to continue, and they supported traditional village leaders. Even the village elders, the *aksakals* (literally, "white beards"), were salaried and confirmed by tsarist authorities after their customary selection by peers. The approach of the Russians was to buttress the traditional political order of the khanates as a guarantee of the status quo. In doing so, they recognized the close connection between the political regime of the khanates and the conservative clerical establishment in the religious schools, and were careful not to meddle in or inhibit the activities of the latter as long as they too supported the status quo. It has been said that their major policy in this matter was to ignore Islam altogether.

In Sinkiang, somewhat different patterns of foreign influence unfolded. In the mid-nineteenth century Sinkiang was shaken by the resurgence of Islam and the political movements based on it. The early part of the century saw repeated attempts by the exiled Afaqi *khojas,* who made their uneasy base in Kokand, to regain their former territories in Altishahr. The attack of Jahengir led, in 1827, to a Ch'ing expedition of reconquest, and a regarrisoning of Kashgar. Subse-

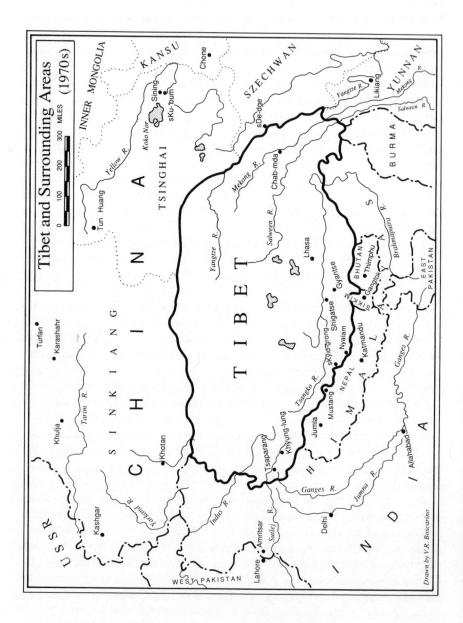

Tibet and Surrounding Areas (1970s)

Drawn by V.R. Boscarino

quently, the Ch'ing imposed an abortive embargo on the Kokand trade, and began to encourage Chinese immigration, so that by the 1830s, for instance, Yarkand had two hundred Chinese residents. These measures simply exacerbated the situation, though, and had to be abandoned. No long-term solution presented itself, and until the 1860s the Ch'ing had difficulty resisting the periodic holy wars of the Afaqi *khojas*.

The situation became further aggravated when Muslim Dungan rebellions broke out in China proper. The so-called Panthay rebellion raged in Yunnan from 1856 until 1873, and Muslims rose in Shensi and Kansu beginning in 1862. This second rebellion of the Dungans was influenced by the "New Teaching," introduced by the eighteenth-century Chinese Muslim Ma Ming-hsin, a follower of the Naqshbandiyya, who had traveled to Bukhara and the Arabian peninsula. As the Dungan rebellion spread along the Kansu corridor, it evoked a major response in Sinkiang. Dungan forces captured Urumchi, while in the south the Afaqi *khojas* attacked again. The result was the creation of a new kingdom in Altishahr, ruled by Yakub Beg (1820–1877).

Yakub Beg conquered all of southern Sinkiang, and drove the Dungans (who as followers of the Shafi'ite school of law, and perhaps as ethnic Chinese as well, were not possible allies) out of northern Sinkiang, capturing Urumchi in 1870. The founding of his kingdom promised a new political status for Sinkiang: his regime's recognition by the Ottomans was announced in 1873, followed by the British, in the course of treaty negotiations, a year later. Fearful lest their own Muslims become restive, the Russians had occupied Ili in 1871, but they supported the new regime elsewhere, as a buffer and potential client. The foreign interest in the new state was a reminder of how much greater Sinkiang's strategic significance was becoming in the nineteenth century.

Ili was of strategic importance, since the Muzart pass controlled access to Altishahr from the west. Britain was concerned about the northern boundary of India, for the passes through the Karakoram seemed to provide an invasion route into India from the Central Asia that Russia was so rapidly acquiring. Britain and Russia nearly came to blows in 1878 over this northwest frontier, and the quarter-century that followed was tense.

In the case of Tibet, Ch'ing support in the war with Nepal in 1792 established a Manchu presence in the Tibetan capital. An *amban,* an assistant *amban,* and a small garrison (all Manchu bannermen, not Chinese) were stationed there permanently, and the Ch'ien-lung emperor delivered a golden urn, from which, it was supposedly agreed, the names of new incarnations of the Dalai Lama would be chosen. It is not clear how far the Tibetans actually followed this practice. For domestic purposes, it was essential that the new Dalai Lama be chosen according to the signs of incarnation recognized by senior holy men. But it served Tibet's foreign interests to promote the impression that to tangle with Lhasa was to tangle with China (see "Political Leadership and Participation," chapter 3).

In the course of the nineteenth century the Manchu presence in Lhasa became rather attenuated. *Ambans* were unable to obtain money from Peking to pay their garrison, and had to rely on loans from the Tibetan government. The Manchu troops married local women and settled down, rather than being rotated on a three-year basis as regulations required. Nevertheless, with Russians and British increasingly probing their defenses, the Tibetans strove to maintain the impression that they were a Ch'ing protectorate, and indeed that the strict policy of exclusion they promulgated originated at the Ch'ing, not the Tibetan, capital.

Exclusion was a popular policy. Tibetans had a rather strong sense of identity even in the nineteenth century. In 1804, when the eighth Dalai Lama died, pamphlets and placards in the capital gave voice to popular opposition to following the Ch'ing-sanctioned method of choosing a successor. A series of British adventurers who sought to reach Lhasa encountered varying degrees of hostility: one, Henry Savage Landor, was brutally tortured. British intelligence in north India sent local people on forays into Tibet to attempt to determine such basic information as the location of Lhasa. But until the end of the nineteenth century, the policy of exclusion was remarkably successful.

Attempts by the Russian military explorer Count Nikolai Przhevalsky to reach Lhasa in 1872 and 1879 failed. A British expedition planned for 1886 was never mounted. In 1888, however, British troops in Sikkim defeated a Tibetan force defending that state, a traditional Tibetan feudatory. The Tibetan military defeat was followed by the conclusion of the so-called Sikkim-Tibet Convention between Britain and China. With the arrival of Curzon as viceroy in India, though, the British finally did enter Tibet, spurred on by hopes of trade, and fears of Lhasa's contacts with St. Petersburg. A small expeditionary force led by Colonel Francis Younghusband reached the Tibetan capital in 1904, after inflicting several military defeats on the Tibetans. He concluded the Anglo-Tibet Convention, a document important because in it Britain recognized Tibet's right to bargain for itself.

In Mongolia, after the dissolution of the Yuan dynasty in China in 1368 and the dissolution of the other Mongolian khanates elsewhere in Eurasia, would-be leaders on the steppe recognized the necessity for a new form of political legitimation in order to achieve political cohesion. Genealogy had proven insufficient: being in the bloodline of Chinggis Khan had not enabled any post-empire Mongolian leader to forestall political infighting.

Altan Khan of the Tumed (1507–1582) opted for a different means to achieve that cohesion. In 1578 he took advantage of the struggle among Tibetan Buddhists between the Yellow Church and the Red Church, siding with the Yellow Church (see "Distribution of Political Power," chapter 3). Although Tibetan Buddhism may have filled a spiritual void among the Mongols, its rapid spread among the Mongols under Altan Khan did not lead to the creation of a new Mongolian nation with unified leadership. In fact, the intertwining of Mongolian secular leadership with Tibetan religious leadership (as evidenced by Altan Khan's great-grandson being formally recognized as the Tibetan Dalai

Lama's next incarnation in 1601) may have weakened the Mongols in the long run. The Manchu Ch'ing dynasty (1644–1912) took full advantage of the precepts and institutional apparatus of Tibetan Buddhism to demilitarize and sedentarize the Mongols.

The Manchus in their conquest of China in the mid-seventeenth century relied gratefully on Mongolian military aid and know-how, but once the conquest had been completed, the Mongols themselves became the objects of pacification campaigns and strategies. The imposition of Manchu authority over Mongolia led to many changes. The range of nomadic migration was, for the first time, limited. The Manchus held to a policy of breaking up traditional clan-based confederations into so-called *khoshighun*, or superimposed nonclan territorial-administrative units, thus legally tying the Mongols down to specific territories for the first time ever (see, for instance, M27, pp. 318–319). The *khoshighun* (Mongolian for "banners") fragmented the Mongols by weakening horizontal ties among different clans and tribes and creating new vertical ties to the Manchu government in Peking. Mongolian tribal and clan leaders became "grounded" local princes, who derived authority from their relationship to the Manchu royal house. Mongolian scholars today write of the "nomadic feudalism" of the period of Manchu supremacy over the Mongols. In the terminology of "nomadic feudalism," the Manchu emperors enfoeffed Mongolian princes with hereditary fiefs *(khoshighun)*, and the enfoeffed Mongolian prince was called a *jasagh* (from which the Manchu *jasak* is derived) (M46).

As the Manchu dynasty itself gradually became sinicized, its control of the steppe became an avenue for the transmission of Chinese ways. Just as some Chinese in Yuan times had adopted Mongolian ways, some Mongols, especially those in the Inner Mongolian crescent, adopted aspects of Chinese culture. Next to their flat-roofed Tibetan-style palaces, some Mongolian princes built new residences with sweeping Chinese-style roofs.

While cultural sinification appealed most to those members of the Mongolian elite who stood to benefit economically, the influx of Han Chinese settlers, which was speeded by the gradual extension of the railway line, posed a profound threat to the Mongolian population and way of life, particularly in Inner Mongolia. By the first decade of the twentieth century, Mongolia seemed destined to be absorbed by the Russian and Chinese empires.

The Challenge of Modernity

As premodern societies are confronted by the challenge of modernity, whether in the form of intrusions by more modern societies or of demands for reform from within the society, the many difficult choices they face are centered on a single issue: should they discard traditional values and institutions and replace them with those borrowed from abroad, or should they seek to adapt their traditional heritage to modern functions?

In the period before rapid modernization was undertaken—in the case of Inner Asia, in the generations before the 1920s—the first impulse was to borrow directly from abroad. It was only much later that it became apparent that foreign institutions could not simply be transplanted, and that some form of adjustment with the traditional heritage had to be made.

In the case of Iran, under strong foreign influence but independent of direct foreign rule, it was natural that its leaders should turn to foreign models. Before Reza Shah Pahlavi rose to the Peacock Throne in 1925, most modernist reform efforts came from the minuscule element of Western-educated Persians. The first Iranian students were sent to Europe in 1811; by 1850 Iranians studying abroad numbered fewer than twenty. Furthermore, attempts at reform were usually accompanied by economic concessions and further penetration by European economic interests.

More fundamental reforms were undertaken in the latter half of the nineteenth century. A legal code was created and some consistency was achieved, but corruption in the courts canceled out most benefits. The Cossack Brigade (see above) helped reform the military. What would pass for a cabinet was created by the shah, although he and his inner circle strove to hold on to absolute power. But economic and cultural reforms tended to favor Western interests. These contradictions laid the political groundwork for the constitutional movement of 1905 (see chapter 3).

Persian newspapers appeared about 1851, but mainly outside Iran, in London, Cairo, and Calcutta. Probably the most influential was *Qanun* (Law), published in London, beginning in 1890. It attacked the corruption, the shah, and his advisers, and wanted fair laws promulgated and an elected parliament created.

Two charismatic personalities had an impact on Iranian modernist thinking, and their ideas and programs spread far beyond Iran. Sayyid Ali Mohammad (1819–1850) founded the Babi movement which evolved into modern Bahaism. He called himself the Bab (Gate) or the Mahdi, successor to the Twelfth Imam, who had disappeared exactly one thousand years earlier. Bahaism is a syncretic religion embracing idealistic elements from most regional religions, with an emphasis on the absence of class distinctions and peace to all humankind. The Bab was executed in 1850, and subsequently many of his followers turned to violence. They tried to assassinate the shah and his chief adviser, and a Babi blood bath followed. Modern Bahaism still exists in Iran, and has spread to Europe and the United States.

The other important reformist was Jamaluddin al-Afghani (1839–1897), who had a great impact on modernist Muslim thinking from India to Russia, across Iran to Turkey and Egypt. He pushed for pan-Islamism, and constantly preached that Islamic nations should use Islamic patterns to modernize. One of al-Afghani's favorite sura from the Holy Koran was: "God changes not what is in a people until they change what is in themselves" (quoted in G30, p. 93).

In Afghanistan, in contrast to Iran, the government did not gain control of the countryside until the end of the nineteenth century. When Amir Abdur Rahman began his reign he controlled only the city of Kabul and had at his disposal a bureaucracy of no more than ten clerks. His main concern was to defend his country against British and Russian intrusions, and his first step was to extend the authority of Kabul to the rest of the country. This policy of "internal imperialism" eventually succeeded, and provided sources of revenue that gave the amir a degree of bargaining power with his imperial enemies.

Abdur Rahman's program was a classic case of defensive modernization, in the sense that he sought to create a strong national state without disturbing the underlying social and economic structure of the society. On the one hand he turned to Western models for administrative, economic, and social reforms, and on the other he sought the support of the various tribal and ethnic groups by stressing the values of Islam and by promoting xenophobia and traditionalism. Many reform programs were launched during Abdur Rahman's reign, but they bore meager fruits in his lifetime. His son and successor, Habibullah, sought to continue his programs, but Habibullah's efforts were largely frustrated by the continuing British-Russian rivalry for control of his country.

In Russian Central Asia it was all but impossible to avoid friction, however predictable, between the indigenous populations and the Russian authorities. Differing customs, habits, and social approaches brought about periodic confrontations over such issues as new health regulations, sanitation projects, and water-control efforts as these projects offended local sensibilities. The large influx of Russian and Ukrainian settlers from 1890 on presented major new challenges for the management of interethnic relations. Their large-scale movement into the Kazakh steppes provoked severe economic and social dislocations among the nomads. These dislocations triggered increasingly acute debates about the nature of Islam and the proper response to such interaction with the Russians. Such questions drew sharply divergent answers from conservative and reformist groups within those communities, setting them at loggerheads with each other. For the conservatives, closer contact with the Russians would mean further contamination by outsiders, abandonment of the community to the source of its decline, and acceleration of Islam's disintegration. For reformists in the area, such interaction with the Russians was an integral part of the attempt to adapt the best of the techniques and knowledge Europe had to offer through its Russian variant, to recapture the original dynamic, undogmatic tenets of Islam in order to reestablish and secure the identity and viability of the Turco-Islamic community within the Russian empire: in the Crimea, along the Volga, in the Caucasus and Central Asia alike.

The Tatar community played the leading role in the search for community reform and renovation. Their dynamism and energy came from several sources. For centuries they had been the major commercial and social intermediaries between the multinational Volga region and the Inner Asian areas. As merchants, translators, and traders, they had established their dominance in those markets, and built upon those positions to create impressive intellectual and cultural credentials as well. In such capacities, especially in the eighteenth and nineteenth centuries, they enjoyed unusual opportunities to travel to Moscow, St. Petersburg, Paris, Istanbul, Egypt, and the Levant where they were exposed to new social and cultural trends, science, and technology. Especially after the Crimean War and the resulting sizable Tatar migration to Constantinople and the cities of Ottoman Turkey, these communities came into contact with intellectual trends questioning traditional Islamic social patterns, calling for a restructuring of institutions, and initiating an intense new search for cultural identity that has continued to the present.

The roots of this phenomenon can be traced to such figures as Khursavi (1783–1814) and Marjani (1818–1889), as they began to question traditional scholastic dogmatism and examine the causes of corruption and decline in the Muslim communities. Bukharan decline was closely dissected by Ahmad Makhdum Donish (1827–1889) and traced to the abuses of wealth and power by the ruling dynasty and aristocracy who had turned their back on Islamic purity. Donish traveled widely in European Russia and posited Central Asian renewal on a close acquaintance with and study of Russian techniques and advances in science and technology, a study that would have to begin with a mastery of the Russian language itself. Donish and later Tatar thinkers combined the call for such an acquisition of European techniques with a call for rethinking and revivifying the fundamental structures of Muslim (and Turkic) societies throughout the region. This search for a "new way" *(jadid)* often took on what seemed to be pan-Turkic or pan-Islamic colorations to the tsarist authorities, who attempted to insulate the other Turkic communities such as the Kazakhs and Uzbeks from such *jadidist* Tatar teachers and journalists. For the most part tsarist administrative measures were successful, and Central Asia was protected from *jadidist* ideas until the end of the nineteenth century.

The most influential *jadid* publicist of the period was Ismail bey Gaspirali (Gasprinski) who originally opened a reformed *maktab* in Bakhchisaray; attempted to design a comprehensive set of language, religious, and social reforms; and published his ideas in the newspaper he founded in the Crimea, *Terjuman* (1851–1914). In his newspaper Gaspirali sought to shape and propagate a standard new Turkic language which would be used by and unite the several Turkic peoples of Muslim Russia. The tangible impact of these ideas and these forms was minimal until after the turn of the century.

The Jadidists had taken an increasingly critical stance on questions of reform within their own communities, and by the eve of the revolution of 1905 began to display new sympathies with reformist and radical intellectual and political trends from Russia and the West. The Russian loss of the war to Japan in 1905 opened up harsher alternatives than those hitherto considered by Russian reformist groups, and such thinking had its effects within the Turkic communities as well. Nevertheless, there was very little or no overt participation by the Turkic populations in the revolutionary events of 1905–1906 in Central Asia. The tsarist authoritites attributed this quiescence to the influence of the conservative Islamic religious establishment which saw the events as a challenge to the status quo. They immediately concluded that it was in their own interest to protect official Islam in the area in its most rigid and dogmatic forms as a major barrier to unpredictable social movements. The social struggle between the traditionalists (Kadimists) and the Jadidists became a major theme until the watershed events of the October revolution and the civil war.

Central Asian Turks played very little role in the Muslim congresses of 1905–1906, assemblies dominated almost entirely by Azeris and Tatars. One tradition that did begin at this time was a more active pattern of newspaper publishing. Various *jadidist* papers appeared briefly until 1908, some schools were opened in Bukhara, and reform trends were put forward. But a massacre of Shi'ites because of a religious clash in 1910 gave Bukharan authorities the opportunity to settle accounts and eliminate *jadidist* critics as well, and many of the reformers went underground thereafter. Small secret societies were formed to collect and propagate new information and new ideas, but these were initially circumscribed in their activity, sponsoring students for schooling in Turkey and bringing books and materials from Turkey and the West to Central Asia. By the time of the First World War, however, their activities had become more ambitious and effective, and were designed to bring in broader layers of the population, to overcome existing ethnic and religious divisions, and to inculcate a sense of more cohesive community unity.

Such activity and criticism reemerged more openly after 1912 as new discussion groups were formed in homes, teahouses, and schoolrooms, questioning the conservative structure and rationale of the Bukharan emirate, the khanates, and the religious establishment. Such *jadidist* analysis began for the first time to trace certain political consequences as it started to look at the alignments between tsarist imperial authority, the khanates, and the conservative religious establishment on the one hand, and radical political groups in Russia and the new *jadidist* trends in the Muslim areas on the other. Nevertheless, such activity remained limited largely to the social and cultural realm, and little or nothing was done before the revolution to embody such concerns in concrete political parties. Furthermore, such trends were limited mostly to the large cities of the Uzbek khanates in the south, and to the Kazakh elites in the steppe country to the north. The Turkmen and Kirgiz areas were relatively untouched. At the onset of the First World War the Central Asian elites had developed little resembling a mature political consciousness or organized political parties, and these deficiencies were magnified against the background of a very fragmented social and cultural landscape.

The war itself was received with apathy by the Central Asian peoples, who saw it essentially as a European matter of little direct concern to their region, especially since the local population was exempt from military service. That attitude changed with the imperial order of June 1916 to mobilize the Turkic population into workers' battalions, a move that was much resented because of a recent influx of Slavic migrants. The ensuing revolt resulted in tremendous destruction and loss of life among the indigenous peoples with perhaps as many as two hundred thousand killed and an equal number fleeing to China. The brutality of the repression touched virtually every subregion of the area, and deepened the chaos of the political scene on the eve of the revolution even further.

In the spring of 1917, after the first stage of the revolution in February, the first regional Muslim Congress was held at Tashkent, bringing together representatives of both the conservative clerical assembly, the Ulema Jamiyati, and the council of reformists, the Shura-i Islamiyah. Agreeing on little except the need to end Russian colonization and the return of confiscated lands to their original indigenous owners, the congress formed the Turkestan Muslim Central Council to represent it in future negotiations with the central government in Petersburg. These and similar bodies that were created over the course of the next months were fragile entities that did not sustain the test of wildly diverse internal divisions or external Russian and Soviet opposition. The last of the series of pan-Muslim congresses was organized in Kokand in November 1917 and proclaimed the establishment of the government of Autonomous Turkestan. This was probably the most serious challenge to eventual Soviet dominance in the area, but it ended in the Soviet capture and sack of the city in February 1918. Similar fleeting challenges were put up by local indigenous groups in Turkmenia and Kazakhstan, but neither was effective or long-lived. The Turkmen National Executive Committee based at Ashkhabad was quickly subdued by the Soviets, while the national-minded Alash Orda in the Kazakh steppes lasted somewhat longer but suffered a similar fate. The Kazakh case was a complicated one in which the Kazakhs were caught between a shifting set of Reds and Whites without, and a complex of competing actors and factions within. The Soviet victory in this instance was more diplomatic and political than military.

With the pacification of the bulk of Central Asia by 1920, the Bolsheviks could proceed to the subjugation of the remaining autonomous khanates of Khiva and Bukhara, a task much simplified by the existence of virulent ethnic and social disputes within those cities. Aided in each case by such internal factions as the Young Khivans and Young Bukharans, Soviet forces were able to weaken, intervene in, and subjugate the khanates. Only the remnants of the Kokand government that formed the nucleus of the Basmachi insurgency in the extreme southeastern regions of Central Asia were able to maintain a desultory guerrilla action for several more years.

Throughout the period of the civil war in the region, no clear or viable indigenous alternative to eventual Soviet rule emerged. No single group had defined or put forward a coherent political vision capable of catalyzing a persuasive national movement. Regional and tribal distinctions and animosities persisted, undercutting any broader political potential. The social and political contexts of events in Kazakhstan, Turkmenia, Kirgizia, Tajikistan, and the

Uzbek areas were radically different with few uniting ties or binding interests across that span. The fundamental conflict between *jadidist* and *kadimist* approaches rent that fabric even further, and caused many within the former camp to cast their fate with the Russian Bolsheviks and against "the forces of reaction." These divisions contributed features of a very real civil war to the Soviet subjugation of the area, whatever the realities of eventual Russian domination of that process. Ethnic, religious, and regional frictions underscored the weakness of the indigenous peoples, but the lack of political maturity and any mobilizing political vision doomed them to be pawns in the process.

In Sinkiang, as in other territories within the Chinese sphere, the rise of foreign influences posed the challenge of modernization to its not very numerous inhabitants. Yakub Beg's moves in this direction included military development as well as efforts to reestablish contact with centers of Islamic learning and military authority. Respectable quantities of weapons reached him from British India. But the Ch'ing forces that soon attacked him had even better foreign weapons, as well as solid supply lines, and no shortage of troops. After Yakub's death, Ch'ing reconquest proceeded rapidly, and the entire territory was incorporated into the Ch'ing empire as a province.

Culturally, however, influences in Sinkiang were diverse. Though the Ch'ing had prevailed militarily, the dynasty itself was becoming increasingly enfeebled, and militarily outclassed by its neighbors, as the war with Japan in 1895 demonstrated. Chinese authorities in Sinkiang practiced an ethnic exclusivity every bit as strict as that of the British in India, but Chinese culture seems to have held less interest for the Turks of Sinkiang than British did for the Indian population. From 1890 the British maintained an informal representative at Kashgar, in the person of George Macartney, a remarkable linguist and diplomat whose mother was Chinese. But the dominant power in the area was Russia. Nikolai F. Petrovsky, Macartney's opposite number, told him in 1897 that Russia would soon annex the area (G56, p. 92). Though this did not occur, the Treaty of St. Petersburg (1881) had given the Russians a preeminent position in Sinkiang, and Russia soon dominated economically. Roads and railways were reaching the borders of Russian Central Asia, making transport costs into Sinkiang far less than from either China proper or British India (G56, p. 26).

The Ch'ing reconquest had been bloody and thorough, and eliminated, for the time being, the local basis for development in Sinkiang. Chinese political control was indirectly strengthened by the Russian conquest of the Central Asian khanates, notably Kokand, which had been the traditional sanctuaries of Sinkiang's Islamic leadership. But despite these factors, Chinese control was gradually displaced by Russian. After the Sino-Japanese war the court in Peking was too pressed to pay much attention to faraway Sinkiang. The overthrow of the Manchus in 1911 further weakened China's grip. Sinkiang became, in effect, the personal fiefdom of Yang Tseng-hsin, who ruled at Urumchi from 1912 to 1928. In 1920 Yang concluded a trade pact with the new Soviet government,

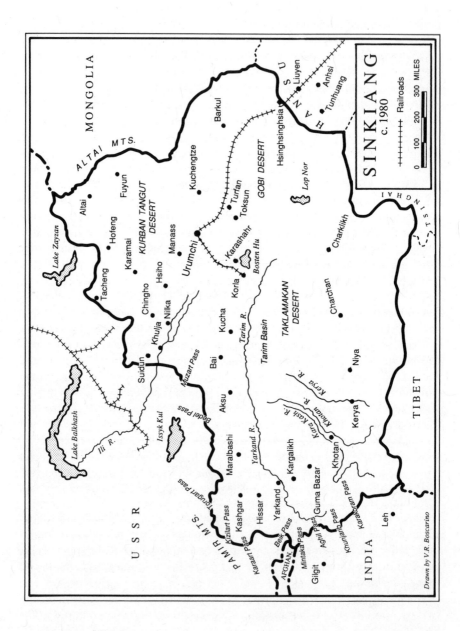

MONGOLIA

ALTAI MTS.

Lake Zaysan

Barkul

KURBAN TANGUT DESERT

Kuchengtze

Fuyun

Altai

Hofeng

Karamai

Tacheng

Chingho

Hsiho

Manass

Nilka

Khulja

Urumchi

Turfan

Toksun

GOBI DESERT

Lop Nor

Hsinghsinghsia

Liuyen

Ahhsi

Tunhuang

HANSU

SINKIANG
c. 1980

++++ Railroads

0   100   200   300 MILES

Karashahr

Korla

Bosten Hu

Charkiikh

Charchan

TAKLAMAKAN
DESERT

Niya

Kerya

TSINGHAI

Suidun

Muzart Pass

Bai

Kucha

Tarim R.

Tarim Basin

Bedel Pass

Issyk Kul

Lake Balkhash

Ili R.

Aksu

Maralbashi

Yarkand R.

Kargalikh

Guma Bazar

Khotan

Kerya

Keriya R.

Khotan R.

Kara Kash R.

Yurungkash R.

TIBET

USSR

PAMIR MTS.

Kizilart Pass

Karaart Pass

Yangart Pass

Kashgar

Hissar

Yarkand

Belk Pass

ARGHAN.

Mintaka Pass

Aghil Pass

Gilgit

Khunjarab Pass

Karakoram Pass

Leh

INDIA

Drawn by V.R. Boscarino

and set up two Chinese consulates in Soviet Central Asia. Soviet influence was enhanced by the completion of the Turkestan-Siberian railroad in 1930. By the early twentieth century Sinkiang was being transformed, but not by its own people.

In Mongolia, the Chinese-Russian rivalry also had a profound influence. The completion of the Trans-Siberian railway in 1905 made it possible for an originally European power, Russia, to establish firm control on the Pacific coast as far south as Port Arthur. Broadly speaking, this represented an important increment to Russia's influence, but it also created new risks. The rather narrow corridor through which the railway passes south of the great crescent of Lake Baikal was vulnerable to attack from Mongolia. The Russians became painfully aware of this problem during the disastrous Russian-Japanese war, and as a result the territory of economically impoverished lamaist herdsmen, who looked vaguely to Urga as a kind of protocapital, suddenly became a key link in the security of a great power. At the same time, the declining Manchus, for more than two centuries masters of Mongolia, were attempting to reassert their control through the massive immigration of Han Chinese into Inner Mongolia. Out of deep-seated and longstanding animosity toward Chinese merchants and moneylenders, the Mongols began to look to Russia for protection, a Russia that already had a foothold in Mongolia.

As Russia began to expand to the Pacific, its influence began to be felt in the still-independent Mongolian territories. The first foreign consulate in Outer Mongolia, a Russian consulate, opened in Urga, site of the Gandan monastery and home of the Jebtsundamba Khutughtu (the supreme lama in Outer Mongolia). The chief Russian diplomatic representative from 1872 to 1907, Ia. P. Shishimarev, had great political influence. Russian Orthodox priests also played a role, notably F. A. Parniakov, who served in Urga from 1914 to 1921, and organized schools and libraries. A few Mongols, such as Ja Lama (Dambijantsan), a Kalmyk (Oirat) military leader who attempted after 1911 to establish his own Oirat separatist state in and around Kobdo in western Mongolia, had spent much time in Russia.

To deal with the "challenge of modernity" that suddenly confronted them, some Mongols began to think in ways that today we call "nationalistic." They tried to establish a common identity that would override the traditional clan and tribal antagonisms. The impulse for much of this thought came from Mongols outside of the heartland: Buriats in Russia and Barguts in Inner Mongolia. Some slight cultural stirrings became evident: newspapers were published, the church came in for criticism, and social theories were debated among Buriat intellectuals. The roots of pan-Mongolism based on the Buddhist church can be traced back to this period.

But above all it was the military challenge that galvanized the Mongols. Fearing the Chinese, the Jebtsundamba Khutughtu had dispatched a mission to St. Petersburg in 1895 seeking aid. Similar missions were sent in 1905, 1907, and 1910, while in 1907 a group of Mongols in Manchuria sought help from the Russian consul at Harbin. In 1911 the Sain Noyon Khan (Sayin Noyan Khan), a lay prince, persuaded the Jebtsundamba Khutughtu to call a congress of princes and lamas at Urga, which again sent delegates to St. Petersburg.

Some breathing space for the Mongols was provided by the overthrow of the Manchu dynasty in 1911. Mongolia declared independence, and the Jebtsundamba Khutughtu became the secular as well as ecclesiastical leader. His not very effective administration was overwhelmed, though, when the battles of the civil war in Russia began to affect Mongolia. In 1921 Baron Roman von Ungern-Sternberg occupied Urga with an army of White Russians, driving the Chinese out for good. Shortly thereafter, ten thousand Red Army troops (and seven hundred Mongols) marched in, and established, in effect, Soviet administration.

This outcome, by no means foreordained, determined the direction of Mongolia's modernization. Chinese were expelled, and trade with China, previously vast, rapidly came to a halt. The political struggles of the Soviet Union were mirrored in Mongolia, and when industrialization was attempted, it was along Soviet lines.

In Tibet, a limited relaxation of the policy of self-isolation following Colonel Younghusband's invasion of 1904 led to some minor contacts with the modern world. An agreement concluded in that year gave the British the right to establish trade marts in several Tibetan towns, and these rights were confirmed by a treaty with China two years later. It is interesting to note that at this time four young Tibetans were sent to public school in England, where they learned excellent English while forgetting Tibetan.

Under the terms of the Anglo-Russian convention of 1907 the two countries agreed not to establish formal diplomatic relations with Tibet or to seek concessions for railways, roads, telegraph lines, mines, or similar enterprises. This agreement did not, however, affect British trading rights in Tibet. When the thirteenth Dalai Lama went into exile in Darjeeling and Kalimpong in 1910, during a Chinese invasion of his country, he became interested in modern institutions and technology. When he returned to Lhasa in 1912 he tried to introduce a modest program of modernization, but he could not convince either his fellow lamas or the secular leaders to change their ways. In these years modernity in Tibet was limited to a telegraph line, an electric generator, and rifles for its small army.

Throughout this period the British treated Tibet as an autonomous state under the suzerainty of China. The term "suzerainty" was drawn from the vocabulary of Western international law, and had no precise equivalent in Tibetan or Chinese. Tibet had accepted the protection of China since the eighteenth century, and China considered Tibet to be within its sphere of influence. The actual role of China in Tibet depended on the ability of the Chinese government to exert influence in this distant territory, but between 1910 and 1950 China did not have such a capacity. Throughout the first half of the twentieth century the British frequently mediated between Tibet and China over frontier disputes and similar controversies.

Conclusions and Comparisons

In seeking to describe the processes of modern change in Inner Asia, it is important to recognize that for some purposes it is legitimate to consider it as a region with significant common characteristics, whereas for other purposes it is a region of great diversity. The political diversity is increasingly evident as seen from a late twentieth-century perspective, and one is tempted to question whether such concepts as identity, foreign influences, and the challenge of modernity are applicable to the region as a whole. Yet when one considers the regional commonalities in the process of societal transformation as compared with other regions of the world, the importance of assessing the relations of the relative and the particular to the general becomes apparent.

One's first impression in considering patterns of identity in Inner Asia is that the overarching influence of Islam in most of the region, and of Buddhism in Tibet, Mongolia, and parts of Sinkiang, provides the common basis for beliefs, customs, and organization that serve as the point of departure for common action in the modern era. On closer examination, however, it becomes apparent that the great variety of sects and outlooks within these religions, interacting as it does with a diversity of ethnic cultures and foreign influences, provides little basis for a common identity. Like Christianity in Europe, the common religious culture has not withstood the pressures of myriad local and regional animosities and conflicts.

In parts of Inner Asia, however, religion has provided the main basis for identity. In Mongolia and Tibet, religion has combined with common historical experiences to form a powerful unifying force. In Iran and Afghanistan, however, local loyalties and ethnic, tribal, and religious divisions predominated before the modern era and have continued to serve as obstacles to national unity well into the twentieth century. To an even greater extent in Russian Central Asia, and in Sinkiang, patterns of religious identity have been fragmented.

It should be acknowledged that throughout the world even today "national" identity is still the exception rather than the rule. Even in the case of such well-established early-modernizing societies as France and the United Kingdom, a society-wide sense of national identity facilitating the pursuit of common policies was not achieved without great conflict, and regional loyalties remain strong. Japan and Russia, although under great pressure as latecomers to modernization, had achieved a strong premodern sense of identity and were able to borrow from more developed societies without danger of losing their independence. In a politically divided Germany, and to an even greater degree in China, regional loyalties, enhanced by local dialects and customs, continue to dilute the larger identities. Given the continuing influence of local identities in most societies, one must conclude that—apart from Iran, Tibet, and Mongolia—the societies of Inner Asia entered the modern era with an unusual degree of fragmentation.

The significance of patterns of identity in premodern societies resides in their capacity to interact with more developed societies as they come into contact with the outer world. Inner Asia was one of the last regions to come under the influence of more developed societies, and this influence followed patterns familiar in other parts of the world. The nature of foreign influences depended on the interaction between the level of development of the foreign country and the capacity of the Inner Asian societies to make use of these influences.

In the case of Iran and to a certain extent Afghanistan, the foreign powers were able to provide significant developmental assistance at a time when the governments of the two countries were prepared to undertake reforms. In this respect, and also in the price exacted by the foreigners, the experience of Iran and Afghanistan resembled that of the Ottoman Empire, Egypt, and Thailand. When colonial societies lacked the capacity to take advantage of the foreign influence, as in Russian Central Asia, such influence tended to serve the security interests of the metropolitan country as much as the developmental needs of the subject peoples. These cases resemble in this respect the situations in many parts of the world where European colonial influence brought the benefits of improved communications, public health, and security, but tended to delay more fundamental reforms by keeping most traditional institutions in place.

In the case of the parts of Inner Asia that came under predominant Chinese influence—Sinkiang, Tibet, and Mongolia—neither the foreign power nor the subject peoples was concerned with modern development. The Chinese influence was almost entirely concerned with the needs of Chinese security, and at the turn of the century China itself in its eastern provinces had been subjected to a semicolonial status not unlike that of Iran.

The capacity of political leaders to meet the challenge of modernity depends both on the foreign influences to which they are subjected and on their ability to absorb them. In Inner Asia such capacity was exhibited only by the rulers of Iran and Afghanistan. Foreign influence in these countries was more often than not exploitative, but the experience gained by local leaders was valuable as well as expensive. The beginnings of modernizing reforms, even though inaugurated under semicolonial conditions, permitted local leaders to meet the challenge of modernity more successfully than if they had proceeded in the absence of foreign influence. Benign foreign assistance, like that provided by international lending institutions in the second half of the twentieth century, was not an available option except to the very limited extent that Christian missionaries supported educational institutions. In this respect the experience of Iran was similar to that of the Ottoman Empire and China.

In the case of the colonial areas of Central Asia, and Mongolia, the challenge of modernity was predominantly intellectual so far as native leaders were concerned. In this respect it may not be too far-fetched to compare their response to the European Enlightenment, as well as to similar intellectual developments in the Ottoman Empire, China, and many other parts of the world. Before leaders in these societies could consider how to adapt their traditional institutions to modern functions and which foreign institutions could be transplanted to native soil, they had to confront the elements in their own cultural heritage that were opposed to change in any form. Intellectuals such as al-Afghani in Iran, the Jadidists in Central Asia, and the early Mongolian nationalists were precursors of the more effective modernizing tendencies that emerged in the twentieth century.

In Sinkiang and Tibet, on the other hand, the challenge of modernity was still beyond the horizon. Native leaders were concerned more with the Chinese military challenge and with the possibility of using Russian influence as a counterforce to this challenge. Chinese influence itself offered little in the way of modernizing inspiration, as that country was still in the throes of confronting European pressures on its maritime provinces while undergoing a still undecisive struggle between traditional and modernizing leaders at home.

3

Political Institutions

Introduction

The ability of a society—or a group of societies such as those comprising Inner Asia—to undertake modern political development depends to a very considerable degree on the extent to which the institutions and values that are convertible to modern functions have been developed before the modern era. The societies that have modernized most efficiently had the advantage of an institutional heritage of well-organized political authority, effective political leadership, and extensive experience in mobilizing skills and resources. It is of course possible for leaders of societies without such a heritage to adopt political institutions based on foreign models, but this involves imposing alien structures and values on populations that may well respond with a strong cultural reaction.

The complexities of political development may for the sake of economy be discussed in terms of three salient features: (1) the distribution of political power between central, regional, and local authorities in premodern societies, and the gradual ascendancy of central political authority in the process of state formation; (2) the role of political leadership, the growth of bureaucracies, traditional forms of political participation, and the incipient conflict between traditional and modernizing leaders; (3) the capacity of premodern political systems to mobilize skills and resources. Premodern governments that have the capacity to mobilize armies and build and maintain extensive public works have a long head start over those that have had little organizational experience.

The formation of states based on common ethnic or other loyalties is one of the most characteristic features of modern political development. Since few societies are ethnically homogeneous, states are normally formed by the forcible unification of local sovereignties at the initiative of a dominant ethnic group. The formation of national states has also involved the breakup of multinational empires, and only occasionally have multi-ethnic states (such as Switzerland, the

United Kingdom, Russia/USSR, and China) survived. The expansion of central political institutions has been accompanied by the penetration of societies by bureaucracies concerned with the mobilization and allocation of skills and resources. Prominent among these expanded activities are the promotion of security, and the allocation of resources to various forms of communication, education, and health and welfare that are characteristic of modern societies.

Premodern societies vary greatly in the extent to which political authority is centralized. Examples range from France and imperial Russia, with a significant degree of centralized administration before the modern era, to the Holy Roman Empire and India, where political authority was predominantly local and regional. The process of political integration is normally prolonged and fraught with conflict—as witness, for example, the experience of the German states and the United States in the nineteenth century. Success in developing legitimate central institutions in the modern era depends in considerable degree on the extent to which such institutions have been established in some form before the modern era.

The key to political development, and to other aspects of the process of modernization, is leadership. The struggle between modernizing leaders and adherents of premodern institutions and values is a central feature of this process. In seeking to determine the prospects for successful political development in the modern era, it is therefore important to explore the availability of modernizing leadership in a premodern society. Such leaders are normally individuals who have come under the influence of modern societies and who possess sufficient leverage within their societies to challenge the incumbent leaders. Experience indicates that modernizing leaders tend to come from the premodern elites— individuals who become convinced that modernizing change is essential to the survival of their society. However, they may also be individuals who are alienated from the traditional elites, whose professional experience (intellectuals, the military) has brought them into close contact with more modern societies, or who represent ethnic and religious minorities seeking redress of grievances.

Related to the question of leadership are the patterns of policy making, and especially the degree of participation of individuals and organized interests. The patterns of interest representation in policy formation vary widely among premodern societies, from those that seek to apply the principle of no taxation without representation to more restricted forms of consultation with organized interest groups. Regardless of the diverse heritages of societies in this respect, the trend is generally toward more expanded forms of political participation.

The capacity to mobilize skills and resources is a prime characteristic of modern governments, which frequently administer programs equaling one-third to two-thirds the gross national product. It is therefore important to determine the extent to which a premodern society has been able to maintain order; to mobilize and support armies; and to undertake projects of society-wide importance such as irrigation and canal systems, highways and other means of communication, and institutions to promote education and research.

It is apparent that, broadly speaking, the societies of Inner Asia have been among the last to confront the political challenges of the modern era. Their periods of significant political achievement in earlier eras were almost forgotten by the nineteenth century, and the process of political integration has developed in response to and under the predominant influence of outside forces.

Distribution of Political Power

Among the societies of Inner Asia, only Iran and Tibet had achieved a significant degree of political centralization by the beginning of the twentieth century.

The Iranian political structure can be traced back to the Achaemenid Empire (7th–4th centuries B.C.) with the development of the satrapy system. Under this system, local rulers, after being conquered or voluntarily submitting to the Achaemenid monarch, would continue to govern their kingdoms. In return, the satraps were required to send requisite tribute to the center annually, and to furnish manpower when needed to fight wars. To keep the satraps honest, the Persian kings stationed military garrisons in the larger cities, and employed spies ("eyes and ears of the king") to report directly to the capital any discrepancies or defections, or plots to regain independence.

The satrapy pattern continued throughout the rise and fall of many indigenous Persian empires. By the Safavid period (1501–1736) the concept of provinces ruled by governors appointed by the shah had become established. Also, standing armies were created, and the bureaucracy was reformed into a more centralized system. The unstructured succession of power in the royal family, however, constantly threatened to unhinge any regime. Charisma, palace intrigues, regional revolts, religious zeal, and fluctuating influence in the military caused constant shifts in the power elites.

European imperialism intruded into the area in the early years of the 1800s, and a continued deterioration at the center during the Qajar period (1794–1925) forced the Persian shahs to become more and more dependent on European nations, especially Great Britain and Russia, for revenue.

Four patterns emerged during the long reign of Nasiruddin Shah (r. 1848–1896): (1) an increase in the political influence of the *mujtahid* (Shi'a interpreters of the Koran and *Hadith*—"Sayings of the Prophet Muhammad"); (2) the rise of an opposition press; (3) the growth of Bahaism out of Babism (see "The Challenge of Modernity," chapter 2); and (4) the growth of nationalism and constitutionalism, fertilized by contacts with European liberalism. The development of new sources of leadership in the twentieth century, as represented especially by the constitutional movement that emerged in 1904, led in due course to the strengthening of central authority under new auspices.

In Tibet a similar degree of political consolidation had evolved. Tibet achieved prominence as a major political power during the seventh to the ninth centuries under the leadership of a royal lineage within a social structure analogous to what is known in the West as feudalism. When the unity of the kingdom was destroyed by rivalries within the royal dynasty, Tibet dissolved into feuding principalities and was only united under a new dynasty with the support of its Mongolian patrons in the thirteenth century. This lineage in turn weakened under internal dissension, but renewed Mongolian influence gradually transferred political authority to a succession of lamas of the dGe-lugs-pa monastic order, known as the Yellow Hats. The title of Dalai Lama (Dalai being a Mongolian word meaning "ocean," implying great strength and authority) was created in the sixteenth century, and Tibet was finally reunited by the Mongols in 1642 during the administration of the fifth Dalai Lama.

The Dalai Lama, resident in the Potala palace in Lhasa, was temporal head of a structure of balanced tensions. The landowning nobles shared political authority with the lamas, but resented their influence. Rival Buddhist sects, in particular the Black Hats and the Red Hats, were also restless under the rule of the Yellow Hats. The Panchen Lama, who resided in a separate residence in a monastery near Shigatse, was sometimes used by the Ch'ing as a counterpoise to the Dalai Lama. This rather tenuous structure, which lasted until 1950, was breached by Jungarian and Nepalese invasions in the eighteenth century, accompanied by civil strife, but order was restored by Ch'ing intervention in 1721, 1728, and 1751.

Ultimate sovereignty over Tibet was never clear, for the Chinese took a direct role in the kingdom in 1720, at the time of the expulsion of the Jungars, and eventually stationed a military mission there. The Tibetans recognized Ch'ing rule, but on their own terms: as lay patronage of a higher spiritual authority, thus reserving ultimate legitimacy to themselves. The Ch'ing, of course, saw things the other way around, with their emperor taking precedence, and uncertainty about the relationship between the Chinese capital and Lhasa continued until 1949.

Religious and secular status intermeshed. Within the monasteries, of which there were about twenty-five hundred containing some 760,000 monks in the late nineteenth century, boys from rich or noble families stood the best chance of advancement. Only one position—that of abbot of Ganden monastery, founded by Tsong-kha-pa—was open to any monk. Other such positions were either hereditary, or filled by a reincarnating lama, whose successive incarnations were often found among the offspring of the leading noble families.

Central Asia, the traditional heartland of Inner Asia, was for centuries the crossroads of major empires, dominant nomadic imperial formations that conquered and held in political subjugation the large sedentary states on their periphery for hundreds of years. The Huns, the Mongols, the Golden Horde, the Turkic khanates of the steppe, all traced their origins to the particular socioeconomic and political dynamics of the Turco-Mongolian regions of Inner Asia. They controlled the agricultural centers of China, Russia, Persia, Afghanistan, and north India. Headed by dynasties that were nomadic and tribal in origin, these empires contributed to the emergence of a high culture and civilization which flourished in the great urban centers of Central Asia: Bukhara, Khiva, Samarkand, Herat. For almost a millennium that culture was a fountainhead of artistic, literary, architectural, musical, and medical achievements, blending the three great streams of Turco-Mongolian military structures and discipline, Persian administrative genius and language, and Arabic religion and philosophy.

From the sixteenth century on, this great cultural and imperial crossroads began to break down into a series of fragmented and subject dependencies, increasingly subservient to the sedentary agricultural states on the periphery. Three major trends combined to bring about this reversal. The gunpowder revolution along with the rapid acquisition of firearms and their use by the European powers, the European opening of the sea lanes to Asia and the concomitant decline of the Inner Asian overland east-west trade routes, and, finally, the increasingly conservative religious establishment in Central Asia which stifled innovation—together these factors undercut the root sources of the area's former dominance and made it the prey of more dynamic and increasingly intrusive external forces.

Similarly Mongolia, which had presided over a world empire in the thirteenth century, was decaying and being absorbed into new empires that were encroaching on its traditional territory. Neither Inner nor Outer Mongolia had an indigenous government, for both territories had become parts of the Ch'ing empire. Tension between traditional Mongolian ways and the political order imposed by the Manchus emerged as a powerful force when the Ch'ing empire was overthrown in 1911.

The Mongols are a traditionally pastoral nomadic people, who have ranged over a vast territory in Inner Asia, from modern Manchuria to Inner and Outer Mongolia, to Jungaria (in northern Sinkiang), and beyond. Like other nomadic peoples, they have at times lacked any state organization above the tribal level. Indeed, even the tribe is not always well defined, although genealogy based on the clan has always played a role in attempts at unification and the legitimation of rulership.

At certain times the Mongols and other nomads have formed themselves into cohesive units, building first pan-tribal coalitions, and then, in some cases, great nomadic empires. Why nomads tended to build extended imperial structures in Inner Asia is the subject of much argument and little agreement among scholars. Certainly, we can dispense with the age-old stereotype concerning a supposedly eternal nomadic greed for the wealth of sedentary neighbors. Episodic trading and raiding (as was the case with the Mongols on the Ming Chinese frontiers) could garner such wealth without the necessity of building an empire. The inherent instability of nomadic economies in Inner Asia, however, may have provided some impetus for unification: unexpected spring blizzards which make iced-over grass inaccessible to herds, and diseases that can decimate sheep flocks in only days, for example, attest to the ecological unpredictability of life on the steppe.

Overcoming the centrifugal forces that seem always to exist in tribal societies, Temujin (Chinggis Khan, 1162–1227) managed to build such a nomadic empire. Upon Chinggis's death, however, his four sons, according to traditional Mongolian custom, were apportioned their "shares" of the empire, and four different histories (Persia, Russia, Central Asia, and China-Mongolia) were the result. Although the Mongolian empire as a single political structure was short-lived, its several heirs continued to exert influence into the sixteenth century.

Under the Ming dynasty several Mongols attempted to reconstruct the defeated empire, seeking first to use personal prestige (as in the case of Esen of the Oirat, not a Chinggissid), but later turning to religion as a possible additional bond to cement a Mongolian polity together. The conversion of Altan Khan to the dGe-lugs-pa or Yellow Church of lamaistic Buddhism is the crucial event: in 1578 Altan Khan met bSod-nams-rgya-mts'o, head of the Yellow Church 'Brasspuns monastery in Lhasa, at Koko Nor and awarded him the title Vajra-dhara Dalai Lama (Oceanic or Universal Lama, Holder of the Thunderbolt) and was in return declared to be the reincarnation of Khubilai Khaghan.

Religion became an increasingly important political force in the life of the Mongols from the sixteenth century on, both changing certain aspects of their way of life, and drawing their destinies into a relationship with those of Tibet, the Manchus, and ultimately the Chinese. Even as political cohesiveness was declining among the Mongols, religious influence increased. Several political leaders received titles from the Dalai Lama; such khans stressed their religious qualities, but none enjoyed success in reconstructing the empire. Instead, internecine struggle among the Mongols led to their conquest and co-optation by the Manchus, who had begun to become powerful in the early seventeenth century, and who gradually consolidated a hold over both Inner and Outer Mongolia, which they ruled as part of their Ch'ing empire.

Sinkiang, unlike Tibet and Mongolia, which by early modern times already had a considerable degree of cultural and political definition, is a territory defined by conquest: the wars of the Ch'ien-lung emperor against the Jungars, which brought under Peking's control a vast and diverse territory (the province of that name today covers 636,000 square miles, more than three times the size of France).

This new territory was placed under military rule. A Ch'ing general was in charge, and his headquarters were at Hui-yuan, a new city, west of the traditional Jungar capital which, renamed Ning-yuan, continued to develop under Ch'ing rule. A major garrison was placed to the east, at Urumchi (Tihwa), and other centers of Ch'ing administration were at Tarbagatai (Chuguchak) in northwestern Sinkiang, and at Kashgar (Ka-shi). The Ch'ing general and military officers controlled a military and civil establishment that was likewise imposed from without: Manchu bannermen and Han Chinese members of the army of the Green standard were garrisoned in Sinkiang, and supported both by local revenues (which were increased as farming peoples were settled to support the troops) and by silver from the Ch'ing capital (see "Identity Patterns," chapter 2).

In addition to the populations of Jungaria and East Turkestan already mentioned, which were ruled as its full subjects, other nomadic populations with much more limited ties inhabited sections of both areas. In the north were Kazakhs, of whom the Ch'ing were largely ignorant, though claiming them as tributaries. Small numbers of Kirgiz nomads were also found in the south, though there the climate was far less favorable to them.

After the conquest, the Mongolian inhabitants of the northern part of Sinkiang were organized in much the same way that the Ch'ing had already organized their other Mongol-inhabited territories, with banners created and hereditary *jasaks* exercising nominal rule, under Ch'ing supervision.

Southern Sinkiang, by contrast, lacked even the degree of cohesion that Jungaria had attained. The Turkic-speaking inhabitants referred to themselves as *yerlik* (or "local"), and merchants and other visitors to the area from western Central Asia found nothing particularly distinctive about the portion of their cultural world that was incorporated into the Ch'ing empire.

The valley of the Tarim River defined most of southern Sinkiang. The oasis cities along the river developed an urban civilization through involvement in the overland trade: Kashgar, Yarkand, and other settlements in the western part of the territory, which contained about 70 percent of the sparse indigenous population, probably three hundred thousand in the early nineteenth century.

Likewise in Afghanistan, until the reign of Amir Abdur Rahman, political authority was diffused among the local tribal and ethnolinguistic regional leaders and the Islamic clergy. Attempts at centralization generally proved ineffective, or created Afghan empires and not nation-states. Invasion from outside often brought about regional unity, to respond to the invader, but it usually dissipated when the threat disappeared. Most empires grew out of the southern (Kandahar), south-central (Ghazni), or eastern (Kabul) areas, home of the Pushtun ethnic group which constituted about half of the total population.

Rural leadership, either in sedentary villages or nomadic camps, was—and still is—collective, based on adult males who meet in a council (called *jirgah* in the south, *majlis* in the north) to discuss local matters. Joint councils met when issues involved two or more villages. All rural peoples avoided contact with government officials, because throughout most of the period before 1920 one-way extraction was the pattern. Those in power took from the rural scene without putting anything back in.

Abdur Rahman, who acceded to the throne in Kabul in 1880, could not, unlike many of his predecessors, construct an empire. He was blocked by Russia to the north and British India to the south. While the British and Russians drew his external boundaries, Abdur Rahman engaged in "internal imperialism." He literally conquered his own country, and spread his influence—if not actual control—throughout what is now Afghanistan. With the drawing of Afghanistan's boundaries, the country went into virtual isolation for the first time in its long history. The amir's resettlement of dissident Pushtun groups (see "Identity Patterns," chapter 2) accomplished three political goals: it removed dissidents from areas of discontent, it guaranteed a force loyal to the Pushtun amir among non-Pushtun peoples, and it provided the first line of defense against any invasion by Russia.

As he conquered, Abdur Rahman administered. At the center, he created an elaborate bureaucracy. Unlike previous Afghan amirs, who ruled as paramount chieftains among equals, Abdur Rahman constituted an authoritarian rule, with ultimate power vested in his person. Afghanistan, before Abdur Rahman, was the freest area in Asia. Under Abdur Rahman, an Afghan had to get permission from local government officials to travel from one town to another. The Iron Amir laid the groundwork for modernization, by shifting from a loose local type of federalism (which bred anarchy), to a centralism that was fiercely resisted by various ethnic groups for more than a decade. During his reign, the Iron Amir fought no fewer than twenty wars of conquest and rebellion.

Abdur Rahman divided the country into ten provinces, which in turn were split into districts. He gave his provincial governors carte blanche as long as they forwarded the requisite taxes and conscripts to the center. Ultimately, provincial boundaries were drawn without regard to prior Pushtun tribal configurations in the south, or the conquered non-Pushtun khanates of the north. Several important patterns emerged: provincial and district governments began to replace the tribal confederations and khanates as loci of power; some government officials confused, consciously or unconsciously, the duty to collect taxes with bona fide ownership of land; religious leaders lost secular power as Abdur Rahman "nationalized" major *wakfs* (religious trusts) and most prominent religious leaders were placed on the government payroll; those who resisted the acts of government officials were forcibly resettled within the province, thereby causing the local kinship-oriented systems to deteriorate further, with an attendant emphasis on the status of the individual in government-people relationships. The army was around to "legalize" all the activities. In fact, the provincial military commanders usually exercised more power than the civilian authorities.

Political Leadership and Participation

In view of the critical role of leadership and the multifaceted transformation with which the societies of Inner Asia were confronted in the twentieth century, it is important to understand the sources of the incumbent leadership in the premodern period and also the nongovernmental groups and interests that were likely to challenge this leadership as the complex problems of modernization began to become apparent. The leadership in modern political development is likely to come from without rather than from within the incumbent political leadership. In either case the transition from traditional to modernizing leadership has generally been accompanied by violent struggles among the various competing groups.

In tracing the emergence of modern political leadership and forms of participation in Inner Asia before the twentieth century, one should make the distinction between those societies that evolved independently, without direct outside
intervention, and those that were to a greater or lesser degree under colonial rule.
Those in the former category, Iran and Afghanistan, enjoyed the advantage of
independence from foreign rule in a context in which the countervailing pressures of Russia and Britain assured them of freedom from occupation. Reforming leaders could therefore borrow from earlier modernizers without facing the
burdens of wars of national liberation.

In the other societies of Inner Asia, political leaders had to interact with
foreign officials if they wished to implement policies of societal transformation.
In these territories the foreign rulers were more concerned with stability than
with change. One must nevertheless make the additional distinction between the
Russians, who encouraged limited social change in Central Asia, and the Chinese, who neither in their homeland nor in their outlying territories were sensitive to the potentialities of the modern era before the twentieth century. Tibet, as
always, was in significant respects unique. Although under Chinese suzerainty, it
retained a great deal more autonomy than most colonies and avoided coming
under predominant Chinese cultural influence because of the tenacity of its native heritage protected as it was by geographical isolation.

In Iran, the political system permitted tribal, regional leadership to remain
intact as long as it did not threaten the central government, which it occasionally
did successfully for the purpose of changing dynasties. This balance between the
incumbent central and regional leaders ensured the continuity of traditional values, which were little affected by the outside world until the twentieth century.
This tendency was strengthened by the secular power of Shi'a religious leaders
who had a continuing impact at the center, with varying degrees of intensity and
success. Central leadership was strengthened in particular during the long reign
of Nasiruddin, supported by his energetic minister Mirza Taqi Khan. Apart from
these centralist-oriented leaders, the traditional tribal and linguistic elites dominated the rural scene. This was especially the case in the non-Persian areas that
surround the basic Persian population: from Azerbaijan to Khuzistan, and from
Turkmenia to Baluchistan. "Regional shahs" gained influence as the center lost
power, a recurring pattern in Iranian history, and the Bakhtiari tribal leadership
maintained great influence in Tehran.

This traditional pattern of leadership did not undergo fundamental change until
1921, when Sayyid Zia ud-din Tabatabai (a political journalist), and Colonel Reza
Mohammed (commander of the troops) rode into Tehran with the Persian Cossacks
and shifted leadership patterns to inaugurate a new era in the history of modern Iran.

Afghanistan lacked a heritage of relatively integrated political authority such as
that represented by the political system in Iran, and did not begin to evolve into a
nation-state until the end of the nineteenth century. From about 1826 to 1978,
political leadership at the national level usually came from the Mohammadzai lin-

eage of the Durrani tribe of the Pushtun ethnic group. It was in the course of the long reign of Amir Abdur Rahman Khan that the first efforts were made to bring the diverse regions and ethnic groups of Afghanistan under central control.

As he conquered, the amir established provinces and appointed governors, usually successful soldiers, to whom he delegated considerable powers in matters of security and the collection of revenue. However, Abdur Rahman maintained control through a network of spies. Before Abdur Rahman the regional civil and military authority had been vested in one man who ruled with virtually no interference from the center as long as he supplied the requisite taxes, conscripts, and concubines. Abdur Rahman separated the two spheres of power, and each served as a check on the other. He encouraged his governors to consult the local leadership. In the countryside, the collective leadership of the *jirgah* dominated, but one elder served as the go-between with the district governor and other officials.

Unlike previous amirs, Abdur Rahman kept his sons and close kinsmen away from provincial power positions. He brought to Kabul the sons of vanquished regional leaders to train as civil administrators and army officers—and to have as hostages in case their fathers revolted. The "hostages" received jobs at the center, thus giving the rural leadership horizontal links into the government structure, important to gain favor with the amir and the court. Only in the zones of easy accessibility along the main routes of communication did the central government maintain relatively tight control.

The bureaucracy exploded to meet the administrative needs of the center, and to link the center to the provinces. Senior advisers to the amir not only came from his Mohammadzai (and other Pushtun tribes and subtribes), but from minority groups such as Qizilbash, Tajik, Hindu, and Nuristani.

Abdur Rahman's two-tiered council *(darbar)* acted more as a sounding board than as an advisory body. The upper *darbar* consisted mainly of favored members of the royal family and the ulema (learned religious leaders) and those in the elite trusted by the amir. Abdur Rahman appointed regional and tribal leaders to the lower council. However, both tiers remained in a state of constant flux for the Iron Amir tolerated no opposition. In addition, each of the uncles and sons of the amir held his own *darbar*, which complicated the institutionalization of power. A man could gain a favorable judgment at one *darbar*, only to find it nullified in favor of his adversary who had petitioned the *darbar* of another *sardar* (prince).

Abdur Rahman used an old Afghan tradition to further centralization. He called three (1885, 1888, 1892) Loya Jirgah (Great National Assemblies) during his reign. The Loya Jirgah consisted of key members of the royal family, civil servants, and military, religious, regional, and tribal leaders.

The amir appointed mayors *(kotwal)* for larger towns and cities, but various wards informally elected their leaders *(kalantar)*, who had to be approved by the government. Although the religious establishment lost much of its secular power under Abdur Rahman, the religious leaders were still responsible for handling civil cases in the courts, using a combination of religious law *(shari'at)* and local custom *(adat)*. Crimes against the state (that is, opposition to the amir) were personally handled by the amir. Abdur Rahman was probably the first Afghan ruler to articulate the "divine right" of a ruler. Thus, he went beyond the Muslim legal "divine sanction" to rule.

Unlike most Afghan rulers, Abdur Rahman died in bed and was succeeded by his son Habibullah I without incident. Habibullah continued his father's administrative policies, and invited members of families exiled by his father to return. Two families, the Tarzis and the Yahya Khel Musahiban, would play major roles in twentieth-century Afghanistan. They had been educated in Ottoman Turkey and British India respectively. Religious leaders regained some of their secular powers until the assassination of Habibullah in 1919.

The politics of Central Asia, in contrast to those of Iran and Afghanistan, evolved within the framework of an imperial system. Before the coming of the Russians into the northern Kazakh steppe in the eighteenth century, the two most important influences on political leadership in the area were the Arab introduction of Islam as a comprehensive way of life, and the Mongolian introduction of the principle of political legitimacy and authority through the line of Chinggissid princes. Together, the principles of Islam and Chinggissid lineage were to shape the political life of the region from the thirteenth century on.

Islam came not as a religion restricted to simple clerical dogma, but as an all-encompassing system combining philosophy, literature, art, and modes of military and political behavior—a system touching all facets of daily life. Yet, introduced in different ways throughout that vast territory, Islam took differing political and social forms in the various geographic subsegments of the region. The peculiar effect of its multiform interaction with the variant subcultures was ultimately politically fragmenting rather than uniting.

Similarly, in its initial effects, the overwhelming impact and impression created by Chinggis Khan's Mongolian onslaught in the thirteenth century served to implant the notion of imperial patterns and authority derived from descent in the Chinggissid line. Nevertheless, princely, tribal, and clan leadership became entwined in a complex genealogical fabric that from time to time pretended to unite, but ultimately served to fragment the area politically. The collapse of the Mongolian imperial system by the beginning of the fourteenth century left a kaleidoscopic political landscape. Although the genealogy of Chinggissid descent continued to provide the legitimating factor of political authority well into the eighteenth century, that authority tended to be segmented and located at local tribal levels, rather than serving as a supracommunal focus. Several energetic attempts were made over the centuries to resuscitate the overarching imperial ideal that was the Mongolian legacy, but little was accomplished of permanence until the Russian intrusion in the nineteenth century. It is ironic that it was to be the Russians, headed by the "white tsar" (as he was known in the Tatar documents of the sixteenth century) who were eventually to reestablish the unity of the region.

On the eve of the arrival of the Russians, the political life of the region was broken into several variant forms. The primary division was between the nomadic and sedentary peoples, with the former basically located in the steppe, desert, and mountain regions in the north, west, and east, and the latter in the south and southeast, in the lowland oases and river valleys of Transoxiana. The political structure of these several areas was primitive and was based on the essentially subsistence nature of these economies. Engaged in nomadic herding and the caravan trade, the Kazakhs, Kirgiz, and Turkmen were organized along patriarchal lines, submitting to a tribal and clan hierarchy based on personal and family loyalties. Internecine strife was frequent, raiding common, and there was little coherent political life. The economic and political life of the south was based on the sedentary agricultural patterns of the irrigated river valleys and oases and centered around the more structured and urban, but hardly less volatile, princely oligarchies of the khanates of Bukhara and Khiva. The economy of these Uzbek and Tajik areas in the south was richer and more diverse, with urban crafts and commerce supplementing the agricultural base, but the urban population probably never reached 10 percent of the whole.

Although some differentiation into diverse groups such as the Kazakhs, Turkmen, Uzbeks, or Kirgiz began to be evident among the Turkic peoples as early as the fifteenth century, there was little sense of identification as such by individuals until virtually the twentieth century. Until then, such groups had no real separate existence as political units, and individuals tended (as they still do today) to identify themselves by regional, clan, or tribal designations or, alternatively, by simple designation as a Muslim. The sense of ethnicity, if it can be called that at all, was restricted to the least possible social denominator and, as such, it never became a political force.

The significance of this loose and chaotic legal framework lay in its extreme diversity, and in the eventually disjunctive political effects it produced, rather than in any unifying Islamic legal system it created. Legal approaches and forms of conflict management and adjudication were intensely personal and local, dependent essentially on the idiosyncratic abilities of leading personages at the local tribal and clan levels. What this produced was not a single cohesive cultural and political world, but a complex set of patriarchal, personalistic, and highly competitive clusters.

The administrative structure established in Central Asia by the Russian overlords in the second half of the nineteenth century included elements of both centralized bureaucracy and political participation at the local level. By the end of the century, after going through several stages of reorganization, the region was divided into two territorial units, the Steppe and Turkestan, each administered by a governor-general.

The General Government of the Steppe, with its capital at Omsk, had an area of 698,965 square miles and included the territory between Siberia and the Aral Sea and Lake Balkhash, inhabited primarily by Kazakh nomads. The General Government of Turkestan, with its capital at Tashkent, was slightly smaller (685,466 sq. mi.). It included the more settled Turkic peoples of the agricultural southern region, and the vassal khanates of Khiva and Bokhara.

The two governors-general were appointed directly by the emperor, and were high-ranking military officers who both commanded the Russian troops of occupation and oversaw the civilian political, economic, and judicial administrative systems. Their regions were divided into provinces *(oblasts)* and counties *(uezds)* along lines similar to the administration of European Russia, and the mixed military and civilian Russian bureaucracy wrestled with the diverse problems of the Russian and Ukrainian settlers and the diverse local peoples.

The Russian and Ukrainian immigrants, who settled principally in the Steppe region, were organized along the lines established in Russia after the 1861 reforms. Each village was administered by a council formed by heads of households, who elected an elder as their leader. Groups of villages formed a district *(volost),* also administered by elected householders. These district councils had judicial functions governing minor offenses, which were adjudicated on the basis of customary law.

The settled native peoples were allowed to keep most of their traditional customs. The villages were headed by elders chosen by heads of households, who were concerned in particular with the allocation and collection of taxes. Justice was administered on the basis of Muslim written law, but the Russians sought to ban the inhuman local punishments involving cutting off hands and feet, confinement in pits, and other picturesque practices. In Khiva and Bukhara, however, such practices continued to prevail.

Administration of the nomads was a more difficult task. The basic social unit was the household *(kibitka),* and these were grouped into *auls,* which were considered equivalent to villages. Here again native practices continued to predominate, and among the nomads elected local judges followed their own customary law *(adat)* rather than Muslim written law.

In Mongolia, the Chinese empire provided a different type of leadership, which in most respects was more loosely organized than that of the Russians. The populace was organized into banners (see "Foreign Influences," chapter 2), which were subdivided into "arrows" *(sumun);* two or more "arrows" made up a regiment *(jalan).* Presiding over the banners were banner princes, or *jasaks,* who served as hereditary rulers. Banners were organized into leagues *(chighulghan),* which met every three years but dealt with little other than internal matters. Descendants of various Mongolian tribes continued to hold the title of *jasak,* but derived no enhanced power from it. The descendants of Chinggis were brought into the Manchu ruling house by marriage, and made to feel superior to the regular bureaucracy, but as the Ch'ing empire became more and more sinified, they too became more subjects than allies. Sovereignty was embodied in the Ch'ing ruler, to whom the *jasaks* presented yearly tribute of steppe goods to indicate their personal subordination.

However, the Mongolian recognition of Ch'ing legitimacy was never complete. Manchu tradition stated that when Ligdan Khan's son surrendered in 1635, the imperial seal of the Chinggissids also came into their possession. The Mongols deny this. The relics of Chinggis, traditionally the locus of Mongolian legitimacy, were not turned over to the Ch'ing, but rather returned to the Ordos, their traditional resting place.

The reorganization of Mongolian life that took place under the Ch'ing had many consequences. The division into banners, and the territorial delimitation of each banner's area, meant the end both to the fully mobile pastoral way of life, and to the possibility of intertribal alliances, the source of political power in the past. From being relatively independent herders, most Mongols were transformed into banner subjects, who owed taxes and services to their banner princes and to the Ch'ing government. Subjects could not leave a banner without the *jasak's* permission, and the *jasak* assigned pasturage rights within his territory. In other words, Mongolian tribal and clan leaders were co-opted by the Manchu practice of doling out titles, privileges, and territorial grants, a practice that the Manchus no doubt borrowed from traditional Chinese methods of dealing with neighbors on the periphery.

In Sinkiang, the cities of Jungaria, as well as Turfan and Kumul, had long histories of relations with China, and were brought without too much difficulty into the Ch'ing empire. The extension of authority into Altishahr, however, proved more difficult. Authority in the area had long been held by Muslim saintly families, the most important of these being the Makhdumzadas, descendants of a famous sixteenth-century shaykh of the Naqshbandiyya. Rivalry between two groups of these families had led to the war that brought the Ch'ing in initially. After that war, although some of the Naqshbandiyya were able to co-exist with the Ch'ing, others fled or were killed. In the nineteenth century, the continued loyalty of Altishahr's population to one or another of the Muslim leaders remained a problem for the Ch'ing, in particular because Muslim doctrine did not provide any legitimate status for a non-Muslim ruler. Continuing trade and cultural relations with the increasingly flourishing state of Kokand, in Russian Central Asia, meant that Muslim leaders could keep in touch with the peoples of Altishahr, and thus maintain sentiment, though the division among the Muslims into followers of the two chief branches of the Naqshbandiyya, the Ishaqiyya and the Afaqiyya, not to mention allegiances to other Sufi orders, made it possible for the Ch'ing to defeat the several uprisings and Kokandian invasions of the early part of the nineteenth century.

However, the Ch'ing empire was shaken by a series of Muslim uprisings later in the century (see "Foreign Influences," chapter 2). These were paralleled by uprisings in Sinkiang: that in Ili in 1863 was easily put down, but the successful uprising of Yakub Beg, who established an independent domain in Altishahr, was put down only with great difficulty. It resulted in the tsarist occupation of the Ili, which lasted until 1881, and the border remains a subject of dispute between China and the USSR.

Yakub was an able politician and general, and his legitimacy was further strengthened by the emir of Bukhara's conferring on him the religious title Ataiq Ghazi (Father Warrior of the Faith), by his strict adherence to Islamic law, and by his patronage of religious schools. In 1873 he was recognized by the Ottoman Empire, and he also received support from England.

Although some at the Ch'ing court favored recognizing Yakub as a tributary, the decision was made to conquer Sinkiang yet again. In 1876 Ch'ing forces left Su-chou in Kansu for Sinkiang. The Ch'ing overcame formidable logistical obstacles, shipping grain from the Yellow River loop, and across the deserts by caravan. Han settlers were moved in, accelerating a trend that had already begun, to man new irrigated farms that were designed to help support the troops. Critical to the success of the conquest, though, was the use by the Ch'ing armies of modern European weapons, including repeating rifles, steel cannon, and Krupp needle guns. These weapons were purchased with the assistance of a loan from Great Britain, China's first foreign debt. They were purchased mainly from Russia, and were shipped across that country to China. Divisions among the Muslims were skillfully exploited, with those who had served the Ch'ing previously being wooed. When Yakub died under mysterious circumstances in the spring of 1876, a succession struggle among his sons in Altishahr broke out, which greatly facilitated Ch'ing operations.

In 1884 Sinkiang was incorporated into the Ch'ing empire as a province and divided into twenty-six counties; administration was reorganized, with the intention of greatly increasing tax revenues, to the point at which the military garrison would become financially self-sufficient.

With the break-up of the Ch'ing empire in 1911, Sinkiang came under the control of Yang Tseng-hsin, a military man who followed a policy of maintaining good relations with the new Bolshevik regime in Russia. Under his rule, and that of his successor, Chin Shu-jen, the Soviet presence and influence were expanded, with Soviet trade agencies being established at many points. In 1933 a coup d'etat ousted Chin, and he was succeeded by Sheng Shih-ts'ai.

Tibet differed from Sinkiang and Mongolia in Ch'ing times by having its own indigenous and virtually autonomous government. Tibet proper maintained its own structure of government (see below), while Tsinghai (northeastern Tibet) and eastern Tibet (eastern Kham) paid taxes to the Ch'ing government. Tsinghai was under the control of a Manchu *amban* in Sining, and eastern Kham was administered by Szechwan.

In theory, Tibet was administered by the Li-fan-yuan (Court of Colonial Affairs), a Ch'ing institution set up to oversee Mongolia, Tibet, Sinkiang, and the rest of Inner Asia, whether within or beyond the borders of the Ch'ing empire. In fact, Tibet's distance from Peking enabled the Dalai Lama, Tibet's theocratic ruler, to govern fairly autonomously, with only formal acknowledgment of Ch'ing sovereignty.

During the centuries of nominal Ch'ing sovereignty, the government of the Dalai Lama exhibited far greater unity and autonomy than that of either Inner or Outer Mongolia: these latter were directly subject to Ch'ing policies, which induced and accelerated political fragmentation. The Lhasa government assigned hereditary lands to Tibetan noble families in return for their giving up one or two sons for government service. The sons of the Tibetan nobility thus joined the lay branch of the dual clerical-lay government structure. The noble family's land and right to serve in government were inherited, but specific government posts were not inherited, as Lhasa tried to prevent a monopoly of the top posts. Pastoral nomads, who constituted only about one-sixth of the nineteenth-century Tibetan population, did not play a role in this system.

The Tibetan government under the Dalai Lama in Lhasa consisted of two equal branches, one clerical and one lay, each with 175 officials. One monk official would be paired with one layman to serve in a regional governorship in Tibet. The Ch'ing presence in Lhasa consisted of one *amban,* one assistant *amban* (both bannermen), and a small garrison. *Amban* was the Manchu (and Mongolian) word for "high official" in the sense of an imperial representive. The role of the *ambans* has been characterized as being little more than that of political observers. As a formality, Lhasa forwarded recommendations for filling bureaucratic offices to Peking for approval, and members of the lay bureaucracy received Ch'ing bureaucratic ranks.

The person of the Dalai Lama, however, was not always supreme in this political structure. While the newly selected Dalai Lama was an infant, regents would rule in his stead. Regents did not always relinquish their power and in some cases continued to rule throughout a Dalai Lama's lifetime. In at least one case, the Dalai Lama chose his own regent to rule in his stead; in 1904 the Dalai Lama fled the capital as British troops were approaching, and he selected a high-ranking lama to serve as regent in his absence. Not all regents were lamas; some were laymen.

The political power of the clerical half of government seems to have been as great as that of the secular branch, even though monk officials had no office lands and were financially less well off as a group than their secular counterparts. Future monk officials were drafted as boys from the main monasteries and were trained for office in the Potala.

Outside of the government-defined nobility, there were prominent local landowning families, *Bon* (indigenous shamanist) priests, and others whose status was derived from nongovernmental functions. Waddell (N42, p. 175) lists "Village Headmen" at the bottom of his list of civil government offices, but it seems that these headmen functioned more as a part of local society than as a part of Lhasa's government bureaucracy. Such headmen were elected for perhaps three years by a "council of elders." The village headmen collected taxes for the

Lhasa government, independent prince, or religious leader, depending on the village's jurisdiction. The position of village elder was lucrative and prestigious and sometimes became hereditary.

Of particular relevance to the authority of political leadership in Tibet was the effort of the Ch'ing dynasty to control the actual selection of a reincarnation of the Dalai Lama. In 1793, in the aftermath of the Ch'ing expulsion of Nepalese forces from Tibet in the Tibetan-Nepalese war of 1792, the Ch'ien-lung emperor decided to exert more direct control over the Tibetan polity. The emperor ordered a golden urn sent to Lhasa; in the urn slips of paper with the names of appropriate candidates were to be placed. Appropriate candidates, from the Ch'ing point of view, were members of Tibetan commoner households, not members of the Tibetan nobility. The name of the next reincarnation of the Dalai Lama was supposed to be drawn out of the urn. To what degree the Tibetans adhered to the Ch'ien-lung emperor's decree on this matter is extremely difficult to ascertain. What is certain is that the Ch'ing method of selection was directly counter to the traditional Tibetan (and Mongolian) means of selection: the child-candidate's recognition of a few items that had belonged to the deceased incarnation. Just as the Ch'ing court by the nineteenth century was lax in enforcing prohibitions against Mongolian nobles being selected as *khubilghans* (reincarnations), so the enforcement of the urn method in Tibet is highly questionable.

Ch'ing patronage and support of the Dalai Lama were not rejected by the Tibetans, in spite of the unwelcome interference in the selection of reincarnations. From the Tibetan point of view, the role of patron was inferior to the figure of the Dalai Lama and the ecclesiastical community. From the Ch'ing point of view, Tibetan acceptance of imperial Manchu patronage signaled subservience.

Mobilization of Skills and Resources

Among the outstanding characteristics of the modern era is the capacity of societies, whether by governmental or private means, to mobilize skills and resources for purposes of societal transformation. The integration of administrative authority and the emergence of political leadership on a society-wide scale are the necessary prerequisites for the accumulation of resources and the organization of enterprises beyond what is possible at a local or regional level. In earlier centuries the peoples of Inner Asia had administered large empires, maintained substantial military forces, and constructed impressive buildings, irrigation systems, and other public works. These capacities had been largely lost by the seventeenth century, and it was not until the end of the nineteenth, under the pressure of foreign influences, that leaders concerned with the creation of modern institutions began to regain the capacity to organize major undertakings.

In Iran the initial achievement of the centralizing leadership, a prerequisite to further developmental efforts, was the mobilization of substantial military forces controlled by the center. A standing army was not established in Iran until the

1920s, but during the Qajar dynasty five military groupings evolved: the professional palace guards; tribal armies commanded by their own chieftains; provincial levies raised in emergencies and commanded by the Qajar nobility; the paramilitary gendarmerie responsible for maintaining law and order in the countryside, created and trained in the early 1900s by pro-German Swedish instructors; and a special group of Turkic-speaking Qizilbash, the Shahsevan, who were the guardians of the northwestern Russo-Iranian frontier. In the late nineteenth century, the Russian-trained and commanded Persian Cossack Brigade replaced the old palace guard, and during the First World War (1916), the British raised the South Persia Rifles, mainly to protect British interests.

Military consolidation was accompanied by increased mobilization of fiscal resources. For taxation purposes, the government relied on tax farmers, who worked through revenue-collection offices in each province. Local leaders remained in power and cooperated with the agents of the shah to collect the requisite taxes and send levies to the center as required. However, customs duties were the most important item in taxation receipts. As 1900 approached, the main sources of revenue came from foreign investments and loans. Concessions to European nations contributed to the creation of an infrastructure of roads, ports, and communications networks. But large bodies of men could be mobilized to build and perpetuate the local irrigation systems necessary to improve agricultural output. Corvée was common. And, to mobilize men for any project, the cooperation of the clergy was essential. Without its approval, any attempts to mobilize could be blocked.

In Afghanistan, Amir Sher Ali (r. 1863–1866; 1868–1879) created the first effective standing army. Prior to this, regional khans and other leaders sent levies, primarily cavalry, to the amir's armies to serve in their winter campaigns. Seldom did the Afghans fight during the prime agricultural and herding season. Before the 1860s, only in winter could large bodies of men be collected, for then they would be either idle or feuding with each other.

With military consolidation came other developmental possibilities. Depending on their energy and developmental interests, provincial governors (and even district governors) had increasing opportunities to use conscript labor for public works projects. In some areas, roads and bridges were built. In others, chains of caravansaries (camel hostelries) were linked together about one day's march (14–15 miles) apart.

In the Inner Asian territories that developed under foreign rule, the interaction between native capacities and imperial practices led to a variety of patterns of mobilization.

In that segment that became *Russian Central Asia* such unity as existed was cultural rather than political, and was represented by the overlay of Islam. Yet the two potentially unifying features of the region, religion and ethnicity, never assumed any significant political contours. These features were functionally shattered by the intense parochialism engendered by patriarchal and tribal structures, as well as by the sheer distances and diverse topography of that huge and relatively underpopulated area. Political habits and interests tended to focus at social microlevels, suspicion and conspiracy seemed to be the primary political fuels, and there was little sense of cooperation or social coordination to achieve common goals, if such goals were even perceived. Attachments were to clan and village units, not to some larger political combination or formation.

Similarly, the concept of Islam was never able to meld the myriad competing local communities into a single, viable political entity. At best, it provided a loose sense of common cultural community, but, in Central Asia as in the Middle East and elsewhere, Islam did not provide a sufficient focus for a unitary durable political unit. Ethnicity and religion were not adequate aggregating factors, and did not shape an essential community of interests. Until the establishment of a dominant Russian presence in the nineteenth century, there was little stability or political integration.

Local political units were never able to aggregate into a sum larger than their parts. Political tensions and cleavages were numerous and frequent. The basic fault lines were those that divided the nomadic and sedentary worlds, the rural and urban worlds, and the distinctive tribal structures. Dominance, booty, and taxes were major motivating forces, and ruler-subject relations were marked primarily by notions of efficient exaction of tribute and service. There were few effective positive linkages between different strata of the populace of a given area, nor were there institutionalized political organizations or patterns of clearly delineated reciprocal obligations capable of holding a supracommunal structure together. After the Mongols, no single political or legal system ever emerged in Central Asia.

This chaotic political landscape was one the Russians were easily able to exploit in playing upon multiple internal divisions. It was not at all difficult for St. Petersburg to implement a policy of divide and conquer in this setting. In the course of the conquest, many of these Turkic groups either betrayed their ethnic kin to the Russians or maintained their internecine conflicts in the face of the challenge.

The tsarist legacy in the area between the 1850s and the First World War is a complex one. To begin with, the Russian incursion opened the closed world of Central Asia for the first time in almost three hundred years. It opened the Turkic elites of the area to dynamic new secular ideas of modernism and nationalism from Europe (as well as from Turkey) and to reform trends within Islam itself. On the other hand, concerned about the very consequences of such exposure, and about possible reform and renascence among the Turkic peoples, the tsarist administration instituted policies intended to buttress some of the traditional pillars of the political and cultural establishment in the area, especially the deeply conservative and orthodox khanates of Bukhara and Khiva, as a guarantee of the status quo. The khanates' accommodation with, indeed reliance on, tsarist military and administrative support only served to postpone any reform of the traditional system of power. The contradictory tensions of artificial political retardation, coupled with exciting new intellectual contacts and opportunities, engendered an increasing cultural, and incipient political, schizophrenia within those communities. Under these circumstances, such mobilization of skills and resources as occurred was the work of the Russian overlords rather than the native peoples.

In Mongolia and Tibet, of the territories of Inner Asia that came under Chinese influence, the principal context for the mobilization of skills and resources was the construction and maintenance of monasteries. In Mongolia under Ch'ing rule the importance of fixed settlements, particularly those associated with monasteries, began to increase. The rapid growth of monasticism—in the nineteenth century one-third to two-thirds of the male population may have taken vows—provided the main impetus for this growth of fixed settlements. The monasteries themselves engaged in trading and money lending, and Han merchants who had hitherto traded only at border stations began to settle in these proto-urban centers. Garrison troops added another element to this process, notably in Outer Mongolia.

It is quite obvious that to build the numerous Buddhist monasteries and temples which by the early twentieth century dotted the Greater Mongolian landscape a large work force—presumably consisting of skilled artisans and unskilled commoners—must have been drafted by the Mongolian princes and, later, by the Buddhist establishment itself. By the early years of this century, an estimated six thousand buildings, all connected with religious sites or monastery complexes (of which there were about 583) existed in Outer Mongolia (M42, p. 125). Estimates of the number of monasteries and temples in Inner Mongolia range from 678 to 1,166 (M41, pp. 29–30). As any one monastery might have an array of buildings from the main assembly hall to storehouses, printeries, guest houses, and monks' quarters, the total number of buildings in Inner Mongolia was indeed impressive for an area whose inhabitants were in the main seminomadic pastoralists.

Although physical descriptions of architectural styles—Chinese, Tibetan, or a mixture thereof—are easy to come by in the Western travel literature of this period, it is extremely difficult to locate an eyewitness account of the actual mobilization of a work crew of builders or a description of the actual construction of a monastery. Once a monastery had become established, its "disciples" (*shabi* or persons attached to monastic estates, sometimes called "serfs") were charged with maintaining and contributing to the physical well-being of the monastery. According to one account, the *shabi*'s duties included "tending the monastery cattle herds, grinding grain, cultivating, transporting goods, [repairing and constructing] buildings, kindling bricks, and preparing *argal* [dung] fuel" (M42, p. 132).

Similarly in Tibet, religion was a powerful mobilizing force. The Manchus tried to keep Mongolian Lamaism separate politically and administratively from

Tibet's Yellow Church, even though Mongolian Lamaism was derivative of, and dependent upon, Tibetan Lamaism theologically (M21, p. 34). Nevertheless, individual Mongols made the pilgrimage to Lhasa in spite of the distance and difficult travel conditions involved. The Manchu policy of keeping Mongolian nobles out of important ecclesiastical positions led to their dictating that reincarnations of high-ranking lamas in the Mongolian church, such as the Jebtsundamba Khutughtu, be found in Tibet, not Mongolia. In spite of this apparent confluence of interests, the Tibetan and Mongolian churches never attempted to mobilize their considerable resources to throw off Ch'ing control or form a unified political-ecclesiastical structure.

The total number of monasteries in Tibet has been estimated variously from about 2,500 (according to a late nineteenth-century observer) to almost 3,500 (according to an early eighteenth-century source; N31, pp. 139–140). Whichever figure was more accurate, the same question vis-à-vis mobilization of skills and resources arises with Tibet as with Mongolia: how were the financial resources and manpower mobilized for the construction and maintenance of such extensive structures? In Tibet, some monasteries were so huge as to constitute virtual cities. Such monasteries grew gradually over the centuries as monastic revenues from landed property, trade, and interest from money lending led to the amassing of great wealth. Monasteries were built and repaired with funds from donors who pledged contributions; monks solicited such funds (N37, pp. 93–97; N31, p. 140).

In the case of sparsely settled Sinkiang, apart from the maintenance of Ch'ing garrisons, the political economy was predominantly local. The possibility of a society-wide mobilization of skills and resources did not arise until the twentieth century.

Conclusions and Comparisons

Measured by the achievements of most other societies, Inner Asia in the 1920s ranked rather low in the degree of political centralization, the emergence of a cadre of modernizing leaders, and the development of a bureaucratic capacity to mobilize skills and resources. At the same time, it is also apparent that the premodern political heritage of the countries and territories of Inner Asia varied significantly. While considering the common features of the societies of Inner Asia, it is also important to give weight to the characteristics that distinguish them.

It is clear that in none of the societies of Inner Asia had central political authority developed in any way comparable to that of China, Japan, or Russia, let alone France or England, before the modern era. The predominant pattern of political organization was local and tribal, often nomadic, and the succession of "empires" that dominated much of Inner Asia over the centuries consisted of loose confederations of local chieftains rather than politically integrated structures. One would have to look to Africa, and South and Southeast Asia to find societies in which tribe, lineage, and other local loyalties played as large a role.

Iran and Tibet developed the most significant degree of political centralization. In both cases, late premodern political development was built on a foundation of relations between the center and the component regions that provided the basis for subsequent political consolidation. In the case of Iran, political development was strongly affected by both the challenge and the influence of British and Russian pressure. In the case of Tibet, geographical isolation and the idiosyncratic nature of the religious-political oligarchy led to a significant degree of central control.

The effectiveness of political leadership depends in part on the degree of central authority in the society, but one can have strong leadership in a decentralized society and weak leadership in a society with a tradition of central controls. Amir Abdur Rahman was a vigorous leader in an Afghanistan that was still predominantly tribal and pastoral, whereas the Dalai Lama provided little innovative leadership in a society in which he had great influence.

One thinks of leadership in terms of energetic rulers, such as Nasiruddin in Iran and Abdur Rahman in Afghanistan, but in practice they governed in consultation with central interest groups as well as with regional and local leaders. Modern democratic forms of political participation in Inner Asia may emerge in the twenty-first century, if then, but one should not ignore the primary and intermediate forms of participation, especially at the local level, that are characteristic of all societies. Only in Iran and Afghanistan were consultative national assemblies created before the 1920s, and they naturally tended to represent the elites rather than the commoners. Similarly the rather complex Tibetan administrative system provided "leadership" only in the sense of maintaining the existing system against foreign intrusion.

In the other areas of Inner Asia, under one degree or another of colonial rule, such native political leadership as existed was predominantly local and concerned more with stability than with change. Leadership at a more central level was provided by foreigners rather than by natives.

With the exception of Iran and Afghanistan, to the extent noted, the premodern societies of Inner Asia had developed little of the capacity for central leadership characteristic of medieval western and central Europe, Russia, or Japan. One would have to turn to Africa to find societies with as little experience before the twentieth century in organized political leadership as Inner Asia.

A valid distinction can be made between the form of political leadership and the functions of mobilizing skills and resources. The latter may be achieved by means other than central direction, such as local leaders or religious organizations. Whether by public or private means, any experience a premodern society may have in building large structures or highways or organizing large groups of individuals for the pursuit of common tasks will stand it in good stead when it faces the challenges of societal transformation.

In Inner Asia in the late nineteenth and early twentieth centuries, only Tibet and Mongolia had retained a premodern pattern of mobilizing skills and resources as reflected in the construction and maintenance of monasteries. Little evidence is available of the administrative and fiscal capacities underlying this achievement, but the proliferation of large monastic structures provides ample evidence that such capacities existed. In earlier times the societies of Central Asia had also had comparable capacities, but by the twentieth century these had long since disappeared.

4

Economies

Introduction

The most familiar feature of modern societal transformation is economic growth, reflected in the rapid increase in productivity per capita resulting primarily from the introduction of machinery. Probably the best measure of the scope of modern economic growth is the long-term change in employment patterns from 80 percent or more of the labor force in agriculture, animal husbandry, and fishing to a similar percentage in manufacturing and services. This transformation has a profound effect on the lifestyles and values of all individuals and is a fundamental feature of the thoroughgoing reorientation of society.

In this as in other spheres the levels of achievement of societies undergoing modernization depend to a marked degree on their premodern economic structure. This in turn, despite a tendency in the West to regard all later-modernizing societies as simply "underdeveloped," varies greatly among premodern societies. Some have a prosperous agriculture with a surplus that can be used for export and that can be taxed to provide resources for society-wide purposes, while others may barely be able to raise enough food for subsistence and live under the constant threat of drought or other catastrophes. Some have an extensive production of handicrafts for domestic trade and for export, while others produce only the limited instruments used locally by families and villages. Some have an active group of merchants with an organized system of periodic markets and with links to other countries, while others have little experience with the exchange of goods outside their own local communities. Some have political leaders actively concerned with the improvement of economic conditions and trade, while in other countries leaders are concerned chiefly with maintaining the existing system unchanged.

The extent to which the traditional economies of Inner Asia were an asset to future economic growth varies, of course, with their premodern economic status.

The productivity of an economy depends in considerable measure on the capacity of the political system to mobilize agricultural and trade surpluses for central services. Such central services include establishment of law and order, construction and maintenance of means of communication and systems of transportation, and regulation of currency and credit institutions. In the Western countries governments performed such services several centuries before the modern era, and provided a strong base for modern economic growth. Similarly in Tokugawa Japan and imperial Russia, the state played a crucial role in the premodern economy. In China, by contrast, the delay in undertaking thoroughgoing modernization in the nineteenth and early twentieth centuries was due to domestic strife and international wars, which prevented the state from maintaining the mobilizing functions developed in earlier centuries. It has often been noted that among the later-developing countries, some that retained their independence suffered by not having the benefits of colonialism. In the long run, the policies of colonial regimes have tended to stimulate premodern economic growth, and it is important to recognize that colonialism brought not only the burdens of exploitation but also the benefits of political coordination and control.

There are few premodern societies in which agriculture and animal husbandry do not represent the principal economic activity. It is primarily the surpluses produced by this branch of the economy that provide the revenues to support the services necessary for economic development. The role of agriculture as a source of wealth depends not only on its productivity but also on the efficiency with which the surpluses are extracted by the political system. While one may think of feudalism and serfdom as forms of exploitation of commoners by elites, they also formed the basis for the extraction of resources essential for economic growth. In assessing the contributions of premodern economics to economic growth, one must therefore be concerned with forms of landholding and with mechanisms for accumulating resources. In parts of premodern Japan and Russia, for example, some 20 to 30 percent more agricultural goods were produced than were consumed by the rural population. Whether such surpluses were used by the elites to support an indolent way of life or for productive activity in other spheres, was a vital factor in premodern economic development.

There is considerable diversity also in the extent to which premodern societies draw on the resources of agriculture and animal husbandry for manufacturing and trade. In China, for example, grains, cotton, silk, and tea were produced for a very active domestic and foreign market. The state regulated the currency and collected taxes which were applied to maintaining order, building canals and irrigation systems, and in emergencies helping areas afflicted by drought. Although most production depended on human labor, water-powered machinery was extensively used. Similarly in Japan and Russia before the nineteenth century, grain and specialized industrial crops provided extensive surpluses for trade. In Japan, this trade was entirely domestic, since the ports were closed to foreign commerce, but Russia was an active participant in world trade. Russia also developed during the period of serfdom a considerable industrial base in mining, metallurgy, and textiles, drawing on Western European technology, whereas technology in Japan lagged until the latter part of the nineteenth century. These examples of relatively developed premodern societies stand in contrast to most others, which had a much lower level of productivity and lacked the central political leadership to guarantee stable currencies, security, and communications necessary for a productive economy.

Economic Structure and Policies

The premodern economies of Inner Asia were based predominantly on agriculture and herding, with nomads, seminomads, and settled populations exploiting the resources in a symbiotic relationship. Trade also played a large role in economic life, with east-west trade predominating until the sixteenth century, when shifts in commercial routes led to the growth of north-south trade, which later declined significantly. In the course of the nineteenth century Britain and Russia sought to control the most valuable products, such as minerals, cotton, and later oil, and their intrusion also brought the beginnings of modern industry. These foreign influences were significant primarily in Iran, Afghanistan, and Central Asia; Sinkiang, Tibet, and Mongolia were only marginally affected before the twentieth century. The characteristic problem confronting modern economic growth in Inner Asia was that of transforming largely peasant and nomadic societies with a conservative social and political outlook based on strong religious beliefs.

Because of inadequate data, it is difficult to make accurate statements about the economic structures of Inner Asia, and the best one can do is make intelligent estimates. *In the case of Iran,* for example, it has been estimated that 75–80 percent of the population were peasant farmers, and nomadic and seminomadic herdsmen (E25, p. 49). Two-thirds of the population occupied one-fourth of the land and were concentrated in the relatively fertile northwest, the area with maximum rainfall. About 50 percent of the rural population were nomadic and seminomadic, but the figure dropped to about 25 percent in the early twentieth century.

Iran did attempt a census in 1860, but it was aborted because of the difficulty in penetrating the harems, resistance from religious leaders, and the simple fact that fathers did not want to declare the number of their sons of draftable age to the government, as well as expose themselves to the possibility of more taxes (E25, p. 33).

The population in 1800 was estimated to be five to six million, and in 1914 ten million. Famine and disease made greater inroads on the population than the many wars. Five successive years of drought caused the 1871–1872 famine, and nine cholera epidemics between 1851 and 1861 drastically interfered with population growth (E25, p. 21). The economic growth rate for Iran during the latter half of the nineteenth century was approximately 0.5 percent, close to the estimate for India during the same period (E25, p. 20).

Different economic patterns existed at various levels of society. By 1880 most agricultural land was owned by absentee landlords living in towns or cities. As farms grew larger and larger the indifference of landlords to the condition of the peasants led to a sizable migration to urban areas (E25, p. 209). European encroachment and economic activities gave further incentive to the rural-urban migration as new factories were built and urban-oriented cash crops were introduced. Irrigation projects near urban centers increased food production, and the cities were then able to support a larger population.

Few large urban centers existed before the late 1800s. Several factors accounted for this: no social and economic advantages existed for either the rural or urban common man; little economic opportunity was possible for an outsider because the bazaar usually consisted of tightly knit guilds; the food surplus necessary for urban expansion was lacking; no credit facilities were available, except to the upper classes (E25, p. 34). Urban centers and the easily accessible areas were controlled by the shah's appointees. The local power elites of nomads and seminomads dominated the political and economic scene outside the easily accessible areas.

In Afghanistan, the government likewise sought to promote economic development. Amir Abdur Rahman used forced labor to construct and repair roads. Local villages were impressed and their village councils were held responsible for the work. The amir also restricted travel in the countryside, and permits had to be obtained to travel from place to place. However, these regulations could only be enforced along the main lines of communication (F10, p. 143).

The amir also attempted to improve the postal service, founded by Amir Sher Ali. The service was exclusively for government communications, and not only used runners, who carried special identification spears, but also carrier pigeons that could fly from Kabul to Herat (F10, p. 144).

Nomads and seminomads usually managed to escape military service and taxes, and they ignored the travel restrictions. To pay for his many internal wars, Amir Abdur Rahman developed a tax system which was so successful that from 1880 to 1919 revenue from taxes increased five times. At the same time British subsidies contributed about 15 percent of his annual budget (F10, p. 161).

In Amir Abdur Rahman's Afghanistan, the many internal wars caused a fall in agricultural production, but the Afghans could still feed themselves. The amir began to tax bazaar merchants arbitrarily, which caused three reactions: some fled to Central Asia or India, others buried their money, and those who remained behind united more closely to protect themselves. Abdur Rahman, unlike the shahs of Persia, who permitted foreign monopolies to exist, created his own monopolies—especially in sugar and tobacco.

The amir tried to establish a unified system of weights and coinage, minted in Kabul. He also issued new coinage about every six months, and canceled all earlier issues, so merchants who hoarded their profits found themselves wiped out. Merchants, however, had a way of getting around regulations, and in most places the old coin remained valid for commercial transactions. The large standing army of Abdur Rahman ate up at least 78 percent of his annual budget (F10, p. 23), and British subsidies helped keep the country afloat. Abdur Rahman did want to develop the mineral potential of his country, but he wanted to do so without being dominated by Europeans. However, he stifled the free economic spirits who could have contributed: the bazaar merchants and entrepreneurs.

The economy of Central Asia was historically divided between the pastoral nomadism of the arid western and northern region and cultivated agricultural and commercial urban areas of the oases and river valleys of the south. The nomadic populations were always numerically inferior to their sedentary neighbors. Because of its arid setting and climatic conditions, this region always had a low population density. The extensive animal husbandry practiced by the Kazakhs required the vast grazing lands of the northern steppes, while even in the south there were relatively few oases and urban areas, and the population was scattered among the several river valleys.

Economic and political leadership among the several nomadic hordes of the north and the west went by age and hereditary distinction to the khans, sultans, *beks, biys,* and *aksakals*. The khans and sultans traced their patrilineal genealogies to Mongolian dynastic roots wherever possible. The primary responsibilities of these elders were to mobilize their nomadic clans and tribes to carry out their seasonal migrations, to enforce customary law, and to raise forces for combat when necessary.

These well-established leadership hierarchies were important not only in protecting and expanding flocks, herds, pastures, and water holes, but in undertaking marauding expeditions as well. Blood feuds and tribal warfare were common, and aggressive habits were often apparent in the struggle for pastures and expansion of grazing areas.

In the pastoral economy of the north there was little or no permanent settlement, and the nomads' livestock provided food, clothing, shelter, fuel, and transport, as well as a surplus to barter with their sedentary neighbors for necessities such as grain and metalware and luxury items as well. The nomadic way of life, which provided training as hunters, archers, horse breeders, and horsemen, gave them striking mobility and military skills, important initial advantages vis-à-vis the sedentary agricultural communities on the periphery.

The horse was virtually an object of cult attention among the Kazakhs and Kirgiz. The Kazakh horse was small and shaggy, but of great endurance, and prestige was attached to large herds. Sheep, however, were of greater economic importance, making up two-thirds to three-quarters of the total of livestock. These provided milk, meat, fat, wool, and hides. There were some camels, but these decreased in numbers as one moved from south to north in the Kazakh steppe lands. Dogs were used in herding, and from the eighteenth century on cattle appeared among the Kazakhs on the fringes of the Russian settlements. The nomads also produced rugs and embroidery on rough portable looms as well as felt, ropes, and leatherwork for their own use and barter with the towns and agricultural settlements.

The nomads enjoyed a symbiotic economic, commercial, and military relationship with the urban settlements to the south of the steppe and desert regions. The northern pastoral nomadic groups needed and were drawn to the agricultural, manufacturing, and trade centers of the settled oases and river-crossing towns of the south. Over the centuries the various Turkic nomadic clans, genealogically distinguished and militarily adept, not only bartered and traded with, but provided the changing dynastic leadership for the southern cities. Kazakh, Turkmen, and Uzbek nomads shared in a remarkable division of labor with the Sarts who formed the original commercial, craft, and administrative elites of the urban areas to shape the distinctive political economy of the region.

In the centuries that preceded the Uzbek wars with the Persian Safavids, this symbiotic economic pattern permitted surplus nomadic goods such as horses, livestock, hides, and rugs to be moved and traded for luxury items, metalware, and specialized weaponry to the Persian cities below Khorasan. Afterward, such trade patterns continued with India and China to the east, but the volume and regularity of such traffic were always dependent on the security of the trade routes and the intensity of intertribal warfare in the region. From the end of the eighteenth century on, the bulk of such traffic was reoriented to trade and interaction with the Russians to the north and west, as tsarist forces and settlers appeared in the Kazakh steppes. The principal raison d'être for Central Asian nomadic imperialism over the centuries had been control over the caravan routes and the trade that moved over them. Nomadic rulers consistently patronized commerce because by controlling and taxing caravans instead of plundering them they assured themselves both a regular revenue and access to the weaponry, metalware, luxury items, silks, jewelry, tea, and precious metals that the trade would bring. The eventual Russian move toward domination of the region was to a large extent motivated by much the same rationale.

A succession of ruling dynasties had standardized the collection of customs and taxes on the trade routes and at the caravan town. They began to introduce systems of weights and measures, sponsored the building and maintenance of a network of caravansaries, craft workshops, and bazaars; stationed post horses; regulated trade procedures; and suppressed banditry in the area. This "pax nomadica" fostered and advanced the symbiotic nature of economic interaction between the major nomadic, agricultural, and industrial actors of the Inner Asian regions, but the phenomenon was a cyclical one, subject to the competition of the various nomadic clans and federations and the destructive and creative cycle that spawned.

Patterns of landholding and ownership in the khanates and surrounding regions were complicated. Most lands in all three of the major khanates of

Bukhara, Khiva, and Kokand belonged to the khan and the government, but much of this was given to various aristocratic families to manage, and was inhabited by a peasantry that held the land in heredity but paid both state taxes to the court treasury and rent to the aristocracy.

From the sixteenth century on, aristocratic families had increasingly struck deals with the ruling khans whereby, through one-time large payments or returns of land, they received substantial lands from the court in perpetuity and were freed from further taxes, with administrative immunity to boot. In practice this process of transference was quite complex, but its ultimate significance was clear: an expanding pattern of tax and administrative exemption for the aristocracy. These properties were known as *mulki-khurri-khalis.*

From the end of the eighteenth century, the rulers of all three khanates attempted to curb this process and to break the hold of the aristocratic families on such lands. Numerous campaigns against the magnates involved both their physical extermination and their conversion into conditional landholding servitors holding service estates. These campaigns were far from successful and the reestablishment of control was far from complete by the time the Russians arrived in the nineteenth century, and such centralizing efforts were weakly carried out not only in Khiva and Kokand, but in Bukhara as well.

One way the great magnate families had secured land control in perpetuity was to turn such holdings into hereditary *wakfs (wakf avlad).* A significant segment of the irrigated and settled lands was in the hands of the Muslim clergy in the form of *wakfs:* approximately 25 percent in the Khivan khanate, for example, or in the Zerafshan valley. Peasants working these lands and those of the aristocratic magnates were sometimes bound to a variety of services and rent, sometimes not, so that the phenomenon of legal serfdom was scattered and unclear. Nevertheless, the binding of the agrarian populace to the magnates was common, and there is some evidence that in sales between magnate families rural inhabitants were transferred along with the land. Slavery existed initially as a form of war booty, prisoners being turned to a variety of household and agrarian services. The buying and selling of slaves, especially in Bukhara and Khiva, became a substantial traffic.

In Tibet, the role of the nomads was more important. A. M. Khazanov, in his typology of pastoral nomadism, describes Tibetan nomads as principal representatives of the High Inner Asian type, along with the Kirgiz of the Pamirs (B7, pp. 65–67). In those areas of Tibet in which the High Inner Asian type predominates, herds consist of yak and mountain sheep in a ratio of 1:4–8. The yak is used as a transport animal; with an active lifespan of thirty years and its ability to thrive at high altitudes, it has long been a valuable animal in Tibet. Cattle are ill-suited for Tibet's altitudes, and the horse was traditionally a symbol of prestige rather than a productive (meat, milk) animal as it was and still is among the Mongols.

Agriculture and pastoral nomadism in Tibet are to a great extent ecologically segregated activities, as the higher altitudes which are ideal for Tibet's High

Inner Asian type of pastoral nomadism are less suitable for agriculture. The lower altitudes which can support agriculture are ill-suited for the yak. Although the pastoral areas were more extensive than the agricultural areas in the nineteenth century, approximately five-sixths of Tibet's population of about six million were agriculturalists (N31, p. 109). Tibetans of all social levels engaged in trade, although the government established monopolies over the most profitable items, such as tea, wool, and rice. The government would apportion monopolies to monasteries and individuals. The government also ran enterprises such as the textile industry and gold mines.

In the eyes of Huc and Gabet, two Lazarists sent by the church in 1844 to collect information on religion in China and Tibet, Tibet was "rich, beyond all imagination, in metals" (D9, p. 146). According to Huc and Gabet, "gold and silver are collected there so readily, that the common shepherds have become acquainted with the art of purifying these precious metals." The Lazarists describe a currency of silver coins which were cut into pieces to produce smaller denominations. From the mid-nineteenth century on, Indian rupees gradually replaced silver coins as the most used currency, a development that reflected an expansion of Tibet's trade with India (N24, pp. 266–267).

Both Tibet and Mongolia generally struck nineteenth- and twentieth-century Western observers as being rich in natural resources but lacking in the means of exploitation and distribution of such resources. In the words of Huc and Gabet, "this country [Tibet] is perhaps the richest, and, at the same time the poorest in the world; rich in gold and silver, poor in all that constitutes the well-being of the masses" (D9, p. 146). The Lazarists, betraying a bias against Buddhism, blamed what they perceived as Tibet's overall destitution on the monasteries' accumulation of wealth: "The Lamas, invested with the major part of the currency by the voluntary donations of the faithful, centuple their fortunes by usury that puts even Chinese knavery to the blush" (D9, p. 147). There is no question, however, that the monasteries and the Lhasa government dominated the economy.

Sinkiang was, apart from Outer Mongolia, the least developed of the territories of Inner Asia, and in the middle of the nineteenth century its population of some two and a half million in the two provinces of Jungaria and Altishahr, divided by the T'ien-shan Mountains, lived mostly in some sixteen thousand villages. The Chinese authorities provided the bureaucratic structure, supported by garrisons in the main towns, which supervised irrigation systems and state farms and oversaw the administration of justice. The expenses of the Chinese administration were supported by taxes in silver, and in agricultural goods and handicrafts. The Chinese interest in Sinkiang was strategic rather than developmental. To the extent that they had economic policies they were directed more toward maintaining stability under the traditional system than toward promoting economic growth.

In terms of the economy of Greater Mongolia in the period before the 1920s, a distinction should be drawn between Inner Mongolia (especially the crescent most proximate to China proper) and Outer Mongolia. Inner Mongolia continued to be the epitome of a frontier zone, an area constantly in flux because of the effects of Han Chinese immigration and Chinese inroads into the Mongolian economy and culture. That immigration was legalized finally in 1860, after at least a century of illegal immigration which had been spurred by China's population growth and shortage of cropland.

Eastern Inner Mongolia, those areas closest to Manchuria, absorbed the greatest number of Han Chinese immigrants during the nineteenth century. This trend was intensified by the opening of Manchuria by the railways in the early 1900s. The completion in 1909 of the Peking-Kalgan-Suiyuan Railway into western Inner Mongolia was followed immediately by a deluge of Chinese colonizers who essentially confiscated lands from the Mongols for farming.

Ecologically, Inner Mongolia is unsuitable for either agriculture or pastoral nomadism exclusively; the region is ideally suited to a mixed economy. But the influx of land-hungry Han Chinese immigrants swung the balance to agriculture. Provincial governors and warlords in the early republican period sent soldier-colonists supplied with agricultural tools, seeds, and animals to expropriate lands from the Mongols.

The proximity to China allowed the Mongols of Inner Mongolia easy access to trade routes, but the policies of the Manchu Ch'ing dynasty prevented the Mongols from taking advantage of that access. It was only under the Ch'ing dynasty that Chinese traders were able to expand markets and reap tremendous profits in both Inner and Outer Mongolia. The first markets established by the Chinese in the seventeenth century were set up near Lamaist monasteries, the only settlements in existence in Mongolia's pre-urban history. Chinese traders encouraged trading on credit, since this allowed them to return repeatedly to Mongolia to collect debts in spite of Ch'ing regulations, which attempted to limit the numbers of traders. For the Mongols, credit was a necessity since pastoral products were ready for market only at specific times of the year (when sheep are shorn or camels shed, for instance), whereas Chinese tea was in demand in Mongolia all year. Already by the middle of the eighteenth century, Mongolian commoners (arad) were deeply in debt to Chinese trading firms. Even worse for the commoners, Mongolian princes became indebted to the Chinese traders, and attempted to repay their debts by levying special taxes on the commoners. All in all, several thousand head of livestock were confiscated yearly by Chinese traders.

The fact that a Chinese trader could return to Mongolia and buy fifty sheep with the profit he had made selling one sheep in China bears witness to the Chinese traders' enormous profits. By the early nineteenth century, there were a few Mongolian traders, but Manchu-imposed travel restrictions limited their mobility. A few Mongols found employment as agents of Chinese firms, caravan leaders, and herders of livestock being transported to China. The expansion of trade in Mongolia profited only the Chinese (and Russians), while destroying the Mongolian economy.

The economy of Outer Mongolia where, on account of ecological factors pastoral nomadism far outweighed agriculture, was also hard hit by Manchu-imposed policies. For the right to use pasture lands the Mongolian commoner essentially paid rent to the ruling prince of the banner in which he pastured. The prince allocated the pasture lands as he pleased. The taxes owed to the Manchu government and to the banner princes (the latter tax was understood to be rent) were so onerous in the nineteenth century that impoverishment and vagrancy (leaving one's legal banner jurisdiction) became common. *Shabi* as well as lay commoners were affected, *shabi* paying taxes to the church (see M4, pp. 89, 106, 150–151; M46).

Agriculture

Throughout Inner Asia agriculture and herding have been the principal source of wealth that has over the centuries supported the cities and provided the goods for trade. *In Iran,* for example, basic technology had changed little since the medieval period. The main crops were wheat, barley, and rice, but olives, fruits and nuts, various spices, and medicinal plants were also grown. Some of these crops were exported to towns and cities, and other items (dried fruits and nuts, medicinal plants) were channeled into foreign trade. In the nineteenth century, tobacco and cotton (exported mainly to Russia) became important in both internal and external trade. The importance of opium increased perceptibly toward the end of the nineteenth century, and was initially shipped to East Asia.

Three types of agriculture developed, depending on the availability of water: (1) unirrigated, mountainside agriculture, which depended on rain and snow meltwater; (2) open, above-ground irrigation, near major river systems; (3) the *qanat* system of underground canals, which led the water to the surface above the normal water table, so that more land could be farmed. The Persian waterwheel, which lifted water from one level to another, was ubiquitous. The last two types required the periodic employment of large bodies of men to build, to repair, and to reconstruct. Government officials and absentee landlords called upon the services of whole villages under the leadership of one or more of the local power elite.

The annual farming cycle in Iran included the time-honored planting, watering, reaping with hand sickles, threshing, and winnowing. Oxen and water buffalo were mainly used for plowing, but threshing was done by any number of livestock, including cattle, horses, donkeys, mules, and even camels. Grain was ground into flour by water-powered mills, although windmills were used along the Iranian-Afghan border.

Basically, agriculture in Iran was seen as involving five elements: land, water, seed, animal power, and human labor. Theoretically, whoever contributed one of the elements received one-fifth of the crop. Often a peasant could only offer his own labor, and received only one-fifth of the yield. In Afghanistan, a similar pattern (with regional variations) existed, but small, independent landholdings constituted about 50 percent of the land under cultivation.

The land tenure system was not feudal as in medieval Europe, because the peasant had few rights codified by legal code, only those sanctified by tradition, as in most Islamic countries. Also, the European lords of the manor lived on the land, not away at an urban center. In addition, those peasants who did own land usually sold their surplus crops to middlemen, who then sold high in the bazaar.

The nomads and seminomads, especially those in the Zagros Mountains, not only maintained large herds of sheep, goats, and camels, as well as horses and donkeys, but often owned much of the land around the villages through which they passed. Their economic holdings easily translated into political power, both regional and national.

Similarly in Afghanistan, the agriculture and herding that supported the towns and cities consisted of the classic wheat-barley-sheep-goat-cattle complex, developed in Western Asia nine to eleven thousand years ago. Also important were rice, maize, peas, beans, melons, grapes, pistachios, pomegranates, and a great variety of other fruits and nuts, immortalized in sensual Persian poetry. Cooking oils came from seed plants (sesame, sunflower) or from the fat of the fat-tailed sheep.

Crops were broadly divided into two major categories: irrigated (usually near extensive river systems, such as the Indus or the Hilmand-Arghandab) and non-irrigated (in the mountains, where the farmers were dependent on rain and snow meltwater). As in Iran, another type of irrigation used underground tunnels or channels, excavated and maintained by specialists, to bring the water to the surface before it would normally do so. These *qanat* exist today in Afghanistan and Iran.

By the nineteenth century, the wooden plow tipped with iron had reached most regions, and oxen were the major plow animals although horses, mules, donkeys, and camels are known to have been used. Enough land was available for agriculture to expand as populations expanded. In fact, Afghanistan and Iran had food surpluses (except in rare periods of famine brought on by either extensive drought or flooding) until after World War II.

In Central Asia the agriculture of the settled rural areas was productive and the population density in these areas was relatively high. The Russian newcomers in the nineteenth century were surprised by the density of this settled populace in the irrigated regions of the Samarkand and Tashkent areas and the Ferghana valley. Such settlement was concentrated in relatively small areas along the rivers. These regions produced high yields of fruits, vegetables, and other agricultural goods: apricots, peaches, melons, grapes, and wines were abundant, and the fruit orchards of Central Asia were famous. Although some wheat, barley, and sorghum were grown at the higher mountain elevations, the basic crops of the region came from these lowland valleys: cotton, tobacco, rice, silk, and dyes. The silk industry was intensely developed with concentrations of mulberry trees near Bukhara and Margelan. Tobacco cultivation was centered around Karshi and Katta-kurgan. Rice was grown mostly around the Samarkand area. Sesame, hemp, and poppies were also produced in abundance and for export, as were all the products mentioned above. Bukhara and Ferghana were primary centers for cotton growing. The local cotton was a short, thick gray variety which proved to be uncompetitive on major world markets, so that after the conquest the Russians introduced American varieties to grow for export.

Agrarian implements were extremely primitive, exemplified by the old, inefficient wooden plow *(omach)* which, held down by hand and pulled by oxen or cattle, would simply cut a shallow crease but not turn over the soil. At harvest a small sickle was used, but the long scythe was unknown. The typical instrument in gardens, small vegetable plots, and the cotton fields was the heavy, long-handled hoe, the *ketmen,* which was reasonably effective but required a sweeping, forceful, and exhausting blow to use. In general, the agrarian process involved a relatively primitive set of implements and quite heavy labor.

Agricultural production was heavily dependent on irrigation, and large-scale irrigation systems went back to the time of the Achaemenids when they were probably introduced by Iranian administrators and engineers. The first half of the eighteenth century had witnessed the substantial destruction of these systems during periodic conflict between the khanates, conflicts compounded by military incursions from the outside. These systems were always vulnerable to manipulation in times of political tension when the competing parties attempted to use them to pressure and control their adversaries. Destroying water and irrigation systems was a major tactic in such confrontations. In the second half of the eighteenth and the beginning of the nineteenth century, several of the khanates initiated a new and impressive reconstruction of these systems, and the period saw a real expansion of irrigated territory.

The frequency of the construction of irrigation networks reported in the sources seems to have been linked to the poor quality and extreme fragility of the systems. Constructed by hand or with the aid only of the ubiquitous *ketmen,* the systems in question consisted largely of earth and wooden branches poorly put together and contoured, and either ineffective or vulnerable to the slightest overload. Continuous natural catastrophes, compounded by willful destruction of the works in the interest of political manipulation, placed heavy burdens on the agricultural populace. On the whole, it is quite remarkable that the agricultural populations did as well as they did, producing substantial quantities of goods not only for local consumption but for export and trade as well.

Towns and cities had been established essentially at key transit points having to do with management of the transcontinental caravan routes: at key river crossings, at the periodic oases where irrigation permitted intensive cultivation and supply services for the caravan traffic, and at logical distributing and manufacturing centers for some valuable local product. Because of the role of these centers in handling the commerce between the major civilizations of the Iranian west and the Chinese east, the culture of these urban elites was strongly affected by Iranian and Chinese influences. Iranian place names intermingled in a complex way with Turkish designations across the urban landscape. The initial carriers of Muslim culture in these towns were the Sarts, a term that until the sixteenth century ethnographically described the Tajik populace of the cities. The Turkic nomads had adopted the term from the Mongols, who had used it to mean "Muslim," describing thereby the essentially Tajik urban dwellers who had earlier converted to Islam. As some Uzbeks began to settle in the towns and assume the sedentary professions of merchant and craftsman, this term came to be ascribed to them as well. Over time, it began to be used exclusively for sedentary Uzbeks in distinction to the Tajiks for whom it was originally coined. The Tajik and Turkic populations worked closely together in the cities, taking advantage of their strategic placement on the lucrative trade routes, building substantial commercial and manufacturing centers in those areas, and shaping a creative bilingual and bicultural civilization in Central Asia.

In Sinkiang oasis farming predominated, and the continental dry climate combined with primitive farming methods resulted in an agriculture that remained little changed until the twentieth century. Sinkiang was famous for its fruits, especially melons, grapes, and apples. Wheat, maize, rice, millet, and cotton were also widely cultivated. The large population of nomads, mainly, but not exclusively, in Jungaria, pursued the age-old tasks of animal husbandry and produced lambskins and sheepskins, as well as wool and meat, for trade.

Agriculture in Tibet was based on barley, which can grow at altitudes up to fourteen or fifteen thousand feet. In addition to barley, which was a staple food of the Tibetan population, buckwheat, peas, radishes, and mustard, and the lower-altitude crops of wheat, apricots, peaches, pears, and nuts were also grown. As early as the fourteenth century, grapes were cultivated for wine production. Other traditional agricultural and woodland products from different regions of Tibet include honey, cinnamon, and bamboo. Bamboo wood went into the production of bows, arrows, and spears, while the fibers of a shrub of the genus Daphne went into the making of paper.

Local conditions varied tremendously, each valley having its own microclimate. Generally speaking, irrigation was a necessity for the valley crops as the runoff from the high mountains and the rainfall were insufficient. Agricultural lands that had been granted by the Lhasa government to nobles were cooperatively irrigated using peasant labor.

The pastoral economy contributed such basic necessities as meat and dairy products as well as wool for clothing. The yak was of paramount importance. Yak hides were made into bags, storage cases, belts, and boats; yak hair was spun and woven into the nomads' black tent coverings; yak meat was a staple as was (and still is) butter made from yak milk. Yak butter was used in Tibetan tea, and monasteries stored yak butter in enormous quantities for use as the fuel in lamps (N39, pp. 135–136).

In Outer Mongolia, the first census ever taken of the population and livestock was ordered and executed by the government of the Boghda Gegen (the last Jebtsundamba Khutughtu) of Urga in 1918. Fortunately for us, the census figures were preserved and made available by I. M. Maiskii, who was to serve as Soviet ambassador to the United Kingdom in World War II. In 1919 he was sent by the All-Russian Central Union of Cooperative Societies as head of an expedition to investigate Mongolia's economy. Maiskii spent sixteen months in Mongolia and traveled over eighteen hundred miles. In the appendixes of his report appear the following livestock figures for Autonomous (Outer) Mongolia in 1918 (M38, appendix 10, pp. 76–77): horses, 1,150,511; camels, 228,640; horned cattle (includes oxen), 1,078,407; and sheep and goats, 7,188,005; for a total of 9,645,563.

Maiskii's figures have been accepted as the official figures for the year 1918 by the Central Statistical Board under the Council of Ministers of the Mongolian People's Republic, which in 1981 published another volume of invaluable information. The only change made in this volume regarding the 1918 livestock figures is to divide "sheep and goats" into separate categories: sheep, 5,700,100; goats, 1,487,900. The *Narodnoe Khoziaistvo* volume also gives livestock figures for the year 1924 (no source cited), figures that demonstrate that in spite of political and military turbulence, the pastoral economy of Outer Mongolia was growing rapidly (M45): horses, 1,339,800; camels, 275,000; horned cattle, 1,512,100; sheep, 8,444,800; and goats, 2,204,400; for a total of 13,776,100.

Maiskii also divided his 1918 livestock ownership statistics into three categories: animals owned by taxable population representing 7,498,115 head; animals owned by Mongolian princes 327,153 head; and animals owned by monasteries and temples, 1,820,295 head. In other words, in 1918 over one-fifth of Outer Mongolia's productive wealth (measurable in livestock, not in agricultural crops which were virtually nonexistent) was in the hands of the secular and religious elite. All in all, the statistics from the 1918 Outer Mongolian census must be viewed with some caution, as the population certainly had reason to hide its livestock resources because of the fiscally extractive purpose behind the census.

Unfortunately, similar statistics for Inner Mongolia are lacking. W. Karamisheff, writing in 1925, gives the following estimate for the livestock of *both* Inner and Outer Mongolia (M29, p. 10): horses, 1,840,817; camels, 365,824; horned cattle, 1,725,451; and sheep and goats, 11,500,808; for a total of 15,432,900.

Subtracting Maiskii's figures for Outer Mongolia from Karamisheff's for both Mongolias, one is left with the not surprising evidence that Inner Mongolia was less wealthy in livestock than Outer Mongolia. This was in part owing to ecological factors and in part to the results of Han Chinese transformation of Inner Mongolian pastoral grazing lands into farmlands.

Karamisheff also offers estimates of yearly production in such pastoral products as cattle meat (46,800,000 lbs.), sheep's wool (23,000,000 lbs.), camel wool

(2,200,000 lbs.), cow's milk (31 million buckets), and mare's milk (34 million buckets). The annual export value of furs (wolf, lynx, bear, deer, sable, ermine, marmot, and others) was approximately ten to twelve million dollars, according to Karamisheff. Ten million marmot furs were exported yearly to Russia (M29, pp. 10–16). Karamisheff's figures, of course, must also be viewed with caution, as he was obviously interested in convincing Russian entrepreneurs of the wealth of raw materials awaiting development in Mongolia. At the time Karamisheff was writing, several Russian-owned butter factories were already operating in Mongolia.

From the Russian point of view, Mongolia was a land of pastoral riches; it is of interest that this view coincided with that of the Mongols who traditionally counted their wealth in livestock, not agriculture. (People who ate crops were to be pitied in the Mongolian view; it was the animal that was supposed to graze on the steppe.) From the Chinese point of view, however, Mongolia's potential lay in the opening of agricultural lands to land-hungry Chinese colonizers. Specific information on the types of grain planted by Chinese farmers in Inner Mongolia is difficult to obtain.

As for the technology used by the few Mongols who tilled the soil of Inner Mongolia, we have the following description by Sechin Jagchid and Paul Hyer (M27, pp. 315–316):

> A unique type of grain planting and harvesting was developed by the Mongols who lived away from the Great Wall, though still south of the Gobi Desert. This form of farming, known in Mongolian as *Mongghol tariya,* was practiced mostly in the northern part of the Juu-uda and Jerim leagues. A special sickle with a long handle, which made it possible to stand upright to cut and remove grass, was used, after which seeds were broadcast freehand and the herds were moved away from the site until the fall harvest of the crop. While the production was very poor using this approach, it was better than nothing. The development of *Mongghol tariya* further confirms the attitude of the nomadic or pastoral Mongols who needed some agricultural products, but did not want to dig in the dirt or stoop in the back-breaking manner necessary when using the short-handled sickles of the Chinese farmer.

As Jagchid and Hyer have pointed out (M27, p. 375), it is only in relatively recent times that the Mongols have begun to put aside their cultural bias against agriculture as a means of production. The development of agriculture and industry has been seen by Soviet theorists and others as a precondition to Mongolia's modernization; pastoral nomadism is thus condemned as the greatest hindrance to economic modernization.

Manufacturing, Services, Trade

If premodern Inner Asia deserves a distinctive place in world economic history, it is because of its role in world trade. From ancient times until east-west trade went into decline, primarily because of the opening of oceangoing trade following the discovery of America, caravans of silk, jade, tea, and many other products were transported overland from China through Kashgar in Sinkiang, over the Pamir passes, and across Central Asia, Afghanistan, and northern Iran, to Greece, Rome, and later central and western Europe. This famous Silk Route was one of the mainstays of international trade, and provided many commercial opportunities for the nomads and settled peoples en route as well as for the merchants conducting the trade. The waning of this trade route was an important factor in the decline of Inner Asia from a mainstream to a backwater, and it was only a memory during the two or three centuries before the modern era. There remained a north-south trade with India and Siberia, however, and manufacturing and services centered on this traditional base. Trade within the area was also maintained, while the beginnings of modern industry, mining, banking, and agricultural improvement were developing under foreign auspices.

In Iran in the nineteenth century most village and nomadic handicrafts were intended for local use. Often, one man in a village would specialize in leatherwork, another in woodcarving, another in butchering. Many of the articles looked on as functional and mundane by Western eyes became little works of art, as each household item was decorated with one traditional design or another. The women tried to outdo each other in fine embroidery, to be included in their dowry. A major export industry did grow out of a handicraft: the making of carpets and kilims. European demand for these fine handwoven works of art intensified decade by decade.

Just as the political elites in the countryside used their power to control the rural economic scene, so the bazaar merchants and artisans translated their economic power into political clout. The merchants and artisans formed guilds which not only fixed prices and trained apprentices (three to ten years, depending on the skill required), but delayed the growth of free enterprise. The economic and political power of the guilds reached deep into the activities of the royal court and, until foreign capitalists interfered, guilds were the main source of credit and loans, at high interest rates, in spite of the fact that Islam prohibited usury.

Nationwide political links between larger bazaar centers developed in the late Qajar period, as European manufactured products steadily replaced the handicrafts of Iranian artisans (E16, p. 28). India was undergoing the same process, as were the Russian-dominated regions of Central Asia. Although the bazaar artisans lost ground, the commercial sector boomed. Imports overwhelmed exports (carpets, kilims, calico, silks, porcelains, leathergoods, felt, flannel). Much agricultural land was converted to cash crops, such as cotton and opium (E16, p. 551). Except for the bazaar merchants, virtually everyone was in debt to someone.

Bazaar merchants with French, British, or Russian commercial ties became part of the rising urban middle class, with entrepreneurial ambitions. They differed from other middle- and upper-class groups, however, "in that . . . [their]

influence rested on individual honesty" (E4, p. 511). While the bazaar thrived and expanded, the central government continually tried to extract more revenue from the populace. The bazaar paid little or no taxes, and government revenue came mainly from: (1) taxation, primarily on land; (2) revenues from crown lands; (3) customs duties; (4) rents or leases on government properties, often from foreign investors.

The right to collect land taxes was sold by the government to the highest bidder, who kept 20–25 percent of the yield. Usually, the collector was a member of the local power elite. The requisite lump sum was collected from the village as a whole, and the absentee landlord tried to hide as much of the yield as possible. Each province had its own budget, and the surplus was sent to a rapacious center. Major expenditures of the central government went first to the army, and then to the royal court, pensions for government officials, the operations of the various ministries (i.e., the bureaucracy), and education—in that order.

In spite of increasing taxation, government expenditures always exceeded income. Foreign loans were easy to obtain and debt servicing increased in high annual increments. The royal court owed more and more money to foreigners, peasants plunged deeper in debt to absentee landlords, but the bazaar merchant class and the absentee landlords got richer and richer and, through economic strength, stronger and stronger politically.

Occasionally, reforms were attempted. In the 1830s and 1840s, Hussain Khan unsuccessfully tried to design a uniform tax collection *firman*. He wanted to shift tax collecting to the village council and eliminate the tax collector (E23, p. 121). At times, flashes of reformist energy struck the indolent royal court. Prime Minister Mirza Aghasi reintroduced sericulture in the Kerman region, and silk became an important export after the 1840s. He also dreamed of large irrigation projects, undertaken generations later, and was one of the key instruments of foreign penetration. The "new economic alignments [with foreigners] were not destined to enrich the people, but only to make a rapacious aristocracy more powerful, while the situation of the cultivators became little better than slavery" (E4, p. 47). Mirza Aghasi's successor, Mirza Taqi Khan (also called Amir-i-Kabir), fired up after a visit to Europe, proposed a three-year plan to reform public administration, encourage industrialization, expand and repair irrigation systems, and build dams (E25, p. 206).

France, Great Britain, and Russia all competed in Iran for economic concessions and political advantage. France remained a major cultural force among the intelligentsia, and Britain and Russia succeeded in gaining economic superiority in southern and northern Iran respectively. Modern banking began in 1888, with the creation of a branch of the New Oriental Banking Corporation of England. Escalating foreign investments led to an increased dependency on foreign loans. The jump in loans was brought about by the royal court's demand for luxuries, the modernization of the military, and the payment of indemnities for broken foreign contracts (such as the British Tobacco Concession of 1890) to governments or individuals (E4, pp. 100–105). An American economist, Morgan Shuster, was hired as treasurer-general of Iran in 1911, and he began economic reform programs. He was relatively successful in reorganizing the Iranian bureaucracy and finances, and the Russians demanded that the Iranians dismiss Shuster—which they did (E25).

During the nineteenth century, much of the land—and even some shops—was held by the Muslim religious leaders as *wakfs,* or religious endowments. The government collected no taxes from these institutions, and many secular Iranians took advantage of the system. They would will land or shops to a *wakf,* but keep the revenue as long as they lived, after which the land or shop would revert to the *wakf.* Administration of the *wakf* could remain in the family as a trust.

Exports went primarily to Turkey, Russia, and India: cotton, tobacco, rhubarb, rice, herbs, fish, gold, silver, iron, cutlery, opium, dried fruits and nuts, textiles, carpets, cashmere, jewels, and coral. By the early twentieth century, Russia dominated the Caspian Sea fishing, and Britain the oil concessions in the southwest.

Several factors delayed industrial development: no infrastructure existed; cheap European goods flooded the bazaars; the power elite was more interested in easy commercial profits than industrial investments; the ulema and tribal leaders resisted foreign influences; low population density made it difficult to obtain labor for factories; the luxury-loving royal court was apathetic. However, loans from foreigners increased, and slowly the outsiders accrued much economic power and political influence.

The main economic classes consisted of the royal court and its sycophants, who exploited all levels of society, and were deeply in debt to foreigners; military officers and civil servants, the bureaucrats who perpetuated the exploitative system decade after decade; religious leaders, to whom political power accrued out of the economic power of the *wakfs;* merchants, who, with their capital base, gave credit and made loans; artisans and craftsmen, who had well-organized guilds, but suffered from foreign competition; absentee landlords, whose estates got larger and larger. Lower on the scale were the nomads, mobile, but the owners of much agricultural land, and gradually evolving into seminomads; rural peasants, usually tenant farmers; and the urban poor, many of whom migrated annually from the cities to neighboring countries, or, later, to work in the Iranian oil fields. In many regions the quality of life for the peasants gradually deteriorated after 1800, and this continued into the twentieth century, partly because of the proliferation of large estates and the problem of underemployment on farms.

Many minority groups engaged in nonagricultural economic activities. Armenians had great influence in the seventeenth century, but began to lose out to others by the mid-nineteenth century. The early Portuguese, Dutch, and British used minority groups in the import-export trade network, in banks, and in communication (telegraph). The Jews had important commercial links with Turkestan,

Afghanistan, Bombay, and even stretching to Europe (textiles from Britain).

At the end of the period under discussion, oil became an important element. After the formation of the Anglo-Persian Oil Company in 1909, Iran would never be the same.

Afghanistan was typical of much of Inner Asia in its earlier experience with international trade, although it was primarily a luxury trade. For example, true lapis lazuli is found only in Badakhshan in the mountains of northeast Afghanistan, and it was a prime object in the trade along the Lapis Lazuli Route which extended from Inner Asia to Egypt, where the stone is found in pharaonic tombs. A second major period in the early centuries A.D. witnessed the growth of the fabled Silk Route trade from China to Europe, and the Afghan area was a hub. Such items as silks, spices, carved ivories, and glassware were exchanged.

Bazaars, with guildlike structures, always played an important role in the transfer of village and town commodities and local handicrafts to cities and manufactured goods to the villages. Often itinerant peddlers performed this role.

The bazaars of Samarkand, Bukhara, Herat, Kandahar, Kabul, and Peshawar maintained a vigorous trading system, with commercial families having contacts as far north as Moscow, as far west as London, as far east as Hong Kong. They sold gold, hides, skins, sheep guts (for sausage casings), carpets, and some handicrafts for Russian "Nikolai" gold coins and British sovereigns. Most of the upper-class affluent traders and shopkeepers in the Afghan cities were non-Pushtun. In northwest India they were mainly Hindus and Sikhs. In the Afghan bazaars, one could also find Hindus and Sikhs, many of whom had been living in Afghanistan since the 1500s—and even earlier. Other groups of Afghan bazaar shopkeepers were Uzbek, Tajik, Qizilbash, Paracha, and a small colony of Jews (Yahudi) with commercial links with other Jews from Tehran through Bukhara and Kabul to Bombay.

Bazaars not only contained traders and shopkeepers, but artisans who lived in particular sections, so that occupational and residential areas coincided, with the residence over the shop. Bazaar shopkeepers often evolved into moneylenders. Sons usually followed their fathers' occupations, but artisans also took apprentices.

In Kabul in the 1890s, thirty-two separate vocations (a traditional number throughout Inner Asia) were listed—and taxed. Among them were coppersmiths, goldsmiths, silversmiths, jewelers, tinsmiths, potters, and blacksmiths. Each occupation had its own guild master, elected periodically as the go-between with government authorities.

Handicrafts were usually made for local consumption, to be used by the immediate family or traded or sold in a nearby town or city bazaar. For sale were sheepskin coats, felt, silk items, carpets, kilims, cotton fabrics, and even weapons until arms salesmen from Manchester and Birmingham began to peddle their wares among the frontier tribes in the late nineteenth century. But the local arms craftsmen continued their trade with hand-operated lathes manufacturing excellent copies of the originals. Hand-made weapons from Kabul, Kandahar, and Herat are works of art, but the most famous arms factories were at Dara Adam Khel, which still functions in Pakistan. The first modern factory, designed to manufacture weapons, was built during the reign of Amir Sher Ali Khan who had created a large standing army. Previously, amirs only had royal bodyguards; levies and armies came together to invade or repel invaders. Brass cannon gave way to iron cannon, and the British captured many of them during the second Anglo-Afghan war (1878–1880); most now reside in the Tower of London's armory.

Amir Abdur Rahman established what would now be called an industrial park *(machine khana)* one-third of a mile long and two hundred yards wide, and imported British and Indian engineers to help build and run the complex, which manufactured candles, soap, furniture, carpets, and blankets, and included a lithographic printing press and a distillery. There was also a boot factory near the Arg (fort-palace). An Englishman was hired to instruct in the tailoring of uniforms. Wood powered the first steam engines to produce electricity. The ecology of some Afghan regions still suffers from the effects. The weapons factory was modernized and increased its production with each of the amir's annual military campaigns. But, whereas the bazaar guilds had been competitive and strict in their quality control, the new factories stressed quantity over quality. Some four to five thousand workers were found in the factories, all of which were government controlled (F10, p. 143).

Important to trade and commerce was the fact that no universally accepted international boundaries existed. The lack of accepted boundaries enabled nomads to move easily from area to area and establish trading partnerships with bazaar merchants. Until the British and Russians engaged in regional boundary-drawing exercises, local princes and khans dominated as much territory as they could militarily control and customs fees were collected accordingly. Because of this, corruption, mainly bribery and the purchasing of loyalties, developed into a fine art, continuing today in many parts of Inner Asia.

Smuggling and corruption run together, but these institutions were accepted as legitimate parts of the economic system, just as they are today. However, each society has its own allowable bounds of deviance. Also, the bribes paid to civil servants were considered a realistic part of their salaries because they were invariably underpaid.

Commercial activities, therefore, spread along caravan routes stretching from Chinese Turkestan down through Afghanistan into India, and even to Iran, but the north-south thrust predominated, and the Indus River became an important artery of commerce. Annual trade fairs were important in Afghanistan and northwest India, when nomad-traders and merchants gathered to sell each other goods, which the bazaar merchants would return to their shops and the nomad-traders would move in long-distance trade.

Although British interests from India established themselves in Iran first, by

1889 Russian goods, much cheaper than British, dominated the Afghan-Iranian marketplace. The Russians had also constructed a rail line toward the Afghan border. The British, for their part, busily built railroads toward the Afghan border from Quetta and Peshawar. Afghan exports to Russian Inner Asia exceeded imports; but the reverse was true with British India.

Amir Abdur Rahman instituted several unwise economic policies, including prohibitive import tariffs, which caused a great drop in the import-export trade. Anglo-Russian economic and political machinations in Inner Asia also contributed to the decline in trade, the Russians gaining the upper hand. British trade from India to Inner Asia dropped 80 percent by 1895 (F10, p. 146). Afghanistan lost its role as economic go-between, and the rise in the importance of Iran with the discovery of oil further shifted the center of economic activity to the west and south.

In Central Asia the towns were renowned for their crafts. Their textiles were much in demand in the eighteenth and nineteenth centuries, and were produced for export to Russia and the countries of Asia. Their popularity and the resulting demand created a major expansion of the industry in the khanates' cities. European observers commented on the lack of any large-scale textile factory or workshop—except for that of the khan's court, which did not produce for the market—but they noted the widespread weaving and production of silken and cotton fabrics for clothing in individual homes, a ubiquitous cottage industry. There was no regulation of such handicraft by the administration of the khanates. The large volume of such production of fabrics and their export, as well as the fabrics' reputation for beauty and durability, were noted repeatedly by travelers from the West.

The technically more sophisticated *charkh (samoprialka)* was used for weaving in the cities, while the nomads got by with simply the *vereteno* for both cotton and wool. The work required both substantial dexterity and long apprenticeship and was an acknowledged skill of the area. Some families specialized in such weaving, and a certain surplus was produced in the cities for trade and export. Substantial accumulation of capital or expansion of the craft was unlikely under these circumstances.

Craftsmen attached themselves to a wealthy sponsor through receipt of a one-time substantial sum, the *bunak* (its size depending on the skill and the individual circumstances of the craftsman involved), with the craftsman (weaver, baker, metalworker, smith) then receiving appropriate individual payment for subsequent goods produced. When the craftsman wished to leave such service to take up employment with another sponsor, he was required to pay back the full original sum received from the current sponsor, although his new benefactor would often cover this sum for him.

Extraction of metals and metallurgy were practiced, though weakly developed. Processing was relatively expensive, inefficient, and wasteful. Some gold was mined around Ferghana and Karategin, silver and lead near Andijan and

Bukhara. Iron, copper, and magnesium were also extracted in small amounts throughout the region, though the extraction of each of these was languishing by the beginning of the nineteenth century, with only lead and saltpeter produced for bullets and powder.

Historically there were three virtually self-subsistent economies in the area which increasingly came to interact with each other over time: nomadic, agricultural, and the craft economy in the towns and cities. Each was differentiated enough internally to produce its own foodstuffs, clothes, and items of subsistence, so that the initial imperatives of trade were minimal. Specialization and interaction grew gradually, but strong features of self-reliance persisted well into the nineteenth century within each of the three communities. The frequent internecine strife and external incursions, which broke down patterns of trade and community interaction and rendered them fragile, tended to reinforce habits of isolated self-reliance. The expansion of trade with Russia toward the end of the nineteenth century, with the appearance of cheaper factory goods from the West, had the effect of driving down prices of local crafts, reducing demand, and eventually undermining the crafts themselves.

Trade with Russia grew markedly over the hundred years from the mid-eighteenth to the mid-nineteenth century. The total value in that trade in the 1750s was approximately a quarter million rubles in each direction, but by the 1850s nearly four million rubles worth of goods were reaching Russia, with three million rubles of goods being exported to the Central Asian regions. Before the nineteenth century, cloth, some cotton yarn and raw cotton, textile dyes, and gold coins came from Central Asia. The export of metals to these areas from Russia was forbidden until 1801, but with the lifting of the prohibition, metals quickly became the chief items of export, with iron, steel, copper, and cast iron being shipped to Central Asia in great quantities for use in the manufacture of agricultural tools, household implements, weaponry, and the like. The khanates themselves imposed high tariffs not only for export and import, but for transit as well, in addition taking a further fee for space in the markets and for the right to sell. These practices impeded the broad development of trade.

The importance of Central Asian markets and raw materials for the Russian economy had grown considerably in the nineteenth and early twentieth centuries. The integral nature of those economies internally and the intensity of external challenges to the Russian and the Soviet state during the period of the revolution and the civil war made it unlikely that the Moscow center would divest itself of those relations easily. The substantial Russian presence in the cities of the region since the conquest in the 1860s, and the commanding role Russian administrators and merchants had come to play in the area during that period, had reduced the position and influence of the indigenous peoples substantially.

In the latter half of the nineteenth century the Russian presence led to the establishment of a separate economy which was superimposed on the traditional crafts and trade of the native peoples. By 1914 some 40 percent of the population of the Kazakh steppe regions was Russian, although further south the settlement of Russians was much smaller and predominantly urban. The impact of Russia was less through the movement of peoples, at this stage, than through government policy.

Railroad construction was probably the most important long-term contribution made by the Russians to the Central Asian economy in the nineteenth century. The Trans-Caspian railroad from the Caspian to Ashkabad was completed in 1881, and was later extended to Merv (1884), Samarkand (1888), and Tashkent and the Ferghana valley (1898). Although this railroad was rapidly built since it covered flat territory, passengers and freight had to be transshipped across the Caspian Sea which resulted in long delays. A second main line from Orenburg to Tashkent, completed in 1906, connected Central Asia more directly to the main Russian network. Other lines were planned to connect Central Asia with the Trans-Siberian railroad, but this work was not completed until after 1917. Although the initial impulse for railroad building was strategic, these lines opened up the region to trade and settlement much more rapidly than would otherwise have been possible (G45, pp. 184–189).

Russian colonization was also accompanied by numerous state-financed programs for irrigation in an effort to reclaim land from the deserts. Private enterprise was also beginning to develop the mining of coal, copper, manganese, oil, and gold and other precious metals. Many of these resources had been exploited at a modest level by traditional methods in the past, but by the turn of the century modern technology was being widely introduced. At the same time, both Russian and native entrepreneurs promoted the growth of light industry for processing agricultural and animal products (G45, pp. 175–182, 190–197).

Tibet, in contrast to the other territories of Inner Asia, had not played an active role in the earlier trade routes, but its incorporation into the Ch'ing empire in 1792 enabled foreign traders to explore Tibet's potential as a market. Although Tibet closed its frontiers to outsiders, the British used Tibetan agents to report back to the East India Company on trade possibilities. Shawl wool called *pashmina,* which could come from the domesticated goat or the wild goat and wild sheep, was of particular interest to the British. Tibet adhered rigorously to a monopoly whereby shawl wool was exported only to Leh in Ladakh, which was a tributary of Tibet; from Leh it was reexported only to the Kashmir weaving industry. Britain was excluded from this highly lucrative trade.

Tibet not only exported shawl wool, borax, sulfur, and black salt to Ladakh, but also reexported certain Chinese goods such as brick tea and silk. In return, Tibet imported from Leh cotton cloth, shawls, household goods, and Indian and European manufactured goods.

Although trade with the Russians came under the same prohibition as trade with the British and other foreigners, tsarist subjects of Asian descent, particularly Buriats and Kalmyks, visited Tibet fairly regularly for religious and trade purposes. In fact, the growing Russian influence in Lhasa, as exemplified by the powerful position of the Buriat confidant of the Dalai Lama, Dorjiev, who also had close ties with Tsar Nicholas II's court, contributed to the British decision to mount an expedition that in 1904 invaded Lhasa and ended Tibet's closed-frontier policy.

In Sinkiang little was left of the Silk Route, with many of the old cities in decline or covered by sand by the nineteenth century, but north of the Taklamakan desert some trade in tea and other products was still conducted between China and Central Asia, India, and Afghanistan. Goods produced in Khotan, Yarkand, and Kashgar, such as silk, metalware, jade, carpets, and furs, continued to find an export market. There were also weekly bazaars where goods were exchanged locally. This very considerable production and exchange of goods was based on traditional craftsmanship, however, and apart from rifles imported from abroad the peoples of the area had little knowledge of modern technology.

In Outer Mongolia, although Chinese merchants and traders still dominated the economy of Urga, the largest "city" (a city of felt yurts and monasteries), by the time the Finnish scholar and traveler Gustav John Ramstedt (1873–1950) visited Urga in 1898, Russian commercial interests were beginning to make inroads (see M51, chapter 3). Urga's downtown district consisted of a monastery with ten to twenty thousand lamas; a separate Chinese residential quarter, enclosed by high walls; and a quarter called by Ramstedt "Meat City" (the butchers' section), where Russian log buildings mixed with Mongolian yurts and Chinese houses. The Russian tea company of Kokovin & Basov conducted trade in many sorts of goods in their large general store in Meat City. About two miles east of the center of Urga, Chinese merchants set up their own market known as *Mai Mai ch'eng* (called *Mai mai khota* in Mongolian). Until at least the early 1980s, this market still had a Chinese section.

The main unit of currency in Urga consisted of the Buddhist prayer scarves (known as *khadak*), produced from silk by the Chinese for export to the Mongols. Another unit of currency, the brick of tea, corresponded to a certain number of Russian kopeks and Chinese liang of silver. The exchange rate between silver and tea changed daily. Brick tea was imported from China in enormous quantities, but for very large transactions, Mongols would use live animals instead of the cumbersome bricks of tea. (In 1898, one camel was worth about one hundred rubles, a horse about twenty rubles.) According to Karamisheff (M29, p. 29), writing in 1925, there were about four hundred Chinese commercial firms in Urga and about fifty Russian concerns.

Generally speaking, the Mongols were late in developing industry and manufacturing because of the absence of urban centers; even in Ch'ing times, when the Mongols of Inner Mongolia led far more sedentary lives than their ancestors, there was still little indigenous industry. The easy availability of Chinese goods and the presence of Chinese artisans are usually blamed for this nondevelopment.

Yet, traditionally, the Mongols have excelled in certain handicrafts: the work of Mongolian blacksmiths, goldsmiths, and silversmiths was held in high esteem. The production of Buddhist images and ornaments as well as armaments occurred on a small scale. The Mongols produced their own very durable and aesthetic boots, and of course all the materials needed to construct a yurt: felt, wooden frames *(khana)* over which the felt is stretched, and wooden doors (see M27, pp. 316–318).

Conclusions and Comparisons

The experience of Inner Asia before the twentieth century illustrates the extent to which economic growth depends on a political leadership that is able both to mobilize resources by taxing agriculture and trade, and to take the initiative in promoting agricultural improvement and the development of mining and industry.

Considering Inner Asia as a whole, the share of the population employed in agriculture was doubtless higher in 1900, about 85 percent, than in Western Europe in 1750, 65–75 percent. In this respect, then, Inner Asia was some two and a half centuries behind the West. Agricultural implements, so far as one can judge, were also two or three centuries behind those of Western Europe, but closer in efficiency to those employed in Russia and Japan. In other respects, however, agriculture was less backward. The various forms of irrigation, especially the construction and maintenance of underground canals, were relatively sophisticated. The diversity of agricultural products was also remarkable, including as it did a wide variety of fruits and vegetables, in addition to grain. In terms of their diet, the peasants of Inner Asia were probably better off than those of Russia or the Ottoman Empire, and perhaps approached the level of the agrarian population of Japan and China. What was lacking in Inner Asia, however, was the capacity to mobilize agricultural surpluses for central purposes. Agricultural products were consumed and traded, but contributed little to the society-wide economies before the introduction of taxation in the late nineteenth century, the income from which was used for internal wars rather than development.

In the realm of manufacturing and trade, there were in effect two economies in Inner Asia in the latter half of the nineteenth century. One was the traditional economy, producing and trading in agricultural products and handicrafts. This economy was dominant in Mongolia, Sinkiang, and Tibet, and continued to play a large role in Iran, Afghanistan, and Central Asia. It had changed little through the ages, but was significantly reduced in volume owing to the decline in overland trade. There is no evidence that the native merchants and entrepreneurs were making significant efforts at innovation in the nineteenth century.

Particularly in the areas under Chinese influence, the emphasis of economic policy was primarily on maintaining the traditional system of agriculture and trade. Ch'ing rule in Sinkiang and Mongolia provided sufficient stability to encourage the development of trade, but economic activity remained within the limits of traditional technology. Like the British in India, the Chinese were particularly concerned with maintaining the existing system as a basis for taxation. Unlike Britain, however, China in its domestic policies did not confront the problems of modern transformation until the end of the nineteenth century and had no basis for promoting economic growth in its outlying territories. Tibet, for its part, remained isolated from the modern world until well into the twentieth century, and its economy remained essentially static.

The second economy was that stimulated by European influence—Russian in Central Asia, and Russian, British, French, and other European in Iran and Afghanistan. In Central Asia, the Russians promoted an extensive development of natural resources and of the textile industry, usually with native labor working under Russian management. Since the goal of the Russians was to incorporate Central Asia into their empire, and included extensive migration of Russians into the region, their methods were concerned more particularly with economic development than was the case with most colonial policies. In this respect their policy bears some resemblance to that of the Prussians in Posen, the British in Ireland, and the Habsburgs in Bosnia-Hercegovina, and also in some measure to United States policy in the Philippines.

Iran and Afghanistan, as independent states with relatively effective leadership, moved more vigorously toward modern economic development than the rest of Inner Asia. Although the British, Russian, and other European participation in the economic development of Iran and Afghanistan led to a form of semicolonialism, it also provided the capital and technology that enabled them to lay the foundations of a modern economic system. In this respect they resembled the Ottoman Empire and Egypt, which likewise evolved from traditional to modern economies with foreign assistance that was both oppressive and stimulating.

5

Social Structure

Introduction

An important aspect of societal transformation is the expansion of the area within which individuals and groups are closely interrelated. In premodern societies, individuals are closely integrated within villages and tribes, but may be interdependent with other social units to only a limited degree. As societies modernize, the areas of social integration expand until individuals within a whole society or nation may be as closely interdependent as were members of villages and tribes in earlier times. The growth of cities, of trade, and of social and political structures, represents steps toward society-wide integration. In advanced industrial societies, this trend is continued to the point at which international integration becomes a reality.

In this as in other respects, premodern societies vary considerably. In the least developed, villages may be located at some distance from each other with few mutual contacts. In others, individuals in villages and tribes may have a considerable degree of integration with the larger society through trade, religious and guild organizations, and the growth of urban areas. The greater the degree of integration in a premodern society, the easier will be its transition to the more highly developed forms of social integration common to modern societies.

Integration involves a wide range of social factors. Because of our limited knowledge of Inner Asian societies, however, we focus on three of these factors: human resources, organizational contexts, and redistributive processes.

With regard to human resources, we are concerned with the size and rate of growth of the population as these relate to the availability of food and other products. Before the modern era, was the per capita wealth of the population increasing or diminishing? Were surpluses available for central purposes growing or declining? Similarly important is the question of ethnic and religious diversity within the societies of Inner Asia, and its implications for social stabil-

109

ity and cohesion. We are also concerned with the growth of towns and cities. Since modern societies are predominantly urban, the degree of urbanization before the modern era indicates with considerable accuracy a society's capacity for modern development. One of the main features of modern societal transformation is the change in the occupation of the labor force from 90 percent in agriculture to a similar percentage in manufacturing and services. We are therefore concerned with the extent to which a diversification of occupations had been achieved before the modern era.

The organizational development of a premodern society is also a factor in its readiness for modern change. Before the modern era most activity is concentrated in families, clans, and villages, which tend to subordinate individuals to a static pattern of life. The growth of intermediate and society-wide organizations—religious, educational, professional, and commercial—promotes greater opportunities for individuals and enhances the coordinated efforts of a society for change. Although such development may weaken the positive role of the family as the authority structure for individual development, it tends at the same time to free individuals from family constraints and to promote society-wide coordination and control.

Among the factors that facilitate social integration, as the area in which goods and services are exchanged expands from a narrowly local to a society-wide level, is the predominance of a common language and culture. The societies of Inner Asia varied considerably in this respect. Tibet and Outer Mongolia had the advantage of essentially homogeneous populations with a common sense of identity that facilitated integration. The other societies of the region, however, were characterized by a considerable diversity of ethnic groups.

The significance of redistributive processes for societal transformation is that they breach the normally rigid and static structure of premodern societies and make them more susceptible to integration beyond the local and tribal levels. In the Inner Asian societies, the principal processes by which goods and services were redistributed were migration, taxation, and upward mobility through government and military service.

Human Resources

In the absence of accurate information, one may estimate that the population of Inner Asia as a whole in the mid-nineteenth century was some twenty-five to thirty million, of which perhaps one-third were nomads. In the absence of a strict definition of ''urban,'' it is estimated that about 5 percent of the population lived in towns and cities. By the turn of the century the population had grown to some forty million.

The population of Iran is estimated to have grown from five to ten million in the course of the nineteenth century, with the urban population growing more rapidly than that of the country as a whole. The two main seats of wealth and power had been in the northwest, dominated by the city of Tabriz, the capital of the truncated (in 1828, by Russian annexation) Azerbaijan province, and along the north-south axis in the central plateau encompassing Isphahan and Shiraz, both eighteenth-century capitals.

As political power shifted into the hands of the Turkmen-based Qajar dynasty, a new capital at Tehran, far to the north on the plateau and closer to the Turkmen home base, was developed. According to estimates based on travel accounts, Tehran grew from a mud town of some 50,000 persons in 1807 to 150,000 by 1910, only a threefold increase in just over a century. The growth rate for Tehran, a city with an expanding bureaucracy and other employment opportunities linked to its status as the capital, was greater than that of other urban centers. By 1900 it had become the major town in Iran. (With urbanization and the rapid growth of central government, its population reached four million in the early 1980s.)

Nonetheless, Tabriz, the seat of the crown prince, and an important commercial link with Europe and Russia, also grew rapidly and retained its position as the second largest town. Tabriz's large non-Muslim, mainly Armenian, population helped in the development of rudimentary banking establishments, especially for foreign trade, even after two foreign banks, the Imperial Bank of Iran (British) and the Discount Bank of Iran (Russian), were set up. As the urban centers grew, they spilled beyond the old walls and, in order to collect the tariffs and taxes from all who benefited from the commerce of the city, ever longer walls had to be constructed to encompass the growing population. Tehran needed new walls twice during the last century.

Tehran and Tabriz both grew in stature partially because, as the two most important administrative centers of government, they became magnets for government employment, albeit not in the modern civil service sense. Former administrative towns like Isphahan, however, underwent a period of decay in the nineteenth century. Not only bureaucrats, but also artisans, shifted to Tehran or Tabriz in search of markets for their goods. This, coupled with the importing of cheap European products, textiles in particular, also contributed to the decline of former artisan centers and of sections of the extensive bazaars in Isphahan and Ghazvin.

Iran's two holy towns continued to function as before. Mashhad in the northeast and Qom, south of Tehran, are venerated as sites of pilgrimage because of the shrines around which have been established several *madrasahs*. The two towns served to attract two kinds of temporary residents: pilgrims and students. These two groups, drawn from the small artisan and peasant sectors, helped to integrate persons from differing ethnic or regional backgrounds. The network of students especially enhanced the ability of the ulema to spread their ideas. Neither the government nor any other sector of society had this ability in the premodern period.

The nomadic population, which remained at about two and a half million from the beginning to the end of the nineteenth century, was gradually affected by sedenterization. This trend also accelerated during the twentieth century, the natural rate being augmented by forced settlement of tribes. In view of the weak structure of the standing army, however, the well-organized tribal fighting units remained both a threat and a support to the Iranian monarchy until the modern period.

The rate of growth of the general population and the rural-urban ratio were affected by the gradual shift toward the planting of cash export crops like cotton and opium, rather than sustenance crops. This trend, fed in part by the opening of external markets and the internal wish for foreign manufactured goods, led to two phenomena: first, wealthy landowners acquired ever larger tracts of land, while more peasants became landless and some moved to cities. Second, the widespread planting of nonedible crops contributed to the great famine of 1869–1872. The fact that fewer peasants were growing food crops for ever larger urban populations where the system of food distribution was poorly developed aggravated conditions at times of stress (such as drought) and brought about much suffering. A second famine, that of 1918, which affected chiefly the north-western part of the country, was caused by World War I and the consequent ravaging of local food stocks and displacement of peasants. In this second major famine, one-quarter of the population of the northwest is estimated to have perished.

In the case of Afghanistan, the absence of reliable population data and the interrelationship of ethnic groups make it difficult to evaluate the significance of human resources. A few population estimates for Afghanistan existed before 1880, almost all made by foreigners, who were mainly interested in the number of fighting men in each region. One estimate reported a total population of 4,901,000 from the Amu Darya to Peshawar (F18).

Amir Abdur Rahman juggled the figures to suit his specific purposes. In 1882, he informed the ruler of Merv that Afghanistan included two million souls, doing this to avoid helping the khan drive the tsarist Russians out of Merv. To impress the British, Abdur Rahman used the figure ten million in 1883. A census was attempted in 1892, but the method used to collect data is not too clear (F15, p. 182). Probably, government officials asked local leaders to send in head counts, but bribes may have reduced the real numbers considerably. However, Abdur Rahman accepted eight million as the official figure in 1894.

Resistance to the census occurred for several reasons. Among them: fathers did not want the total number of sons to be in government files for fear of conscription; most feared an increase in taxes; the custom of purdah made it difficult to ascertain the number of females.

Before the end of the eighteenth century urbanization declined perceptibly. Several factors accounted for this, including the drop in overland trade, the disintegration of what little centralization existed, and, finally, the encroachment of European imperialism. The lack of central authority caused a breakdown in law and order and an increase in brigandage in rural areas. Also, the unpredictability of customs duties collected by local rulers compounded the insecurity of trade through Afghanistan. However, Abdur Rahman attempted to regulate customs fees and standardize weights and measures. These were noble efforts, but largely unsuccessful.

The shift in trade from overland to sea routes caused many in the non-Pushtun urban minorities to migrate, either individually or as groups to Central Asia, Iran, or British India. Herat, once a major hub in international trade, suffered the following drop in population: 100,000 (1810); 40,000 (1826); 20,000 (1845), partly caused by the ten-month siege (November 1837–September 1838) by Iranian troops with Russian advisers (F10, p. 53).

The capital was moved from Kandahar to Kabul in 1775–1776. Kabul continued to grow because of the size of the court and the increases in administrative cadres. The bazaar in Kabul grew to be one of the more significant in the region, with its fabled Charsu (covered bazaar) as the hub. After the British burned down and looted the Charsu in 1842, the great bazaar never returned to its former prominence.

Kandahar was another of the few urban centers that continued to grow. Provincial governors took three censuses in the late nineteenth century in order to increase taxation and improve methods of conscription. From 1880 to 1891 the population increased from 29,000 to 31,514. The annual growth rate during this period was 0.636 percent. For the same period, however, the rural population around Kandahar rose from 0.5 percent to 1.00 percent annually.

Virtually all the large cities in Afghanistan seasonally increased in population as large groups of nomads camped nearby for varying amounts of time, engaging in trade and barter. For example, the population in the environs of Jalalabad jumped tenfold each winter as nomads moved into the foothills surrounding the town.

Why was the rate of population growth so low? The reasons are both cultural and biological. The so-called bride price (really an exchange of economic goods, and, anyway, usually within the extended family or clan) often dictated that men other than the wealthy married late, therefore delaying fatherhood. Mothers often breast fed children two years or longer, thus delaying another conception. Infant mortality was high, and approximately one-half of the children died before the age of three. Feuds and warfare also made dents in the potential male parent generation. Young widows, under familial and other social pressures, sometimes never remarried. The prevalence of homosexuality also helped keep the population down.

Younger children and older persons died in smallpox epidemics. The smallpox epidemic of 1886 was especially devastating from Kabul to Herat. Frequent cholera epidemics (1885, 1889, 1891, 1892, 1899) killed many in Afghanistan. Chicken pox also claimed many victims (F15, p. 184).

Natural disasters also contributed to population control. Afghanistan is situated along the great earthquake faults which finger up from the Rift valley of the East African Horn to Central Asia. An 1842 earthquake did great damage to Jalalabad town and destroyed large sections of the walls of the fort of the British garrison. Heavy snowfall and subsequent flash floods at times caused great loss of life.

The enormous territory of what was to become *Russian Central Asia,* some one and a half million square miles in area, was more sparsely settled than Iran or Afghanistan. Estimates for the 1860s found two and a half million Kazakhs, three hundred thousand Kirgiz, and three hundred thousand Turkmen, predominantly nomads occupying the steppe region. They maintained their age-old way of life, organized by clans which in fluctuating patterns were loosely grouped into hordes. To the south were another three and a half million Uzbeks, predominantly settled peoples who lived in the khanates of Kokand, Bukhara, and Khiva, and numerous smaller states with constantly shifting boundaries (G45, pp. 8–13).

Reliable estimates of the distribution of the Central Asian population are difficult to find. A foreign estimate of 1889 put the regional total, including the khanates of Bukhara and Khiva, at six million. The first accurate count was the census of 1897 which gave the total population of Turkestan, minus the territories of the two khanates, at five and one-quarter million. By 1913–1914 this number had grown to six and three-quarter million, totaling eleven and one-quarter million with the addition of the khanates. The census of 1926 showed a growth to roughly thirteen and one-half million, despite the losses incurred during the revolution and civil war. In the Kazakh, Kirgiz, and Tajik areas in 1926, the indigenous groups made up slightly over half of the populace in each case, whereas in the Turkmen and Uzbek areas they made up closer to three-quarters of the total. Also in 1926, the percentage of urban population in each of these regions was still low: ranging from a low of 9 in the Kazakh areas, to 10 in what was to become Tajikistan, 12 within the boundaries of the future Kirgizia, 14 in Turkmenistan, and 22 in Uzbekistan. The share of the indigenous peoples in those urban totals was of course lower because of the presence of Russians and other Slavs in the cities. Given the low percentage of urban dwellers as late as 1926, it may be assumed that the urban-rural ratios in earlier centuries were even lower. Tsarist estimates and descriptions from the late 1800s speak of a substantial increase in the number of urban dwellers from the 1860s on, with the influx of the Russians.

The largest city in Central Asia was Tashkent, which grew from 80,000 at the time of the Russian conquest to 120,000 or more by the end of the century as the main Russian administrative center. As was the case with a dozen or more lesser administrative cities and towns, a modern Russian quarter was built adjacent to the native city to house the Russian administrative personnel and the garrison. In the course of General Von Kaufman's fourteen-year term as governor-general, the Russian section of Tashkent was developed as a major administrative center with a theater, a museum, a library, an astronomical observatory, gardens, and newspapers. Until late in the century the Russians and the native population lived and worked separately, and the khanates retained a significant degree of autonomy (G45, pp. 95–106).

The overall population of Tibet in the nineteenth century has been estimated at about six million with five-sixths of this total consisting of agriculturalists and one-sixth pastoral nomads (N31, p. 109). A strict delineation between agriculturalists and pastoralists is, however, far more difficult to draw in traditional Tibet than in traditional Mongolia. In central Tibet, for instance, the economy was characterized by an "agropastoral subsistence pattern" consisting of both agriculture and pastoral nomadic herding, and ranging along a broad continuum from mainly agricultural at one end to mainly pastoral at the other (see N11 and N12).

In the late nineteenth century, an estimated 760,000 Tibetans lived in the approximately twenty-five hundred monasteries as monks and nuns (N31, pp. 139–140). Large cities grew around important monasteries. Lhasa itself in 1910 is estimated to have had 50,000 inhabitants, while the three great monasteries near Lhasa—Ganden, Sera, and Drepung—according to late nineteenth-century estimates had altogether approximately twenty thousand resident monks. In eastern Tibet, Chamdo's population of 12,000 included some three thousand monks (N31, p. 139).

In Sinkiang, administrative unity was imposed by Chinese conquest in the eighteenth century and reconquest in the nineteenth, but it was never matched by a corresponding social unity. The indigenous bases of social cohesion in traditional times did not coincide with the new boundaries imposed by the Chinese, and even today the area's political structure is supplied from outside.

What today is northern Sinkiang was traditionally a westward extension of the Mongolian world. The most important elements in its population were the Kazakhs, Turkic-speaking nomads, who numbered 319,000 in the 1940s, and who inhabited the highlands of Jungaria and the Ili valley; and the Kirgiz, also Turkic-speaking nomads, who numbered perhaps 65,000 in late Republican times, and who lived in the T'ien-shan and Pamir highlands.

Southern Sinkiang, or traditional East Turkestan, was by contrast an extension of Muslim Inner Asia. Its primary population group consisted of Uighurs, Turkic-speaking and largely sedentary agriculturalists who inhabited the oases of the Tarim basin, the area of Turfan and Kumul, and the Ili valley. By the 1930s they numbered perhaps 2,941,000 (O4, p. 6).

At the time of the Chinese conquest, these population figures were far lower. The entire indigenous population of East Turkestan was then probably about three hundred thousand, of which perhaps 70 percent lived in the western part of the Tarim basin, in the vicinity of Kashgar. Between the Ch'ing conquest in 1759 and the 1920s, both this East Turkestan population and the amount of farmland under cultivation appear to have doubled (A10, p. 69).

The Mongolian population of Outer Mongolia stood at 540,000 in 1921. This figure does not include the approximately 100,000 Chinese and 5,000 Russian residents of Outer Mongolia (figures on Outer Mongolia from M32, p. 92). Another estimate gives the 1918 population as 647,800, a figure that must include Chinese and Russian residents in Outer Mongolia (M45, p. 35). Over 40 percent of the male population of Outer Mongolia were lamas. Population estimates for Mongols in Inner Mongolia in the 1930s vary from 900,000 to 2,500,000, depending on which territories are included as part of Inner Mongolia (M41, pp. 25–27). Eastern Inner Mongolia was far more densely populated than the western portions. Estimates of the population of Inner Mongolia by banner between 1912 and 1940 reflect a steady decline in overall population. The population decline that both Inner and Outer Mongolia experienced in the nineteenth and first third of the twentieth centuries should not be surprising. As stated above, at least 40 percent of the male population of Outer Mongolia consisted of lamas (who had taken vows of celibacy), and 40–60 percent of the male population of Inner Mongolia were likewise celibate monks (M41, p. 27). Educated Mongols realized that Buddhism was contributing to the noticeable population decrease. Injannasi (1837–1892), author of the fascinating literary work *Koke sudur* (The Blue Chronicle, 1871), wrote: "Furthermore, the Chinese are a prolific race, and they do not make their children monks in order to make them Buddhas like the Mongols do which decreases the population" (M16, pp. 79–80).

It is no exaggeration to say that the survival of the Mongols as a people was threatened far more by demographic factors than by external political factors. A high infant mortality rate in combination with the ravages of plague, smallpox, and syphilis also contributed to the decline in overall population. The Mongols' lack of resistance to, and deep-seated fear of, smallpox are well attested in Chinese sources (M67, pp. 41–63). When an epidemic hit one of the larger monasteries, as, for instance, when "a fever illness" hit the Badghar monastery in western Inner Mongolia in 1933, hundreds of monks might perish in a year's time (M24, pp. 137–138).

In terms of the urban-rural distribution of population in prerevolutionary Outer Mongolia, I. M. Maiskii was not too far from the truth when he wrote in 1921: "Here there is no diversity of activity; here everybody has only one occupation—cattle raising. Here the entire people is composed of herdsmen" (M38, p. 109). In less impressionistic terms, the census of 1918 as recorded by Maiskii lists an urban population of 140,000 or 22 percent of the total population. Yet only 50,000 of the 140,000 urban inhabitants were Mongols; 85,000 were Chinese and 5,000 Russian. And 40,000 of the 50,000 Mongolian urban inhabitants were permanent inhabitants of sedentary monasteries. (Maiskii's figures are cited in B4, pp. 56–57.)

The monastery played a role as the core area around which a town or city might grow, and as a market center. Monasteries were often located on trade routes. Most important was a monastery's annual fair at which nomadic herds as well as the monastery's own herds would be traded to Chinese merchants. Such fairs included religious ceremonies and athletic contests in addition to business transactions. Some monasteries also held periodic markets (perhaps four times a year), but it is difficult to generalize on the timing of such markets (see M41, pp. 108–110, and M24, pp. 116–117).

Organizational Contexts

The family is generally the primary framework within which human activity is organized, and in premodern societies it plays a significantly more important role than in advanced societies. As the societies of Central Asia moved toward wider forms of social organization, their course was deeply affected by the degree to which the populations shared a culture and language.

In urban and settled rural settings in Iran, the extended family unit formed the basis for organization. In tribal settings, however, lineage and the divisions into clans and tribes formed the basis for relationships. Because of the power of the monarch to appoint, dismiss, reward, and punish members of the government, the status of the aristocracy was not fixed but rather fluid. Members of the aristocracy could buy a tax farm and could also be deprived of it and the income it provided. They could hold on to ancestral lands by circumventing Muslim laws of inheritance or marrying within the extended family unit. But even the most established families remained susceptible to monarchal whim and relied on social forces and connections to retain their positions and fortunes. Legal recourse was impractical. By the nineteenth century, rebellion often led to exile, frequently to the Ottoman Empire or to the tsarist Caucasus.

The monarch could and did elevate men from poor backgrounds to responsible and rewarding positions. Mobility thus achieved, however, was fragile. Thus the cement of society was marriage. Family ties with the monarchy provided a certain assurance against whimsical arrest though this did not always work. The most striking example is that of Mirza Taqi Khan, the first prime minister of Nasiruddin Shah, who was the son of a cook, but married to the shah's sister. When he fell victim to court intrigue, Taqi Khan was murdered with court connivance.

In the society at large, although endogamous marriage, specifically marriage with the father's niece, was preferred, health arguments were used for marriage outside the extended family unit.

Reflecting the hierarchical organization of the monarchy, much of the tribal organization in Iran has also been hierarchical. The Baluch provide a contrast to the Pushtun and demonstrate the difference between Iranian and Afghan modes of power structure and organization. The latter form councils of equal men who rule by consensus, whereas the Baluch have chiefs whose councils are merely advisory.

Among urban dwellers in the middle and lower classes, the guild system served to create a network among artisans and related professionals. Concentrated in the bazaar, and enjoying close ties with the ulema, guilds supported political endeavors during the late Qajar period, particularly in the struggle against foreign concessions. Guild members often were among those who suffered most from the influx of foreign goods. Many guild systems were strengthened through long association, the system of passing a trade from father to son, and intermarriage. Therefore, the guilds provided a ready basis for political organization by the ulema, a factor that became important at the time of the Constitutional Revolution (1905–1911).

Religious organizations affected mainly urban dwellers and were of two varieties: the loose organization of a particular town quarter around the local mosque and that of the Sufi orders. The latter drew devotees from all parts of a town, possibly also from a particular guild, and from multiple layers of society. Though banned in periods of strict Shi'ite orthodoxy, Sufi orders enjoyed a return during the premodern period. In Tehran, Shiraz, and other towns were located prominent and well-endowed Sufi hostels. Even when *madrasa* and mosque construction lagged, as in the new quarters of rapidly growing towns like Tehran, Sufi *tekiya* appear to have flourished.

Membership in a guild or a Sufi order, and residence in a particular quarter of a town provided for several allegiances and corporate identity for individuals. Such identities together with ethnic and regional identities gave, to urban individuals especially, layers of loyalties that could help in politically uncertain times.

The least developed of the integrating institutions of nineteenth-century society in premodern Iran was the military. Unlike its neighbor Turkey, Iran's attempts to develop a standing army during the nineteenth century were limited to a brief period in the early part of the century. Instead, the monarchy and aristocrats employed private mercenaries who were little more than ruffians with no training or discipline. For this reason, tribal levies were occasionally used, but controlling their political direction was not always certain. High-sounding military titles were sold much like tax farms, and the purchaser pocketed pay for the soldiers while the latter searched for other means of feeding themselves. The sole trained and equipped military unit that was reliable was the Russian Cossack Brigade, formed in 1879, and used in Tehran to protect the monarchy. From this unit came Reza Shah, the corporal who became king of Iran in 1925.

In Iran Shi'ism and Persian culture constituted the main commonalities until the modern period, when nationalism gained in acceptance and also served to advance social integration. Yet even this religious and cultural identity did not permeate the entire population. Iran, since the eleventh-century Turkic incursions, has been a country with large and influential pockets of Turkic-speaking people, both settled and nomadic. Even among the Iranian-speaking population, again both settled and nomadic, several language communities exist. These communities, such as the Kurds and Baluch, retained their own popular culture quite distinct from Persian culture. Added to these are Arabic-speaking communities, once again divided between settled and pastoral nomadic. Although most of these groups belong to the Shi'ite branch of Islam, important sections also profess Sunnism and little known heterodox sects. Added to such diversity are the non-Muslim communities, two of them, Zoroastrians and Jews, essentially Persian-speaking together with Armenians and Assyrians. The Bahais, so prominent in the mid-twentieth century, began to make their mark in the late nineteenth century. By the turn of the century, roughly 95 percent of the population was Muslim, but non-Muslims living in urban centers influenced change to a degree beyond their numbers. Generally they remained outside the main social divisions of society except in the case of prominent converts to Islam.

This ethnoreligious diversity, a challenge to national integration, suffered further subdivision into rural and urban elements between which few lines of communication existed. Thus Iran, up to the beginning of the modern period, was a country with a dispersed and diverse population, organized along centuries-old social, economic, and political patterns that were ill-suited for the adoption of the basic infrastructure demanded by modernization.

Similarly in Afghanistan, ethnic and religious diversity has been a continuing obstacle to social integration. The dominant Pushtun tribes had to contend with Tajik, Uzbek, Turkmen, and other ethnic groups equally intent on preserving their separate interests. This pattern of ethnic rivalries was further complicated by the religious division between the four-fifths of the population who were Hanafi Sunni and the balance who were mainly Imami Shi'a.

Professional guilds, somewhat loosely structured, did exist in towns, but became much more highly structured and better organized in the cities. Common occupations clustered together, so it was easy for the guilds to organize and present a common face to the outside world, especially in matters of taxation, usury, and rents. Usury, although forbidden in Islam, was widely practiced. Many villagers found themselves in perpetual debt to landlords, itinerant peddlers, nomads, or town shopkeepers, who also functioned as moneylenders.

Seldom were all town bazaar shops open all the time, but special bazaar days occurred each week, usually no more than two. Favored days were Monday and Thursday. Animal fairs, reminiscent of medieval Europe, were held in some areas, particularly in central Afghanistan where many nomadic groups came together in late summer.

Villagers would bring agricultural produce and handicrafts to the town on bazaar days to barter or sell and buy items from town artisans and merchants. City merchants would come to the towns to purchase items to sell in their urban shops. The town bazaar, especially the tea house, acted as an important disseminator of news from village to city and vice versa. Nomads passing through village areas performed the same function.

The city was a major commercial, administrative, and communication center, linking the interior with the outside world. The importance of cities varied or shifted as power shifted hands. For example, Kandahar was originally the capital of the last Afghan empire, the Durrani, but in 1775–1776 the capital was shifted to Kabul for political reasons.

As in most Inner Asian cities, the pre-1920s cities of Afghanistan consisted of an "old city" and a "new city," usually divided by a river or some other natural feature such as a series of hills. Usually, the "new city" arose in response to administrative needs, the governing of an empire or a province. The "old city" consisted of the bazaars and residential areas of the general populace. In the bazaars, similar occupations of artisans and merchants clustered together in tight guildlike structures. Laborers and others often lived in ethnically oriented wards, each reflecting a group that migrated to the city. In Kabul, for example, the Tajik, Qizilbash, Hazara, and Pushtun all had their separate quarters, and few dared cross over to the others' zones.

In Russian Central Asia the territory was so sparsely settled and the ethnic groups were so diverse that social integration beyond the tribal level was not a significant issue. The native peoples retained until the end of the nineteenth century a traditional way of life that was characterized by relatively little social cohesion. Even in the twentieth century the five republics into which the region was divided—Kazakh, Kirgiz, Tajik, Turkmen, and Uzbek—each contained a considerable variety of ethnic groups; and by the end of the nineteenth century they were already in the process of being infiltrated by Russian and other European settlers.

Among the Kazakhs, for example, the family was more likely to be nuclear than extended, and two to eight families were often grouped to form *auls*. These families in turn were grouped into an escalating hierarchy of clans, tribes, and hordes, but these were loose and fluctuating alliances of convenience which did not exert a significant central control over their members. The Muslim religious institution likewise did not provide an organizational context for the nomads. The nomadic way of life was not suited to organized religion, the nomads had no mosques, and they practiced their own variant of Islam which included strong elements of their earlier shamanism.

In the areas to the south settled by the Uzbeks, the three khanates and the smaller principalities were autocratic polities which provided few links between the government and the peasants apart from the mechanism for collecting taxes. The Muslim clergy was associated with the authority of the government, and did not provide a separate structure of organization. Since trade played an important role in the Central Asian economy, one should also consider the organizational role of the bazaars as centers of merchant activity, and of the guilds which regulated the work of the craftsmen. The bazaars and the guilds were under government supervision, for purposes of both taxation and regulation.

Urban crafts had a long history of being highly specialized in Central Asian towns and cities. Individual craftsmen almost invariably produced only a single type of article, and most often they themselves would sell it directly rather than through middlemen, except when it was for the foreign market. They had their own guild organizations which established and maintained norms. The guilds had written statutes and customary social traditions, maintained themselves as self-governing communities, and even owned their own lands. One progressed within the guilds through three stages, from student *(shagird)* to apprentice *(khalfa)* to master *(usto)* with years, often decades, between each step. To become a master one had to own one's own house and equipment, and the stages were often prolonged by the master in order to benefit from the labor of his students and apprentices. Members of a given craft guild often worked in a cohesive neighborhood area in the towns and elected their own guild heads, senior wealthy and influential figures who were then confirmed by the khans and given administrative and judicial autonomy within their neighborhood areas. These craft concentrations fed the phenomenon of the bazaars, which played a significant role in bringing together not only the urban and rural populace for exchange of goods and produce, but the nomadic peoples as well.

What is particularly significant about the peoples of Central Asia is the gap between the peasants and the rulers. In Bukhara, for example, the very substantial revenues collected by the emir were expended primarily for his personal use for palaces and travel, and he devoted little attention to public services. The coming of the Russians imposed a separate organizational structure on that of the native rulers, but not until the end of the century did Russian influence begin to introduce modern organizational forms such as trade unions and political parties.

In Tibet, except for outcaste groups for whom marriage outside the clan was frowned on (though still possible), exogamous marriage was the rule. Polygamous marriage was practiced usually only by the wealthy and noble families, whereas polyandry was widespread among all socioeconomic groups and in most geographic areas (N31, pp. 94–97). In the region of D'ing-ri in southern Tibet, north of Nepal, Barbara Nimri Aziz found polyandry, polygamy, monogamy, and frequent remarriage all to be common (N2).

Power in the typical Tibetan village was held by village officials called *genbo* ("elders"). In the village of Samada in central Tibet, there were two such elders appointed by a village council for indefinite terms of office. The village council itself consisted of the heads of the tax-paying, hereditary serfs (as opposed to the "human lease" serfs; see "Redistributive Processes," this chapter). In Samada there were eight such tax-paying serf families who held hereditary rights to agricultural lands and pastures, which were owned by the government. Since government officials cared only that the village pay its taxes, the village council had considerable leeway in internal administration. One of Samada's two village elders assessed and administered tax affairs while the other managed official business with outsiders who came to the village. Methods of recruiting village elders varied in central Tibet from hereditary transmission to rotating the position among heads of tax-paying serf families. Clearly the elders were agents of the tax-paying serf families, not independent power brokers. (The above is from N12, pp. 1–27.) The village elder in the D'ing-ri region of southern Tibet played a similar role (N2, p. 199).

Landed estates and monasteries constituted the two main institutions that ordered the lives of people in traditional Tibet, but the Lhasa government's military force (about which very little has been written) should also be mentioned. In addition to taxes in barley, hay, and money, villages owed the central government a military tax. According to the government's record books, the village of Samada in central Tibet owed six and one-quarter men who would serve in the central government's regiments (N12, p. 14).

In southern Sinkiang, the Ch'ing were initially aware of the hostility of the people to non-Muslims, and attempted to avoid provocation. Where possible, they followed traditional patterns, so that "patterns of land tenure, taxation, and service obligations in Eastern Turkestan in 1800 were essentially a continuation of pre-existing customs which were very similar to patterns obtaining in other parts of Muslim central Asia" (A10, p. 74). Some changes were of course unavoidable, but by and large the Ch'ing sought to minimize them: indeed, they took active measures to prevent the extension of their administrative power from destabilizing traditional patterns.

The Ch'ing sought to exclude Han merchants from southern Sinkiang, for fear they would take over the area economically, as they were beginning to do in Manchuria and Mongolia, and thus cause unrest. They sent military forces in only on a temporary, rotating basis. Instead of bringing in farmers to support their forces, they leased government lands to local people. No Chinese civilians were allowed to migrate west of Hami. "The authorities would not admit Han civilians into any part of East Turkestan without good reasons and properly validated passports" (A10, p. 77).

Where a Han presence did exist, it was rigorously segregated from the native inhabitants. Special walled citadels housed Ch'ing garrisons, administrative offices, and nonindigenous personnel. Such settlements were located outside the native city walls, and regulations forbade Ch'ing officials from entering native cities or villages except as prescribed, and severely limited their economic activity, such as moneylending and the hiring of native labor. Disputes between Muslims and Ch'ing personnel were resolved following Muslim law (A10, p. 77).

Such policies were modified a bit in the nineteenth century as a result of the chronic unrest in the area. After 1834, Peking began to encourage poor Chinese to migrate to southern Sinkiang, and by the mid-1830s Yarkand had two hundred Chinese merchants as fixed residents, in addition to many others who came and went. The Chinese language began to be used (A10, p. 374). But even these measures were only partially successful, and the Han Chinese population of southern Sinkiang has remained low even in the twentieth century, while the tension that led to the original Ch'ing policies of segregation and tolerance has by no means disappeared.

The caution of Ch'ing policy in southern Sinkiang meant that the imposition of Chinese influence, which we might expect to lead to a gradual mixing of the peoples, the development of a new social and political cohesion, and a gradual mobilization of indigenous peoples into structures imposed from outside, was prevented from having any such effects. Far from trying to reconstruct Sinkiang, the Ch'ing tried to maintain an equilibrium there both by insulating native people from contact with their conquerors, and by keeping the conquerors themselves segregated in their own areas. At the same time the Ch'ing did very little to control either trade or religion, the two mutually reinforcing elements that maintained the ties of the indigenous people of southern Sinkiang with their cousins and co-religionists across the border. Premodern development in Sinkiang, in other words, did little or nothing to prepare the area for a future as a modernizing component of a Chinese state. Quite the opposite: it helped to maintain ethnic and religious features of the area that would reappear later as obstacles to such incorporation.

Among the Mongols, tribes and clans constituted the largest indigenous suprafamily units until very recent times. Even by Ming and Ch'ing times, the tribe was no longer "a homogeneous group of people claiming common descent" (M67, pp. 63–75, esp. p. 64). Tribes consisted of people from different clans, although the name of a tribe was usually the name of one of its most influential clans. The same clan name often appeared in different geographic areas of Greater Mongolia and among different tribes. In theory exogamy was practiced by members of a clan, though it is questionable whether by the nineteenth century Mongols other than nobles consistently adhered to this custom.

Manchu rule over both Outer and Inner Mongolia fragmented the Mongols as a people. It was not in the interest of the Manchu Ch'ing government to integrate regions or groups of Mongols. Rather, the Manchus reorganized the Mongols into the arbitrarily superimposed administrative territorial units known as banners *(khoshighun).* Gradually, the names of banners tended to displace clan names as official identification, although most Mongols knew their own clan names. The institution of banners was meant to disrupt tribal and clan organizations and to supplant clan authority. In order to co-opt the Mongolian nobility (a genealogically legitimated nobility limited to the descendants of Chinggis Khan and his brothers), the Manchus invested Mongolian nobles with titles and offices such as that of *jasak,* or head of a banner. Ever conscious of the possibility of a resurgence of Chinggissid power, the Manchus limited the Mongolian princes' privileges to the economic sphere: they were granted tax and service exemptions and a free hand at exploiting Mongolian commoners.

Military weapons, much less indigenous military organizations, were strictly forbidden among the Mongols. The banner units with their subdivisions were, however, liable for quasi-military duties such as relay and watch-post services. On occasion, the Manchus mobilized Mongols as soldiers, as in the Ch'ing wars with the Jungars (western Mongols) from the 1730s to the 1750s; desertions to the Jungars and sabotage of Manchu war matériel, however, made the Mongols a less than trustworthy military force (M4, pp. 100–106). Ch'ing law forbade the buying of arms by Mongols without a certificate from the Ch'ing Ministry of War. Infractions were punishable by fines in livestock for Mongolian nobles and by eighty lashes for commoners. As Jacques Legrand notes (M34, p. 129), such laws against weapons reflected the Manchus' fear of a reconstitution of Mongolian power.

The Mongols' traditional council of princes and military leaders, the *khuriltai*, whose roots go back to the twelfth century, apparently continued in some very limited form in Ch'ing times. (It is not clear what the participants of banner *khuriltai* and league [*chighulghan*] *khuriltai* discussed [see M27, p. 341]. Apparently a Manchu envoy was always present at *chighulghan* meetings in Outer Mongolia [see M34, p. 97].) Unlike the *khuriltai* of earlier centuries at which a new khan would be selected and military options reviewed, the *khuriltai* of the Ch'ing era seems to have been an empty shell with no political authority. The old institution of the *khuriltai* was reborn in different guise in 1924 when the Great Khural (Mongolia's Supreme Soviet) was instituted.

Since virtually every Mongolian family had a son who was a lama, the Buddhist monastery played an important role in the lives of the Mongols. It must be stressed, however, that each local monastery was an autonomous unit. Although ultimately responsible to Peking, the monastery was more of a local institution than a part of an integrated network (M41, p. 141). As a market center, as the recipient of constantly solicited donations, and as a place to send one or more sons when Ch'ing-imposed restrictions on grazing lands made the family economy unstable, the local monastery had both positive and negative effects on the individual herder's family. It was not, in the final analysis, a socially integrating institution.

Overall, Manchu prohibitions on travel between banner units led to restricted communication, which in turn led to a growth in localism at the expense of the development of a national consciousness among Mongols at large.

Redistributive Processes

In societies such as those of Inner Asia in which the gap between rulers and ruled was large among the settled population, and the pressure of Russian and Chinese settlers was being imposed on the relatively egalitarian nomads, the question of redistributing wealth and status became increasingly important in the course of the nineteenth century.

In Iran in the late nineteenth and early twentieth centuries seeds were planted for the social changes that occurred in the modern period. Some of these changes, though antithetical to modernization, nonetheless prepared the way for it by creating grounds for unrest. Among the most important changes was the emergence of a large class of landless peasants whose properties became absorbed into crown and other large estates. This trend continued into the Reza Shah period and ultimately led to considerable unrest.

The growth of urban areas, associated with landlessness, increased the political base for the ulema but changed the patterns of urban settlement in two ways:

first, the peasants were not easily incorporated into the guilds but formed a large poor working population. Second, the old quarters that had housed both rich and poor and formed patronage communities gave way to quarters made up mostly of the poor and artisan classes. Living conditions in these areas were rarely affected by improved sanitation, pure water supply, health care, roads, schools, or communications networks. Thus the poor came to form separate sections of town without the traditional links to landlord or rich neighbors that had helped to mollify class differences in the past.

Additionally, the movement toward urban areas brought ethnic populations in contact with each other despite the fact that they would live in different sections of the same town. More Christians and Muslims begin to interact, but even more important was the movement of Turkic groups into Persian-speaking urban areas. The populations of Tehran and eventually Shiraz and Isphahan were thus reshaped. Urbanized Azerbaijanis living in Persian towns adopted Persian language and culture as never before, while retaining their language in the family. Gradually, as public-school education spread in the cities, Azerbaijani families, with no access to education in their own language, changed to the exclusive use of Persian. To a lesser degree, the case of Azerbaijani assimilation is duplicated for Kurds, Turkmen, and non-Muslim groups.

The urban picture also was affected by the presence of substantial and influential immigrants from former tsarist lands. In the aftermath of the Russian revolution, many Persian families who had either remained in the Caucasus from the pre-1828 period or moved there for trade, education, or in times of religious strife (true in particular for Bahais), became repatriated in the 1920s and 1930s. They brought with them secular perspectives and certainly many Western ideas. Their role in influencing social mobility, the professions, education, and culture was substantial, particularly in the case of Christian ethnic minorities.

The rural picture too was affected by the installation of Soviet power because of the substantial numbers of Turkmen and Kurds who left Soviet areas. These settled in very small towns or rural areas in northern Iran and formed pockets of Sunnis in largely Shi'ite areas. The Turkmen community in Khorasan, its position within its region, and its relationship with central government are particularly interesting.

In Afghanistan migration, both forced and voluntary, was an important means of redistribution. In his effort to defend his power at the center, Amir Abdur Rahman shifted dissident Pushtun groups from the south to north of the Hindu Kush. These forced migrations caused several shifts in social, political, and economic patterns. Abdur Rahman removed internal threats to his regime, and the Pushtun sent north supported the Pushtun amir against the non-Pushtun peoples of the north: Tajik, Uzbek, Turkmen, and Aimaq.

Later, some Pushtun voluntarily emigrated when the amir made the lands of conquered non-Pushtun peoples available to the Pushtun. Also, when he conquered the Hazarajat in 1895–1896, he reduced many Hazara to virtual slavery, and awarded their lands to loyal Pushtun.

Initially, the forcibly migrated Pushtun attempted to maintain links with their kinsmen in the south and east. Transplanted Pushtun would come south, seeking brides for their sons, but the southern branches usually refused to send their daughters north. Because of this, some Pushtun males were forced to seek brides among non-Pushtun females. Probably few marriages occurred between non-Pushtun males and Pushtun females.

In the latter half of the nineteenth and early twentieth centuries, refugees from the tsarist conquests in Central Asia poured into northern Afghanistan, thus increasing the non-Pushtun population. Pushtun, however, retained political control of most village councils in the north.

Also, some provincial governors in southern Afghanistan began, consciously or unconsciously, to mistake the right to collect taxes with ownership of land. Amir Abdur Rahman gave the governors a free hand in internal matters as long as they submitted the requisite taxes and conscripts to the center.

Provincial governors used the army to force dissidents to move to other parts of their provinces. Therefore, many villages with only one clan or lineage and its clients became multilineage, and even multi-ethnic. This pattern began to break down tribal loyalties without, however, creating loyalties to a larger nation-state.

Abdur Rahman did succeed in extending his influence—if not actual control—over what was to become modern Afghanistan. His control over accessible areas gathered momentum year by year and provided new opportunities for upward mobility. Centralization required an expanded bureaucracy, and to meet this need, Abdur Rahman brought some of the sons of his conquered subjects to Kabul for training as military officers and civil administrators (see "Distribution of Political Power," chapter 3).

A further dimension of social integration in Afghanistan was represented by the nomads. Numerically inferior to the sedentary populations, nonsedentary peoples have always had great political clout, especially in Afghanistan. Two nomadic movements have dominated through time: horizontal and vertical. Horizontal movements were more common among steppe, semidesert nomads, who traveled between oases. Vertical migrations (also called transhumance) entailed movements between winter pasture lands in the lowlands to summer pasture lands in mountainous, alpine ecological zones. These movements took nomads through settled areas of peasant farmers, and often several weeks passed before nomads reached their pasture lands. Any deviation from routes of migration usually meant poaching on the routes of other nomads and could result in conflict.

Although conflicts also occurred between the settled peasants and the nomads, usually the relationships were symbiotic. Contrary to popular belief, nomads do not necessarily deflower the landscape, but are actually the perpetuators of the loessy grasslands and semideserts (even in the foothills of the Hindu Kush) through which they pass twice a year. Sheep and goats are among nature's more prolific defecating machines, and as they eat they deposit natural fertilizer on the landscape. The decomposition of this nitrogeneous material helps keep the grasses growing. In addition, nomads returned to their winter pasture lands in late summer just after the farmers had reaped their wheat. Cooperative agreements permitted the livestock to graze on the stubble. Once again, manure from the sheep and goats helped replace the nitrogen in the soil lost through cultivation.

In societies such as those of Russian Central Asia, where the main division of status among the settled peoples was between rulers and subjects, there was little opportunity for the development of "classes." Such classes as existed, such as government officials, clergy, merchants, and craftsmen—although the last two groups were taxed—tended to be grouped around the rulers. Customarily, sons followed the professions of their fathers, and peasants had little opportunity to improve their status. The nomads, for their part, had a much simpler social structure. Their division of labor by gender traditionally allocated most of the hard labor to women, including the construction and transportation of the prefabricated tents in which they lived. Some individuals specialized in handicrafts, but not to the extent of developing separate professions. Probably the progression from family member to clan elder and military leader—requiring a combination of age and skill—was the principal opportunity for upward mobility in a nomadic society.

In the case of the Russians after the 1860s, there was a sharp division between the colonial administrators and the immigrant peasants. The administrators were civil servants, by definition members of the privileged group in Russian society, and their task was to supervise and facilitate the process of immigration and settlement. There was a formal Resettlement Administration, which set aside land for the immigrants and provided them with financial and other assistance. By the early twentieth century, some 40 percent of the population of the steppe territories and 6 percent of those in the settled areas to the south were Russians. Under the influence of the Russians and the development of trade, industry, and education, Central Asia was beginning to exhibit the characteristics of a modern social structure.

The classic means of redistributing wealth and status in Central Asia was through migration, but by the nineteenth century there were no major new migrations of the native peoples of Central Asia apart from the move of some Kazakhs into Sinkiang and Mongolia to escape the pressures of the Russian immigrants. The great new migration was of Russians and other Europeans, of whom some two million settled in Central Asia in the last four decades of the nineteenth century. The colonial administrators sought to protect the traditional pastures of the nomads, but in practice the settlers often found the pastures to be particularly suited to agriculture and the movements of the nomads were increasingly constrained.

The native system of taxation in Central Asia was designed primarily to redistribute wealth from the poor to the rich—from the peasants to the rulers. Although in principle taxes on land were not unreasonable, the tax farmers normally overtaxed the peasants for their own benefit. There was also a wide range of taxes on agricultural products and crafts, which kept the populace in poverty.

With the development of cotton growing, an intensive crop requiring hired labor, peasants were often reduced to poverty, indebtedness, and even the loss of their property. The native system of land tenure also tended to discriminate against those who worked the land. The Russians were concerned about the inequities of the native system and did what they could to introduce greater equity. The most dramatic measure was the land reform of 1867–1868, which gave the land to those who worked it—a much more drastic reform than that enacted in Russia in 1861. By other changes in the very complex native system, the pressure on the peasants was somewhat relieved. The Kazakh nomads of the steppe region were the first to feel the effects of the Russian colonization. As the colonization restricted the availability of pasture lands, many nomads sought relief in sedentary agriculture which required them to give up their communal practices in favor of private property rights. It is a matter of dispute whether these developments benefited the former nomads.

Tibetan society has most often been characterized as having three social classes—commoners, nobility, and clergy (N31, p. 92). More recent case studies of Tibetan villages have sought to clarify the traditional contours of Tibetan social classes and to establish the existence of subgroups within those classes. Aziz's case study of D'ing-ri (N2) describes four distinct social groups. First is a hereditary clergy whose members married and whose sons inherited the status of clergy; second, nobles of which there were none resident in D'ing-ri, although some D'ing-ri land was owned by absentee nobles; third, commoners who constituted 90 percent of D'ing-ri's population and who worked as agriculturalists, itinerant laborers, artisans, and traders; and finally, "outcaste people," who were prohibited from holding land and who were allowed to work only at such lowly tasks as butchering and preparing hides. Outcastes occasionally intermarried with commoners, but such marriages were much criticized. Carrasco (N7, p. 214) has noted the existence of endogamous outcaste groups in central Tibet (fishermen, ferrymen, smiths, corpse cutters, butchers) and in western Tibet (musicians and smiths of Indian origin).

In D'ing-ri, agriculturalists held lands leased from the government or other landlords. Aziz rejects the notion that the status of such tenant farmers can be understood by a peasant feudal model, and points out that the tenant had the right to transfer hereditarily his leased landholding, and that tenants could become prosperous through engaging in commercial trade or expanding their herds. Nonetheless, in terms of social mobility, it appears that D'ing-ri's tenant farmers, although able to achieve differing levels of economic prosperity, were not able to abrogate the fundamental duties owed to their landlords. Also, it is unclear how typically Tibetan the frontier zone Aziz studied actually was.

The debate about stratification and interclass mobility in traditional Tibet has been addressed head-on by Melvyn C. Goldstein, whose research is based on a case study of the village of Samada in central Tibet. Goldstein embraces the notion of a "pervasive serfdom" in traditional Tibet, but argues that traditional Tibetan social organization allowed "a significant potential for personal mobility within a matrix of hereditary and pervasive serfdom" (N11, p. 521). Tibet's lay population included only 250 to 300 aristocratic families; the rest were hereditary serfs. Most serfs were legally bound to their lords' estates (in some cases the government was lord), with tax obligations clearly delineated in written documents. According to Goldstein, mobility between lord and serf was nonexistent, and mobility through becoming a monk or nun was dependent on a serf's receiving his or her lord's permission to leave the estate to join a monastic order. Monks and nuns were released from their estate obligations for as long as they remained members of the clergy, but upon leaving the clergy, they reverted once again to serf status. Estates in Tibet were owned by aristocratic families, monasteries, and offices of the central government.

In spite of this apparent lack of interclass mobility, there was one type of serf who remained free to live and work where he or she wished. This type of serf obtained what is called "human lease" to seek work where he wished as long as he paid an annual cash sum to his original lord. This arrangement allowed significant personal and geographic mobility, as the "human lease" serf was a much sought-after worker in rural Tibet where there was a chronic labor shortage and underpopulation (because of the monastic tradition). Usually a serf obtained "human lease" by first running away from an estate, and because the estate lord had few means by which to trace runaways, the lord would issue the "human lease" after the remaining relatives of the runaway had mediated the issue. Marriages between individuals of different estates would usually lead to the issuing of the "human lease" to the girl. Although "human lease" was considered by agriculturalists as preferable to bound serf status, certain disadvantages (separation from family, breaking ties with one's home area, lack of protection by a lord) prevented the majority of serfs from fleeing their lands.

In the village of Samada, which was a "corporate village" since its lands were owned by the central government, the population consisted of 40 to 45 members of the eight tax-paying serf families and about 240 "human lease" serfs, whose labor was crucial to the village's ability to operate and pay its taxes. Villages essentially competed for the much needed labor resources embodied in "human lease" serfs. The institution of "human lease" reflected the realities of the limitations of the lords' actual control and the high value placed on human labor in an underpopulated land. (This section relies heavily on N2, and N11, pp. 521–534.)

In Sinkiang, migration and trade were the most significant redistributive processes. Incorporation of the diverse territories and peoples of Sinkiang into the Ch'ing empire was a critical factor in late premodern developments. There had been a Han Chinese presence in modern Sinkiang off and on for centuries, beginning, perhaps, with the conquests of Wu-ti of the Han (r. 140–87 B.C.). But significant demographic movement began only in the eighteenth century. The

Ch'ing rulers brought with them substantial military forces. The effect of this movement on northern and southern Sinkiang was quite different.

By the beginning of the nineteenth century the garrison forces in the northern part of Sinkiang probably numbered about 100,000. They consisted both of Han Chinese soldiers of the Ch'ing Army of the Green Standard, and of Mongols and Manchus from the dynasty's banner forces. They constituted "in effect, an immigrant population permanently established in Sinkiang with their families and all their belongings" (A10, p. 60). In addition to soldiers, the Ch'ing brought settlers into those parts of northern Sinkiang where irrigation made agriculture possible. Sedentary people from East Turkestan were moved into so-called Muslim colonies which produced food to support the military and civilian populations. Called Taranchis, these people numbered over 34,000 by 1800 (A10, p. 65). Even more significant was the decision to move in civilians from China. By the turn of the nineteenth century hundreds of thousands of Chinese Muslims (so-called Hui or Tungan) and non-Muslim Han Chinese had settled in northern Sinkiang. By 1777, north of the T'ien-shan, more than 11,000 immigrant households were cultivating more than 35,000 acres. In the nineteenth century this immigration picked up, and by 1808 the amount of civilian farmland in the districts under the jurisdiction of Urumchi had increased tenfold over what it had been in 1775 (A10, pp. 65–66). The indigenous Kazakhs and Kirgiz were treated by the Ch'ing as foreign tributaries, and lived with very little interference from the authorities. Official trade was sanctioned with the Kazakhs at Ili and Tarbagatai and with the Kirgiz at Kashgar (A10, pp. 62, 64).

But southern Sinkiang was quite different. The people there had long been settled in the oases of the Tarim basin, and belonged to the Muslim civilization of Central Asia. Identity was local: people thought of themselves as belonging to the community of the oasis in which they lived, not to any larger political community. They had extensive trade ties, however, and the oasis towns derived much of their livelihood not just from agriculture, but from trade with northern Sinkiang and Russia, with India, Tibet, Afghanistan, and Central Asia. These patterns of trade reinforced the territory's ties with the larger religious world of Islam. The people of southern Sinkiang followed the leadership of rival lines of *khojas* within the Naqshbandiyya order. After the Ch'ing conquest many of their religious leaders were across the border, in Bukhara or elsewhere in Central Asia, and links were maintained by family and by merchant connections along the trade routes. Such a pattern of religious affiliation conflicted with the Ch'ing territorial demarcation.

In Mongolia, Manchu Ch'ing policies accelerated the process of social stratification by defining legally the distinctions between nobles *(tayiji)* and commoners *(arad).* By the nineteenth century, so much of Mongolia's wealth in livestock and livestock products had come to be concentrated in the hands of the monasteries and the few princes that widespread poverty was everywhere apparent. In the eastern half of Outer Mongolia, the number of paupers, some on the verge of starvation, had risen to nearly seventy-one thousand by the years 1884–1885 (M4, p. 142). Among the destitute were princes who had fallen deep into debt to Chinese merchants.

Although leaving one's banner jurisdiction was illegal, these déclassé elements had no choice but to become vagrants and laborers. Charles Bawden (M4, p. 143) has referred to this destitute group as a "new proletariat" with no industry to absorb its labor. Some vagrants became bandits, and the folktales of the nineteenth century are full of Robin Hood figures. The unequal distribution of wealth caused by banner princes' levies and Chinese merchants' moneylending practices transformed a previously semi-egalitarian society into one of the most economically and socially stratified pastoral societies.

As Chinese settlers took more and more pasture lands from the Mongols, which forced a reduction in the Mongols' herds, some Mongols attempted to imitate the Chinese in agricultural pursuits. Lack of experience in, or knowledge of, cultivation and fertilization techniques made the Mongols poor farmers. Mongols who by circumstance rather than choice had turned to agriculture and who then failed to eke out an existence would turn to banditry or rebellion (M20, pp. 165–168). Heissig (M20, p. 177) estimates that by 1930 two-thirds of eastern Inner Mongolia had been colonized by Chinese. The result was a displacement of those Mongols to more barren grazing lands near Outer Mongolia.

For the Mongols at the turn of the century, "redistributive processes" can refer only to involuntary sedentarization (for those who were forced to give up herding), involuntary migration to inferior lands (for those who tried to keep their herds), or a turn to banditry. Agriculture, railroads, and marketing systems took root on Mongolian soil, but their benefits bypassed the Mongolian people.

Conclusions and Comparisons

Conclusions and comparisons are both inhibited by the dearth of precise data on the countries and territories of Inner Asia in the nineteenth century, and this in itself is of course an indication of their relatively nonmodernized status.

In discussing human resources, for example, we have no reliable information on the populations of these societies, on their rates of growth either absolutely or in relation to the production of food and other resources, or on the share of the populations living in towns and cities. Both analysis and comparisons must therefore be made with caution, and with due recognition of their limitations. It is interesting to note that in 1800, some 30 percent of the population of England and somewhat less than 20 percent of the population of France and Japan was urban. In the absence of reliable estimates, one may conjecture that in Inner Asia the urban population at the end of the nineteenth century was not much over 5 percent. One may therefore estimate that in this respect the Inner Asian societies were in 1900 some two centuries or more behind Western Europe. Not only were most of the inhabitants peasants and herders, but only Iran was beginning to develop the mechanisms for mobilizing surpluses for central purposes. Even in Iran these efforts were weak, since it was able to rely to a considerable extent on foreign loans and by the beginning of the twentieth century on oil revenues as well. In all of these respects the unusual cultural heritage of Tibet makes it an anomaly, since the entry of some 40 percent of the male population into the monasteries both limited population growth and restricted the development of other professions.

The organizational development of the Inner Asian societies was also very limited. A society like the United States has a great many nonprofit membership organizations of national scope, in addition to myriad local and regional organizations, as well as political structures, and manufacturing and commercial enterprises. To make a more reasonable comparison, Japan and Russia in the nineteenth century were complex societies with many organizational structures that competed with the family in offering opportunities for individual development. China, by contrast, was relatively lacking in such organizations. In the societies of Inner Asia, organizations beyond the local level were limited. These included the Muslim religious establishment, the Sufi mystical organizations, the guilds that regulated the craftsmen, and the bazaars which were the business centers. The last two of these categories were certainly adaptable to modern transformation, although the bazaar merchants tended to be closely associated with the mullahs in their attachment to the traditional culture. Here again Tibet is an exception, when one considers the dominant role of the monasteries.

Redistribution processes of Inner Asia were also very limited. There was significant geographical mobility in Afghanistan during the period Adbur Rahman was forcing the movement of tribes in his effort to gain control over the country, but this did not have positive consequences for modernization. There was little occupational mobility, with the possible exception of the small number of natives of Central Asia who were drawn by Russian colonization into the beginnings of a modern economy by the end of the century. There is nothing resembling the examination system in China, for example, which offered opportunities for advancement to anyone who had a talent for study. Again, there is nothing resembling the periodic and regional markets in Japan which were the medium for an active commerce, or of the extensive emigration in Russia which offered peasants the opportunity to acquire larger plots of land to cultivate and freedom from the constraints of the village communes. Such education as was available in the *maktabs* and *madrasahs* prepared the youth more for immobility than for mobility, and by the beginning of the twentieth century only a small fraction of the urban youth had access to advanced modern education.

An aspect of redistribution that has been given inadequate attention is the status of women in Islamic and Buddhist societies. The gap between male and female roles was significantly greater than that between rich and poor, and was eventually to provide leverage for the Soviet efforts to penetrate and disintegrate Muslim conservatism. Women did much of the physical labor, were in effect lacking in legal rights, had a limited education, and were generally treated more as property than as human beings. Although native proverbs and later Soviet propaganda may have exaggerated their low status, and some accounts suggest that women could assert their influence within the family, the question of the status of women in Inner Asia deserves much more attention than it has thus far received (see G36, and E51).

6

Knowledge and Education

Introduction

In the early-modernizing societies, recognition of the potentialities of societal transformation, and research and educational institutions designed to develop and perpetuate this knowledge, were essential preconditions of modern development. In a book on France or England a discussion of knowledge and education would be the first in a series of topical chapters. One could in fact go back to the reorientation of Western thought in the twelfth century to find the beginnings of a rational approach to the human environment.

The later-modernizing societies, however, developed in an environment in which the advancement of knowledge had already begun and was being carried forward in the more developed societies, which their members could visit and from which they could borrow. For later-modernizing societies the initial task was not the production and distribution of knowledge, but the creation of modern political, economic, and social institutions. Although these aspects of development are closely interrelated and evolve in a more or less synchronous fashion, the creation of a national system of education is one of the later developments not only because of its great cost but also because of popular resistance to new values. The fact that in most advanced societies today there are large and often influential pockets of resistance to a rational approach to the human environment, is a measure of the problems that societies have to overcome in this respect.

In this as in other aspects of societal transformation there is a wide range among premodern societies in their capacity to adopt a modern world view and to promote elite and popular education. The principal distinction is between those premodern societies with substantial literacy and with elites that have had long experience with written law codes and literary works, and those that are essentially nonliterate and where even the elites have little experience with the written word. Closely associated with this distinction is that between outward-looking and inward-looking societies. Russia and Japan, for example, had both borrowed significant elements of their premodern culture from other societies—from Byzantium and China. India likewise had a considerable experience with other cultures. For them, changing their orientation toward the West was much less of a trauma than for societies that were predominantly self-contained—such as China, for instance. Also relevant, of course, is whether their status is one of independent state or colony. The differentiations among premodern societies are much more complex than these brief remarks would indicate, but they point in the direction that one should look in seeking to understand the role of knowledge and education in societal transformation.

We approach this problem here in terms of three issues: world views, elite education, and popular education. The significance of the world views held by members of a society has to do with how they see themselves in the context of other societies. To what extent are they aware of other societies? Do they see the world primarily in terms of conflicting religions—Muslims versus Christians and other beliefs? Do they have other indicators by which they measure themselves against others? Do they see themselves as vulnerable and in need of reform? These and many other questions arise in this context.

"Societies," of course, do not have world views. One must turn to individuals and groups among them for more specific answers to these questions. Elites, those with the highest status and the most influence, are those to whom one naturally turns first. To what extent do their education and experience differentiate them from the commoners? At what point do they become aware of the capabilities of more advanced societies? What educational institutions are established to train them? What is the curriculum of these institutions? To what extent is a modern outlook promoted by the elites by means of periodicals and other publications? In all of the above, one must not think of "elites" as individuals with uniform views. Quite the contrary. There are few issues more controversial than the policies a modernizing society should adopt, and in particular the extent to which traditional institutions should be adapted or even jettisoned. One looks for debates and conflict rather than conformity within an elite, just as conflicting political parties and civil strife characterize the continuing controversies within and among advanced societies.

Popular education in a modern context is normally long delayed. What is of concern is the extent to which popular values are compatible with a modern outlook, and the processes by which the gap between popular and elite values is gradually closed. One is impressed in particular by the tenacity with which fundamentalist views survive into the modern era. Just as the great religions have often had to incorporate earlier beliefs and customs into their theology, so there are all sorts of adaptations one should look for between popular beliefs and modern values.

World Views: Between Tradition and Modernity

Iran, as the Inner Asian society most open to Western influences in the nine-teenth century, is a natural starting point for a discussion of the transformation of world views. The structure of Iran's society during this critical period of change provides a key to understanding the domestic reasons for resistance to change. Iranian society was divided both horizontally and vertically. The horizontal divisions relate to ethnic differences reinforced by region and religion (for example, Sunni Baluch) and separation of secular and religious institutions. Vertical differences are seen in the pyramid structure of political institutions in the loosely centralized monarchal system as well as the even more decentralized Shi'ite hierarchy. The separation of elites from the masses, the absence of intermediary classes, and the predominantly rural habitat of the population, were factors that complicated the domestic debate concerning the goals of modernization and the appropriate methods for their implementation.

Until the period of Reza Shah (1925–1941) the world view of Iranian elites was formed chiefly by contacts within the region. To a large extent, therefore, Western influence was filtered through tsarist Russian contacts, with limited and select influence from France or Frankified intermediaries. Symbolic of this process are the trips made by Nasiruddin Shah to Europe via Russia. It is only during the Pahlavi period (and the consolidation of Communist rule in former tsarist lands) that Iranians made the leap across to Western Europe and later still to America in search of a modernizing world view.

Although much that was not traditional arrived in Iran as a result of competition and then cooperation with Russia, Iranian elites also looked to the Ottomans for models of change. The Turkish model remained for Iran a source of ideas and inspiration at least to the period of World War II.

Military defense of Iran from Russian (and Turkish) incursions provided the preliminary impetus for change. In the early nineteenth century, when Iran suffered humiliating losses of territory to Russia (1828), many among the elite circles embarked on the process of questioning the paradigms that governed Iranian life internally and its relationship to the outside world. Periodically during the next eighty-odd years, leaders gained power who attempted reforms on various levels, many having to do with education. But these efforts were invariably cut short because of the fear of loss of power and influence by the majority of the elites, the meddling of foreign powers (Russia and Britain), the complex position of the powerful Shi'ite ulema, the lack of a political base outside the circles of power, and the inertia of the vast majority of the population. Crown Prince Abbas Mirza (d. 1833) initiated military modernization, brought in French and British instructors, and sent students abroad to study. A second short-lived effort under Mirza Taqi Khan Amir Kabir (d. 1852) resulted in the establishment in 1851 of the Dar ul-Funun, an institution for technical and scientific instruction in Tehran; translation of Western books; the publication of the first Persian

textbooks; and the beginnings of education for government officials. Many reforms were cut short by the increasing suspicion of the long ruling Nasiruddin
Shah concerning the loyalty of reformists.

At about the same time, Western missionaries, French, American, and British,
followed by Germans and Russians, arrived to establish educational institutions
that flourished while their conversion efforts languished among Muslims. These
religious efforts were redirected toward Iran's religious, particularly Christian,
minorities with far-reaching effect. Educational levels among minority elites
soared, allowing many of them access to professional posts, in medicine for
example, previously unavailable to them. The support of foreign missionaries
also fostered education abroad and emigration among minority Christian elites,
such as the Assyrians and Armenians, as well as stirrings of ethnic nationalism.
The world view of these minorities, especially in the northwest of Iran, favored
"Christian" Europeans, a view that, when translated into political terms in the
context of World War I, led to their massacre and dispersion. Consequently the
educated elites of these communities spread throughout Iran and formed an
important component in the technocratic structure of the country.

The presence of foreign instructors and missionaries encouraged the elites to
learn foreign languages, especially French and later English. For Muslim elites,
this came at the expense of Arabic. Acquisition of foreign languages and study
opportunities abroad, married with a shaken faith in the viability of their own
traditions in a changing world, eventually led to a considerable alienation of the
elites from the masses of the Iranian people. The single best portrayal of
Iranians' disaffection with each other may be seen in a 1920 short story that
demonstrates the inability of three sets of Iranians, a Western-educated youth, a
mullah, and provincial officials, to communicate with each other in their native
Persian language. The Western-educated youth clutters his sentences with
French loanwords (and dresses in European fashion), the mullah punctuates his
speech with Arabic words and phrases, and the provincial officials are befuddled
by the entire situation.

For all these groups of Iranians, except the religious minorities, Islam, together with Iranian customs and traditions, formed the basis for daily relationships. Within this framework, the Shi'ite religious establishment continued to
wield power, perhaps even more than it had in the past because the Qajar dynasty was weak and without the religiously venerated status of the Safavids who
could claim a heritage of Shi'ite high descent. Moreover, because the major
schools (madrasas) and strength of the Shi'ite clergy lay outside the territory of
Qajar Iran (that is in Najaf and Kerbala in Ottoman Iraq), Iran's secular authorities exercised even less power over them than had previous dynasties. Because of
the social and political force that religious leaders could exercise in far-flung
areas of the country, they could block the introduction of laws or institutions that
they deemed dangerous. As the ruling elites allowed themselves to be drawn
deeper into obligatory debt relationships with foreign powers, and as the growing

urban population became more conscious of the tyranny and corruption of the court, the religious leadership emerged in the role of patriots seeking reform. This reform movement brought together clerics and educated liberals who joined to press for a constitution. The Constitutional Revolution marks a turning point in the world view of a large number of politically active Iranians. The period of struggle pitted patriotic Iranians against foreign powers and a dated system of rule. Although the ultimate success of the revolution may be questioned, it came to symbolize in later decades the high point of reform possibilities generated not from the top down but from the combined energy of a multitude of factions from among the ordinary people themselves.

On a theological level, the struggle to shift basic paradigms in order to become more attuned to the modern world involved the emergence of the Bahai religion, which may be considered Iran's major contribution to world thought in the modern period. The Bahai faith, based on a new prophecy by Baha'ullah who declared himself in 1863, promulgates a cosmopolitan, pacifist, and liberal doctrine outside Islam but encompassing it as well as other major religions. To the orthodox Shi'ite clergy, the Bahais together with their precursors the Babis (followers of the Bab, hanged in 1850) represented heretics par excellence. For this reason, both the Babis and the Bahais suffered terrible persecution at the hands of Shi'ite zealots, at times in collusion with the government. Nonetheless, for many elites the Bahai message offered the answer to the chief dilemma of their time: how to remain true to the national Iranian heritage without the constrictions imposed by traditional Shi'ism on adoption of new social, economic, and political values. Also attracted to Bahaism were elites of certain minorities such as Zoroastrians. Like their counterpart the Ahmadiyya of Pakistan, who suffered a similar fate in their own homeland, the Bahais' interest in modern education and the equality of women were among their modernizing differences with traditional society.

In Afghanistan likewise, the dominant world view well into the twentieth century was defined by the outlook of the Muslim religious establishment. Members of the clergy were firm in their belief that their traditional teachings represented all the knowledge that was worthwhile, and they rejected modern education and especially the natural sciences as subversive. This traditionalism was encouraged by the relative isolation of the country from outside influences, and also by the lawlessness of Afghan society which prevented its members from confronting the problems of the modern world in a coherent fashion.

Not until the beginning of the twentieth century did a modernist movement known as the Young Afghans emerge to present a critique of the country's dilemmas and to propose a reform program. The most prominent leader of this small group of intellectuals was Mahmud Tarzi (1866–1935), who edited the newspaper *Seraj ul-akhbar-e afghaniyah* (Torch of Afghan News), which was published biweekly in Kabul from 1911 to 1918 with the support of Amir Habibullah.

The main concern of the Young Afghans was that their country was declining because it had failed to adapt its cultural heritage to modern trends. They were well aware that wholesale adoption of Western institutions and values was both infeasible and unwise, but they also rejected the view that Islam was incompatible with modernity. They were aware of the transformation that Russia and Japan were undergoing, and urged the Muslim establishment to return to the essential values of Islam—which had in earlier times nurtured science and objective scholarship—rather than rejecting the West on the superficial grounds of differences in clothing and social customs.

The Young Afghans were conducting a campaign that had been fought in one form or another by all earlier modernizers, and their program for reform followed familiar lines. They were particularly concerned with the importance of education, and in their journal they published summaries of scientific and technical developments in the West. They emphasized that Afghanistan had not only to borrow modern weapons, but also to incorporate the whole range of modern knowledge into a system of public education. The Young Afghans also urged the development of railroads and industry in order to raise the standard of living, and encouraged the adoption of Pashto (instead of Persian) as the official language as a means of strengthening national identity.

Tarzi and the Young Afghans were of course well ahead of their times, and their vision of a modern world view was only tenuously adopted a century later. The dominant outlook well into the twentieth century remained that of the Muslim establishment, as the numerous isolated tribes, communities, and ethnic groups proved exceptionally resistant to outside influence.

The peoples of Russian Central Asia have historically lived at the crossroads of Inner Asia. Culturally the region looked both east and south for cross-fertilization and, increasingly in the premodern period, to the west as well for inspiration. This region helped to knit together all of Inner Asia. When, as a result of the decline of traditional political structures and tsarist incursions, the area lost its ability to serve as a crossroads, the entire region lost its coherence. To assess the change in world views in this area, it is necessary to return to the period before the Russian impact had become significant and before the Great Game between Russia and Britain had begun, indeed to the period when this region served as the arena for the merging of the Turkic and Iranian cultures.

Knowledge and education in this area were governed by two elements: first, Islam and second, local traditions. These local traditions in turn were formed from the Iranian underlay and a Turkic overlay. The Islamic and the traditional influences differed in the predominantly settled and nomadic areas. Islam as practiced in the settled oases areas followed mainstream traditions, whereas among the nomadic peoples, both the elites and the masses, Islamic practice was less formal and more subject to the practical demands of nomadic existence. In the same manner, the Iranian underlay of culture is more readily recognizable in oases areas where it more clearly relates to the settled culture of Afghanistan and

Iran than it does in nomadic areas. This is not to imply, however, that the Turkmen or the Kazakhs swept before them the previous Iranian culture. Indeed, we have little information about the Iranian nomadic cultures that preceded them. Thus from the start the world view of the two groups of people in this area, though united by Islam, differed as a result of the circumstances of their environment.

By extension, knowledge was disseminated for the elites through the scriptural schools *(madrasas)* in the oases areas, but rarely was a nomad youth drawn into their courtyards and study cells. The *madrasa* system was strongest in towns such as Bukhara, Samarkand, and Khiva, with the first boasting up to two hundred such institutions by the mid-eighteenth century. Although a few Turkmen boys and a stray Kazakh might be found pursuing studies there, the main student population was drawn from among urban elites and bright village boys, often Uzbek or Tajik, with Sarts predominating. A special *madrasa* for Turkmen boys, however, was endowed in Karshi.

Among the nomadic peoples the dissemination of knowledge often took a more markedly oral form; the lack of a tradition of written materials also lent even greater importance to the memorization of genealogy, critical in this tribal setting, as well as narrative poetry, both heroic and nonheroic, which was often accompanied by a musical instrument when recited. Through their narrative poetry, the nomadic people retained not only a vague history of their relationships with neighboring peoples, but also preserved the values of their societies. While elites may have relied on minstrels for retention of their traditions, and may not have attended *madrasas* or have even been literate, it was not unusual for wealthy Kazakh or Turkmen chiefs to retain an educated man to serve as scribe and chaplain as well as tutor in the camp.

Among the nomadic peoples, therefore, the differences between the elites and the masses on the cultural level were not reflected in their ease of access to an educational system. The differences depended on material possessions and lineage, and the world view before the Russian conquest did not differ among classes.

In the case of oases dwellers, however, class differences involved land and position as well as material wealth and, to some extent, education. The family that was able to provide all of these could also certainly send its son or father (or even female members) on pilgrimages, an event that exposed the pilgrim to the great world beyond his oasis. Such an opportunity was usually open only to the well to do. Pilgrims usually engaged in trade, study, or the practice of their craft during the long months, or even years, they were away from home. As the areas traversed by pilgrims underwent change, the traveler returned home with new knowledge imbibed en route. For example, the large number of Uzbeks stopping in Istanbul necessitated the establishment of an Uzbek *tekiya* (Sufi hostel) in that city. This hostel, and others like it in Jerusalem and elsewhere, were established as charitable endowments. Hostel records indicate that some travelers needed to stay for long periods to earn money for their return trip. Few persons in the premodern period of Central Asia went as far as Istanbul without making the pilgrimage to Mecca and Medina and vice versa. Some stopped also for a time in Egypt, attaching themselves to al-Azhar, the intellectual center of the Arab world in the late nineteenth century. Both Istanbul and Cairo during the nineteenth century were seething with new ideas about reviving Islam, repulsing the foreigners, and modernizing Islamic society.

Some Central Asians, unwilling to face the humiliation and expense of travel through Russian lands to Istanbul (and unwilling to risk travel through Iran), made their way to British India and took ship at Bombay for the holy shrines and beyond. Just such a trip, for example, was undertaken by a leading Bukharan Jadid, Abdurrauf Fitrat (d. 1932?), before 1917. Here again, travelers could and did imbibe the spirit of change that was sweeping the subcontinent. Nationalism, modern educational institutions, and advanced communication systems impressed many who, returning home, used the knowledge to press for change (G41).

Despite the introduction of non-Islamic values and traditions, life in oasis societies was governed by the dictates of Islamic law *(shari'at)*, the Hanafi Sunni code in particular. The Central Asian ruler Mohammed Shaybani Khan (1451–1510) had waged bitter warfare against the Safavid Shi'ite rulers of Iran for dominance in the region. As a result, the border areas between Iran and Central Asia continued into the nineteenth century to suffer the strains of religious intolerance. This factor, combined with the rerouting by sea of European trade with East Asia, isolated Central Asian oasis areas from their prime means of contact with the heartlands of Islamic culture. Gradually Central Asia receded into the periphery of Islam rather than continuing to serve as a base for the dissemination of Islamic learning. This process was accompanied by the rapid turkification of the area as pressure from Mongolian groups, in turn pressed by Russian expansion eastward, pushed the Kazakh and Kirgiz further south to vie with settled cultures for control of towns like Tashkent, and as important, the mountain passes to East Turkestan.

Mainstream Islamic social structures, which were becoming increasingly stultified, were somewhat modified by the presence of strong Sufi orders. The most important of these orders, the Naqshbandiyya, originated in Central Asia. Unlike Sufism in Iran, however, mysticism in the oases was closely associated with the governing circles. Moreover, the Naqshbandiyya advocated participation in society rather than withdrawal from it. The difference between the ulema and the Sufi leadership lay in their separate functions and audiences. The Sufi orders served to draw into the religious circles men who were not necessarily educated or even literate beyond the offerings of the local mosque school. The *murshid-murid* (adept-apprentice) relationship bonded men from distant rural regions, and sometimes spanned ethnic differences. In any case, the Sufi orders served as intermediaries between the elite Islam of the *madrasas* and the Muslim masses. In this manner, the Sufi orders served as broadcasters of orthodoxy as well as structures for rallying the people. This last factor gained in importance in the late nineteenth century as ordinary people mounted resistance to Russian rule.

The practice of Sufism was widespread throughout southern Central Asia and included even the Turkmen. Shrines memorializing the burial places of Sufi saints dotted the landscape throughout Turkmen, Tajik, and Uzbek areas. As often as not the true history of the shrines remained shrouded in legend, but it is quite likely that many sites (often near a water source) remained sacred from the pre-Islamic Iranian past. This phenomenon symbolizes the widespread co-option into Islam of pre-Islamic customs and practices.

The conquest of the Kazakhs and the Kirgiz and the subjugation of Tajik and Uzbek areas by tsarist armies resulted in two patterns of change in the Central Asian world view. First, significant groups of elites, particularly among the northern nomads, took advantage of the Russian-style education offered to them, and adopted Russian for writing as well as Russian material values and outlooks, to the extent that they become not only part of the Russian administration but also alienated from the main body of Kazakhs. This attitude is reflected in the higher value placed on Russian culture and criticism of Islam and of nomadic culture.

A second group, more numerous and important, attempted to upgrade and reform native society by borrowing ideas filtered through Russia or from more progressive Turkic societies to the west. The latter group came to be known as Jadidists—from an Arabic word meaning "new." A period of transition and conflict ensued that was halted only with the destruction of the Jadidists during the sovietization of the area. The main thrust of the Jadidists was in the field of education. The Russian conquest finally shattered the confidence of many native elites in the wisdom of complacency about the traditional values of their society. Convincing the entrenched political and religious hierarchy of the need for change fell to men like Mahmud Khoja Behbudiy (1874–1919), Ahmad Makhdum Donish, Fitrat, and Sadriddin Aini (1878–1954), to name a few.

Patterns of knowledge and education *in southern Sinkiang* in the traditional period were, broadly speaking, comparable to what existed elsewhere in Muslim Inner Asia, but with some variation. Islamic thought did not admit the category of non-Islamic ruler, which meant that the Ch'ing monarch could not serve as secular patron of Islam after the conquest of Sinkiang in the way he could fill that role for Buddhism in Tibet. The result was that the integrated structure of politics, religion, and education found elsewhere in the Islamic world was necessarily disturbed after the Ch'ing conquest in Sinkiang. Religious officials continued to have a variety of social functions, which were carried out under the supervision of regular Chinese administrative officials. They served as "a native judiciary and provided the organization and leadership of the population's religious and cultural life" (A10, p. 79).

Elsewhere in Sinkiang, religious officials were regularly used in government, and it appears that in Komul and Turfan "the local rulers had the right to use mullas in government as they saw fit" (A10, p. 74). But in the rest of Sinkiang, the *akhunds,* religious functionaries who enjoyed official rank, lost the kind of political power they had enjoyed before the Ch'ing conquest.

The effect of this was to open up a gap between rulers and ruled, which was exacerbated by the degree to which even the indigenous rulers had to adopt certain Ch'ing ways. Although Ch'ing tolerance was extensive, it was not complete. The year might follow the Islamic calendar, and traditional dress be maintained, but the highest ranking *begs* in the administration had to wear the queue, and at the beginning of every month had to appear at the Confucian temple, early in the morning, to prostrate themselves before an image of the emperor. The education of such officials also contained elements derived from the Ch'ing: they would be likely to know both Chinese and Manchu, as well as more traditional subjects (A10, p. 79).

The considerable co-optation by the Ch'ing of the highest ranks of the religious and civil hierarchy in East Turkestan, and the gap that was thereby created between rulers and subjects, may be one of the factors that made the area fertile ground for Islamic revival and rebellion, which repeatedly rocked the whole area in the nineteenth century.

The world view of Tibetans of virtually all socioeconomic classes, all occupations, and all geographic areas was heavily suffused with Buddhism, specifically with that "highly Tibetanized form of Buddhism" known as Lamaism (M2, p. 28). Tibet's Great Vehicle (Mahayana) Buddhism took the form of Lamaism, a term that correctly underscores the central role played by the lama as spiritual master or teacher (N32, pp. 164–165). The gulf between clerics and lay people, however, was great. Lamaism was a religion centered on monks, and as Stein (N31, p. 172) has written, "it is inaccessible to ordinary believers." Lay Buddhists were essentially spectators on the sidelines whose main religious activity consisted of accumulating merit through charitable contributions to monasteries, making pilgrimages, and asking lamas for blessings.

Tibetan Lamaism incorporated many aspects of indigenous pre-Buddhist religions, including *Bon,* much as Lamaism in Mongolia incorporated what it failed to exterminate of pre-Buddhist shamanism. There was a small number of Tibetan Muslims, but the cultural life of Tibet was dominated by Lamaism.

Unlike Greater Mongolia of Ch'ing times, whose accessibility to China proper allowed Chinese cultural inroads and where Chinese and Tibetan influences competed, Tibet was largely immune to outside cultural influences. Although high-ranking Mongolian lamas went, when possible, to Tibetan monasteries to further their religious education, comparatively few Tibetans left their homeland for India. Tibetan monasteries functioned as universities, and monks had to travel from one such institution (and teacher) to another, since monasteries offered specialized teaching, and since certain books, despite the introduction of wood-block printing from China in the late eleventh century, were scarce (N31, pp. 156–160). A Tibetan monk's career thus involved a great deal of travel—within Tibet itself.

During the two and a half centuries of Manchu-Ch'ing sovereignty *over the Mongols,* the gap between the educated and privileged and the less educated and underprivileged widened enormously. In elite circles, an additional gap between a Chinese-centered world view and a Russian-centered world view appeared in the nineteenth and early twentieth centuries. Those Mongolian nobles living closest to China proper imbibed Chinese cultural values, while those Mongols (the Buriats) who lived within the tsarist Russian cultural orbit and were educated in Russian schools and universities spread a Russian world view among educated Khalkhas in neighboring Outer Mongolia. Indeed, the core group of Mongolian intellectuals and revolutionaries in the early twentieth century consisted of Buriats.

For most Inner Mongolian nobles, identification with a Chinese world view meant alienation from the Mongolian *arad.* Yet, for at least a few privileged Mongols in Inner Mongolia, an education in Chinese book learning and Chinese social values could be turned into ammunition for social criticism. Injannasi, a noble educated in the Mongolian, Manchu, and Chinese languages, and as conversant with the Chinese classics as with Buddhist teachings, refused to serve the Ch'ing government in any official post (M7, p. 14). Identifying with the Mongolian commoner, Injannasi went so far as to suggest (tongue in cheek) that the Mongolian nobility be made commoners: "If they are a useless lot, why not make them commoners and have them serve the empire, instead of feeding them for doing nothing?" (M16, p. 67). Castigating the many Mongolian nobles who turned their backs on Mongolian culture and literature—"Those of our light-headed ones who had learned to read a few words in Chinese would immediately regard Mongolian writings with contempt" (M16, p. 58)—Injannasi urged his fellow nobles to devote their efforts to reconstructing the Mongolian past through the wealth of both written and oral folklore materials in Mongolian then available. If one ever needed to be convinced of the existence of such materials, one need only read Injannasi's offhanded reference to his sorting out " 'five-and-a-half cart-loads' of old Mongolian, Tibetan and Manchurian books from his late father's library" (M20, p. 27; see also M16, pp. 12, 68).

Injannasi had nothing but contempt for "these so-called learned men [who] did not care to investigate their own origin and instead wasted their time by devoting precious hours to the worthless literature of the T'ang and Sung periods" (M16, p. 57). He sought to restore authentic Mongolian history and to restore cultural self-confidence by stripping away centuries of Chinese historiographical distortions and Tibetan Buddhist religious overlays. Although the Mongolian Buddhist clergy did not escape his criticism, the Mongolian prince's most severe words were directed at his fellow nobles whom he saw as contributing to the demise of Mongolian culture.

Far to the north, the Khalkha Mongols were exposed to an increasing Russian influence and presence. In 1860 the first Russian consulate was opened in Urga (M4, p. 135). Russian-educated Buriats and Kalmyks quickly became part of the core revolutionary group in Urga in the 1920s. The Buriats Ts. Jamtsarano (1880–1940?) and Rinchino, who served often as Russian-Mongolian interpreters at high-level meetings, were intensely concerned with both Mongolia's modernization and its transformation into an autonomous nation. Ramstedt recalled meeting several Buriats in Urga in 1912, among them Jamtsarano, who was hard at work editing the first Mongolian-language magazine, promoting popular education, and collecting Mongolian heroic epics (M51, p. 228). Educated Buriats have been referred to as the "cultural avant-garde" and introducers of revolutionary ideas among the Mongols of Outer Mongolia.

To what extent this type of elite activity, in both Outer and Inner Mongolia, filtered down to the popular level is extremely difficult to gauge, not in the least because publications of the Soviet Union, the Mongolian People's Republic, and the People's Republic of China invariably stress the backwardness of the prerevolutionary era in order to accentuate gains made since their respective revolutions.

Elite Education, Research, and Publishing

Religious education has a long tradition in Iranian life and the *maktab* and *madrasa,* the institutions for the training of the literate and educated of society, were the single most important source of education for most Muslims before the 1920s. The aristocracy often hired tutors for its children, but this education too tended to be traditional with greater emphasis on the Iranian classics than on a modern education or the acquisition of modern values. Western-style schools with secular curriculums were established first by Western missionaries among Christian minorities, but these schools were attended also by Muslim boys (and a few girls). The Dar ul-Funun became the focus for the education of the sons of the aristocracy who then could win scholarships to Europe. In addition, two military colleges were established (in Isphahan and Tehran), as well as a translation school. Although the constitution made provisions for public education (1909), funds were not generally available and administered until 1926. By 1925 there were altogether 648 modern primary schools administered by state officials, private boards, religious communities, and foreign missionaries, with about fifty-six thousand students enrolled. In addition there were 74 modern secondary schools with 25 percent of them missionary run. These schools had risen at the expense of *maktabs* and *madrasas;* in 1925 official Pahlavi-regime documents record about twenty-nine thousand students in the first and six thousand in the second (E2, pp. 144–145).

Training for modern fields such as medicine was often accomplished abroad or at the missionary schools, but professional schools for medicine and the like also came into being during the late nineteenth century. Libraries other than private ones were slower to appear and access to them was limited. Educational institutions, both *madrasas* and secular schools, including the Dar ul-Funun, had their own libraries. But the national library, the Kitab-Khaneh-ye Majlis, did not come into being until the Pahlavi period (1926). By the end of World War I, about five hundred Iranians were studying in Europe, chiefly at government expense. Thus after the Constitutional Revolution, among a growing sector of urban society that cut across class lines, a sentiment in favor of training what were called *rowshanfikran* (the enlightened) was growing. The turn had been made toward accepting the necessity for modernization. The dispute remained as to the details of what modernization meant.

The dispute, though discussed in the *anjumans* (or societies, some secret) that were formed, was aired mainly through the new medium of the printed word, and especially through the periodical press. In Iran the history of the periodical press holds much import and is complex. In the nineteenth century the exile press was a far greater force for political change than the internal press. Ethnolinguistic groups, under the guidance of Western sponsors, developed an early capacity to publish periodicals with religious and educational materials in their own languages. Although the Persian-language press was slow to start (the first newspaper appeared in 1851 for a limited circle), by the start of the constitutional era, that number had increased to ninety. Strict censorship in later periods reduced the quality and number of the publications, but never succeeded in stifling their enormous impact. Edward G. Browne, an early chronicler of Persian cultural history, described the periodical press in Iran as "the most powerful modernizing influence" (E16, p. 468). Iranian periodicals provided the instrument not only for the dissemination of foreign and selected internal news, but also for the conveying of Western thought and values. Periodicals serialized European novels and short stories. More important, they carried items about Iranian history and culture, key elements that led to the formation of a secular Iranian identity. This revived interest in the pre-Islamic past of the country was enhanced through archaeological discoveries during the latter half of the nineteenth century.

Outstanding in influence in the exile press were the newspapers published by Jamaluddin al-Afghani and Malkom Khan (d. 1908), both Iranians who attempted to nudge Nasiruddin Shah toward reform. Failing to remain in the good graces of the shah, both men turned to the task of mobilizing opposition to the ways of the court and to reforming Iran. Their activities were a factor in the formation of the opposition movement that resulted in the Constitutional Revolution. The impact of al-Afghani reached far beyond Iran, and he has come to symbolize the first generation of those in the Islamic world who engaged in the dialogue with Europe over the reason for the decline of the Islamic world and the formulas for its reemergence.

Modern education in Afghanistan, as in most modernizing countries, was introduced from the top down rather than from the bottom up. For the great majority of the population such education as existed remained in the hands of the Muslim religious establishment, and at the end of the century no more than 2 percent of the population was literate. The establishment of a national system of primary and secondary education was entirely beyond the financial and administrative capacities of the national government. The founding in 1904 of Habibiya College, a secondary school supported by the royal treasury, was the first small step toward the establishment of a modern educational system. Its curriculum included both traditional and Western learning, including instruction in English and in the natural sciences. There was also a Royal Military Academy with a more narrowly professional curriculum (F10, pp. 184–188).

This educational innovation by Amir Habibullah was inspired in part by earlier developments in the neighboring Muslim provinces of India. Particularly significant was the influence of Sir Sayyid Ahmad (1817–1898), who brought about a revolution in Indian Muslim thinking. He condemned ultraorthodoxy as being too rigid in its interpretations of modern life, and insisted that liberal education in the Western sense would liberate the dormant Muslim spirit, and give it the intellectual tools to compete with both Hindus and the British. Out of the fire of his thinking and the dynamism he possessed, Sir Sayyid founded in 1875 one of the better universities in colonial Asia, the Anglo-Oriental College at Aligarh. Hindus and Christians also attended the college in large numbers, for its curriculum emphasized secular, not religious, instruction.

In early premodern Central Asia, as in the other Muslim areas of Inner Asia, the ability to perform the religious duties necessary for a Muslim was considered the reason for education. This included being able to read the Koran and recite parts of it. Therefore, most boys attended a mosque school at some point for however brief a period. The Koran being in Arabic, children did not usually study their own language, but they also never really learned Arabic except in rote recitation. Thus the level of literacy was not perceptibly affected by the presence of mosque schools, widespread though they were, particularly in the oases.

A boy began his traditional education at the age of six or seven in a *maktab,* his parents paying the local mullah a regular sum of money plus a cloak when the child finished the work at about age thirteen. Not all boys could afford to stay in school that long. Among the few who completed the *maktab* were some who, being poor, were eligible for scholarships to attend the *madrasas,* institutions of higher learning translatable into English as scriptural schools, seminaries, or even universities. The curriculum at the *madrasas* had not changed substantially since the fifteenth century or earlier. Theology dominated, but included in the 137 books of the curriculum were treatises on history, logic, rhetoric, mathematics, astronomy, and poetry. Although much of this material was in Persian, with a few works in the local Turkic literary language, Chagatai, the bulk was read in Arabic. It could take some students all their lives to finish this curriculum although many left without completing it.

The *madrasas* had libraries of manuscripts in the three languages of the area, and advanced students often worked to copy particularly popular manuscripts, religious and secular. The costliness of this method prevented the existence of widely held or large libraries. The ruler of Khiva, Said Muhammad Rahim

Bahadur II (r. 1865–1910), had one of the large libraries of Central Asia.

The products of the *madrasas* were qualified to fill any job in the society that called for education. They could become poets, judges *(qazis)*, administrators, professors, and the like. A bright but poor boy might have to spend part of his time serving in the home of a rich man before finishing, but once finished upward mobility was probable. Most merchants were literate, as were many individuals in the towns. Education was not the sole sign of success, however, as is illustrated in the *jadidist* play by Behbudiy criticizing a wealthy but illiterate man. Moreover, the philosophical basis of education was acquisition of religious knowledge fossilized in form and content. Therefore, although the reformers (Jadidists) themselves were products of the *madrasa* system, they attempted to replace the institution with modern schools whose curriculums and pedagogical approach prepared students for the challenges of the modern world. The Jadidists worked in Tashkent and Samarkand, but also in the protectorates of Bukhara and Khiva, and in Andijan. Here as among the Kazakhs, the inspiration for reform came from the Crimean Tatars. Russian influence also served to advance reformist ideas. The first Uzbek reformist school was opened in Tashkent in 1901. The first Tajik school appeared in Bukhara in 1907.

The Kazakh steppe from the earliest period of Russian expansion into Central Asia came under heavy and direct Russian influence. Significant parts of the Kazakh aristocracy became co-opted and russified at an early period, owing to organized measures adopted by the tsarist regime and the influx of Russians and Ukrainians. To undermine the influence of the Tatars who were transferring the zealous and revivalist Islam of Kazan to the Kazakhs, the Russian authorities barred them from teaching among Kazakhs (1850). They replaced the Tatar schools with Russian-Kazakh ones where the dominance of Russian was only weakly challenged by a Kazakh culture into which a new literary language was then being introduced. Moreover, the establishment of a military school for Kazakhs in Omsk together with a translation school attracted aristocratic Kazakhs into these institutions where the replacement of their native world view with a Russian one was accomplished, often to the point of eliminating use of the Kazakh language.

Two critical byproducts of the reformist movement in education emerged that had far-reaching effects in the entire area. First, the pedagogical emphasis on learning subjects in one's own language forced the issue of ethnic identity to create rivalry, particularly between the Turkic and non-Turkic elements. Traditional bilingualism in Turki and Persian had long marked the urban elite. The school curriculum, with its emphasis on Arabic and the classics, eschewed the language question. However, the *jadidist* schools were conducted in the vernacular, and this raised the issue of identity to a politically potent level. Thus Tajiks demanded their own vernacular schools, in part to counteract the undercurrent of pan-Turkism that was sweeping over the elites of the area. Associating ethnic consciousness with language served to fragment the cultural landscape, which facilitated the Soviet dismemberment of the area into five ethnolinguistic republics.

Second, the new schools required vernacular textbooks. Thus there arose an interest in the establishment of a press, which led to a slow but steady spread of local journalism and publication. In turn the press replaced and finally eliminated the traditional kinds of books, such as anthologies of local versifiers, commentaries on the Koran, and local histories, as well as works from the wider Islamic world, either hand copied or lithographed. Since central authority can more easily control the press than it can individual copyists, the introduction of the press, after a brief period of relative liberalism, made tight control over information possible. Censorship in the tsarist period was transformed in the Soviet period into the information control used to transform knowledge of the past and of the outside world.

Nonetheless, in its early period, the *jadid* press served to promote the new ideas about progress and change. The first newspapers, aside from the official tsarist local-language newspaper, appeared only after 1906. Many clashed with censors, were closed, and their publishers and editors imprisoned. The opposition to the reformists, the conservative clergy in particular, began its own newspapers. In the press, as among elites in general, the lines of conflict were drawn in a triangle: the Russian authorities, the reformers, and the conservatives formed the three angles. The Kazakh elites fell along the line between the Russian authorities and the reformers. The masses were caught between them.

In Sinkiang Ch'ing rule probably impoverished local cultural life, both by prompting the withdrawal of much of the indigenous cultural elite, and by limiting further development. A vacuum was thus created, which came to be filled by imported books and ideas.

Kashgar, for instance, had long been a bastion of traditional Islamic culture, and indeed it remained such until the twentieth century, at a time when elsewhere in the Islamic world new ideas were making themselves felt. Rather than having an indigenous culture, it carried on a culture that was being modified in areas under British or Russian control. Thus in the nineteenth century, according to Jarring, "the greater part of Eastern Turki literature available to the literate part of the Kashgar population belonged to the categories history, classical Arabic-Persian literature in translations and to different kinds of Islamic theological and philosophical-moralizing literature, most of it translated from Arabic or Persian. Especially the last genre of literature must always have had a strong influence on the guiding principles of life in a secluded Islamic society. . . . Reading aloud from such works played a great role in forming the Islamic-moral conceptions of the illiterate people" (O7, p. 10).

This derivative character of East Turkestan culture was reinforced by the way that books were provided. What books there were, for instance, were either copied by professional scribes, or else imported. An account of a visit to Kashgar in 1873–1874 notes how, in the bookshops, "the volumes are mostly Turki manuscripts on religious subjects, but amongst them there are some lithographed books on medicine, history, and theology, and all in Persian from India. We search in vain for any historical records of the country, or for any native literature in poetry and prose. Such works do exist, but are sacredly guarded in the monasteries attached to the many shrines of the country, or are concealed in the possession of private individuals'' (O1, p. 278).

Even in the 1920s and 1930s there was little printing in Kashgar: "The only printed editions of Turki literary works which occasionally were available in Kashgar were books lithographed in Tashkent or in other towns of Russian Turkestan. Printed or lithographed books from Kazan might appear from time to time in the Kashgar bazaars. In the 1930s books lithographed in Delhi and other cities of India were also imported" (O7, pp. 9–10).

In Tibet, the pattern of elite education was significantly different from that in the Muslim sphere. Every Buddhist monastery of any substantial size had its own press. The monastery would store its own wooden and copper printing blocks, and at one of the larger monastic printing houses, such as Narthang, hundreds of thousands of such blocks were stored (N39, p. 199). The two great scriptural canons, the Kanjur and the Tenjur (the former containing works that expressed a buddha's words, the latter containing commentaries), both translated from Sanskrit, were produced in printed editions at various monasteries, including Narthang (N31, pp. 250–251).

Some lamas were prolific authors, producing not only religious works but also historical works, linguistic, and philological ones, as well as treatises on such subjects as astrology, medicine, and agricultural technology.

Even after the use of printing spread, hand copying of manuscripts was often less expensive and therefore preferable. To get a work printed, one would have to travel to a perhaps distant monastery where the wood blocks were stored, and pay for the ink, paper, and labor of monks to carry out the printing. A donor would acquire religious merit by having a text reproduced (by either copying or printing); religious merit along with the satisfaction of seeing one's name mentioned in the sponsored edition obviously contributed to the growth of book production (N31, p. 160).

Scholarship and expertise in such fields as medicine were inextricably bound up with religion in Tibet. Each Tibetan medical book ended with religious phrases invoking divine power to facilitate a successful cure. Indian and Chinese writings on medicine reached Tibet, as did drugs, herbs, roots, powders, and plants (N39, pp. 163–164). Smallpox was apparently as feared in Tibet as it was in Mongolia. Huc and Gabet witnessed the panic ensuing from a rumor that a caravan that had just arrived in Lhasa from Peking a few days earlier had brought smallpox. Along with smallpox, rabies and leprosy were common (D9, vol. 2, pp. 198–199).

For most Mongols before the 1920s, education meant religious education in Lamaist monasteries where texts were read in both Tibetan and Mongolian. Not all lamas, however, were literate.

Much of traditional Mongolian culture had revolved around the military arts, yet the period of Ch'ing sovereignty saw a withering away of the Mongols' military skills. As Injannasi in his *Koke sudur* bitterly complained, "Even if the Mongols did not possess intelligence and talent for learning, do they not possess the raw brawn from eating mutton and beef? Well, at least their military training could be examined to provide them with some opportunity, but their military arts are not being examined" (M16, p. 65). The Ch'ing excluded the Mongols from the Chinese military and civil bureaucracies. No matter how learned a Mongolian noble might be in Chinese philosophy, history, and culture, he was nonetheless barred from the civil service examinations. Education was thus not a steppingstone to a bureaucratic career (M16, pp. 19, 63). The three traditional military "sports" among the Mongols—horse racing, archery, and wrestling— were confined to monastery-sponsored fairs (today they are confined to the national holiday, Naadam, on July 11 in Outer Mongolia).

Prince Gungsangnorbu (1871–1930) tried to change this situation by establishing in 1902 what has been referred to as "the first modern school in Mongolia" (M28, p. 148). After visiting Japan in 1903, Gungsangnorbu returned to Inner Mongolia to found a military school and a girls' school employing Japanese instructors. A few Mongolian students, presumably drawn from the nobility, were sent to Japan to study also. After the abdication of the Manchus in 1912, Gungsangnorbu was appointed director of the Mongolian-Tibetan Affairs Office by Yuan Shih-k'ai. As director, Gungsangnorbu oversaw the establishment of a Mongolian-Tibetan Academy in Peking. Several future Mongolian leaders in both the Inner Mongolian Kuomintang movement and the Communist movement were students at the academy.

The existence of publishing activities and large private libraries is well attested in Inner Mongolia. An Eastern Mongolian Literary Society was founded in the early 1920s in Peking by a group of Mongolian students at Peking University including Bokekeshik, an "industrious and ardent champion of an independent Mongolian literature" (M20, pp. 28–29). Bokekeshik and the others sought to print and distribute Mongolian literature and educational books in Mongolian as a counterweight to Chinese cultural influence in Inner Mongolia. The book-printing endeavors of the Eastern Mongolian Literary Society are particularly noteworthy because hand copying of Mongolian manuscripts was the norm well into the twentieth century. Around the turn of the century, writing poetry and proverbs, often with political undertones, into notebooks became quite common throughout Greater Mongolia. Much anonymous social criticism (directed largely against the Chinese) is preserved in this genre (M16, pp. 179–182).

In Outer Mongolia, the development of education and publishing activities was sponsored by the Russians after 1911. A military school was established near Urga, and a secondary school was opened in 1912. The teachers at the secondary school were mainly russified Buriats, and most of the students were sons of Mongolian commoners, not nobles (M4, pp. 201–202). In 1913 ten graduates were sent to continue their education at schools in Buriatia (Khiakta and Irkutsk). The first Outer Mongolian newspaper and the first Outer Mongolian magazine were both edited by the Buriat Jamtsarano in Urga (see M55, pp. 131–132). The Russian diplomat I. Korostovetz had his consulate finance the magazine, in his own words, "in order to be better able to advance Russian influence by means of the printed word" (A7, p. 79). Jamtsarano, in fact, proved to be far more radical than his Russian sponsors, who ordered him to stop printing criticisms of the Buddhist church in the Mongolian-language newspaper he edited (M56, p. 14).

Popular Education and Literature

One of the costs paid in a society that possesses a high literary culture is the lack of value placed on its popular culture and literature. For this reason, few examples of popular written literature have survived and still fewer are known among those who would evaluate them. Popular culture deals with many themes similar to those characteristic of elite literature: religion, history, and romance. In addition there are minor genres such as fable, proverb, anecdote, and farce that form the ingredients of the education and culture in rural areas.

In Iran, for example, much of popular culture was disseminated through performance. The *ta'ziyah* (the Shi'ite passion play based on the martyrdom of the Caliph Ali and his son Husayn) was performed widely by amateur and professional groups during the first ten days of the holy month (lunar) of Muharram. During the Qajar period, these plays were elaborated upon and expanded as well as professionalized for the court and by extension for elite circles. These performances reinforced Shi'ite popular beliefs as well as strengthening an Iranian religious identity. The performances were only part of the display of popular religion accompanying the commemoration of the days of martyrdom. Additional memorial parades, eulogizing recitations, formal almsgiving, and sermons built an atmosphere of emotional religiosity. Other forms of drama that existed in Iran, such as *ru-howzi* (farce improvisations along set lines), pale in general appeal compared to the *ta'ziyah.*

A major strength of Persian literature has been the romance or epic poem, at times based on history but chiefly deriving its subject from legend. During the nineteenth century, many popular versions of these romances that had survived for centuries in improvised oral tradition were committed to print. The *Shahnameh* (Book of Kings), the most widely disseminated of Persian manuscripts (and the poem credited with preserving Iranian identity for over two millennia), was first printed in Calcutta in 1827. Itinerant storytellers continued to relate and improvise on the epics and romances up to the modern period as part of the entertainment in villages and small towns. The storyteller interspersed lines from high literature into his largely prose recitation. Thus while the education of the elite differed from that of the masses who were barely literate, both groups had some exposure to similar subject matter and to parts of the grand Persian poetic tradition. This phenomenon gains in importance as we approach the latter half of the nineteenth century when, in literature as in other aspects, Iranian elites came to acquire different cultural values from the masses. While elites read Molière and Voltaire in translation, the large segment of Iranian society continued in the old traditions based on religion, popular history, and romance. The more the elites absorbed Western concepts such as secularism and popular government, the greater grew the gap between them and the Iranian masses.

An early twentieth-century movement to simplify language and adopt new modes of expression led to a further cleavage in cultural outlook. Secular drama appeared in Iran, some of it in translation (from Turkish as well as European languages), and made its impact in printed as well as stage form. Poetry too changed to reflect personal feelings and to express thoughts in unequivocally clear terms rather than cloaking them in the by-then stilted expressions of the classics. Political content crept into verse. But the greatest change came with the development of prose literature. Although verse continued as the most popular form of literature, prose became a legitimate form of expression under three influences: the periodical press, foreign literature, and the prose traditions of the popular romances. Prose as travel literature served the double purpose of promoting a new form of literature and introducing foreign places and ideas. Nevertheless, in literature as in other aspects of modernization, Iran became divided between those who accepted the need, if not the desirability, of new form and content, and those who remained oblivious to change or fought it.

In Afghanistan the great majority of the population remained nonliterate into the twentieth century. Such education as existed took place within the Muslim *maktabs* and *madrasahs* and as with the other Muslim peoples of Inner Asia consisted primarily of rote memory of written texts. The various forms of Islam practiced in Afghanistan were influenced by many pre-Islamic customs, including supernatural practices and local cults entirely alien to sophisticated Muslims. These deeply held tribal and village beliefs served as a firm barrier to outside influences.

Beyond the religious realm, popular knowledge of the past, which served to define the identity of the different peoples of Afghanistan, was conveyed by folklore. In addition to providing entertainment, which plays a large role in folklore, the stories passed on by folk tellers relate historical events with special emphasis on tribal wars, define the ideals of ethnic groups and their superiority over others, describe the limits of appropriate behavior and the punishment for those who transgress, and also serve as a form of consciousness raising that promotes group cohesion. The consequence of this popular culture was an inward-looking society, which did not question its circumstances and resisted involvement at a national level.

In Central Asia likewise, folk literature together with folk Islam formed the basis of popular culture in the premodern period. High literature, on the other hand, was based on the general Middle Eastern style with some stylistic and language variants peculiar to Central Asia. The outstanding overall feature of the literature, however, was its dual language base: Persian and Chagatai (respectively called "Farsi" and "Turki" locally).

The Turkic culture of the nomadic people of Central Asia comprised a rich body of epic and folk literature, some based on remembered historical struggles of the past (as with the Russians and Kalmyks) and some reflecting intertribal struggles for supremacy. The hero embodied the admired values of the society. Women characters, both model figures and evil ones, were important in this literature. This material, however, was disseminated orally either by paid, wandering minstrels (who themselves at times became the heroes of legends) or simply within the family or clan.

The oral literature stressed group identity, with family and tribe given paramount importance. The Islamic content of this literature is incidental and certainly an accretion. This rich literature was not incorporated into high written literature. For this reason, its preservation depended on the continuation of the old social system. When that system began to break down under the pressure of colonization, the oral tradition became endangered and difficult to retrieve in later years. Since Kazakh (and Kirgiz) identity was so bound to the values of the oral tradition, its decline and replacement with a russified education system or with a relatively alien *jadid* system resulted in a period of confusion that has lasted into the modern period. In any case, the epics held no real value as modernizing elements in society, and the translations of Russian works that replaced them formed the basis of the new literature emerging in the latter part of the nineteenth century.

Likewise for Central Asians who were agriculturalists or urban dwellers, the oral tradition formed an important part of popular education. Turkic epics even entered into the folk literature of the Tajiks as exemplified in the Goroghlu cycle. Nonetheless, the settled population enjoyed greater access to traditional Middle Eastern cultural elements as well as Islamic elements, particularly as developed through the *maktabs*. The introduction of *jadid* schools during the early twentieth century hardly affected the general population in outlying areas. Thus the world view of the main population continued to be contoured through the Sufi orders, the minimal education received through the *maktabs,* and the values embodied in the folk literature.

The growing effect of improved educational systems, however, may be seen in literacy figures from Central Asia taken during a tsarist census. Overall literacy remained well under 10 percent up to the 1920s. Uzbek male literacy in Tashkent, however, was a high 27 percent with overall Uzbek literacy at 18 percent (G3, pp. 369–370).

High literature in the oasis areas combined the Persian classics with a sprinkling of Chagatai works by such authors as Mir Ali Shir Nawa'i (d. 1501). Mystical writers from the subcontinent, such as Mirza Abdulqadir Bidil (d. c.

1721), were particularly popular. Many educated men were versifiers, patterning themselves on the classical poets rather than using the simpler meters and rhyme patterns of folk poetry, which in any case is better suited to Turkic languages than the Arabic prosody of the classics. An awakening to the value of the indigenous folk literature, however, was not discernible in the premodern period. Rather, in terms of language the new trends in literature were toward simpler structure and vocabulary, but especially toward the greater use of local dialect on a written level. In terms of form, the trends were toward the adoption of prose fiction and drama, two genres with weak roots in the indigenous literature but with growing importance in neighboring Islamic cultures as well. Travelogues too came to be used to express the need for modernization, as was the drama in particular.

A key difference between the Persian literature of Iran and that of Central Asia, which affected the world view of the intellectuals of the two areas, was the extent to which literature reinforced identity and preserved language. Both areas were, in the premodern period, characterized by mixed Turkic and Persian ethnicity, with the Turkic elements often holding positions of power. Yet Iranian identity prevailed in Iran largely because high Persian literature, which incorporated Persian folk themes and epic, reinforced it. This was not the case in Central Asia. The high literature came from Iran, and contained Iranian identity elements. The Turkic oral literature did not become a part of high Turkic literature, which remained bound to Persian style and content. This derivative nature of Central Asian Turkic literature, together with the tradition of bilingualism, reduced the effectiveness of literature in reinforcing a Turkic identity. During the *jadid* period, therefore, the break from the past in Turki literature was more pronounced than in Persian literature. Moreover, when intellectuals attempted to construct a strictly Turkic heritage, particularly among the Uzbeks, perforce they had to turn to the oral traditions to supplement the weak Chagatai classical tradition. For this reason (not to mention the overriding political ones) Russian literature was more readily accepted into the Uzbek literary heritage (L1).

Sinkiang, before the coming of the Ch'ing, had been under the loose control of two rival lines of Makhdumzada *khojas* of the Naqshbandiyya brotherhood. After the Ch'ing conquest, these religious leaders and their followers fled, but they maintained close contact with their former followers. Although the Ch'ing tried to take on the role of patron of religion in East Turkestan—confirming the tax-free status of religious lands and buildings, and maintaining tomb sanctuaries and other holy places, even including the tombs of the Afaqi *khojas* at Yaghdu near Kashgar—they could not be completely successful, and popular religion was probably an important component of popular culture, and one inimical to Ch'ing interests (A10, p. 75).

Knowledge and education in southern Sinkiang in traditional times thus followed in general the patterns found elsewhere in Islamic Central Asia. As part of their effort to control the region, however, the Ch'ing narrowed the scope of permitted cultural activity, and limited the role of religious personnel, the traditional cultural leaders, in politics, while inducing those local officials who remained in administration to adopt a culture that contained certain Chinese elements. The result was a reduction of vigor in local culture which, ironically, had the effect of increasing its dependence on ideas and literature from the rest of Islamic Central Asia, a pattern that was already evident in the rebellions of the nineteenth century, and that would continue to be manifested in the twentieth century.

In Tibet, as in the other Buddhist areas of Inner Asia, popular literacy and interest in literature were more widespread than they were in the Muslim areas. Theoretically anyone in Tibet could order a copy of a work from a monastery where the printing blocks were stored, although this was expensive. It is exceedingly difficult to gauge the degree of literacy among either laymen or the clerical population. The fact that a layman could afford to commission a text to be printed did not in itself attest to more than the desire to attain religious merit; it did not necessarily prove literacy. Tucci (N39, p. 199) describes the Tibetan layman's respect for books as such:

> The texts they did not read or understand could be used by lamas invited to perform any prayers and rites the patron wished; in any case, as verbal embodiments of the Buddha, they would imbue the place with sanctity and ensure the protection of its inhabitants by simply being there. This fact explains the great devotion Tibetans have to books, whether they can read or not: the book is a divine presence, and so must be treated with the utmost respect.

Smaller monasteries typically printed the collected works of famous local monks or biographies of local saints. Guidebooks for pilgrims were quite popular among laymen: these guides would describe a monastery's history or a region's sacred sites. A small-scale book trade conducted by book merchants for profit existed at fairs and festivals. The most popular books sold on such occasions were lives of saints and guidebooks for pilgrims (N39, pp. 199–200).

For the illiterate, mime, drama, and epic provided religious instruction as well as entertainment. Masked dances accompanied by music (but no words) were performed to educate lay people about deities. These ritualized dances were carefully choreographed and "scripts" or directions for the dances were written by monks (N31, pp. 189, 268, 276).

Plays took as their subjects Buddhist "birth stories" and the lives of great lamas. The structure of drama was Indian, but the style of singing and mannerisms appear to have been closer to Chinese opera (N31, p. 278). Oral epics, such as the famed Geser Khan epic, known in variations to both Tibetans and Mongols, were of course meant to be recited; the prose was chanted while the verse songs were set to melodies.

The topic of popular literacy in Mongolia must be approached in an impressionistic manner rather than through statistics which simply do not exist. Charles Bawden has attempted to correct the stereotypical picture of a mass of illiterate nomads in nineteenth-century Mongolia, writing that "neither was there the complete sterility and mass illiteracy that some modern Mongol apologists, from their one-sided Marxist viewpoint, have tried to present as the lot of Mongolia throughout the century" (M4, p. 86). This point is dramatically underscored by the reports of various Scandinavian expeditions and of Walther Heissig, who traveled throughout Mongolia in the 1930s. Whenever word got out that a foreigner was willing to pay for books, streams of herdsmen would arrive at his door to present all sorts of manuscripts in Mongolian for inspection and sale (M20, pp. 96–106).

This is Heissig's description of the immense popularity of Injannasi's *Koke sudur:* "I came across it frequently and in the most unlikely places—a shepherd's tent, the miserable mud hut of a Mongol who had abandoned the nomadic life, the guesthouse of a Buddhist monastery in mid-winter—where a Mongol would either be reading it alone in some corner or reading it aloud to a whole group of people" (M20, p. 30). In addition to an edition printed by the Eastern Mongolian Literary Society, several hand-copied variants of the *Koke sudur* were available, and parts were printed in the Mongolian newspapers that had come into existence by the 1930s. Bawden has warned that we should not be taken in by the official doctrine of the Mongolian People's Republic that Mongolia had no culture prior to the revolution of 1921; he argues convincingly that "the libraries of Europe alone contain enough examples of cheap copies of stories and poems, both native and translated, written out on brown Chinese paper of poor quality well thumbed, greasy and torn, to prove that the Mongols were lovers of books, not ignorant savages, and that there was material for them to feed their curiosity on" (M4, p. 87).

Heissig, scholar of Mongolian religions, folklore, and literature, has shown that popular theater existed in eighteenth- and nineteenth-century Mongolia, and that it was derived from the Tibetan masked dance performances known (in Mongolian) as *cham.* In the *cham* performances, masked and costumed personifications of Buddhist gods would struggle against the enemies of the religion. (For an extensive description of the *cham* [Khalkha *tsam*] ceremony, see M50, pp. 505–521.) From these religious pantomime dances, a more secular theater with dramatic songs, often love songs, emerged. In spite of monasteries' bans on such secular entertainment, it became common among both princes and commoners. There were even playwright-monks and monks with reputations as great singers and poets of nonreligious themes (M20, pp. 211–230).

Although monasteries provided what we would call "elementary education" for novice monks who generally entered the monastery between the ages of seven and ten (M50, p. 191), it is not clear how basic literacy spread among average herders, unless by family tutelage. There were no secular elementary schools for commoners, although Bawden (M4, p. 86) has described banner-financed schools to train students in banner administration. The course of study at such schools included the Mongolian and Manchu languages (Manchu was used for correspondence with Peking), and law. Presumably, sons of banner princes constituted the student body.

Conclusions and Comparisons

As is the case with most later-modernizing societies, the initial challenge to traditional world views and to the form and content of elite and popular education in Inner Asia has come from abroad rather than from within. Only after the achievements of more modern societies have become evident, more often than not as a result of military pressure, have indigenous leaders come forward with reform programs.

In the case of Iran, the challenge to premodern world views came primarily from military contacts with Russia and Turkey, first as enemies and later as models. In due course Christian missionaries and Western economic interests evoked a variety of religious and secular responses, which were met with firm resistance by the Muslim religious establishment. This confrontation, which continued in the twentieth century, illustrated the remarkable tenacity of traditional institutions and values. To an even greater extent in Afghanistan, the clergy dominated elite and popular outlooks and was in large measure successful in resisting the reform program of the Young Afghans. A somewhat different pattern is represented by Central Asia, where the Russians moved in vigorously with railroads, irrigation systems, and agricultural improvement, but operated primarily within the context of Russian settlements. In the cities the Russians and the native population lived in separate quarters, and in the new enterprises the native peoples participated as workers but rarely as partners. Apart from the few aristocrats among the native population who were assimilated by the Russian elites, such transformation of world views as took place among the peoples of Central Asia was the result of *jadidist* influence and of visits to India, the Ottoman Empire, and occasionally to the West, by the few individuals who could afford such travel.

The Chinese, still locked into their traditional world view, did not play a modernizing cultural role in Mongolia or Sinkiang. Their main concern was political order and commercial penetration, and Mongols who came under Chinese influence were moving from one traditional culture to another. Among the native peoples of Inner Asia, the Tibetans had the most developed and complex traditional culture. Its very sophistication, however, like that of the Chinese, was a strong barrier to the intrusion of modern values.

Comparing world views is no simple matter, but it is clear that the countries and territories of Inner Asia were among the last major areas to accept modern institutions and values. Iran, in most respects the closest to the West of the societies we are studying, was two or more generations behind the Turks of the

Ottoman Empire in adopting a modern world view. The Ottomans, in turn, were ahead of the Chinese in this respect, but also well behind the Japanese and the Russians.

If one wishes to think of Inner Asia in terms of those peoples that maintained independent states—Iran, Afghanistan, and, in effect, Tibet (a dependency rather than a colony of China)—and those that were colonized, one sees that the former were reluctant to give up their traditional culture and the latter were little influenced by—or did not benefit from—colonization. The Russians were modernizing colonizers, but until the twentieth century their influence was predominantly as settlers and to some degree as exploiters, and they did not have the capability, or the interest at this stage, to undertake the transformation of the native societies. In the case of the Inner Asian territories of China, as already noted, the colonizer was not concerned with modern world views. It is often said, and it is probably true in general, that one of the benefits of colonialism is that the indigenous peoples are introduced to modern institutions and values at a rather low cost. This was not the case in Inner Asia in the nineteenth century, however, where in this particular respect the independent states fared better than the colonies.

When it comes to elite and popular education, comparison is less difficult. Nonliteracy was almost universal throughout Inner Asia, and only in Iran, Tibet, and Mongolia did more than 2–3 percent of the population have the ability to read. Higher education, apart from missionary institutions in Iran, was also entirely lacking in the region. Like Albania, Black Africa, and a few marginal areas elsewhere, Inner Asia was one of the last regions to enter the modern world in this particular respect. To say this is not to denigrate the native Muslim and Buddhist cultures of the region, preserved primarily in an oral form, or even to say that modern knowledge is "better" than traditional—a question that can be debated. It is to say rather that—in an era characterized by the worldwide adoption of modern institutions and values—the peoples of Inner Asia were among the later latecomers.

7

Conclusions

The Premodern Heritage

In considering the bearing of the premodern heritage of the societies of Inner Asia on their capacity to modernize in the twentieth century, it is important to take into account the diversities among them as well as their common premodern characteristics. There was a time when students of this subject were inclined to treat so-called third-world countries as an undifferentiated group of societies. Subsequent research has led to the conclusion, which seems obvious once one starts thinking about it, that relatively nonmodernized societies are in fact much more diverse than those that are relatively modernized. The purpose of this study is to enrich our understanding of the process of modernization by adding another area to those already studied as a means of broadening the basis of comparison.

In terms of their confrontation with the international environment, for example, the societies of Inner Asia as a group did not have a common identity despite the powerful influence of Islam in Iran, Afghanistan, Russian Central Asia, and southern Sinkiang, and of Buddhism in Tibet, northern Sinkiang, and Mongolia. The sectarian and ethnic divisions within the two dominant religions outweighed the unifying influence they might have exerted. Among the individual societies, however, Tibet had the strongest sense of identity. Likewise Mongolia and Iran, in their different ways, preserved a historic memory of past achievements that enhanced their capacity to deal with the outside world. Nevertheless, none of these societies, let alone Inner Asia as a region, possessed a sense of identity in any way comparable to that of Japan, China, Russia, or the Ottoman Empire before the modern era.

When the identity of these societies was confronted by the challenge of modernity as represented by the encroachment of foreign influences in the nineteenth century, only Iran, and to a lesser extent Afghanistan, demonstrated the capacity to take advantage of foreign assistance without significant loss of sovereignty. This achievement was nevertheless due more to their position as buffers between Britain and Russia than to their innate capacities. In most of Central

Asia the predominantly nomadic tribes lived in relative isolation, with important, but only limited contacts with the settled peoples, and did not have a sense of societal cohesion beyond the tribal level. Although the emirate of Bukhara and the khanate of Khiva retained their sovereignty until the end of the nineteenth century, their autonomy was due less to strong identities than to the Russian policy of nonintervention.

A significant characteristic of the international environment of the peoples of Central Asia, and also of their subsequent political development, was the encroachment of Russian and other European settlers in the second half of the nineteenth century. This was a particularly significant factor for the Kazakhs, who numbered some 2 million in this period and occupied a territory of some one million square miles—equal to over three-quarters the area of contemporary India, which supports a population of 683 million. These vast open spaces naturally attracted the attention of the land-hungry peasants from European Russia, whose population in the Kazakh territories numbered some 1.5 million by 1911. Under these circumstances modern development in Central Asia was essentially a Russian achievement, and in this period the native population was largely bypassed.

Tibet retained its autonomy, but it was under no great pressure from outside influences at this time. Moreover, none of the Inner Asian societies, with the limited exception of Iran, sought actively to understand the modern world and to anticipate the need for reform.

Closely related to their failure to confront the outside world is the limited extent to which the traditional societies of Inner Asia possessed the capacity for political control and coordination. Such capacity alone is not necessarily an asset for future modernization without the presence of a modernizing leadership, but neither can such leadership be effective in the absence of political structures. Among other later-modernizing societies, Japan, Russia, and the Ottoman Empire all had well-organized and centrally guided political systems long before the modern era. These could be adapted in due course to modern needs once their leaders decided to take that route. China likewise had this capacity, although in the century after the 1840s it was significantly weakened by civil strife and foreign intervention. Among the societies of Inner Asia, only Tibet possessed the central political control and coordination that would have permitted it to undertake modernizing reforms if its leaders had so desired. The building of large monastic establishments also demonstrated the Tibetan capacity to mobilize skills and resources. Until the end of the nineteenth century, only Iran among the other Inner Asian societies exhibited such a capacity.

Iran and Afghanistan, under foreign pressure, took important steps toward political centralization before the end of the premodern era. These efforts met with great resistance from local tribes and pastoral nomads, however, and the principal effect of the reforms was in the capital cities and among the elites. Similarly the consultative national assemblies established in Iran and Afghanistan before the 1920s were limited primarily to the central elites. The emirate of Bukhara and the khanate of Khiva likewise had governments with a significant degree of political consolidation, but their leaders were concerned almost exclusively with protecting their turf and they had little interest in the modern world.

In the economic realm, traditional forms of herding, agriculture, craftsmanship, and trade predominated in Inner Asia until the twentieth century. The efforts that were made to improve agriculture and to develop manufacturing and trade were more the result of foreign influence than of native initiative. In Iran, and to a lesser degree in Afghanistan, the foundations of modern manufacturing were laid with the assistance of British, French, and Russian capital. The exploitation of oil resources in the early 1900s which was to be the basis of Iran's future development was likewise the work of foreigners. In Central Asia the Russians stimulated the development of cotton textiles, irrigation projects, and exploitation of natural resources. There was no comparable initiative on the part of China to stimulate modern economic development in Sinkiang or Mongolia, however, and Tibet in particular remained locked in its own isolation. None of the Inner Asian societies, including Iran, exhibited the vigor of a Japan or an Ottoman Empire in seeking to understand the West.

The predominant concern of the peoples of Inner Asia with agriculture and herding in the century or two before their modern transformation served to maintain a system in which loyalties were to family, tribe, and locality rather than to society-wide institutions. There was little shift in the flow of trade toward regional or central patterns, and urban growth was limited. There were also few intermediate organizations to bridge the gap between locality and society. The Muslim and Buddhist religious establishments were the most important such organizations—and in Tibet the religious and political structures were closely related. The guilds of craftsmen and the bazaars also served to organize important interest groups within society. Such organizations did little, however, to counterbalance the essentially locally oriented character of these societies.

In the realm of knowledge and education, the societies of Inner Asia were alike in their conservative outlook and their resistance to modern knowledge, the acceptance of which is the key to a modern way of life. The fact that both Iran and Afghanistan, the closest to the West, were the first to appreciate the significance of modern knowledge points to the importance of the "inner" characteristics of Inner Asia. Nor was the static quality of these societies relieved by significant opportunities for upward mobility. The limited commoner education in the Muslim and Buddhist schools tended to confirm the students in their existing status, and opportunities for modern elite education were extremely limited. Not until the end of the nineteenth century did books and periodicals begin to open doors to modernity.

How did these various aspects of the premodern heritage of the societies of Inner Asia equip them for modernization in the twentieth century? An important asset for those Inner Asian societies that came under European influence in the nineteenth century—Iran, Afghanistan, and Central Asia—was the beginning of manufacturing and agricultural improvement, and in the case of Iran and Afghanistan political and educational reforms affecting the elite. A further asset of these societies is the existence of a strong tradition of law and order based on their Muslim and Buddhist heritages. Despite significant divisions within each religion, what they had in common was acceptance of the need for both a theoretical and a practical set of rules if societies were to be properly administered. Although these rules were "traditional," and antagonistic to modern values, they at least provided a solid base from which change could take place. This characteristic of the societies of Inner Asia stands in contrast to the newly formed states of Africa, for instance, which had much more limited common value systems as a basis for adapting to modern concepts of law and order.

As against these limited assets, most aspects of the Inner Asian heritage must be listed as liabilities to future modernization. The most important of these was the rejection of modern knowledge by the Muslim and Buddhist religious establishments. The problem was not with the fundamental tenets of Islam and Buddhism, which like those of Christianity were adaptable to modern knowledge, but rather with the prevailing conservative outlook of the religious leaders, who saw Western values and customs as heretical and as a threat to the traditional culture. As a consequence of this outlook, neither elite nor popular education was developed to any significant degree. The *jadidist* movement of Tatar origin, and native reformers in Iran and Afghanistan, had by the end of the nineteenth century exerted only a limited influence on public policy.

To this most critical liability, one should add a weak sense of identity beyond the kinship and tribal levels; limited interaction with more modern societies; unstructured political systems, with limited ability to mobilize skills and resources, and few political leaders concerned with modernizing reforms; agricultural production limited by ecology and technology; a large emphasis on herding by pastoral nomads whose way of life was essentially incompatible with modern institutions and values; limited development of manufacturing beyond the level of craftsmanship before the intrusion of foreign influences; scarcity of people trained for the professions and administration; organizational structures focusing predominantly at the kinship and tribal levels, with few organizations with the capacity to foster society-wide cohesion.

Although the societies of Inner Asia varied in some degree in their conformity to such a balance sheet of assets and liabilities, it seems clear that the similarities among them are greater than the differences. A good case can thus be made for a common Inner Asian premodern heritage, especially before the intrusion of European influences in the mid-nineteenth century.

In this respect Tibet represents an anomalous case. On the one hand it had a strong sense of identity, and was cohesive from an organizational standpoint. The prevailing religious establishment administered a society-wide political and economic system. It had relatively high literacy, and a distinctive ability to mobilize skills and resources. Yet its religious values were so antagonistic to modern world views, and the area was so isolated geographically, that Tibet was the last rather than the first of the Inner Asian societies to respond to the modern world.

II

The Modern Era

(1920s to 1980s)

8

Introduction

The watershed we have adopted for distinguishing between the premodern and modern eras in Inner Asia is the breakdown of the imperial systems that had held the societies of this region in thrall. The "1920s" is a very rough definition of the watershed between the colonial era and the period in which these societies had the possibility, and in some cases the ability, to take charge of their own destinies. More specifically, the overthrow of the Ch'ing dynasty in 1911 gave Mongolia, Sinkiang, and Tibet the opportunity to form more or less independent polities. The 1917 revolution in Russia offered similar opportunities to the peoples of Central Asia, although they did not have the capacity to take advantage of their temporary freedom. The First World War did not bring the British Empire to its knees, but it weakened it to the extent that the Great Game between Britain and Russia ceased to be a dominant factor in the development of Iran, Afghanistan, and peripherally Tibet and Sinkiang.

The specific requirements and problems of societal transformation in the dimensions of international context, political development, economic growth, social integration, and knowledge and education are set forth in the introductions to chapters 8–12. There are two more general issues, however, that concern all aspects of the process of change we are studying. One is the much-debated question of "tradition" and "modernity." Is this an appropriate context for discussing the relevant processes, or is it a false distinction that only obscures reality? The second general issue concerns the relationships among the five dimensions we are employing. To what extent should they evolve synchronously, or do some take precedence over others?

It has frequently been observed that the diffusion of modern ideas and institutions from Western Europe to the world beyond resembles the diffusion of Buddhism, Christianity, Islam, and other great religions. The doctrines and the rhetoric are in due course adopted by the faithful, but they interact in many diverse and unexpected ways with the preexisting culture. The teachings of the

167

religious innovators are confronted by a variety of local cults, myths, and cosmologies which are absorbed by the new religions but which also influence and distort them in myriad ways. In due course the religions become divided into mutually exclusive and often conflicting sects, each of whose members claims to be the true disciple of the founder.

Modernization is of course not a religion, but there are close parallels in the way differing programs of modernization have reflected the earlier values and the diversity of political strategies of a great variety of societies. The term "third world" was coined in the belief that the common predominantly agrarian and nonliterate character of these societies was all one had to know about them. What was often forgotten was that in Europe too modern requirements met the resistance of local cults, myths, and cosmologies, and that even in the late twentieth century many premodern values have survived. No less than in the West, and actually more so because of the much greater pressure for development beyond the West, the important distinction must be kept in mind between the technological and instrumental uses of modernity and the social and spiritual value systems within which they must be applied.

As the academic debate on the interaction of the cultural heritage of a society with the requirements of modernization has progressed, it has evolved from a dichotomous to a dialectical perspective. The dichotomous perspective saw the developing countries as in effect abandoning their diverse cultural heritages and adopting Western institutions and values in their place. The great equestrian statue of Peter the Great in Leningrad, for example, erected in 1782 at Catherine's behest a little over half a century after the emperor died, shows Peter facing the West on his great horse, with the rear hoofs of the horse crushing a serpent, which represented the old, Muscovite Russia. This statue reflects the dichotomous, Westernizing view: you abandon the past, and simply change from Muscovite to Western clothes and ways of thinking.

American textbooks on what is called "Western civilization" often adopt this Eurocentric position. They start with Mesopotamia, survey Greece, Rome, and the Middle Ages, and then in the modern era bring in other countries as they seem to be adopting Western values: Russia with Peter the Great, Japan in the 1860s, China in 1911, and other countries more recently.

This outlook may well be the result of the American historical experience. The United States modernized the easy way. Most European immigrants came to the New World voluntarily to escape the restraints of European society. They emigrated because they had a more modern outlook and wished to get away from tradition-bound Europe. They came to establish a new society. In a sense they tried to walk away from their cultural heritage, although of course they inevitably brought much of it with them. No other major country in the world has been formed in quite this way. Americans have not had the experience of transforming a premodern society, and have had some difficulty in understanding countries that have developed in a different context.

The dialectical perspective, by contrast—the view that stresses the interaction of diverse cultural heritages with the requirements of modernity—is reflected in the experience of all the other countries that have had to transform peasant societies into industrial societies. In all these cases there was no sharp break with tradition—like migrating from Europe to America—but rather a gradual and usually painful and violent form of adaptation, in the course of which the powerful forces of tradition have resisted change at every step.

Some writers seem to think that modernization makes societies more civilized, but there is no more violent period in world history than the modern era. It cannot be emphasized too often that modernization should not be equated with progress. It is characterized by an enhanced human control over the environment, and this new power can be employed as easily to destroy humankind as to raise world standards of health, education, and welfare. The moral dilemmas that have always been with us have been sharpened by the advancement of knowledge.

The dialectical perspective may be illustrated by the differing effects of the individualist and collectivist heritages on the way a society conducts its affairs. Individualism is not a universal value—it is essentially a Western value—and the two differing heritages cast a long shadow into the future. Most of the peoples of the world—Arabs, Asians, and in many respects the Russians—have a heritage of collectivist values. In this view individualism is not a virtue but a vice—it means trying to get ahead on one's own at the expense of family, friends, and associates. Collectivism, by contrast, stresses the importance of family, kinship, and community.

In societies with a collectivist tradition, there is more respect for hierarchy and less inclination to grant initiative to subordinates. There is also a greater tendency to seek consensus through discussion rather than to depend on the decision of a single leader. At the same time, experience has shown that modern institutions can be created within the framework of both value systems. Many traditional patterns of conducting public affairs are adaptable to modern functions.

More generally, as much in the West as elsewhere, the heritage of institutions and values never fails to exert a pervasive influence on the way the requirements of modernity are met. This is particularly the case with the societies of Inner Asia, where the cultural heritage has deep roots in the past and modern influences are recent and even in the 1990s relatively superficial.

The interrelationship of the five dimensions of modernization employed in this study—international context, political development, economic growth, social integration, and knowledge and education—is also an important consideration in interpreting the development of the Inner Asian societies in the twentieth century. One cannot embark on a policy of modernization, the political aspect, without the knowledge that modernization is desirable and possible—the modern values introduced by Western influence. In the early-modernizing societies this cognitive transformation—the recognition and acceptance of the scientific and technological revolution—developed slowly over the centuries. Later-modernizing societies, like those of Inner Asia, could borrow modern knowledge in a very short time from those that had already achieved it. Political development is an essential prerequisite to economic growth. This in turn leads to urbanization, the lowering of death and later birth rates, and the other developments that come under the heading of social mobilization. The acceptance of modern knowledge by the great majority of a population through universal education, publication, and research is usually a relatively late development.

What is important about these interrelationships is that the different aspects of modernization are parts of a single process. No one aspect can develop very far without pulling the others along with it. In later-modernizing societies, the introduction of modern values from abroad is necessarily the first step. The political, economic, and social aspects, however, develop at differing rates depending in part on a society's cultural heritage, in part on the nature of the foreign influences to which it is subjected, and in part on the policies adopted by its leaders.

Political development is a good example of the influence of cultural heritage, foreign models, and political leadership. In a society with a long tradition of individual participation, like France, democratic institutions in the Western sense developed more rapidly than economic growth. In a society with a long tradition of authoritarian government, like Russia/USSR, political participation developed much more slowly than economic growth. In both cases, however, political participation was an essential element of the modernizing process. One cannot build an economy that requires many thousands of university-educated scientists, engineers, and managers without giving them a role in policy making. The question is not whether political participation will evolve, but whether it will come early or late. The longer political participation is postponed, by comparison with other aspects of modernization, the more likely that it will come as a result of confrontational rather than evolutionary processes. A wise leadership will seek to promote the synchronous development of all aspects of modernization, within the framework of the cultural heritage and international constraints of the particular society.

In this respect there is a very significant difference between earlier- and later-modernizing societies. The former developed gradually over many years, and had time to experiment and gain experience. The latter are under pressure to change with a speed that is often beyond their capacity.

Consider, for example, the British experience with representation. In 1215 the Magna Carta established the principle, to simplify somewhat, of no taxation without representation. The reform of 1832 made provision for a million voters out of thirteen million people. The reform of 1867 provided for two million voters out of twenty-two million people. In 1872 the vote became secret. In 1911, the powers of the House of Lords were restricted. It could no longer veto legislation but it could still delay it. In 1918, universal suffrage was introduced: age twenty-one for men and age thirty for women. (They thought women matured later than men—little did they realize the opposite is the case.) Finally, in 1948, universal suffrage was legislated for everyone over eighteen.

One has to make a distinction between political development in the sense of replacing traditional with modern leadership—in effect, revolution—and political development in the sense of democratic participation in the formation of public policy. In the latter sense there is no such thing as instant democracy. Some aspects of modernity are easily acquired. A country can establish an airline with jet planes, a computerized communications system, or a capital city with great boulevards and high-rise buildings, by training or hiring a few thousand specialists. Changing the habits and outlook of the 80 percent or more of the population who are nonliterate peasants, however, is an inexorably slow process.

If it took the British from 1215 to 1948 to get universal suffrage; if the French went through four republics and two empires, until they finally got a fifth republic they seem to like, although it is in some trouble still; if the United States could not organize its political development without a major civil war—the most destructive war in the world between 1815 and 1914—or without having slavery for almost a century and tolerating severe forms of segregation for another century, why should one expect later-modernizing societies such as those of Inner Asia to build modern political systems in only a few decades?

While the overarching generalization in this respect would seem to be that political, economic, and social change should evolve synchronously, in fact the experience of the early modernizers suggests that political development is slower than economic or social. The conclusion is suggested that the larger the portion of the population that is involved in a process, the more slowly that process is likely to develop. Political development involves the institutions and values of a whole society to a greater extent than does economic growth or social integration, and faces much more difficult problems in the adaptation of traditional forms to modern functions.

This process has been greatly complicated by the tendency of many leaders of later-modernizing countries to adopt Western institutions at the expense of their own traditional heritage. It usually takes a generation or two before countries that are set on this course come to realize that the real problem is the adaptation of their own institutional heritage to new tasks, and that the models of the earlier-modernizing societies are of only limited value.

9

International Context

Introduction

The immediate background of the transformation of Inner Asia during the period from the 1920s to the 1980s was the tremendous upheaval of the First World War and the political dislocations engendered by the ensuing breakup of the Chinese and Russian empires and the weakening of the British position in India. The revolutionary states that replaced these empires were to play a much more active role both as models of political, economic, and social change and as intrusive forces seeking to subordinate the peoples of Inner Asia to their interests.

In seeking to cope with this new international environment, the peoples of Inner Asia faced different challenges from those they had confronted earlier in the realms of identity, foreign influence, and modernization programs. Of particular significance in the twentieth century has been the distinction between the societies that maintained or created an independent statehood—Iran, Afghanistan, and Mongolia—and those that were provinces of larger states—the five republics of Soviet Central Asia, and Tibet, Sinkiang, and Inner Mongolia in China.

As societies evolve from traditional-agrarian-rural to rational-industrial-urban values and institutions, the question of identity becomes increasingly important. Before the modern era identity patterns are significant principally in defining the relation of societies to outside influences. The extent to which leaders of later-developing societies can count on loyalty to native institutions and values plays an important role in their ability to confront these influences.

In the phase of evolving modernization, the question of identity becomes particularly relevant to domestic consolidation. As political, economic, and social relations within a society become increasingly organized on a society-wide basis, and in many respects centralized, the need for the development of a homogeneous culture becomes acute.

Societies have confronted this issue with varying degrees of intensity. Japan is one of the few that was to an unusual degree homogeneous before the modern era, and it has retained much of this cultural homogeneity down to the present. In the United States it took a civil war before agreement could be reached on a common political culture. Germany and Italy in the nineteenth century gained unity through a process of intense civil conflict in the course of which the questions of which dialect should predominate as the national language, how loyalties to smaller constituent sovereignties should be adapted to the new national sovereignty, and (in the case of Germany) how the two main branches of Western Christianity should be related, were to a large extent resolved. In societies such as Nigeria and India, the inclusion under one sovereignty of peoples with a wide variety of languages and dialects led to the adoption of English as the dominant language of business and government. In the Republic of South Africa, ethnic differences continue to raise obstacles to a common culture to which no solution is in sight.

In the Inner Asian societies the problem of achieving distinct ethnic identities with the capacity to confront foreign influences and to form the basis for national political systems has encountered two obstacles. One is the diversity of ethnic groups within each society. This obstacle is not confronted uniformly in all the societies, since Tibet was until the 1950s and the Mongolian People's Republic is essentially homogeneous, while at the other extreme the peoples of Afghanistan were only beginning in the 1980s to recognize a national identity that predominates over tribal and other local loyalties.

The second obstacle to the formation of strong identities is the intrusion of foreign settlers. This factor is particularly significant in Soviet Central Asia—and in Tibet and Sinkiang since the 1950s—to the extent that the indigenous peoples in some cases become minorities within their own societies. In these cases the energies mobilized by the rise of nationalism are directed less toward state building and economic development than toward the struggle against foreign rule.

Since the 1920s foreign influences on modernization no longer involve such peripheral matters as loans and other forms of assistance being used by foreigners as instruments of penetration, and by native leaders for purposes of defensive modernization. Instead, in those societies that have gained independence, foreign models are normally sought out by native leaders for all aspects of their own societal transformation. Historical examples abound: the role of the Napoleonic Code in Central Europe; the influence of the American constitution in Europe and Latin America; Kemal Ataturk's adoption of the French civil code, the Swiss criminal code, and aspects of the Soviet state investment system (étatism).

In the twentieth century the Inner Asian societies could draw on a wide variety of foreign models. Turkey as the model for Iran in the 1920s is a typical case; more generally, models changed from British and French in the 1920s, to German in the 1930s, to American in the 1950s. The developments were also significantly influenced by the new Great Game between the United States and the USSR in the West and between China and the USSR in the East. These rivalries are certainly a central feature in Iran, Afghanistan, Sinkiang, and Mongolia. Foreign influences were significant in terms both of native leaders looking outward and of pressure exerted by foreign countries. The balance between the two differs by country and period. Here again, there are important distinctions in Inner Asia between sovereign societies and the societies under foreign rule.

The challenge of modernity in the twentieth century, for the societies of Inner Asia, involved both foreign and domestic dimensions. The foreign dimension predominated, since all conceptions and models of political development, economic growth, and social mobilization came from outside the region. The foreign challenge in the case of the sovereign societies—Iran, Afghanistan, and Mongolia—represented a continuation of the premodern conflict between the desire to gain foreign assistance and at the same time prevent excessive foreign intrusion into domestic affairs. In the case of the societies under foreign rule—Central Asia, Tibet, and Sinkiang—the initiative in modernization was taken by the occupying societies, and the indigenous peoples played only a limited role.

The domestic dimension of the challenge of modernity affected primarily the sovereign states, and took the form of debates among policy makers as to how far and how fast, and in which direction, they should go in adapting their cultural heritage to modern functions. This debate reached the stage of violent civil strife in Iran, and also in Afghanistan until the Soviet occupation came to occupy center stage.

Identity Patterns

Iran and Afghanistan form an interesting contrast in regard to their efforts to develop a national identity. In Iran, which had the most developed political system among the Inner Asian societies, the dominance of Persian ethnicity was enhanced during the administrations of Reza Shah (1925–1941) and Mohammed Reza Shah (1941–1978). Petroleum and strategic location gave Iran the capacity to assert itself in its struggle against foreign domination, and a European-style nationalism prevalent among the Persian-speaking minority came to prevail.

The ethnic composition of Iran nevertheless affected the international context in which it operated during the twentieth century to a greater extent than in the earlier period. It is significant that the association of the various ethnic and tribal groups with foreign trade and general economic relations, as well as the virtual client relationship with foreign powers, resembles less the situation in Afghanistan than that in the Ottoman domains. Not only were Christian, Bahai, and Jewish minority groups involved with Russians, British, and American representatives, but Muslim ethnic and tribal groups too allowed themselves to be drawn into foreign power machinations to control all or parts of Iran.

In the period of uncertainty following World War I, the *Jangali* movement, a regional rebellion among Gilaki Iranians of the Caspian area, which was later over-run by Soviet-style Iranian Communists, facilitated the landing of the first Soviet troops on Iranian soil. Among these were many Central Asians, co-religionists, if not co-ethnics, of local Iranians. This pattern of using co-ethnics and co-religionists from Soviet areas to influence events in Iran was repeated during the "demokrat" period of 1944–1946.

Examples also appear during the 1940s among the Kurds and the Azerbaijani, both of whom evolved threateningly autonomous rule associated with Soviet military or diplomatic backing. The Khamsa tribal confederacy in the south, under British tutelage, posed a military threat to the stability of Iran, as did the virtually autonomous Muhammara (later Khurramshahr) region of ethnically Arab Shi'ites.

The explanation for ethnicity surging into political action lies in general inter-national conditions as well as changes within Iran. Unlike the Qajar period where pride in things Iranian had assumed the traditional pattern, during the Pahlavi period, Reza Shah aggressively promoted a Persian-based Iranian nation-alism. The requirements for use of Persian (set forth in the electoral laws promul-gated during the period of the Constitutional Revolution) called for prohibition of the use of non-Persian languages. This policy, activated in the newly funded public education system as well as in the bureaucracy, alienated ethnic minori-ties, especially in Azerbaijan.

The Turkic population of this area had long participated in Iranian political developments, especially during the late Qajar period when the support of the constitution focused in Tabriz. The easy bilingual relationships between Azeri Turkish and Persian began to give way to an imposed persianization policy. This internal policy, together with the Soviet nationality policy in the same period that elevated Soviet Azeri Turkish to an instituted republic language, created ill will in much of Azerbaijan. Repression of opposition during the 1930s drove dissent underground. But with the forced abdication of Reza Shah in 1941, the dam opened and ethnic regionalism became the prey of international politics. The issue of the treatment of Iran's non-Persian ethnic minorities remains unresolved. In the case of the Azeris, the Kurds, and the Baluch, and to a lesser extent the Arabs, use of these minorities in international affairs occurs and is accepted as a given in regional politics. Iraq has replaced Britain as a potential manipulator, and the Soviet ability to continue menacing Iran through threat or use of its minorities has remained constant. Only with the success of the Islamic revolution has Iran itself initiated steps that indicate its recognition of the vulnerability of the Soviet Union to cross-border ethnic and religious manipulation.

Iran's predominantly Shi'ite Muslim identity has endowed it with a solitary yet threatening position since the Safavid period (1501–1736). Its centuries of conflict with the Ottomans, the Uzbeks, and later with the Turkmen and Af-ghans, hinged around the issue of religion as much as territory. None of Iran's neighbors seriously questioned the value of Iranian culture, and Persian, the vehicle of this culture. In most surrounding areas Persian influence all but swamped the politically dominant Turkic or Pushtun cultures. But Shi'ism never achieved this acceptance, and continued to be regarded as a lesser form of Muslim expression if not outright heretical. For this reason, neighboring states, although wary of the power of Shi'ism and of Iran, persecuted Shi'ites, especially in the eastern countries, prompting Iranian reaction. In this respect, the case of what is now Soviet Azerbaijan is peculiar. Overwhelmingly Shi'ite, the Azerbaijanis experienced much conflict in allegiance during the Russian civil war; as potential separatists from the tsarist state they were torn between ethnic identity with Turkey and religious identity with Iran.

Among non-Persian Muslim ethnic groups within Iran, the divisions along Sunni-Shi'ite lines only partially affected loyalty and allegiance: the Arabs are largely Shi'ite, as are the Azeris, while the Kurds span the range from Sunni to Ja'afari Shi'ites to groups that even the last consider heretical. Other Turkic and Iranian tribal groups profess Shi'ite Islam, a factor less important in their identity patterns than tribal identity. A policy of steadily weakening Iranian tribes during the Pahlavi period, continued since the replacement of the monarchy, has reduced Iran's vulnerability to foreign interference in tribal affairs save in the case of the Kurdish and Baluch tribes. Moreover, within the spectrum of Iranian internal affairs, the tribes have exercised little influence on the religious establishment and may even be viewed as more secular than the sedentary or nontribal communities.

In Afghanistan, despite the development of central political institutions during the reigns of Amanullah (1919–1929) and Mohammed Nadir (1929–1933), and the administrations of General Mohammed Daoud (1953–1963 and 1973–1978), the traditional patterns of religious, ethnolinguistic, tribal, and geographically oriented identities continued to prevail. When Western writers discuss the rise of Afghan nationalism in the first quarter of the twentieth century, they refer to the international recognition of Afghan sovereignty rather than to the type of integral nationalism that developed in Western Europe. In the 1980s, some four-fifths of the peoples of Afghanistan were Sunni Muslims, and the balance were Shi'ites of several sects. About half the population was Pushtun, some 13 percent were Tajiks; 7 percent were Uzbek, Kirgiz, and other Turkic-speaking peoples; and some 6 percent were Hazara. These linguistic groups were further divided into tribal and regional loyalties which usually provided the predominant sense of identity. Even the prolonged Soviet occupation served to moderate these divisive identities to only a limited degree. Only in the relatively small urban areas, and particularly among the intellectuals, do individuals begin to feel part of a nation called Afghanistan.

The Mongolian People's Republic is confronted with identity problems that combine elements of both independence and colonialism. Unlike Iran and Afghanistan, its problem is not one of a multi-ethnic heritage but rather of its close control by the Soviet Union. Despite overt and heavy-handed Soviet pressures, however, the Mongols have largely succeeded in maintaining their cultural identity. "Sovietization" has occurred within superficial strata, but has not penetrated the core of the culture. Political, economic, and educational institutions have all been reorganized along Soviet lines. Nonetheless nationhood, achieved in 1921, has protected the Mongols from the types of disastrous cultural policies to which the minority peoples of China, including the Mongols of Inner Mongolia and the Tibetans, have been subjected, particularly during the Cultural Revolution (1966–1976). Acceptance into the United Nations in 1961 and diplomatic recognition by Western European nations and finally the United States (in 1987) have legitimized the independence of which the Mongols are proud, in spite of their readily acknowledged lack of autonomous policy making resulting from Soviet hegemony.

In terms of cultural identity, the Mongolian government's imposition of the Cyrillic alphabet in the early 1940s has been seen as an attempt to bring the Mongols into the Soviet cultural orbit and to separate them culturally and linguistically from Inner Mongolia where the Mongols have continued to use the traditional Turkic Uighur script. Recently, however, the attempt by both China and the Soviet Union to keep the Mongols on either side of the Sino-Soviet line of influence insulated from one another has been relaxed somewhat. The Turkic Uighur script is now being reintroduced into Mongolian schools for grades seven through ten, and in Inner Mongolia, the study of Mongolian in the Cyrillic alphabet is no longer prohibited (M15, pp. 11–12).

In the other societies of Inner Asia that remained under foreign rule in the twentieth century, the problems of maintaining national identity were equally formidable. *The Tibetans* have had particular problems in their efforts to maintain their cultural identity. In spite of the fact that China in the twentieth century has perpetuated Ch'ing-dynasty claims that Tibet is an integral part of the Chinese polity, most Tibetans today, as in Ch'ing times, do not subscribe to this view. The geography, culture, and social customs of Tibet have always served to protect its people from attempts to exert control over the region. Since the invasion of Tibet by Chinese troops in 1950, however, Tibetans have faced the greatest challenge to the preservation of their cultural identity. The fact that Tibetan Buddhism, the core of that identity, survived the massive onslaught during the decade of the Cultural Revolution, when virtually all monasteries suffered at least partial destruction, argues strongly in favor of the continuation of traditional Tibetan culture. In spite of the influx of Han Chinese military and administrative personnel since 1950 and the emphasis on learning and using the Chinese language, especially during the Cultural Revolution, Tibetans have succeeded in keeping their written and spoken language alive.

Similarly in Sinkiang external forces have been influential in setting its course of development. Even its territorial definition was imposed by conquest, and British, Russians, and Chinese have played more of a role in its modernization than have the indigenous peoples. The territory itself is vast and diverse, culturally part of the Middle East, and until the twentieth century it was inhabited almost entirely by Uighurs and Kazakhs, Turkic peoples of traditional Muslim faith. Strategically, however, it is potentially vital to Russia to the north and west, India to the south, and China to the east. In the twentieth century, the strategic needs of neighbors have by and large overridden the rather tenuous local sense of identity, and created an entity whose status is based more on external than internal factors. This is perhaps inevitable for the territory that Owen Lattimore called "the pivot of Asia."

In the period before the great neighboring empires encroached on it, the territory that is Sinkiang today contained a collection of peoples having strong local identities, but no particular sense of collective regional identification. To the extent that people looked beyond their affiliations with village or tribe, religious identifications were most important, and these linked them with the larger world of the Middle East and what today is Soviet Central Asia. Because Sinkiang was relatively isolated compared to other parts of the Muslim world, these identities were often preserved there after they had begun to change elsewhere. Thus Gunnar Jarring, arriving in Kashgar in the 1920s, found it a perfectly preserved example of a medieval Islamic city of a type no longer to be found elsewhere.

Much of the impulse for change came from outside. Sinkiang's present political shape was imposed in 1884, when the Ch'ing government, which had initially acquired the territory in the eighteenth century, reconquered it in the wake of a series of rebellions. These rebellions manifested the old, more organic order of the area: they were religiously inspired, and to some extent arose in Kokand, outside of the Ch'ing-imposed border. Peking's reaction foreshadowed the general pattern of modern times in Sinkiang: essentially intervention by a foreign power having strategic interests in the area, followed by attempts to create cohesion or even a new identity within the imposed artificial boundaries.

The Ch'ing incorporated the territory as the province of Sinkiang, or "New Territory." But the Ch'ing did not attempt to sinify the area, or transform its society—though the important city of Urumchi began its life as a Ch'ing garrison. Even while the declining Ch'ing still controlled Sinkiang, the Russians, and the British in India, sought to develop influence there through their consuls. These efforts increased after the Ch'ing abdicated in 1912.

Yang Tseng-hsin, a Chinese general who seized power and ruled until 1928, continued the Ch'ing pattern of avoiding direct confrontation with local interests, while relying on British influence in the south to offset Russian in the north. Yang's assassination, however, brought internal instability, and thus invited a larger foreign role. His successor, Chin Shu-jen, another military leader, triggered one rebellion in 1931 by unwisely annexing Hami, previously permitted a quasi-independence like that of a native state in British India, and in short order was faced by another rebellion in the south, which saw the proclamation in 1933 of the independent Turkish-Islamic Republic of Eastern Turkestan.

Such developments were manifestations of an indigenous process of redefinition of identity in reaction partly to foreign conquest, but also reflecting new currents in the Muslim world. They found parallels as Muslim polities, starting with Turkey, attempted to modernize and redefine themselves in line with the nationalism that was sweeping the world in the wake of the First World War. In Sinkiang, the idea of an Eastern Turkic identity, language, and culture stirred as well.

For powers seeking to control the area, these developments were both a problem and an opportunity. The power in charge was usually threatened by manifestations of local feeling. A competing power, however, might seek to mobilize these feelings to serve its own political aims. In the 1920s and 1930s Chinese nationalism, while theoretically embracing non-Chinese groups such as Turks, Tibetans, and Mongols, was in fact inextricably tied to the aspirations of ethnic Chinese in Sinkiang. The Soviet Union, however, took a strong interest for strategic reasons, since instability in the area was particularly worrisome to Moscow. Having initially sought to co-opt the local nationalisms that swept Central Asia after the fall of the empire, it was in the process of subjugating its own Muslim subjects. The period of greatest Soviet influence occurred during the rule of Sheng Shih-ts'ai (1933–1942), a well-educated left-leaning military officer, originally from Manchuria, who eventually joined the Soviet Communist party. In the course of Sheng's administration, Soviet ideas of nationality, based on those already being used in Soviet Central Asia, were applied to Sinkiang as well.

Nor did the victory of the Chinese Communists in 1949 resolve Sinkiang's identity issues. The slogans of the new regime extolled class solidarity and revolution, and clearly sought to make the expression of a hitherto-suppressed local sense of identity the basis of Sinkiang's incorporation into the People's Republic. But almost inevitably, the ethnic Chinese character of the new regime quickly asserted itself. By the end of the Cultural Revolution, "local" literature consisted almost entirely of translations of Chinese works, and the local language had been heavily infiltrated by Chinese vocabulary. The rapid retreat from sinification following Mao's death in 1976 suggests that the attempts to incorporate Sinkiang's native population by making them into Chinese had not succeeded.

In Soviet Central Asia, during the period of revolution and civil war that engaged the entire country, the indigenous peoples had the opportunity to reevaluate their relations with the Russians and to assert their ethnic interests. There was extensive consideration of the option of independence, especially among the Turkic peoples, but the divisions among them were such that they found it impossible to conceive or construct a unifying political consensus or structure that would allow them to present a united front to the Russian outsiders or to shape a common political destiny. The extreme fragmentation of these groups did not just divide them from each other. Internal divisions within each of the groups caused certain factions to fight with the Russians, some to fight against

180

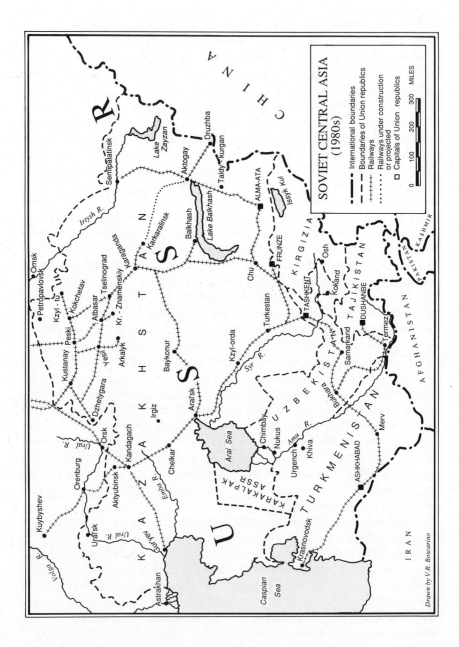

SOVIET CENTRAL ASIA
(1980s)

International boundaries
Boundaries of Union republics
Railways
Railways under construction
or projected
□ Capitals of Union republics

0   100   200   300   MILES

Drawn by V.R. Boscarino

the Russians, and others to attempt to make common cause with English, Turkish, or Afghan outsiders.

In the later 1920s, after the Soviet reconquest, the Central Asian region was divided into distinct republics, and literary, cultural, and social innovations were introduced from the outside, primarily by the newly dominant Russians. Nevertheless, much of the implementation and configuration of these programs was carried out with the assistance of the Turkic and Islamic minority peoples themselves, as the Soviet establishment managed to co-opt substantial numbers of ethnic elites and cadres. *Korenizatsiia,* or the widespread use of ethnic cadres in local administrative settings, became a major principle in the republics. This was combined with an intensive search by regional ethnic elites for a specific role within the structure of the Soviet state, with a federalist principle as the defining goal. In addition, many among the Turkic and Islamic Central Asian elites were attracted by their potential role as a revolutionary example to socially and economically backward ethnic and religious brethren across immediate international borders. There was substantial commitment among these groups in the 1920s to the goal of "bringing light to the peoples of the East," a commitment matched by an active involvement in revolutionary activities in the contiguous states of Turkey, Iran, Afghanistan, and China.

In the 1930s, however, much of the early Soviet ethnic leadership was liquidated as Stalin attempted to break the back of his real and imagined opposition. As Europe moved toward the Second World War Stalin took advantage of growing international tension to create an atmosphere of ubiquitous suspicion and denunciation, eliminating potential opponents both at the political center and in the outlying republics. In Central Asia this was accompanied by a major attack on the traditional structures of Muslim society and a reversal of the relative tolerance of the earlier period. In a comprehensive effort to shatter the mold of traditional identities in the region, the Soviet establishment mounted major campaigns to transform the family, the mosques, the Islamic religious establishment, the independence of the *wakfs,* the profile and management of the water and irrigation system, the character and detail of local alphabets and languages, the structure and purposes of school systems, the themes and direction of literature and culture, and the commitments and allegiances of local political elites.

During and after the Second World War a tentative and partial set of tactical compromises was made with traditional society as the Moscow center sought to retain the political allegiances of the outlying periphery under the crisis conditions of the war and its aftermath. This new policy included a selective relaxation of pressures on local cultures, and a controlled new permissiveness for the spiritual directorates of official Islam. Important patterns of limited autonomy evolved in the economic, social, cultural, and local political spheres in return for local guarantees of ultimate regime adherence and fundamental public order. This was tantamount to a limited but significant social contract, under which a new tolerance was available for the cultivation of Turkic and Muslim identities, including a carefully aesopian search for roots in pre-Soviet sources. This search for the roots of ethnic and religious identity intensified substantially from the early 1970s on, encouraged by a spreading disenchantment within Soviet society with the adequacy of artificial Soviet forms, as well as a general new global fascination with the significance of ethnicity and nationalism. These explorations exposed an intriguing, and potentially explosive, core of common Turkic characteristics and unifying cultural indicators which resembled embryonic pan-Turkic trends. These dynamic cultural trends were paralleled by the evolution of a flourishing second economy as well as patterns of economic and political corruption that took substantial areas of local society out from under central establishment control.

The new reform era after 1985 has been marked by several striking new departures: an end to affirmative-action approaches within the system; a crackdown on local economic and political corruption; a substantial purge of local ethnic leadership; a veto of increased central investment for economic diversification in the region; new pressures on local linguistic and cultural patterns, plus a major insistence on the need to observe revolutionary internationalist canons; and central pressure to end the flirtation with the search for pre-Soviet roots and identities. This period has witnessed the beginnings of a new stage of orthodox Soviet internationalism as the Moscow leadership attempts to eradicate those features of inefficient localism and regionalism that have crippled the effectiveness of the Soviet economic and political system as a whole.

Foreign Influences

Foreign influences in the internal affairs of Iran in the early part of this century culminated in the Anglo-Russian treaty of 1907, which allowed only a narrow strip of Iran to remain outside the sphere of influence of either European power. Subsequent events blurred the lines of control but allowed opportunistic entry at will. During World War II, for example, Iran served as a corridor for Allied supplies to the Soviet Union, and the stationing of Allied troops reduced the country to a puppet of the American, British, and Soviet troops. The forced abdication of Reza Shah, a ruthless but capable national leader, spelled the end of the first phase of Iranian independent action, which had begun in the early nineteenth century.

Reza Shah had relied heavily on the model of Ataturk's Turkey. His policies were marked by a narrow definition of Iranian interests, concentration on internal consolidation of power, reforms aimed at technical progress, and withdrawal from regional conflicts. A supreme confidence in the durability of the Iranian nation manifested itself in actions that restored a sense of pride in being Iranian. With his removal in 1941, his neglect of social and political issues rent the power consolidation for which he had worked and nearly undid the territorial integrity of Iran. Whether the rise of the left and republican nationalism, or the increased expression of clerical political power, would have occurred had he not abdicated is a moot question. But grievances against his tight control of political power made the period until 1953 a very fragile one in Iranian international affairs. From the delicate use of international pressure to dislodge the Soviet army from Iranian Azerbaijan in 1946 to the strangling of the nationalists through British and American economic pressure and the return of the Mohammed Reza Shah with American aid in 1953, Iran's international affairs remained unstable. Emerging from the period of instability, Iran found itself increasingly bound to the Western camp in the Cold War. As this Western camp evolved into an American- rather than British-led group, so too Iran's international affairs functioned in tandem with United States policy in the region. As a member of the Baghdad Pact, renamed the Central Treaty Organization (CENTO) after the withdrawal in 1958 of republicanized Iraq, Iran by the 1960s appeared as the likely regional leader in the area. Its relations with Turkey and Pakistan reached the level of active cooperation with the formation of the Regional Development Authority, and its seizure of the two Tumb islands and Abu Musa in 1971 marked its willingness to replace the British as guardians of the Persian Gulf region. These islands at the mouth of the gulf allowed Iran to assert hegemonic power. The shift from the shah to clerical rule prompts second thoughts on the legitimacy of this move, which at that time passed virtually unquestioned.

Foreign influence within Iran increased with its oil wealth and its role as a regional power. Iranian students from many levels, including first-generation-literate boys from villages, crowded into Iran's mushrooming system of higher education, especially during the 1960s. By this time a widespread educational system, augmented by a literacy corps which formed part of the "White Revolution," had fostered literacy throughout many Iranian villages. Pressure for continued education led to generous and numerous scholarships for foreign study, an important form of foreign influence. The preferred country came to be the United States, replacing France and England, where previous elite generations had gone, mainly at their own expense.

Among ordinary people, foreign influence took indirect forms. A steadily increasing number of Americans, from Peace Corps volunteers to Western corporate personnel who trained weapons specialists, worked in Iran. Added to this dominant foreign presence was personnel from European countries—France, Germany, Belgium, and Britain. The Soviet presence, though not extensive, functioned somewhat differently. The few Soviet projects brought in a large number of Soviet citizens living in enclaves (as at the Isphahan steel mill). The Soviet government also made a special effort to reach the ordinary people, or at least the intelligentsia. Similar Western attempts, though generously funded, nevertheless managed to reach mainly secular, politically acquiescent elites. The Soviet emphasis on knowledge of Persian among its cultural personnel was effective, as was its employment of Persian-speaking Central Asians in such posts and as interpreters. These facts are interesting as a reflection of the contrast between

Soviet and Western attitudes. They also indicate that Iranians were not interested in learning Russian, whereas they enrolled in English classes in large numbers.

Having achieved its position as a regional power, even though public opinion was inclined to regard this position as being that of a surrogate of American power, Iran attracted much regional interest. Afghan, Korean, and Filipino workers arrived to fill menial and semiskilled positions eschewed by Iranian youth who preferred underemployment in the bureaucracy to employment in manual labor once they had achieved a high school degree. Of the three groups, the Afghans most easily entered Iranian society because of the similarity of cultures. The influence of Iran on Afghanistan is further demonstrated in Iranian interest in healing rifts between Afghanistan, Pakistan, and Iran over boundary issues and in the generous plan to fund Afghan development in part through the creation of a transit route through Iranian Baluchistan and the port of Shah Bahar.

Thus in the modern period, Iran changed from a country to be influenced by its neighbors to one that wielded influence. Because of the nature of the ties between Iranian secular elites and the United States, however, and the long history of xenophobia among the people, few Iranians realized the extent of the country's changed position.

In Afghanistan, as in Iran, the significance of foreign influence was closely related to the changing role of the major foreign powers with a strategic interest in the area. Amanullah recognized the Soviet Union as soon as he came to power in 1919, but the British retained their position as the most important foreign influence. At the same time, the French made great inroads on the cultural scene with their high school for boys and girls and their archaeological mission, which began its work in 1922. Also, many in the urban elite, including members of the royal family, preferred to attend French universities.

Habibullah I, Amanullah's father, had founded Habibiya College in 1903, modeling it after Muslim Aligarh College in British India. The French founded Istiqlal Lycée in 1923, the Germans, Nejat College in 1924, the British, Ghazi College in 1928. Foreign teachers and languages dominated the upper classes in the schools until the Soviet takeover. The Soviets came late to the educational scene, establishing a Polytechnic Institute in 1967. Each school turned out clones of its own educational systems, and the students (except most at the Polytechnic) were substantial partisans for the countries represented. This issue became particularly acute when the former German-educated students agitated against the Allies in World War II, although officially the Afghan government remained neutral, just as it had during World War I.

The Soviet Union made significant inroads in Afghanistan during the Amanullah period, partly because of the Anglophobia of several of the king's closest advisers, including his father-in-law, Mahmud Tarzi, an influential Islamic modernist. Tarzi's newspaper, *Seraj ul-akhbar-e afghaniya,* was systematically banned in British India (see "World Views: Between Tradition and Modernity," chapter 6, and "Elite Education, Research, and Publishing," chapter 13).

Afghanistan was one of the first countries to recognize the Bolshevik regime, and the two nations established diplomatic relations in 1919. Thus, official contacts between Afghanistan and the Communist world to the north began early, and were not a product of the Cold War as many believe.

The Russians sent Amanullah a gift of thirteen airplanes, plus pilots, mechanics, transportation specialists, and telegraph operators. Before 1928, the Soviet Union established an air route from Moscow to Kabul via Tashkent. It also laid down telephone lines between Herat-Kandahar and Kabul-Mazar-i-Sharif. Earlier, the German Junker aircraft firm had obtained exclusive rights to establish an airline from Germany via Turkey and Iran.

Even before Amanullah's royal grand tour of Europe in 1928, several other important nations had recognized Afghanistan and exchanged diplomatic missions: Iran (1921), Britain (1922), Turkey (1922), Italy (1922), and France (1923). The European tour produced diplomatic treaties with (among others) Finland, Latvia, Liberia, Poland, Switzerland, Egypt, and Japan. However, a mission to the United States failed to gain American recognition, which only came in 1942 when the American diplomat Cornelius van Engert was sent to Kabul as minister plenipotentiary.

In the 1930s the Afghans continued to develop the private-sector small-scale industries begun after World War I. They sought development assistance from Germany, Italy, and Japan, three nations they thought would be the least troublesome in Inner Asia. Then came World War II, and the British and Soviets invaded Iran in 1941. In October of that year, the British and Russians demanded that the Afghans expel all nondiplomatic Axis personnel. The Afghans felt their honor threatened and agreed only after the British promised to give the Germans, Italians, and Japanese safe conduct through India. The British did not keep their word and placed some Axis personnel in concentration camps.

Afghanistan's constitutions since 1920 have all been influenced by other constitutions, while attempting to embody the basic principles of Islam. Amanullah's 1923 constitution was based on the 1906 constitution of Iran and the Turkish administrative codes of Kemal Ataturk.

The 1931 constitution of King Mohammed Nadir eliminated what was perceived to be "European liberalism" and embodied a hodgepodge of unworkable elements. It was adapted from the French, Turkish, and Iranian constitutions—plus acceptable parts of the 1923 constitution—and combined with many aspects of the Hanafi Shari'a of Sunni Islam. Most of the constitution's 110 articles and sixteen parts seemed to have been borrowed at random from these various sources. The 1931 constitution created the illusion of popular participation without proper enforcement provisions. In reality, central power remained vested in the royal family, creating a veritable oligarchy.

The next Afghan constitution was promulgated in 1964. For over a year the Constitutional Commission appointed by King Mohammed Zahir (1933–1973) met officially with French and British, and informally with American and Soviet, constitutional experts. The resulting constitution can best be described as essentially secular but based on Islam.

The 1977 constitution of Daoud's second administration (1973–1978) was the most secular constitution to that date, and drew on advice from Western experts, particularly Americans. The monarchy had been overthrown and a Republic of Afghanistan came into being.

A leftist-flavored coup occurred on April 27–28, 1978, and the Democratic Republic of Afghanistan was born. The coup was the result of a series of accidents (discussed in chapter 10), not of Soviet intrigue as many believe. But Soviet influence, unwelcome as it is to the bulk of the Afghan population, has been dominant since the Soviet intervention of December 1979, and the resulting war took a grisly toll. The constitution of 1987 is a combination of Islam plus communism designed by the Democratic Republic of Afghanistan to present a facade of independence.

The post–World War II period was characterized by intense competition between the United States and the USSR to gain friends and influence people. The Soviets were obviously more successful than the Americans in creating indigenous cadres. Influence in varying degrees was also exerted by the American Peace Corps, and by French and German technical assistants. Modernization was carried out both by foreigners and by Afghans trained in foreign universities or other institutions. These two sets of specialists reinforced each other's concepts and prejudices about development, but seldom did either understand Afghan cultural patterns, particularly in the rural areas.

Outer Mongolia, which became the third independent state in Inner Asia, had long been a traditional area of Chinese-Russian rivalry. The Chinese revolution of October 10, 1911, was greeted in Urga by a proclamation of Mongolian independence in December 1911. (For the Chinese Republic, 1912 is Year One, whereas for the Mongolian Republic, Year One is 1911.) The Tripartite Treaty of Kyakhta of June 1915, signed by representatives of tsarist Russia, the Chinese Republic, and the Mongolian Republic, set the borders of what in 1921 became the Mongolian People's Republic (MPR). The period 1911–1921 witnessed decreasing Russian activity in Mongolia, as the First World War and the Bolshevik Revolution distracted Russian attention from that area. Anti-Chinese nationalism grew as the Chinese general Hsü Shu-cheng and his troops late in 1919 returned to Urga and revoked the autonomous status of Mongolia. When in 1921 the anti-Bolshevik Baron von Ungern-Sternberg took Urga out of the hands of the Chinese and proclaimed himself ruler of Mongolia, he inadvertently created the pretext for the Red Army's entry into Mongolia and for what has turned out to be a lasting Soviet military presence in the country.

Since 1921 Soviet influence has far outweighed Chinese influence in the Mongolian People's Republic. The Mongolian People's party, formed in 1920 in Urga—renamed Ulan Bator, or "Red Hero," in 1921—held its first party conference in Kyakhta, in the USSR, in March 1921, and its earliest members were oriented toward the USSR, not China. When Suke Bator, the leader of the revolution of 1921, met with Lenin in November 1921, the basic premises of the USSR-MPR relationship and advice on how the MPR should develop were dictated by Lenin: the Mongols were advised that Mongolia was strategically important to the Soviet Union. This was true not only with regard to the menace of White Army troops and a potential Chinese threat, but in the 1930s and 1940s with regard to the Japanese military presence in Northeast Asia. The Mongols were also advised to bypass capitalism by forming "islands of socialism" in their economy, and to develop a proletariat.

The impact of Soviet domination over the MPR has been felt in the economic realm—the first futile attempt at collectivization occurred from 1929 to 1932— and in the religious realm—the 1930s saw government persecution of Buddhism and the closing of most monasteries. Since the late 1950s and early 1960s the Soviets and several East European countries have poured substantial aid into the MPR to create an industrial base for the economy. The Soviet decision to create and build up the industrial city of Darkhan in the north of the MPR was in part motivated by a Chinese offer to send in a three-hundred-thousand-man labor force and build a steel mill for the Mongols in 1960. The offer was refused under Soviet pressure (M56, pp. 81–82). Chinese laborers were first sent to the MPR in 1955 and several buildings and bridges in Ulan Bator were constructed by them. They were expelled from the MPR in 1962 as Sino-Soviet relations deteriorated.

Every year thousands of Mongolian workers go to the USSR, Czechoslovakia, East Germany, and other socialist countries on industrial training sabbaticals. Since the late 1920s, over twenty-seven thousand Mongolian students have studied in the USSR and in "other fraternal countries" (M36, p. 42). There is little doubt that Soviet influence will continue to predominate in the MPR.

The twentieth-century history of Inner Mongolia, by contrast, consists of the efforts of various Chinese (warlord, Kuomintang, and Chinese Communist) groups to win by military force, negotiation, or some combination thereof, the support of the Mongolian people. The Mongols of Inner Mongolia seem to have been wary of all such attempts to win them over, regardless of the benefits promised to them. As early as 1911, Mongols who were aware of the then-current revolutionary slogans of Sun Yat-sen were alarmed by the implication that Manchus and by extension Mongols were to be condemned for their past history of conquest and rule of China (M26, p. 103).

The overall lack of popularity of Han Chinese administration in Inner Mongolia explains the appeal of the Japanese to certain elements within the Mongolian population in the 1930s. Within the puppet state of Manchukuo, created in March 1932 by the Japanese, a Mongolian region called Hsingan was founded. The Japanese attempted to cultivate Mongolian loyalties by establishing Mongolian-language schools and by actively supporting the Buddhist establishment. Indeed, the Kanjurwa Khutughtu, a high-ranking reincarnation from Inner Mongolia, recalled the "gracious hospitality" his Japanese hosts extended to him and to several other lamas during their 1943 visit to Japan (M24, p. 152). It seems that many Mongols in Inner Mongolia preferred Japanese sovereignty to Kuomintang overlordship. When the Japanese withdrew from Inner Mongolia and China, many Mongols in Inner Mongolia opted for the Chinese Communists, who promised the creation of an autonomous region, over the Kuomintang.

In Sinkiang, even before the fall of the Ch'ing dynasty, foreign influence was evident in the creation of garrisons, most importantly Urumchi, to which Chinese and Manchu soldiers were dispatched. Even today, some of the few remaining groups of Manchu speakers in Sinkiang are the descendants of these soldiers. This process created a pattern of strategically conceived settlements in the territory alongside the more economically and culturally determined patterns that already existed. Major demographic change, however, did not come until after the Chinese revolution in 1949, which was accompanied by massive Chinese immigration.

Foreign military intervention was repeatedly an important factor, and Western armaments had facilitated the Ch'ing conquest in the nineteenth century. In the early twentieth century, Sinkiang's Chinese rulers looked to Britain and Moscow for small-scale assistance. Moscow, however, became deeply involved in the territory's development beginning in the 1930s, when it apparently engineered the coup that brought Sheng Shih-ts'ai to power (A5, pp. 283ff., O18). Soviet troops entered Sinkiang in the following year to crush the rebellions and help Sheng consolidate his rule. When rebellion broke out again in 1937, Soviet assistance was once more critical.

This Soviet military role was accompanied by political influence and economic privilege. After 1937, internal affairs were in the hands of Soviet security police, while Soviet companies developed Sinkiang's oil and mineral deposits. To many it appeared that sooner or later Sinkiang would be incorporated into the USSR.

The German invasion of the USSR, however, forced the withdrawal of many Soviet forces, and the initial poor Soviet showing apparently encouraged Sheng to consider activating his nominal ties with the Chinese government in Nanking. The complex maneuvers that followed led to the eclipse of Soviet influence in the area, and Sheng's departure for Nanking. In 1944 a revolt in Kuldja marked an apparent Soviet attempt to reassert influence, but it ended in 1945 when Moscow seems to have shifted focus to Manchuria in the northeast.

Chinese influence, thus reestablished by the Nanking government at the end of the Second World War, was jeopardized, however, by the outcome of the civil war. Although that conflict brought the Chinese Communist armies of Wang Chen into Sinkiang, the new regime appeared pro-Soviet, and Mao Tse-tung himself acquiesced in the reestablishment after 1950 of many features of the earlier period of Soviet influence, including so-called joint-stock Sino-Soviet companies for the development of Sinkiang's resources.

But Chinese political power in Sinkiang grew steadily in the early 1950s. It was supported by the influx of troops, many of whom were employed in agriculture and construction, and wave upon wave of Chinese immigrants. In the wake of Stalin's death, the USSR made many concessions to China, the joint-stock companies were dissolved, and Soviet influence effectively ended.

Chinese policy in Sinkiang generally presents itself as being popularly based, as drawing on the emergent sense of local identity that other powers had sought to crush as the basis for revolutionary incorporation into the People's Republic of China. The reality of the Chinese role, however, has been rather different, and the same sorts of tensions between local identity, religion, and political loyalty that characterized earlier periods have persisted, and at times been exacerbated by events.

The Great Leap Forward, for example, created severe problems: hunger and political dissatisfaction led in 1962 to street demonstrations, and the flight of an estimated seventy thousand Kazakhs to the Soviet Union. Some five years later, the Cultural Revolution was similarly disruptive: fighting was reported between the local population and Chinese immigrants at oil fields, and wholesale sinification policies led to bitterness, fanned by the USSR through radio broadcasts. But since Mao Tse-tung's death in 1976, Chinese policy toward the region has become, superficially at least, more tolerant.

These fundamental shifts in military hegemony have been accompanied by economic and cultural developments. In traditional times, Sinkiang was linked to Central Asia by the caravan trade. As this lost its relative importance, the territory gradually became reoriented toward Russia, particularly after railroads made European Russia relatively accessible from Asia. The Russian orientation continued into the 1950s, but then the completion of the railway from China to Urumchi, and the political turn away from Moscow, brought Sinkiang, somewhat unnaturally, back into a primary economic relationship with China proper. In the post-Mao period, trade across the Soviet border began once again, and the Soviet-Chinese rivalry continues to be a factor in the area.

In Tibet likewise, Chinese influence has not gone unchallenged. In spite of the well-taken argument that no central government of China in modern times has exercised "effective authority" in Tibet (A15, p. 4), the one constant foreign presence in Tibet's twentieth-century history has been that of the Chinese. In the period before 1950, however, Chinese influence was somewhat restricted in the military sphere.

After the 1911 revolution in China and the withdrawal of Ch'ing troops from Tibet, the British attempted once more to become involved in determining Tibet's status, this time—in 1914—proposing that Tibet become a buffer zone between China and India. The British convened a conference in India to discuss the creation of a Tibetan buffer zone; the Tibetan delegate to the conference was given status equal to that of the Chinese and British delegates (D6, p. 35). The delegates agreed to a convention dividing Tibet into an outer zone (the areas of

Lhasa, Shigatse, and Chamdo) that would exercise self-administration, and an inner zone (most of eastern Tibet) subject to a Chinese military and administrative presence. China's republican government, however, would not ratify the convention.

The Chinese Republic late in 1917 stationed administrative representatives in eastern Tibet, but for most of the period from the 1920s through the 1940s Tibet, while paying lip service to the Nationalist government, was left on its own. Kuomintang interference in Tibet's internal affairs, as in the case of Kuomintang involvement in the selection of a reincarnation as successor to the ninth Panchen Lama who had died while residing in China, was much resented by Tibetans. The Lhasa government meanwhile chose a different young reincarnation to be the tenth Panchen Lama.

The Lhasa government's expulsion of representatives of the Chinese Nationalist government from Tibet in July 1949 was accompanied by a declaration of Tibet's independence from China. The Chinese Communists, however, chose to interpret Tibet's declaration of independence as the product of British and American agents in Tibet, though in 1949 there were no Americans and only three British citizens there (D6, p. 88). Tibet, for its part, had not taken advantage of its de facto independence for the four decades before the arrival of the Chinese People's Liberation Army in 1950. The Tibetan army, which had not drilled since 1933, was unprepared for the events of 1950. Any hope for British involvement in determining Tibet's future waned as Britain was engaged in granting India its independence. At this point it was evident that Tibet's future would be tied directly to Chinese policies and priorities.

Soviet influence has been predominant in Central Asia since its reconquest in 1917–1921, and the territorial and linguistic demarcation of the five Central Asian republics from 1924 on guaranteed fragmentation of the political landscape. It divided the region culturally and linguistically, and prescribed a major new social role for Russians. The determined attack on the fundamental institutions, structures, and elites of the traditional society in the 1930s represented a concerted attempt to eradicate the traditional cultural markers and characteristics of the local society in order to clear the landscape for "internationalist" patterns introduced from Moscow. In later years, especially during the Brezhnev administration, there was a substantial and structurally significant respite. Since 1985 Soviet influence has once again been intensified, and the central question now is how crude an approach will be taken by Moscow in the latest crackdown on Central Asian mores, and how broad ranging Moscow's intent to transform might be across the political, economic, social, and cultural spectrum. Can Moscow achieve an effective balance between international and national themes and motifs in its approaches to reform in the system, or will it overstep sensitive bounds in imposing new restrictions on the highly valued semi-autonomy of these peoples?

Within the framework of Soviet predominance, consideration should be given to Turkey, Iran, Afghanistan, and China, each of which has exerted a variety of peripheral influences in Soviet Central Asia over the last decade. Because of strong linguistic and cultural associations, Turkey has been of substantial interest to the Muslim peoples of the region, and formal exchanges established in the 1980s as Moscow has sought a more stable relationship with Ankara have brought an expansion of contacts. The particular brand of fundamentalist Islam practiced in Khomeini's post-1979 Iran has presented a special set of challenges for Moscow's management of its Central Asian landscape. The potential attraction of such patterns, should crude mismanagement by Moscow trigger serious new anti-European attitudes among Soviet Muslims, deserves careful analysis. This potential trend may have been reinforced by the protracted, costly, and brutal Soviet presence in Afghanistan, where ethnic and religious attitudes might eventually take on destabilizing forms because of the impression of Russian contempt for these populations. The competitive example of China could also come into play in important ways, as a more sophisticated and flexible approach taken by Peking in the 1980s introduced a series of improvements in the situation of the Muslim and Turkic peoples of Sinkiang and western China.

The Challenge of Modernity

The international environment plays a vital role in the way later-modernizing societies meet the challenge of modernity. For their leaders it is not an abstract issue of how they can adapt their cultural heritages to the new functions made possible by the revolution in science and technology, but rather the very practical one of selecting among competing foreign models and negotiating among domestic interest groups over the extent to which the heritage of institutions and values can be preserved.

Typically, as in the case of Iran, the adoption of modernizing reforms was accepted as a goal by most leaders, but they disagreed about the priority that should be accorded to this objective and about the price to be paid for technological achievement. This disagreement came to be expressed most clearly by the secular technocrats and the clerical leaders. Underlying the ideological gap was the ever-present struggle for temporal power that marks Shi'ite ambivalence about the legitimacy of earthly rulers.

A corollary to this basic disagreement related to the extent to which foreign experts should engage in management as opposed to technical services. The tendency in the modern period had been to train Iranians to take over technical aspects of modernization, from the military to the oil industry. But the technocrats, trained overseas and in Iran itself, were disturbed by the relationship of modernization to their basic values. For some the conflict occurred on a purely subliminal level. In the process of absorbing modern technology they rejected traditional values without a conscious decision. For others, making decisions became very painful. In an atmosphere where discussion of such matters implied adoption of unacceptable political attitudes, the necessity for decision became a part of political action.

In addition, the official recognition of the dilemma of modernization was complicated by the secular nationalist answers vigorously promoted by the monarchy. In effect, the traditional values of Iran were distorted through a nationalist prism that filtered out traditional religion and morality and adopted values based on the creation of secular Iranian traditions hinging on twenty-five hundred years of monarchal history. The stress on Iranian nationalism at the expense of Islam made it easy for Iranians to blame foreigners and foreign influence for the vacuum in their lives created by this voiding of their past. The technocrats elevated to managerial positions were ill equipped to deal with the philosophy of modernization. The petroleum windfall allowed them to offer financial answers to nonmaterial questions. Dissenters could be bought off with foreign fellowships, lofty positions, and fancy equipment. Meanwhile the challenge to modernization as wholesale rejection of the reality of the past could be ignored. But only so long. When oil revenues declined and totalitarian resolve crumbled, the dissenters rose to assert themselves. The modernization paradigm gave way to other priorities such as purging a corrupt society and renewal on the basis of moral Islamic models that predated technical modernization.

Similarly in Afghanistan, the abortive reforms proposed by King Amanullah struck at the vitals of traditional Afghan cultural patterns, and the culture struck back. Later attempts at internal reforms came from the external impact on Afghanistan's growing intelligentsia, educated within local foreign-language high schools, with advanced education in the outside world, mainly Western Europe and the United States, but also some in the USSR and Japan. The "Liberal Parliament" (1949–1952) was a noble experiment that failed. Encouraged by Western-educated young Afghans, Prime Minister Shah Mahmud made modest attempts to bring about free elections. Of the 120 members elected to the parliament, 40–50 were reform minded. They questioned individual ministers about budgetary matters, and in a nation where corruption often served as a major path to riches and power, such investigations can deeply upset entrenched patterns.

The first administration of Mohammed Daoud left behind several significant reforms. In the short period of a decade, Afghanistan moved from relative inaction to relative action. The solid achievements are many: a reaffirmed nonaligned policy brought in increased foreign aid, from both East and West, the impact of which initially appeared to be beneficial, but also was partly responsible for the Soviet intervention.

Although most of Daoud's achievements related to the economic establishment, probably his most important legacy was the voluntary removal of the veil from the women and the abolition of purdah, moves that struck at the roots of ultraconservative Islam and directed women toward the mainstream of Afghan life, particularly in the urban areas.

A much wider range of reforms was instituted under the Democratic Republic of Afghanistan after it came to power in 1978, but these alienated virtually every segment of Afghan society.

In Mongolia, wedged between the Soviet Union and China, ideas and strategies for modernization inevitably came via its two neighbors. The foremost Buriat Mongolian scholar of Mongolian culture and early revolutionary leader Jamtsarano is said to have hoped that Mongolia would be "neutral like Switzerland" (M56, p. 34; M5, p. 809, n. 54). For such an idea and for his attempts to find common ground between Marxism-Leninism and Buddhism, Jamtsarano was labeled a petit-bourgeois nationalist, a rightist agitator, and a subverter of Mongolian-Soviet relations (M5, p. 233). Jamtsarano was arrested in Leningrad in 1937 and never resurfaced.

The MPR purges of the 1930s, a replica of Soviet events, narrowed the path to modernization, allowing only one option—following Soviet-dictated policy. An alternative political-cultural option, pan-Mongolism, did not survive long enough to come to grips with questions of modernization. Pan-Mongolism, especially in reference to the desire for a union between Outer and Inner Mongolia, predated the revolution of 1921 and reemerged during the 1930s with greater support. The Japanese manipulation of both the pan-Mongolist and pan-Buddhist movements in Inner Mongolia in order to extend Japanese influence and criticize Soviet persecution of the Buddhist establishment in the 1930s only reinforced Soviet and MPR official condemnation of those movements.

In spite of avowed aims of building up a proletariat and an industrial base, the MPR's road to modernization via industrialization has been rather slow, in part because the Soviets in the decade after the Second World War assigned low priority to aiding Mongolia's development. During the 1950s very little industrialization occurred. It was only in the 1960s that the Soviets invested in the development of the city of Darkhan (a flour mill), and it was not until the 1970s that the Soviets created the industrial center of Erdenet where copper and molybdenum are mined. Both cities lie in the northern railway corridor between Ulan Bator and the Soviet border.

From the Soviet point of view, successful modernization in a traditionally nomadic country such as Mongolia must be accompanied by the sedentarization of the herding population. Sedentarization is achieved along two main avenues: first, by convincing part of the pastoral-nomadic population to change livelihoods, that is, to become involved in trade, transport, construction, agriculture, government, and service industries; second, by encouraging herdsmen and their families to join collectives and to change their ways of raising livestock (B4, pp. 120–121). Yet both the Soviet and Mongolian governments have been hesitant to commit the necessary aid to modernize livestock production or to risk the social upheaval that might accompany such enforced modernization. Full-scale sedentarization, which at least one Mongolian economist has predicted will occur soon after the year 2000, and which in Soviet theory is a prerequisite to the modernization of Mongolia, seems unlikely to occur (B4, pp. 79–80).

Likewise in the territories under Chinese sovereignty, the indigenous peoples played only a limited role in promoting economic growth and social change. *Tibet's declaration of independence* in 1949 had no practical results. Its historical isolation, continuing up through 1949, combined with its lack of experience in international diplomacy, prevented any effective effort by the Lhasa government to convince foreign powers of Tibet's legitimate status as an independent nation. Other factors in addition to isolation and lack of diplomatic ties contributed to Tibet's failure to achieve nationhood and independence from China.

Primary among these factors in 1949 was the lack of unity among Tibetans themselves. The feud between the Dalai Lama and the Panchen Lama, a feud that had continued long after the deaths of the two original rivals, benefited only the Chinese. Whereas the Nationalist government in the 1930s and 1940s had not been able to take full advantage of this division in the Tibetan Buddhist hierarchy, the Chinese Communists from the very beginning were quite astute in manipulating the pro-Chinese Panchen Lama and his followers. Traditional tensions between secular and ecclesiastical authorities, as well as tensions between Lhasa and local authorities, also made Tibetan unity in the face of a Chinese military challenge virtually impossible. Thus, by default it was the Chinese who determined Tibet's path to modernization. The traditional isolation that had helped preserve Tibetans' cultural identity so well proved to be a negative factor in the political arena.

In confronting the challenge of modernity, *Sinkiang* has absorbed ideas from other parts of Central Asia, from British India, from Russia and the USSR, and from China, in a sequence that follows, roughly, that of political influence. In the present, which appears to be a period of cultural redefinition for China, changes are underway in Sinkiang, such as the officially sanctioned rebuilding of mosques, that suggest the same sort of process is going on in Sinkiang as well.

In Sinkiang both the challenge of modernity and the framework for local response have been determined by foreign powers, and indeed much of the work that has contributed to twentieth-century modernization has been carried out by foreigners, mostly Russian and Chinese. Furthermore, the purpose of much of this work has as often as not been strategic: like London and Moscow in earlier periods, Peking has been above all concerned with securing Sinkiang against foreign conquest, and it has been easier to do this by implanting a more-or-less self-sufficient Chinese establishment in the territory, with the Chinese in a majority in the north, than by winning the loyalty of the local people and fostering their development.

This process appears to be irreversible and means that, barring some extraordinary development, Sinkiang will remain part of the People's Republic of China. It nevertheless bypasses, rather than solves, the problem of modernity for the local people. Furthermore, by defining modernity in terms that are culturally alien to them, it makes it likely that they will seek culturally more congenial models, perhaps from Islamic and Middle Eastern sources. These, in turn, will prove politically troublesome for the larger polity, in China as already in the USSR.

In Soviet Central Asia the original revolutionary experience offered the promise of federalism and internationalism, but the potential cohesiveness of the area was undercut when the basic tribal structures were very early divided into somewhat artificial and competing political units. The traditional social institutions were subjected to devastating attacks in the 1930s as old elites and cultural patterns were crushed to clear the landscape for Soviet internationalism. The attendant purge was an external mechanism imposed on the region by dominant Slav outsiders. The ethnic minorities received new breathing space and social latitude after the death of Stalin, and especially after the accession of Brezhnev. From 1965 to 1985 they were able to evolve a significant pattern of relative semi-autonomy in local economic growth, social change, and cultural development. This degree of indigenous initiative was permitted by Moscow in return for tacit guarantees of public order and continued adherence to the regime. These groups used this period to develop a substantial parallel second economy, important patterns of petty political and judicial corruption, and an intense literary and artistic search for ancient ethnic and cultural roots and sources of identity. The period came to an end in 1985 with Gorbachev's appointment and the beginnings of a revived Soviet internationalism. Whatever the specific features of this internationalism, its basic approaches might well be perceived by the indigenous peoples of the Central Asian republics, indeed by Soviet minorities as a whole, as a new form of russification. The care and finesse employed in such approaches—or the lack thereof—will strongly condition their success or failure.

Conclusions and Comparisons

The societies of Inner Asia have not fared very well in their confrontation with the international environment in the twentieth century. And by the late 1980s only Iran and Mongolia were functioning as independent states. The reasons for this political weakness vary with the circumstances of the individual societies, but at a general level they reflect an inability to form viable political systems.

Of the Inner Asia societies, only Mongolia and Tibet did not face serious problems of identity because of ethnic, religious, or tribal differences. The others to a greater or lesser degree had weaker identities than most European societies on the eve of the modern era, and their problems of achieving unity out of diversity resembled more those of the new African states. Japan was of course unique in its sense of identity, while in both China and Russia the dominant ethnic group was sufficiently strong to hold their societies together. The Ottoman Empire, on the other hand, was less firmly controlled. By the end of World War I almost all of its minority peoples had seceded.

It is interesting to note that in Iran and Afghanistan the process of state formation resembled that in Germany and Italy in the nineteenth century. Within the framework of internationally recognized frontiers, the Persians in Iran, and the Pushtun in Afghanistan—like the Prussians in Germany and the Piedmontese in Italy—sought to create national entities out of a population divided by ethnic, religious, and other local loyalties. In Iran this effort was essentially successful, despite the continuing opposition of Azeri and Kurds. In Afghanistan the central government never gained full control over the countryside, and its nationhood remained something of a fiction even at the end of the twentieth century.

Although Tibet and Mongolia possessed the sense of identity called for by modern nation building, they lacked the capacity to meet the challenge of modernity that might have given them the ability to avoid foreign domination. In neither case did they take advantage of the opportunity provided by their relative independence after the fall of the Ch'ing dynasty—a period of four decades in the case of Tibet, and one in the case of Mongolia—to reorient their societies toward a more modern way of life. This task was left to the Soviet hegemony in Mongolia after the 1920s and to the more drastic methods applied by the Chinese in Tibet after the 1950s. This is not to say that even under modernizing leadership the Tibetans or the Mongols would have been able to play a more active role under foreign rule. The Tibetans in particular, protected by their mountain fastnesses and endowed with a government potentially capable of mobilizing skill and resources, neglected an opportunity to undertake economic growth and social change that would have greatly strengthened the case for independence they were later to make.

The other peoples of Inner Asia, the Kazakhs, Kirgiz, Tajiks, Turkmen, and Uzbeks, and the Uighurs in Sinkiang, had neither the sense of identity nor the political skill to confront—or even to recognize—the challenge of modernity. They were entirely overshadowed by their Russian and Chinese overlords and have become minority peoples in terms of political powers—and in some cases in numbers as well—within their own territories.

10

Political Development

Introduction

We examine the political structures of the societies of Inner Asia, and the ways in which they have developed over the course of the twentieth century, in terms of the distribution of political power, the role of leadership and participation in policy making, and their capacity to mobilize skills and resources.

At a very general level, our knowledge of what to look for is derived from the experience of the earlier-modernizing societies. At a more specific level, however, we are concerned with the ways in which the premodern institutions of the Inner Asian societies have been adapted to the challenges of the modern era, the debates within each society on how much of the traditional heritage should be kept and to what extent foreign institutions should be borrowed, and the outcome of this process. The policies that a society should adopt in relation to these issues have never failed to be a subject of great domestic controversy, leading to revolution and other forms of violence. We wish to understand both the commonalities among the societies of Inner Asia and the differences that divide them.

One of the political characteristics of the modern era about which there is little disagreement is the accumulation of political power by central governments at the expense of local political, ethnic, religious, and tribal organizations. The great empires and autocracies of earlier centuries are often referred to as exercising a heavy hand on the peoples they ruled, but in fact their bureaucracies were small and did not extend much beyond control of the cities and regulation of trade. The villages, where four-fifths of the population lived, were more often than not scarcely aware that a central government existed.

Even by 1900, after a century of state building and nationalism, government expenditures in Western Europe and the United States amounted to only some 5 percent of gross national product. By 1930 this figure had reached 10–15 percent, and by the 1980s it had risen to 35–55 percent. This is only one indicator of the redistribution of political power that has occurred in the West, but it illustrates dramatically the political changes that are characteristic of the modern era. Comparable indicators for later-modernizing societies are not available, but it seems safe to assume that the concentration of political power in central governments is roughly proportional to the level of development measured by economic and social indicators.

The political aspect of modernization is characterized not only by the centralization of political power but also by greater cooperation in policy making between leaders and individuals and groups. The particular form this takes depends on the political culture of a society. In predominantly democratic societies, interest representation interacts with individual participation through the electoral system. In predominantly authoritarian political systems, interests are represented exclusively through bureaucratic, economic, and other organizations. In the last analysis individuals are of course the only participants in policy formation, but there is a wide range of patterns of influence between individuals acting alone or as members or leaders of organizations.

Modernizing leaders exert influence from the top down, and interest groups from the bottom up. Were the various assemblies and parliaments established in Inner Asia in the twentieth century imposed from above (imitating Western institutions), or did they arise from internal pressures? Did the major interest groups (landowners, clergy, bazaar merchants, intellectuals, tribal leaders, ethnic minorities, and others) press their claims chiefly through representative institutions, or by other means such as direct pressures on the bureaucracy, lobbies, violence, and various forms of bargaining?

The evolving capacity of political systems to mobilize skills and resources is another useful indicator of their modern development. Traditional societies were able to mobilize armies, usually through the intermediary of local elites; to control towns and bazaars, guilds, and religious establishments; to tax domestic and foreign trade; and to build great cathedrals, public buildings, and monuments in a few central cities. As with political authority more generally, however, such premodern mobilization affected only a small portion of the population.

At a later stage of development, governments built railroads and established educational institutions, although usually this could be accomplished only with foreign assistance. Only a highly developed government, however, has the capacity to administer value-added and personal-income taxes. Advanced industrial societies usually pride themselves on the prosperity and freedom of their citizens, but they exert far greater control over their income and property than the most oppressive of traditional empires.

Distribution of Political Power

In Inner Asia the question of political centralization arises principally in the independent states of Iran, Afghanistan, and Mongolia. In the societies that became territories of the Soviet Union and China, by contrast, a variety of adjustments had to be made to the centralizing tendencies of the two multinational states.

In the case of Iran, the change in perceptions of where political authority should lie emerged during the Constitutional Revolution. Surviving periods of political freedom and repression, the ideas articulated between 1905 and 1910 continued to mold the theories about the distribution of political power. With the withering of Qajar authority after World War I and the emergence of new power elites, whether Iran continued as a monarchy or accepted republican government as had Turkey lay in balance. Finally, in 1925, the former Cossack colonel Reza, having eliminated his constitutionalist allies, crowned himself and proceeded to acquire the accoutrements of monarchy: lands, wealth, a court, a military, and a royal lineage linked to the last non-Muslim dynasty of Iran. The dynastic name, Pahlavi, refers to this past.

But Reza Shah became far more than a mere replacement for a previous monarch. He became the sole source of power in the country and the wellspring of modernization as he recognized that process. Autocratic and authoritarian, he forced through projects that had languished for decades before. The most notable of his modernization projects lay in the fields of secular education, communications, and the military. The last he restructured from personal armies and a professional Cossack brigade into a modern conscript army with an able, well rewarded officer corps. This became his base of power in confrontation with those who sought to challenge his authority, particularly among the central tribes of the country. Despite the presence of a legislature decreed by constitutional law to share political authority, Reza Shah usurped all political power. He also consolidated political power by eliminating the historic challengers of central authority—the ethnic groups, Islamic forces, and traditional landed power elements.

International events forced the collapse of his form of one-man rule in 1941, when he abdicated to save his heir's position and died an exile in Johannesburg. His son, only nineteen upon accession, had neither the experience and opportunity, nor originally the inclination, to follow his father's authoritarian pattern of rule. From 1942 to 1953, therefore, political power became dispersed among various groups including emerging political parties. The legislature, long a rubber stamp for the monarch, asserted its position as did successive prime ministers. The presence of foreigners, especially that of Soviet troops in Azerbaijan who remained despite international agreement even after the end of war hostilities, encouraged the formation of autonomous ethnic regions, as well as the Iranian Communist party (Tudeh) which asserted its power and gained many adherents as the best organized organ for political dissent.

The rise of Mohammed Mossadegh and the collapse of his regime marked the end of the phase of jockeying for redistribution of political power. Clerical elements, National Democrats, and the Tudeh as well as other nationalist Iranians, rallied around the issue of the nationalization of the oil industry. This issue also became involved in a struggle over the form of government. Fleeing into exile, the shah returned only when outside intervention and internal dissent cut short the possibility of a viable alternative government. With his return, the shah relied heavily on the military forces that had cooperated in his return, and continued to build his base of power within the military structure. Devices to create acceptable forms of political participation through centrally created political parties, alternately two-party and one-party systems, all failed. As the single largest employer in the country, the government was able to require membership in these parties, but not participation, loyalty, dedication, or faith in them. Real political action took place outside the official parties. From 1953 to the overthrow of the Pahlavi monarchy and the declaration of a republic in 1979, the opposing forces occasionally took action but more often remained impassively watching.

Political power alignments leading to the overthrow of Mohammed Reza Shah coalesced around Ayatollah Ruhollah Khomeini, a cleric who had been exiled subsequent to his role in leading the 1963 riots in Tehran. These riots, manned by bazaar elements, had been supported by the National Freedom Front, the heir to Mossadegh. Although suppressed by paratroopers and the Iranian secret police (SAVAK), the two factions, secular nationalists and religious elements, remained potent though quiet forces within the country, ready to re-emerge. The active dissenters of the 1960s and 1970s within the country and abroad became the youth and student elements who launched urban guerrilla war with much loss of life to SAVAK. Among the two most important of political-action youth organizations were the Mujahidin-e Khalq (Islamic Fighters for the Masses) and the Fadayin-e Khalq (The Sacrificers for the Masses). Royalist propaganda attempted to paint both groups as Marxist and Communist, and indeed splinter or branch groups in these umbrella organizations did espouse various shades of secular or religious socialism. But in fact few links were formed with the pro-Soviet Tudeh party, which remained aloof from the opposition groups and has generally been regarded as patently Moscow's surrogate since the 1940s.

Just as it had been surprised by the religiously led riots of 1963 but willing to lend its support, so too the National Front cooperated in the demonstrations that led to the removal of the monarchy. The youth groups too fought for the same ends in 1979. The surprise for both youth groups and the National Front came when the clerical group eased both factions out of effective political leadership. Although the National Front continues to be represented in the legislature, its role in policy making and implementation is minimal. The youth groups, on the other hand, have resumed their external and internal opposition activities. The alignment of the Mujahidin-e Khalq with Iraq in the Iran-Iraq war has seriously diminished its credibility in the country.

As for the monarchists, their position, stated from exile, was adversely affected by the Iran-Iraq war which elicited a strong nationalist response. While some old upper-level bureaucratic families are resigned to exile, others wage war against the revolution from Iraq. The pretender to the throne remains uncommitted to leadership.

Throughout the period of turmoil, political authority remained little better distributed than it was in other periods of instability, although it may be said that the will of the urban and rural underclasses is better served. This does not mean that these groups have become politically active or involved, but rather that the current clerical leadership reflects better their value system. The effect of a less confrontational alignment of people and authority now than in the period of the Pahlavis may bode well for successful technical modernization. The fact that Iran was able to mount a technically modern war under the reign of clerics may indicate a workable relationship exists between technical modernization and traditional Iranian values.

Political leaders in Afghanistan, unlike those in Iran, have made little progress in unifying the country. The amirs and kings have often been repressive, but they have not achieved national unity. Each successive ruler has been first among equals, unless he was able to accrue power by armed force, or take advantage of regional rivalries, or both.

To introduce change from the top, as Amanullah attempted to do, a national leader needed a base of power. If the power did not come from the traditional tribal, ethnolinguistic, and religious elites, it had to come from a loyal, effective military—often combined with an efficient secret police system.

Amanullah had been impressed by the modernizing strides taken by Ataturk, Reza Shah, and Stalin, and he returned from his European tour of 1927–1928 eager to tackle his reform programs: education, reshaping a corruptible bureaucracy, women's rights, free elections, and a parliamentary system.

Ataturk had warned Amanullah not to start large-scale social and political reforms without a strong army, and promised to send some of his best officers to train the Afghans. Amanullah, however, always underestimated the relationship of force to drastic reforms and announced elaborate programs immediately on his return from Europe. The Turkish officers arrived, but too late to do anything but observe the debacle that followed.

A key figure in Amanullah's ideological growth was his father-in-law, Mahmud Tarzi. All his life, Mahmud Tarzi had preached reform, but he always recommended a strong foundation. He advised the reorganization of the government administration with the help of Ataturk's Turks. He wanted the king to raise the salaries of civil servants in order to fight bribery, and Tarzi agreed with Ataturk on the importance of a loyal army to combat regional power elites and conservative religious elements that opposed reforms.

Before the end came in 1929, Amanullah had surrounded himself with "yes men." Even the venerable Tarzi left the entourage, his advice unheeded. Amanullah's plans collapsed with cruel swiftness. Tribal, regional, religious, and conservative literates combined to overthrow the regime.

General Mohammed Nadir returned from his self-imposed exile in France and successfully overthrew Amanullah's successor, the Tajik usurper Habibullah II, in 1929. The non-Pushtun tribes of the north, with few exceptions, supported Habibullah II, but the Pushtun of the south and east of Afghanistan and several Pushtun tribes in British India joined Nadir Khan's *lashkar* (tribal army) as it marched toward Kabul.

The successful overthrow of Habibullah II by Mohammed Nadir Khan heralded the return of the Mohammadzai Durrani lineage to power, a period that lasted until 1973. The assassination of Nadir Shah by a tribal rival in 1933 brought his son Mohammed Zahir to the throne. Zahir Shah reigned but did not rule until 1953.

A generational shift took place in 1953 when a first cousin and brother-in-law of Zahir Shah, Lt. General Mohammed Daoud, seized power in a bloodless palace coup. The first administration of Daoud broadened the base of secular political power and somewhat diminished the political power of the religious establishment. With Daoud's resignation in 1963, a new era began: an attempt to create a constitutional monarchy based on "free" elections and a free press. Since Daoud's coup in 1973, the political scene has been clouded by several patterns: competition, at times violent, between the leftist factions, particularly Parcham (The Banner) and Khalq (The Masses); the Soviet effort since 1979 to pacify the countryside in association with the puppet army of the Democratic Republic of Afghanistan; limited unity among the resistance political groups in Peshawar; and growing regional unity among the resistance groups fighting inside Afghanistan—for the war was a regional war, not a unified war of national liberation.

Mongolia, unlike Iran and Afghanistan, entered the twentieth century without experience in independent government. When the Mongols of Outer Mongolia were preparing to declare their independence from China in November 1911, a message was delivered from the head of the Buddhist church in Outer Mongolia to the Manchu administrator of Urga which read in part: "The Mongols have decided to establish a Mongolian state with full powers, and to elevate the Jebtsundamba Khutughtu to be its Emperor, to defend all their territory and themselves" (M44, p. 108). For most Mongols of the early twentieth century, political power could be envisaged only in religious and imperial terms, as the wording of the above message shows. Who else but the head of the Outer Mongolian Buddhist ecclesiastical hierarchy could fill the political vacuum created by the departure of Ch'ing dynasty administrators? And how else could a head of state be envisioned other than as "emperor"?

When several thousand Red Army troops marched into Urga accompanied by about four hundred Mongolian troops and established a new revolutionary government, the Mongolian People's party had only twenty members altogether (M43, p. 28). The revolutionary government of 1921 was actually a dyarchy, with the Jebtsundamba Khutughtu as ceremonial head of state and the tiny Mongolian People's party under Soviet guidance training its cadres as administrators.

The Jebtsundamba Khutughtu provided in his person the only possible rallying point for the Mongols, and thus no attempt was made to wrest political power from him. Indeed, the ranks of the growing Mongolian People's Revolutionary party (MPRP; the name was changed in 1924) in the 1920s were filled with former lamas and princes—the only fully literate people in Mongolian society. Political power at this stage had to be shared with those who would eventually be condemned as "class enemies," and the crackdown on Buddhism had to wait until the 1930s.

As early as 1921–1923, however, what was to become a familiar pattern of managing political power had already emerged. Between the July 1921 revolution and the death of Suke Bator in February 1923, Suke Bator is credited with "discovering and liquidating" the first of several "counterrevolutionary enemies"; the hunt for enemies of the revolution had begun almost immediately (see M44, pp. 170–172). Just as Stalin was the only Bolshevik of the Politburo of thirteen to survive the 1930s, the Russian-educated Choibalsan (1895–1952) was the only one of the original "Khalkha Seven" (the first Mongolian delegation to go to the USSR in 1920 to request assistance) to live past 1939. Suke Bator died (probably from tuberculosis although the Buddhist church is officially accused of poisoning him) in 1923; two others were executed in 1922; one in 1924; and the remaining two in 1939 (M56, p. 30).

During the 1920s, political power was still shared with the church. In western Outer Mongolia, for instance, the membership of the MPRP consisted of only sixteen individuals in the Uliasutai region in 1922, and at least some of them came from a Buddhist background. The Diluv Khutughtu, a high-ranking reincarnation, was deemed progressive enough to be appointed governor of the western Mongolian town of Uliasutai in 1921. In 1930, however, faced with the government's confiscation of his property and with the accusation that he was a traitor with Japanese contacts, the Diluv Khutughtu fled as a political refugee into Inner Mongolia (see M33). With the death of the Jebtsundamba Khutughtu in 1924 and the government's refusal to allow a search for his reincarnation, the Buddhist church lost its symbolic leader and protector. Many Buddhists followed the Diluv Khutughtu's path of flight; those who remained faced full-scale governmental persecution in the 1930s.

Political authority had by the late 1930s become concentrated in the hands of party and government. The only potential rival for power—the Buddhist establishment—had been silenced. The formal outline of political leadership and participation as drawn up in the 1940 and 1960 constitutions is discussed in the following section.

Modernization in Soviet Central Asia has to a great extent resulted from Moscow's imposition of external political mechanisms and managerial structures driven by Slavic overseers. In the period following the establishment of Soviet power in Turkestan during the civil war, it was this externally imposed pattern that brought the question of modernization to the fore for the first time. The pattern has been strongly reinforced by the regime's successful recruitment and co-optation of indigenous ethnic elites, which helps to give the process regional coloration and shape and make it an organic part of the local landscape. The mixture of external imposition and local co-optation distinguishes the pattern of modernization in Central Asia from other patterns studied in this series.

The political elites in the prerevolutionary period were extraordinarily fragmented. The area that fell under the control of St. Petersburg and became known as Russian Central Asia had not enjoyed a unified political life for centuries. The northern, eastern, and western segments of this vast region were dominated by migratory nomadic groups, with the Kazakhs to the north, the Kazakh-Kirgiz groups to the east, and the Turkmen to the west. Furthermore, these separate groups did not individually enjoy a unified political life, but were internally divided into a sometimes bewildering variety of tribal, clan, and family subunits, all of them often competitive with each other. The southern and central segment of this region was dominated by the urban-based sedentary khanates of Bukhara and Kokand, and the emirate of Khiva, which were similarly constantly at loggerheads, each repeatedly attempting to expand its influence at the expense of the others.

The nomads on the periphery functioned under hierarchies of distinguished notables, *biys,* and chieftains, whose interests were local, parochial, and decidedly competitive with those of neighboring tribes and clans. The ruling khans and emir of the sedentary urban complexes were supported by extensive aristocratic oligarchies as well as by the conservative religious establishment of the Islamic theological schools. None of these groups was able to rise above its own petty interests and project a broader, common political vision for the region. They were unable to unite in the face of a common external danger when the Russian armies appeared in the steppe regions in the middle of the nineteenth century, and they continued not only to fight with each other as the Russian armies advanced, but often collaborated with the Russians to subjugate opposing clans and tribes for what they perceived to be short-term advantage.

Similarly, commercial groups within the cities often turned to the Russians for assistance against the ruling aristocracies of their own ethnic kinsmen for what they saw as the longer-run benefits of expanded trade with the rich and technologically advanced Russian metropolitan areas to the west. Liberal intellectual groups within the cities, often as the result of extended and creative cultural contact with Russian, other European, or Turkish sources from the outside, were alienated from the traditional religious communities of their own societies and came to play a similar anti-establishment role. Many of these *jadidist* reformists, either as individuals or groups, eventually sided with the advancing Russians. Embryonic political parties, in the very early stages of formation and with little or no political experience, such as the Young Khivans or Young Bukharans, frequently sided with the Bolshevik newcomers in the struggles that marked the period of the revolution and civil war. No one group was able to work out a persuasive and practical political vision to substitute for the imperial structure brought first by the tsarist, then the Bolshevik troops. Even the ultimate conquest by Russian troops was substantially aided and abetted by various indigenous ethnic forces participating by then in a virtual civil war.

When Russian forces initially came into Turkestan in the mid-nineteenth century, the decision was taken by tsarist authorities to concentrate all civil and military power in the hands of the military, permitting former local judicial institutions, as well as village political institutions to continue. The decision was similarly taken to avoid any intrusion into affairs of religion, thereby bolstering the authority of the traditional conservative establishment, retarding any liberalizing reformist trends, and inhibiting the emergence of any syncretist cultural movements that might have political consequences. Traditional political cleavages were thereby perpetuated, and native elite orientations were fragmented and retarded in their development.

By contrast, the establishment of Soviet power at the beginning of the 1920s witnessed a much more vigorous and intrusive effort both to suppress the power of traditional political elites and to impose new political forms on these indigenous communities. Basic political and developmental guidelines were evolved at the Moscow center, and the essential forms of party and governmental control were designed and imposed from the outside.

The successes of the Red Army secured the area for Soviet rule by the early 1920s, and the importance of that military arm should not be underestimated. The command structure of that force was then, and remains today, heavily Slavic, with the general staff and senior officers corps largely Russian, and a large percentage of the noncommissioned officers Ukrainian. Force distribution has also been important, with a basic principle of the military being that ethnic contingents by and large do not serve in their own republics or regions. This pattern has long served essential internal security considerations.

The establishment of Communist party control in the Central Asian regions was marked by a similar ethnic pattern. Based on Russian urban workers' groups working on the railways or in other industrial concentrations, the party organization was heavily influenced by Moscow and, through a variety of institutional lines of command and communication, retains that subordination. Party controls continue to take precedence over government organs, and the chain of authority leads clearly back to the all-Union center at Moscow.

Throughout the Soviet period, the Moscow center maintained firm political control over regional and political party and governmental establishments through both the *nomenklatura* system and the use of "second secretary" appointments to manage the apparatus. Key command positions and offices throughout the state and republican bureaucracies were reserved for nominations from a centrally approved list of candidates. These candidates were identified and selected by the central Moscow leadership for their political reliability and the personal patron-client subordination on which such reliability was built. Even in republican situations where the figurehead first secretary was an indigenous ethnic representative, real control within the apparatus flowed through the second secretary position, which was usually filled by a Slavic *nomenklatura* appointee from the Moscow center. Within these limits, native cadres came to fill the ranks not only of the lower and middle levels of the political structure in Central Asia, but of the upper levels as well, and began to play appropriate roles in carefully circumscribed decision-making functions. Very few of the indigenous Turkic and Iranian elites were able to move out of their immediate republics to become part of the all-Union political apparatus centered in Moscow.

The pattern of ethnic appointments to key positions within the republics has shifted over time. In the immediate postrevolutionary period and during the course of the 1920s, party authorities attempted to attract and staff the local republican apparatuses with indigenous ethnic personnel from the minorities. The effects of the territorial demarcation of the 1920s and 1930s on confirming the regional ethnic and economic divisions of these peoples into the distinct republican structures of Kazakhstan, Uzbekistan, Kirgizia, Turkmenia, and Tajikistan cannot be underestimated. The talents of indigenous elites and peoples were effectively diverted into substructures guaranteeing the political fragmentation of the Central Asian region and its clear subordination to Moscow. At the same time, local skills and energies were developed, mobilized, and put in the service of these new political entities. This attempt at "sinking roots," *korenizatsiia,* did achieve substantial success in recruiting and involving native revolutionary elites in the dramatic experiments to transform the traditional society, as these Turkic and Iranian cadres saw themselves as beneficiaries of the system with an immediate stake in its success and expansion.

In spite of these successes, the 1930s witnessed a radical reversal as Stalin's decisions and personal paranoia at the center spurred the collectivization and purges that struck so disastrously not only at Soviet elites in the central apparatus of the party and government, but at minority elites in the outlying republics as well. The collectivization campaign wreaked havoc in the Kazakh and Uzbek countrysides, and to a lesser extent in the Kirgiz, Turkmen, and Tajik regions as well. Uzbek and Kazakh elites were similarly ravaged, as Stalin, for reasons of both policy and personal power, destroyed real and imagined enemies throughout the system. Many new Slavic appointees were brought into the region in the process. This pattern was reinforced during the war years of the early 1940s when many European and Russian party functionaries were evacuated from the western regions of the USSR as those regions were overrun by the Germans and many industrial and manufacturing enterprises were moved to Central Asia.

It was not until after Stalin's death in the early 1950s that new regional elites began to reposition themselves in leading positions at upper and middle political levels in the republics. The period from the mid-1950s to the mid-1980s witnessed a substantial spread of minority cadres throughout the political system in Central Asia, as these peoples began to assert themselves more actively and openly, and assumed increasing control over broad sectors of local republican life. During the Brezhnevite period, the Moscow center allowed the Central Asian republics and their indigenous political elites substantial flexibility in directing their own internal affairs in social and cultural matters. To a lesser extent, and subject to the fulfillment of a core set of guidelines and plans dictated by central Soviet authorities, such flexibility extended to local economic and political matters as well (see "Identity Patterns," chapter 9). Within this setting, the ethnic and cultural identity of these peoples flourished as they actively sought out the historical roots of their pre-Soviet past and attempted to use this base in reshaping their present societies.

The appearance of a new reformist leadership at the Moscow center in 1985 signified a break with the permissive approaches of the prior two decades. Major political stress was put on internationalization and the interchangeability of cadres throughout the system. The stagnation and inefficiency of the political economy as a whole had put a premium on talent, modernization, and the need to weed out corrupt habits and structures. To the extent that the permissiveness of the previous twenty years had allowed local forms of corruption and inefficiency to spread in the Turkic republics, central authorities were determined to crack down, and they did. The first secretaries of the party establishment in each of these republics were removed, sometimes under spectacular circumstances like those surrounding Dinmukhamed Kunaev's fall in Kazakhstan, and widespread purges of corrupt ethnic cadres were carried out at all party levels. The campaign in effect sounded the death knell to habits of affirmative action, as new appointments were to emphasize talent, skills, and modernizing efficiency over any considerations of ethnic balance and distribution. Although driven by understandable concerns about the efficiency and competitiveness of the Soviet system as a whole, this campaign endangered the treasured cultural gains that had been made by indigenous elites over the prior two decades, and raised concerns over the emergence of new and potentially destabilizing forms of ethnonationalism in the area.

The societies of Inner Asia that became territories of China in the twentieth century faced a different set of problems from those confronting Iran, Afghanistan, and Mongolia. Although they were confronted in some degree by the problems of political consolidation that had preoccupied the independent states, they lacked the organizational strength to consider independence as a practical policy. Tibet's period of independence should be attributed more to the temporary political vacuum of its international environment than to its inherent strength. Nevertheless in each case efforts were made to mobilize sufficient political strength to negotiate some degree of autonomy.

For the Mongols of Inner Mongolia, the years immediately following the 1911 revolution offered limited options for the development of political autonomy. Some Inner Mongolian princes continued to support the Manchu imperial house, while other Mongols looked with great interest to the independence movement in Outer Mongolia. A small group of Mongols who later rose to prominence in the government of the Inner Mongolian Autonomous Region studied during the 1920s at the Mongolian-Tibetan Academy in Peking. Among these Mongols was Ulanfu of the highly sinicized Tumet Mongols. It is said that Ulanfu learned how to speak Mongolian only after 1960; Chinese was his native language. Ulanfu, who cast his lot with the Chinese Communists in the mid-1920s, was also one of about seventy or eighty Mongolian students to attend the Far Eastern Communist University in Moscow in the 1920s (M23, p. 30).

Another activist of this period, Prince Demchugdungrub, also called Te Wang, set up an autonomous Mongolian government with headquarters in Kalgan in the 1930s. The anti-Communist movement of Te Wang lasted until its final stand in western Inner Mongolia (the Alashan region) in 1949. Te Wang had cast his lot first with the Kuomintang, and then, out of frustration with its divide-and-rule policies, with the Japanese. It is evident that even the most nationalist of Mongols—and Prince Te was certainly that—felt constrained to accept aid from questionable sources in the period between 1911 and 1949.

Political development in Sinkiang in the twentieth century followed a much more erratic path. In traditional times, such political structure as Sinkiang had was local and religious; no notion of a unified polity existed. Nevertheless, political power and influence did exist in the area, and the primary theme of its political development in the modern period has been the interaction of local sources of authority with the outsiders, who since the Ch'ing conquest, have had paramount influence. In retrospect, one can see how these outsiders have attempted, variously, to divide and rule, to rule by force alone, to co-opt local authorities, and to create a new local identity.

Before the twentieth century, political power resided in the local and tribal leaders, many of them religious, of the Sinkiang peoples. Initial Ch'ing policy was to keep such peoples divided among themselves, and to co-opt their leaders. Power at the top would be held by Peking's appointee, but local power structures would be little affected. Our era has seen a steady centralization of power in Sinkiang, first to the garrison city of Urumchi, and then to Peking. The Ch'ing garrison ruled militarily, and sought to interfere as little as possible in the life of the people. After the abdication of the Ch'ing in 1912, however, the Chinese generals who ruled the territory had to rely more on their own resources, and developed a series of tightly organized military regimes. These, however, proved vulnerable to local dissatisfaction and independence movements, and ultimately the aid of the Soviet Union was necessary to deal with them. After 1949, however, real power over the province shifted to Peking, with rule enforced by a greatly increased garrison, still centered in Urumchi.

Even today, Sinkiang's political structure is essentially divided into two not entirely compatible components. Peking controls the province firmly, which is understandable given its strategic importance, and the presence there of Chinese nuclear installations. And the more than five million Chinese inhabitants provide a population base, absent in earlier periods, for that control.

But integration of local people into this Chinese political structure is proving difficult, and certain international developments may even be working against it. Better communications make local people more aware of the culture they share with their relatives across international boundaries; such ties are likely to be strengthened as trade increases.

In Tibet, during the four decades following 1911 during which it benefited from the inattention of its larger neighbors, no efforts were made to reorganize or otherwise strengthen the political system. The Dalai Lama and his administration were therefore in no condition to confront the Chinese when they were again ready to assert their influence in this region. When negotiations between China and the Lhasa government were undertaken in the aftermath of the arrival of units of the PLA in Tibet in October 1950, the Chinese arranged to have three separate factions of Tibetans represented among the delegates. These three factions, which were at odds with one another, consisted of representatives of the Dalai Lama's government in Lhasa, Khambas from eastern Tibet, and representatives of the Panchen Lama. The ensuing Seventeen Point Agreement, which was negotiated in Peking in 1951, reaffirmed the Chinese point of view that Tibet was an integral part of China and had no independent status of its own. The agreement, which represented a sort of ultimatum to the Tibetans, set the tone for Tibet's future relationship with China.

In the period from 1951 to the revolt of 1959, Tibet was treated as if it were made up of three, co-equal, separate parts, corresponding to the signatories of the 1951 agreement: that is, the Lhasa government of the Dalai Lama; the Shigatse government of the Panchen Lama; and the province of Chamdo, the easternmost part of Tibet. Chamdo was ruled by the Chinese directly without conferring with the Lhasa government, and in Shigatse, the Chinese exerted control over the Panchen Lama's administration by exploiting his hostility toward the Dalai Lama (A15, pp. 40–43). As for Lhasa, Tibetans who had been in office in the pre-1951 government were kept on in their same offices. Since there was still only one cadre school of the Chinese Communist party in all of Tibet in 1955, the Chinese had no choice but to proceed slowly until Tibetan party cadres could be trained. In fact, because of the total lack of groundwork before the 1950 invasion, it was not until 1956 that the first seven Tibetans became members of the Chinese Communist party.

In 1955 a Preparatory Committee for the Formation of a Tibetan Autonomous Region was set up to function as an arm of the Chinese central government until an autonomous region was indeed established. The membership of this committee again testifies to the fact that the Chinese were attempting to keep control of political power by distributing it among various hostile groups. Members of the committee included representatives of the Dalai Lama's administration, representatives of the Panchen Lama's administration, representatives of the government in Chamdo, representatives of various of the larger monasteries, and representatives of Chinese living in Tibet.

The 1959 revolt in Lhasa changed the Chinese policy of moderation and gradual reform in Tibet. Mao's 1957 promise of no "democratic reforms" in Tibet for the next five years was shelved in the aftermath of the revolt. With the Dalai Lama and much of his entourage across the border in India, the first move of the Chinese after the revolt was to replace the old Lhasa government with an administration directly under Peking's jurisdiction. Peking furthermore redivided Tibet into seven new administrative units in order to break up traditional land-holding patterns.

Political Leadership and Participation

In Iran, the political and economic bases of political leadership have been the landed gentry, the technocratic elites, the religious leadership, and the royal family and entourage. Missing from this picture are ethnic elites which, with the exception of the Azerbaijani, have not participated in the political process at the center of government.

The landed gentry of the modern period differed from that of the premodern period, particularly in key areas such as Azerbaijan, Mazandaran, and Gilan. In the process of consolidating his power, Reza Shah had stripped many large landholders of their property. Some of these lands and villages were redistributed to supporters, but much of it passed into royal possession making the Pahlavis the largest single landholders. The landed gentry thus came to consist of the new royal family and its entourage.

The technocratic elites, formed over several generations, came from somewhat different backgrounds. The first generation of doctors and engineers were sons of landed gentry sent to Europe by their families. Next came a generation from among urban middle classes whose education was funded in part by the Iranian government, while the latest group comes from a much more diversified background, including rural students.

The religious leadership differs from the others both in training and in background. Sons of small merchants and landowners of rural and small-town background, the religious leadership is usually *madrasah*-trained in Qom or Mashhad with advanced training in Najaf (Iraq). Its foreign language is Arabic, and in fact the families may come from Lebanon, Iraq, or other Muslim areas. As Shi'ite, this leadership does not participate in the intellectual developments at al-Azhar or Aligarth but evolves in settings confined to Iran, Iraq, and Lebanon. Religious endowments have freed it from dependence on the government, and it has jealously fought to retain this economic independence, by maintaining control of the *wakf* system and opposing the distribution of endowed lands.

Suffrage was originally envisioned along economic lines during the early part of the century. Women were denied the vote when the issue was brought before the *majlis* in 1911. During the period of Reza Shah, when elections to the *majlis* had little political impact, the issue of who may vote did not appear important.

More important were questions of who was prohibited from standing for elections or the fact that candidates were chosen by committees appointed by the monarch. But since elections were widely known to be rigged, voter turnout and the number standing for election were limited. The exception to this rule came in 1949 when, under pressure from nationalist elements, a rigged election was declared null. New free elections were held that brought to the *majlis* clerical and nationalist elements who engaged in the debates that led to the profound economic and political changes of the early 1950s. Even in the relatively free elections of 1963, members of the National Front who declared themselves candidates were jailed, and it is estimated that even for the important elections of the politically charged 1980 parliamentary vote, voter turnout was only 50 percent.

Given the shaky grounds for executive or legislative rule, legitimacy of government has been a key issue in the modern period. Reza Shah and his son used symbols of Iranian history to lend legitimacy to both the monarchy and their heading of it, while controlling those who disputed their legitimacy through force. The constitutions of 1906 and 1979 assert that ultimate sovereignty rests with God, but that the powers and sovereignty of the state rest with the people. Under the Pahlavis only superficial attempts were made to legitimize sovereignty through the expression of the genuine will of the people. Likewise in the republican period, various participants in the revolution, notably the left, have cast doubt on the ability of the masses to make political decisions, preferring to leave decisions to the leading cadres.

In Afghanistan the pendulum swung more widely between autocratic rule and experiments with democratic participation than in Iran, but the reality underlying these institutional changes was a central government that had few firm links with the multi-ethnic tribes and peasants in the countryside.

The unreality of the early Afghan experiments is illustrated by the Loya Jirgah, called by Amanullah in 1928. It was composed of a combination of regional and religious leaders and home-grown and foreign-trained sycophants and intellectuals. One of Amanullah's first acts at the Loya Jirgah was to take two group photographs of all the delegates gathered in the stadium of the race track at Paghman, which the young king had roughly designed after Epsom Downs. Horse racing rapidly became popular with the upper class of Mohammadzais and their supporters. In the first photograph, the thousand or so delegates wore traditional clothing. In the second, they were forced to dress in Western clothes—largely purchased or rented from Hindu tailors in the Kabul bazaar. Modernization often begets weird manifestations.

In a similar spirit, the 1931 constitution of Mohammed Nadir Shah created a parliamentary facade, whose purpose was to rubber-stamp government decisions. While the educated elite grew slowly and functioned mainly as government bureaucrats and technocrats, undercurrents of reform-oriented groups began to surface in the 1940s. The free elections of 1949 and the resulting "Liberal Parliament" were the product of these efforts, but the government curbed the reform movements and imprisoned the leadership.

After Mohammed Daoud seized power from his uncle in 1953, the parliamentary system reverted to rubber-stamp status. Prime Minister Daoud had spent much of his adult life serving in the provinces and had many links with the leadership in the countryside. He tolerated no dissent at the center, but gave the rural leadership full rein—as long as requisite taxes and conscripts flowed to the center annually.

Daoud's resignation in 1963 was not the result of internal political agitation, although resistance to his policies did exist, and occasionally flowed to the surface. The closing of the border with Pakistan over the "Pushtunistan" issue made it necessary for either President Field Marshal Mohammed Ayub Khan of Pakistan or Daoud to step down. Daoud took the step.

The next ten years witnessed a remarkable—though flawed— experiment in a parliamentary monarchy. Political parties flourished from right to left. Each party published manifestoes and newspapers, some of which were shut down, only to spring up again under different names.

Elections in 1965 and 1969 produced some interesting consequences, one of which was the result of one of the many political patterns instituted by Amir Abdur Rahman. In addition to sending dissident Pushtun north and encouraging others to emigrate voluntarily, the Iron Amir had brought the sons of defeated regional leaders to Kabul to train them as loyal civil and military officers (see "Political Leadership and Participation," chapter 3, and "Redistributive Processes," chapter 5). By the 1965 elections two or three generations of the transplanted sons had evolved into "Kabulis," although many maintained their territorial, tribal links, especially in the pursuit of brides—and bribes. When the regionally oriented elections were announced, many of the Kabulis returned to the homes of their ancestors to run for the Lower House (Wolesi Jirgah). Most of the 216 members came either from the second line of power currently living in villages, or from their urban kinsmen, the Kabulis.

Several leftists were elected: Hafizullah Amin (Khalq); Babrak Karmal, Dr. Anahita (Babrak's mistress), and Nur Ahmad Nur (the last three Parcham). In spite of their small numbers the leftists made more noise and had a greater impact than most of the other parties combined. Legally, no political parties could exist, but the government turned a blind eye to those groups that were obviously organized parties.

Under the 1964 constitution, the parliament should have had a partly elected eighty-four-member Upper House (Meshrano Jirgah): one member elected from each of the twenty-eight provinces; another elected by the Provincial Councils; and twenty-eight appointed by the king, theoretically to give the Upper House more intellectual balance. The Meshrano Jirgah could not veto laws passed by the Wolesi Jirgah but could initiate legislation.

One of the great failures of the constitutional period was the inability of the various cabinet members, virtually all Western educated, to produce and implement the reform programs necessary to move toward modernization. Some cabinet members complained of interference from certain members of the royal family, particularly Queen Homaira and the king's son-in-law and cousin, Major-General Abdul Wali, Commander of Central Forces Kabul, which extended from the capital to the border with Pakistan. Also, under the constitution, the king was enjoined to appoint an independent Supreme Court, which he never did.

Other flaws appeared in the legislative branch. The constitution called for the election of municipal and provincial councils, but elections were never held. Therefore, the Meshrano Jirgah functioned with one-third of its required membership absent, so some legal experts viewed the entire constitutional period (1964–1973) as unconstitutional.

The constitutional decade ended in chaos as the parliamentary experiment under a constitutional monarchy failed to make substantial strides toward socioeconomic and political development, in part because the Western-educated elitists appointed by the king could not break through generations of bureaucratic inertia. In addition, Zahir Shah, advised by conservative sycophants and members of the royal family, did not take steps either to implement the constitution or to suppress the growing opposition to the government's political lassitude.

The July 17, 1973, coup was led by former Prime Minister Daoud in association with certain Afghan military officers and bureaucrats, who, although trained partly in the USSR, and some in the United States as well, were more nationalist than Soviet-oriented Communists. Most were members of the Parcham branch of the leftist (socialist, Marxist)-oriented Jamiyat-i-Demokratiki-Khalq-i-Afghanistan (People's Democratic Party of Afghanistan—PDPA), founded on January 1, 1965, and led by Babrak Karmal. The other major branch, Khalq, led by Nur Mohammed Taraki and Hafizullah Amin, preferred to sit out the coup.

From July 17, 1973, to April 27, 1978, the government (the new Republic of Afghanistan) halfheartedly attempted several reforms in social, political, and legal institutions. For example, the laws of Afghanistan were codified in four massive volumes. Land-reform programs were drawn up but not implemented, and Daoud made a noble attempt to reform the bureaucracy, one of the major constraints to Afghan development.

But after the promulgation of a new constitution in February 1977, Daoud reverted to being a classic tribal khan and in March appointed a cabinet that consisted primarily of conservative sycophants, sons of sycophants, and even collateral members of the royal family. Also, by March 1975, President Daoud had succeeded in politically defanging his Parcham support by sending most of the young, enthusiastic cadre members to the countryside, where they ran headlong into the rural power elites. These frustrated reformers either accepted the fact that change would have to be slow and consistent with existing cultural patterns to succeed, or turned as corrupt as their predecessors. Others, also disillusioned, returned to Kabul and resigned—or were dismissed for leaving their posts without permission.

In response, the two leftist wings, Khalq and Parcham, remarried after a ten-year divorce, which had been brought about by personality and policy differences. Karmal of Parcham was a nationalist opportunist, who professed the desire to unite with all antimonarchist groups to seize power. Taraki and Amin were also nationalist oriented, but insisted on the primacy of the class struggle. Both groups had contacts with the Soviet embassy, but neither was dominated by the Soviets. The groups reunited in July 1977 in an obvious antigovernment front.

Probably, the Soviets expected to eliminate the unreliable and unstable *khalqi* government, replace it with a more pliable, puppet *parchami* regime under Babrak Karmal, and leave within ninety days, having effectively extended their political control about six hundred miles south of their Central Asian frontier.

Relatively speaking, only a small percentage of the Afghan population was actively engaged in resistance before the Soviet invasion. But the invasion triggered a culturally oriented response. Many Afghan groups who were traditional enemies linked up to fight the invaders.

Afghan sociopolitical units are, with varying degrees of intensity, based on vertically structured, segmentary kin units. These units extend from nuclear family to extended family to lineage to subtribe to tribe, which are territorially neighbors to other similar groups. These neighbors often engage in feuding during the off agricultural season. However, when an outside horizontal force threatens the vertical kin-group structures, the tribes, or other ethnolinguistic identities, unite locally and loosely to resist and, if possible, throw out the invaders.

Traditional enemies, such as the Mangal and Jadran in Paktya province; the Wardak Pushtun and the neighboring Hazara in Ghazni; the Panjsheri Tajik and their less than friendly neighbors the Nuristani, Mushwani Pushtun, and Gujar in Kunar, among others, ultimately united to resist the Soviets, just as they had rejected the British one hundred years earlier. Political unity may come later, growing out of military cooperation.

The prewar rural elites in Afghanistan exercised their power through collective leadership, not a single village chief. Westerners usually seek out *the* leader in a power situation, but in Afghanistan, *the* leader seldom exists. Naturally, from time to time, one *rish-i-safid* (Persian) or *spin geray* (Pashto, both refer to "white beards") in a village council can become dominant, but this is not the ideal, nor usually the reality.

The village council consists of the heads of lineages (or some such kin unit) and each is a specialist: in water rights, marital problems, or property rights; the war chief (who leads in the feuds); and the "go-between" with the nearest government offices. Often, outsiders identify this last individual as the *malik* (or khan, beg, boyar—the names differ in different regions). The go-between, however, would never make a spot decision on an important issue, but would refer the matter to the village council for a collective consensus.

In addition to the traditional leadership, two other types of *maliks* have evolved because of the war. The military commanders inside the country have achieved lasting importance and will be integrated into whatever power patterns exist after the Soviet withdrawal.

The war accelerated a process that had already begun in the 1960s, after a fair system of conscription was introduced. Draftees served for two years in the army, air force, police, gendarmes, or labor corps, and then most returned to their home villages. Like veterans everywhere, they frequently banded together to compare their common experiences, which had occurred *outside* the normal village cultural patterns. These informal rural groups were evolving into local de facto (if not de jure) power groups before the war. Seldom did they openly challenge the traditional "white beards," but made their collective input felt in the decision-making processes.

Many of these younger men have become commanders and subcommanders because of their previous military experience—and their charisma. Some are also members of families represented in the traditional village councils. Others are local religious leaders, but no matter what their prior role and status, the military commanders will definitely become a part of the postwar de jure power elite.

The third type of *malik* is the man who has returned from the Persian Gulf, Saudi Arabia, or elsewhere with a small fortune and extensive experience in dealing with outsiders. He often becomes the go-between for the refugees with the Pakistani officials, United Nations, and volunteer agency administrators. Whether or not he can retain a role in the postwithdrawal power elite will depend on his personal and financial contacts, loans he has made, and his own charisma. Probably, most will lose their status and role, which had functioned in the unnatural cultural pattern of the refugee situation.

In May 1985, the seven major political parties in Peshawar were forced into a shotgun marriage by Pakistan and other interested parties, such as the United States and Saudi Arabia, as well as many inside commanders who insisted that if they could organize cooperative military operations inside Afghanistan, the least the parties could do would be to present a common front to the outside world. Although shaky, the Islamic Unity of Afghan Mujahidin (IUAM) has held together. Actually, the parties performed two valuable functions after the Soviet invasion: they have been a major face to the outside world, and they were the main conduit of supplies to the resistance.

However, of the seven leaders, only Yunis Khalis (Hezbi Islami) has a traditional, territorial base of power. This is among the Khugiani Pushtun of the Surkhab region near Jalalabad, and even his base is being challenged by other local leaders. The rest, supported by major outside resources (including the United States, Pakistan, Saudi Arabia, and others), have followers, and followers have the habit of following anyone with the goodies. This does not mean that the six will have no roles to perform in the postwithdrawal period, but they will probably have to accommodate themselves to the commanders and the traditional leadership inside, rather than vice versa.

One major fault with the IUAM as it is constituted is that it includes none of the Shi'a groups, which probably make up about 15–20 percent of Afghanistan's population. Other minority groups, such as the Aimaq, Nuristani, and Baluch also lack adequate representation.

Politics in the Mongolian People's Republic differed from that in Iran and Afghanistan for several reasons. The MPR had a small and homogeneous population; it had only limited experience with modern government, although it had a centuries-long tradition of tribal administration; and its political institutions were developed within the framework of the Soviet hegemony.

The Mongolian People's Republic adopted its first constitution in 1924. This constitution declared the state's intention of ending the "feudal theocratic regime" that had existed in Outer Mongolia. The year 1924 also marked the creation and convening of the First People's Great Khural, the supreme state authority. The notion of rule through assembly was not new to the Mongols. *Khuriltai*, or assemblies of princes and military leaders, constituted the main decision-making forums among twelfth- and thirteenth-century Mongolian tribes and clans. The MPR *khural*, though philologically related to the *khuriltai* of the past, was patterned after the USSR Supreme Soviet. Elections to the Great Khural are held every three years, with one deputy for every twenty-five hundred people. Until the constitutional reforms of 1949 there was also a Small Khural, elected by members of the Great Khural, which carried out legislative business between working sessions of the Great Khural (M61, pp. 16–17; M43, p. 99).

Parallel to the government administration is the Mongolian People's Revolutionary Party (MPRP). Lenin in his meeting with Suke Bator in 1921 had advised the Mongols not to use the name "Communist party" until a proletariat had been developed. The parallel to Soviet party organization is evident: there is a Central Committee of the party, a Mongolian Revolutionary Youth Union, and a Suke Bator Pioneer Movement.

In 1940 a new constitution was promulgated marking the end of the "imperialistic and feudal yoke," and announcing "a noncapitalistic approach to the development of the country to pave the way to socialism in the future" (M43, pp. 145–146). Under the 1940 constitution class enemies were explicitly deprived of the right to vote and it was not until 1944 that universal suffrage from age eighteen was introduced (M12, p. 140). Class enemies as specified in the 1940 constitution consisted of exploiters, usurers, Buddhist dignitaries, nobles, and former serf owners (M11, p. 491). In 1960 a third "socialist" constitution announcing Mongolia's transition to a fully socialist state was promulgated. Under the 1940 constitution elections had been indirect; the 1960 constitution proclaimed that "the Khurals of people's deputies are elected by the citizens of the MPR on the basis of universal, equal and direct electoral rights through secret voting" (M12, p. 147).

Local government administration, as established by the constitution of 1940, consisted of three levels: provinces—of which in the late 1980s there were eighteen; districts; and rural communities, later eliminated. The cities of Ulan Bator, Darkhan, and Erdenet have been given special status as autonomous municipalities on the same level as a province. People's Deputies Khurals, akin to local Soviets in the USSR and elected by direct vote, conduct the affairs of local government.

One scholar of MPR government institutions has referred to the MPR as conducting a "conscious drive for the rapid modernization of administrative techniques in the context of the still rather primitive socio-political conditions of a backward community" (M11, p. 505). Just what effect the transplantation of Soviet government institutions into the MPR has had on actual political participation by the Mongols is difficult to gauge. The structure of MPR government is easy to document; how governmental institutions interact with the general population is extremely difficult to judge. We have little knowledge of the existence or alignment of bureaucratic interest groups in the MPR for instance. The Soviet model of government in theory calls for mass political participation; it puts in place the machinery for mass democracy, and in fact instills in the individual a familiarity with the electoral process. Yet, we know virtually nothing about the nature of MPR elections; apparently all such elections are uncontested (M72, p. 218).

In Sinkiang, the Ch'ing pattern of firm but unobtrusive rule was maintained after 1912 by Yang Tseng-hsin, a warlord from Yunnan. Effectively independent of China proper, he kept his personal power by relying on relatives and fellow provincials from Yunnan, while accentuating regional and ethnic differences among the Sinkiang people, and rigidly excluding foreign influences.

His successor Chin Shu-jen, however, interfered more actively with local life, perhaps most flagrantly by occupying Hami, where he awarded lucrative jobs to Chinese and imposed new taxes on the local population. The rebellion there and elsewhere revealed both the power of local aspirations and the way they were developing outside of the political framework provided by Chinese rule.

These aspirations drew on currents from the Middle East and the USSR. In the north, where the Soviet example was close at hand, dissatisfaction tended to crystallize around radical and socialist ideas, whereas in the south, the area of British influence, pan-Turkish and Islamic currents were paramount.

Along with the tensions among local groups and the quarrels of contenders for power, these ideas made stability elusive in Sinkiang for most of the twentieth century. Among the most important outbreaks of unrest was the attempt in the 1930s to create a Turkish-Islamic Republic of East Turkestan (TIRET), with its capital in or near Kashgar, which would look to Turkey and the Middle East, and unite Muslims of various backgrounds around religious ideas and shared anti-Chinese sentiment. Mobilizing as it did powerful indigenous feeling, and apparently benefiting from some foreign assistance, the rebellion that swirled around this republic was too strong for local Chinese authorities to deal with.

To destroy it, Sheng Shih-ts'ai turned, as we have seen, to the Soviet Union. But he made use not only of Soviet troops, but also of some of Stalin's political techniques as well. Rather than work with old identities, the Soviet approach was to create new ones—a "Uighur nationality," for instance. Sheng introduced this idea and many other components of Soviet nationality policy to Sinkiang, heralding the province's transformation into a "model Soviet republic," in which all nationalities would "enjoy a happy and prosperous life."

Following such a Soviet blueprint, however, required fostering local culture and elevating local people to at least symbolic power. Sheng therefore appointed Uighurs, among them Khoja Niyas Hajji and Yulbars Khan, both leaders in the 1931 Hami revolt, but not of TIRET, to seemingly important positions. From the Soviet point of view, such measures probably prepared the way for Sinkiang to join the USSR.

The return of the Nationalists, however, placed the model republic once again in Chinese hands. To counter this the Soviet Union appears to have attempted to mobilize more extreme Islamic and anti-Chinese sentiments, by sponsoring the establishment of another potentially secessionist government, the East Turkestan Republic (ETR), proclaimed at Ili in 1944. Although the ETR dissolved the following year, its creation, like the emergence of its predecessor TIRET, and Sheng's own attempts to accommodate, testified to the power among the people of potentially threatening currents of thought.

To deal with these challenges, the Chinese Communists relied not only on the army garrisons in Sinkiang, but also on their own attempt to create a new identity for the people. The Uighur concept was stressed: in 1954 the name of the province was changed to the Sinkiang Uighur Autonomous Region. But whereas in the Soviet case, Uighur nationality is subsumed by a larger, "Soviet" citizenship, in the PRC that larger citizenship is "Chinese." Of course such "Chineseness" is explained as being free of ethnic connotation, like "Soviet" citizenship, but in practice its imposition has amounted to attempted sinicization.

This policy was initially held in abeyance. Although Chinese generals were always first secretaries, Saifudin, a Sinkiang Uighur and early Communist convert, partly educated in Tashkent, and until 1950 a member of the Soviet Communist party, held high office in Sinkiang up to the Cultural Revolution.

That period, however, with its wholesale sinicization, and the disgrace even of the most loyal Uighur Communists, highlighted, like Chin Shu-jen's, the dangers of too much interference with local affairs. Although Saifudin returned as first secretary in its wake, enmity between local people and Chinese appears to have grown, and it is by no means clear that attempts to ameliorate the situation by repairing mosques, tolerating Islam and local culture, and giving local people some modicum of political role, will be sufficient.

In Tibet, after the revolt of 1959, the Chinese staffed the new governmental administration in Lhasa with Tibetans educated in China. Specifically, in August 1959, one hundred Tibetan graduates of the Central Nationalities Institute in Peking were sent back to Tibet to aid in land redistribution (D6, p. 169).

A year after the Tibetan Autonomous Region was formally established in

1965, the Cultural Revolution began in China. In August 1966, the Cultural Revolution was inaugurated in Tibet by Red Guards who destroyed images in Lhasa's main temple, the Jokhang. By November 1966, about thirteen hundred Han Chinese Red Guards were residing in Tibet. It has been estimated that the ethnic Tibetan participation in the Cultural Revolution was limited to about 1 percent of the entire Tibetan population (D6, p. 218). It is clear that the influx of Han Chinese into Tibet during the years of the Cultural Revolution left a legacy of even greater Tibetan animosity toward the Chinese. The Cultural Revolution was quite obviously an alien movement with no indigenous roots and no benefits at all to Tibet. According to one Tibetan refugee who fled Tibet in 1975, even Tibetans who had been on the "Chinese payroll" since 1959 were subject to expulsion from their government jobs during the Cultural Revolution (N36, p. 178). The Panchen Lama has noted that "as a result of the 'cultural revolution,' these ties [between Chinese cadres and Tibetans] were impaired" (M6, vol. 1, p. 15). This is most certainly an understatement, as even the most sympathetic accounts of China's governance of Tibet refer to "psychological scars which have created a breach between the Han and the Tibetans which will take decades, if not generations, to heal" (N14, p. 181).

In Soviet Central Asia, Moscow introduced an extensive hierarchy of bureaucratic structures and institutional mechanisms calculated to bring the indigenous populations and their elites into the modernization process. Whatever the initial intent of the Soviet leadership in having these mechanisms serve the purpose of co-opting these peoples into the transformational experiment designed by the dominant party apparatus at the Moscow center, one substantial and very important byproduct was the provision of multiple new organizational opportunities to the indigenous Turkic and Iranian populations, which has allowed them to begin to influence the mechanism of governance and the political establishment itself.

Republican governmental, party, economic, social, and cultural organizations have multiplied dramatically the points of entry into, and possible influence on, the political system, and have provided an extensive training ground for potential political leadership and talent. In addition to the myriad ministerial bureaucracies of the republican governmental units, parliaments, municipal and district committees, academies of science, trade unions, youth organizations, women's groups, and special-interest volunteer societies of all kinds have absorbed and channeled indigenous skills and talents into a variety of quasi-political public service functions. The importance of this complex hierarchical web as a breeding ground for political and managerial ingenuity should not be underestimated.

The statistics on the increase of numbers of cadres employed in any of these categories of public life are predictably dramatic and impressive. Taking Uzbekistan as an example, one finds that the number of Communist party members rose from approximately eighteen thousand in 1925 to over half a million at the beginning of the 1980s, those with a higher education rising from 36 to almost 150,000. Using the same base years for various other groups and associations with political roles or influence, one finds the following: trade union membership went from well under one hundred thousand to over half a million; the Young Communist League expanded from some thirty thousand members to almost two and a quarter million; the number of specialized workers with a higher education employed in the industrial sector went from almost nil to approximately one million. Both the absolute numbers of specialists and those among them with a higher education working in parallel areas of science, education, medicine, or communications were correspondingly high; and, of course, the membership, institutional structure, and outreach activities of such propaganda bodies as the Ilim or Znanie (knowledge) societies were given a special stimulus. Soviet statistics show that in 1976 alone members of the republican branch of the Znanie society gave over 904,000 lectures to popular audiences in Uzbekistan on political, economic, and scientific themes. Needless to say, these statistics must be seen in perspective.

The first question that must be asked is whether such institutional diversification and the accompanying personnel development and recruitment were designed to serve the emerging purposes and aspirations of the indigenous peoples themselves or the control purposes of the Moscow center. There can be little doubt that, in its historical origins and structural models, this institutional experiment was meant to consolidate the center's control over the peripheral minority areas, imposing a series of organizational mechanisms that would bind that periphery more closely. The complex and variegated apparatus installed in the Central Asian republics was meant to serve as a transmission belt for directives from Moscow rather than as an enabling mechanism to bring local Turkic and Iranian aspirations to the fore.

The development of such indigenous talents and skills has not automatically translated into concomitant political roles and influence. Such otherwise natural returns have been limited by the peculiarities of Soviet political culture, which has historically concentrated power in the center and subordinated republican governmental and party institutions to central structures in Moscow. Thus, industrial, agricultural, and cultural ministries in the Central Asian republics were from the 1920s subordinated to all-Union ministries, the governmental structures themselves are subordinated to close party controls, and local republican party structures have furthermore been strictly subordinated to Moscow through the *nomenklatura* system of personnel review and approval. This strict hierarchy has severely limited local political autonomy and initiative.

Nevertheless, paradoxical as it might seem, the system's very intense concentration of political attention on affairs at the center resulted in the Brezhnevite period in an evolution within the peripheral republics of patterns of quasi-autonomy. As habits of revolutionary zeal and belief in Leninist internationalism faded in the 1960s and 1970s among the Moscow leadership, and parallel patterns of political corruption grew, the center quite simply began to lose interest in monitoring the day-to-day activities of the outlying republics. Although it is technically true that from the mid-1960s through the mid-1980s political power remained concentrated in the centralized party apparatus in Moscow, in reality such power increasingly devolved to broader networks of local social and public organizations in the republics, which began quietly to control and guide everyday practice and policy. At that point, the earlier establishment and somewhat artificial proliferation of such public organizations assumed political significance, and these bodies began, albeit modestly, to wield actual political influence.

The point is not that local political structures achieved their de jure independence from the Moscow center, which they did not, but that the center's growing lack of interest in managing the everyday life of these societies, combined with the sheer multiplication of new indigenous public organizations, brought increasingly broad sectors of public and political life in the republics under the de facto control of local political and social units. Areas of political, economic, social, and cultural life that had formerly been considered the proper domain of the central authorities in Moscow were increasingly left to various forms of local initiative and jurisdiction, as long as such practice did not challenge the ultimate authority of the centralized system.

Under these circumstances, patterns of local governance continued to evolve over the decades of the 1960s and 1970s, tapping the energies and resources of both the indigenous elites and the masses as a whole. By the beginning of the 1980s, one could begin to see the emergence of embryonic interest groups and the articulation of new patterns and visions of locally designed modernization and development which could over time come to challenge the patterns and plans of the center.

Mobilization of Skills and Resources

Iran is the only country among the societies of Inner Asia that has in modern times faced both east and west. The eastern dimension includes its geographical characteristics, the continued role of nomads in its population, and in particular its important cultural impact on Central Asia over the centuries. These "inner" characteristics are counterbalanced by its political and cultural contacts with the Middle East and the developed West, which brought it into the modern world early in the twentieth century.

Iran is distinguished in particular from the other Inner Asian societies by the revenue from the concession granted in 1901 for the exploration and exploitation of its oil resources. From the first oil struck in 1908, to the formation of the Anglo-Iranian Oil Company in 1909, its nationalization in 1951, and its subsequent development, oil production rose from a negligible forty-three thousand barrels to some five million barrels a day in the mid-1970s with an annual revenue of some $20 billion. Iran's economic development is discussed in the following chapter, but it is significant that oil revenues provided opportunities for the development of skills and resources unmatched by the other societies of Inner Asia.

From the perspective of the 1980s, the development of Iran's military capabilities is impressive. The capacity to mobilize large numbers of recruits from the villages and to make use of advanced weapons evolved rapidly over the years. In this as in other spheres, a heavy dependence on foreign advisers and on officer training abroad was gradually outgrown. The performance of Iran's armed forces in the war with Iraq, during a period of relative international isolation, reflects the maturing of native capabilities.

Progress in education was also impressive. In the course of the twentieth century physical facilities grew from one to two thousand secondary schools, and from one institution of higher education to seventeen universities and some two hundred other specialized institutes.

The development of numerous other public and private enterprises, including highways, railroads, air transportation, mines, irrigation projects, and manufacturing establishments gave evidence of significant management skills. Some of these developments were slowed by the clerical revolution of 1979, but Khomeini's ideology was not in its essence antimodern. What it sought was to evolve policies that would reconcile science, technology, and industrialization with Islamic social and moral values as interpreted by the Ayatollah. Although the outcome of these policies is still in doubt, it is apparent that the mobilizing capacity of the Iranian government has not been significantly affected.

Mobilizational capacities in Afghanistan developed much more slowly than in Iran. The Amanullah period began with many hopes, promises, and grandiose schemes, but ended in a nightmare of unfulfilled dreams. Amanullah began a new city outside Kabul to serve as his administrative capital, and built a narrow-gauge railroad to connect the old city with his new city—the only rail line ever constructed in Afghanistan. The line consisted of two locomotives which gathered rust in sheds after Amanullah's downfall.

Under Nadir Shah several unpaved motor roads were constructed, particularly one from Kabul to Mazar-i-Sharif over the Hindu Kush, which linked the north and the south. Nadir also forced leading entrepreneurs to purchase land in northern Afghanistan and encouraged them to go north to grow cotton, among other commodities. Private enterprise and not the government developed the rich lands of the north. In subsequent years there was slow progress under the leadership of private enterprise and nominal control by the royal family.

After World War II, Afghanistan became an economic, cultural, and ultimately political battleground in the Cold War. With the assistance of the United States and the USSR, and other nations, Afghanistan's infrastructure grew rapidly, and the good roads, airports, river ports, and communications network made it easy for the central government to expand its influence into the countryside—and also made it easier for the Soviets to invade, if not to control. The *mujahidin* have developed their own infrastructure off the main roads, including roads over some of the three hundred or so passes, many of them previously inaccessible, that exist along the Afghan-Pakistan border from the high Pamir to Baluchistan.

A major provincial reorganization occurred in 1964, when twenty-eight provinces were created out of the previous seven major and seven minor provinces. A twenty-ninth province, Paktika, was launched during Daoud's second administration. The new administrative system was designed to make central government control easier, and economic development more coordinated.

In the late 1950s, Daoud began to revamp the Afghan army and air force with massive Soviet assistance. The armed forces remained mainly a conscript force, but an elite class of officers, loyal to Daoud, was created. Only a few officers were converted to Soviet-style communism but, as it turned out later, these few were enough to change the course of Afghan history.

In spite of vigorous efforts, the Democratic Republic of Afghanistan (DRA) has not been able to mobilize the support necessary to call itself representative of the people of Afghanistan. The army has become a revolving door. Conscripts are grabbed off the streets, and sent to the front after a minimum of training. Most desert at the first opportunity. Some have been redrafted as many as three times.

The prolonged domestic struggle since 1979 has called for unprecedented efforts at mobilization by the government and the *mujahidin* alike. It remains to be seen to what extent this experience will affect the future development of Afghan society.

In Central Asia, the tsarist regime in the nineteenth century had left most indigenous social structures in place, preferring to maintain the framework and behavioral patterns of the traditional societies while seeking primarily to ensure social order and political allegiance to the tsarist state. After the revolution, the civil war, and the establishment of Moscow's control in the region in the 1930s, the Soviet administration introduced a comprehensive program of social engineering designed to mobilize the local peoples for new political and economic purposes, and to alter the structures of these societies in a radical way.

In a set of transformational measures essentially shaped by the Moscow center, the region was fragmented into five major territorial subunits, and an impressive battery of party, governmental, police, and military structures was elaborated to absorb and direct the energies and ambitions of the indigenous Turkic and Iranian peoples. The local populations and their elites were vigorously recruited and provided with substantial initial incentives to join and staff these new ministries and bureaucracies. Whole new career patterns evolved, opening up unprecedented social mobility for the recruits and providing access to material advancement, power, and prestige.

Participation in the multiple bureaucracies of the new republican administrative structures developed technical, managerial, and political skills in these neophyte functionaries. They came to staff the ministries and run the new agricultural and industrial complexes that were built in the republics, and they began to play foreign policy roles in the shaping of Muslim national communism in Inner Asia. Several successive generations of such managerial and clerical elites came to benefit from and develop a personal stake in maintaining and furthering the regime. These peoples gained substantial experience in the diverse political, economic, social, and cultural bureaucracies of the several republics. Their skills were employed and tested in the administration and implementation of the all-Union five-year economic plans; in the traumatic collectivization of agriculture; in the intensification of industrial planning, the construction of hydroelectric stations, new railway lines, and other major industrial projects; and in the widespread mobilization of societal resources such as that represented by the Hudzhum movement in the 1920s and 1930s, the aggressive recruitment of women for the public workplace which was simultaneously intended to weaken traditional Muslim family cohesion. They have continued to be employed in the postwar era in the more modest but creative development of resources represented in the expansion of the system of primary and secondary education; the elaboration of programs of health and medical services; the construction of housing and public buildings; and the design of extensive cultural, artistic, and recreational facilities and outlets.

Although this experience and new skills would over the long run work to the advantage of the Turkic and Iranian peoples of the region, the initial stages of this process represented an extraordinary redirection of indigenous energies and attention to public and state purposes. In the first half-century of the Soviet experiment, mobilizational policies and efforts were essentially designed and initiated by the central state apparatus: such developmental programs were meant to serve the purposes and goals of the all-Union state. The political campaigns mounted against the *maktabs* and the *madrasahs,* against the traditional religious law courts that administered the *adat* and the *shari'at,* against the *wakfs,* and against the traditional institutions of water, crop, and price management, were all executed with the assistance and participation of substantial numbers of local native cadres. The price of these efforts was high and the brunt of the costs was borne by the indigenous people, both masses and elites, themselves. The ultimate political purpose was to clear the institutional landscape for the establishment of Soviet structures and the transformational experiments that were to come. Nevertheless, as experience accrued and bureaucratic and managerial skills were developed, the mobilizational base was laid for a potential growing autonomy of these peoples in designing and managing their own political, economic, and social affairs.

These trends accelerated during the Brezhnevite period (see the previous section). Since the mid-1960s local aspirations have grown for more formal and explicit control over public policy in the republics, and increasing tensions have arisen over the conflicting priorities of the Muscovite center and the Inner Asian periphery. Uzbekistan, Kirgizia, and occasionally other republics have begun to argue for agricultural diversification and substantial new investment in industrial complexes in Soviet Central Asia, but such diversification and expansion are dependent on both Muscovite political approval and increased capital inputs. So far, such requests and demands have been stymied. The perceived needs of the all-Union economy have continued to take precedence over changing regional and republican aspirations, and the stage has been set for a potential significant divergence of goals between the Moscow center and the Central Asian periphery. The irony of this evolving situation is that the basis for such a potential confrontation was laid in the very creation by the center of the complex and increasingly sophisticated institutional and personnel structure of the republics.

In the case of the Mongolian People's Republic, mobilization of skills and resources since the 1920s must refer to governmental, not private, mobilization. Since 1924, when ecclesiastical authority was banished from the government structure, the MPRP and the MPR government have taken over the role of chief organizing units in society.

For both military and civilian projects, the MPR from its very inception has been hindered in its mobilizing efforts by a chronic manpower shortage. This problem, which continues in spite of government financial inducements to encourage larger families, has necessitated heavy reliance on Soviet, East European, and, for a while, Chinese laborers. Not only is the Mongolian population numerically limited, it is also a population with a limited number of skilled laborers. Statistics concerning the number of foreign workers in the MPR are lacking. Nonetheless, official MPR descriptions of the ambitious construction projects of the 1960s and 1970s always pay homage to Soviet assistance. It is clear that the expertise and manpower for constructing a heat and power station in Ulan Bator, a food industry plant in Choibalsan, three new state farms, two housing developments, a trade union palace, and a wedding palace (in Ulan Bator)—just some of the projects completed during the Fifth Five Year Plan (1971–1975)—came in large measure from the USSR. Certainly the construction of the two large industrial cities of Darkhan and Erdenet—from scratch—in the north of the MPR would not have been attempted without Soviet technical assistance and manpower.

Not only is there a labor shortage, but the MPR government's ability to mobilize the skills and resources of the country has been limited by what Robert Rupen has labeled "motivational and attitudinal problems" among workers (M56, p. 108). Various factors have been advanced to account for these problems. Blame has been put on Buddhism, the nomadic way of life, socialist economic organization, and "the laborers' lack of interest in working hard to satisfy Mongolia's debts to the USSR" (M56, p. 108). This motivational problem has been acknowledged by the Mongols themselves. The MPR historian D. Maidar points to the rapid "social-psychological transformation" that has occurred in only one generation as the source of the problem. In one generation, the first workers, the first professionals, indeed the first Mongolian cosmonaut (from a family of herders) have all appeared. According to Maidar, the younger generation has adapted quite well, but the older generation still retains the characteristics of "torpor, passivity, and so-called *margashism*" (*margash* means "tomorrow" in Mongolian; M36, pp. 41–42). As Maidar notes, "The creation of a new personality—this is a complicated, multi-staged process" (M36, p. 42).

The Military Construction Branch of the Mongolian People's Army donates large numbers of soldiers to work on civilian construction sites. The labor shortage is apparent, though, even in terms of the Mongolian People's Army's ability to guard the frontiers of the MPR. Starting in the late 1960s, Soviet divisions were stationed on the MPR-PRC border (M56, p. 116). Obviously, USSR security needs also played a role in the use of Soviet soldiers in such a sensitive frontier zone.

Likewise in Sinkiang, mobilization of skills and resources in traditional times was almost entirely at the local level, with the best example perhaps being the construction of the extensive irrigation systems found around towns such as Turfan. After 1912, Chinese rulers of Sinkiang had to deal with local people, but they avoided bringing them into positions of real power. They preferred, like the British and other imperial powers elsewhere, to rely on military force in the hands of trustworthy foreigners.

The most substantial Sinkiang-wide development projects came during the period of Soviet predominance, when Sheng Shih-ts'ai held power. Both mining and oil-drilling projects were carried out, with extensive Soviet participation, as was local development, such as road building. Although these developments had economic significance, they were not by and large organically linked to the needs of the local area: Soviet interest in Sinkiang, both political and economic, was conceived of in Soviet terms.

The same may be said of development under the People's Republic. Infrastructure construction has been substantial—notably the railroad that now connects Urumchi to China proper. Construction of the continuation of the line to connect with the Soviet railway system has, however, been postponed—even though arguably the link with Soviet Central Asia is more "natural" than that with Peking. Much of the infrastructure construction serves the needs of the Chinese population of Sinkiang, many of whom are involved in military activities. Although precise information is difficult to obtain, it would appear that much of the "modern" population—such as the factory work force and the university population—consists of Chinese immigrants and their children, and not of the local population (though of course, as in the USSR, local people also participate).

Tibet's capacity to mobilize skills and resources before the mid-twentieth century is reflected in the construction, maintenance, and staffing of monasteries under the management of the Buddhist church. Under the government of the PRC since the 1950s, however, Tibetan manpower has instead been harnessed in such massive government-directed projects as road building. Linking Lhasa with Ch'ing-hai, Sinkiang, and other parts of China was a priority for the Chinese in the years after 1950. According to Chinese sources, in the early 1960s more than forty-five hundred Tibetans were employed maintaining the Ch'ing-hai-Tibet highway alone. Conscription of thirty-five thousand Tibetan laborers by the Chinese PLA for work on a rail line linking Lhasa to Lanchow was reported by other sources in the early 1960s (A15, p. 158).

Reports by Tibetan refugees reflect great resentment toward Chinese conscription techniques as well as toward the nature of the projects for which laborers are conscripted. A Tibetan who left Tibet in 1975 reported that the Chinese had indeed constructed many roads and bridges, but that these roads and bridges were used to transport troops and arms. At least in 1975, there was not one public transportation vehicle for civilian use (N36, p. 191). Labor was also conscripted for the construction of airstrips around the country.

The conscription of Tibetans for state projects undoubtedly interfered with landlords' use of labor, and thereby conflicted with local economies (D6, pp. 165–166). In the late 1950s, the granting to Tibetan CCP cadres of exemptions from labor obligations owed to their landlords was intended to encourage Tibetans to join cadre training programs.

Collectivization proceeded slowly in Tibet, with the first communes in the Lhasa area being set up only in June 1966. By June 1970, only 34 percent of Tibet's villages had been organized into communes (D6, p. 231). Not surprisingly, Tibetan attitudes as reflected in refugee reports are uniformly negative concerning the institution and operation of the communes.

Conclusions and Comparisons

The societies of Inner Asia, with the exception of Iran, remained throughout the twentieth century particularly weak in the realm of political development. Despite a rich cultural heritage, and memories of conquest and empire in earlier centuries, they were unable to create political systems strong enough to resist the intrusion of outside powers. As compared with Burma, Thailand, and Vietnam in South and East Asia, and some of the African states, the Inner Asian peoples failed to form political entities commensurate with their needs and circumstances.

In seeking to assess their limited political development in the twentieth century, one must take into account both the overwhelming power and the determined influence of the USSR and China, and in the earlier years, of Britain, and the essentially localized and tribal character of the indigenous settled and tribal peoples. The foreign influences were particularly powerful because they reflected the security interests of the great powers. Central Asia and Tibet and Sinkiang also offered significant economic benefits. Both the USSR and China encouraged settlement in the Inner Asian territories to satisfy the needs of their land-hungry peasants. In the case of Central Asia, the native cotton culture was also a major asset. Moreover, in contrast to the overseas empires of the West European nations, the Soviets and the Chinese formed territorial empires that were gradually integrated into the metropolitan political system. In this respect, relations were comparable to those of England with Wales, Scotland, and Northern Ireland.

Even within the degree of autonomy provided by their position as buffers, neither Afghanistan nor Mongolia—for different reasons—was able to develop the degree of centralization, participation, and mobilization requisite for an independent existence. Similarly Tibet, during the four decades (1911–1950) in which it had the opportunity to gauge the nature of the modern world and to prepare for the inevitable later tests of strength, failed to assert any significant initiative. In the case of Sinkiang, and the five provinces of Soviet Central Asia, it is more understandable that the lack of political heritage and the disproportionately powerful nature of foreign intrusions would have inhibited the development of modern political institutions if they had sought to create them.

Toward the end of the 1980s, a subtle but significant change took place in the relations between the foreign influences and the indigenous peoples. The Soviet Union moved from confrontation to détente in its relations with the United States and China, and its domestic problems came to have a higher priority than Inner Asian issues. At the same time, the indigenous peoples began to assert greater independence: the end of the war with Iraq gave Iran more freedom to proceed with domestic reforms; the Soviet withdrawal from Afghanistan set the stage for the formation of a new political system; the Muslim peoples of Central Asia began to assert their desire for greater autonomy in an era of *glasnost* and *perestroika;* and the Chinese moderated their policies in Tibet and Sinkiang for fear of arousing local antagonism. Especially in Soviet Central Asia, one can see the beginnings of a process similar to that which took place earlier in India and the other European colonies where the indigenous peoples appropriated the foreign institutions imposed on them as a means of asserting their aspirations for greater autonomy.

11

Economic Growth

Introduction

Patterns of economic structure and growth have been systematically studied, and can in principle be more accurately described and measured than patterns of international context or political structure and development. One must say "in principle," however, because for most of the societies of Inner Asia, reliable data that can serve as a basis for comparative indicators of structure and growth are sparse up to the last decades of the twentieth century.

At a very general level, the experience of the developed societies provides guidelines for the types of change one should look for in those that are less developed. Societies can be described as evolving from a primary stage, in which some four-fifths or more of the labor force is engaged in agriculture, through a secondary stage in which industry is the principal feature of economic activity, to a tertiary stage—sometimes referred to as "postindustrial"—in which as much as three-fifths of the labor force may be engaged in services. The widespread use of computers and robots, in particular, permits one to envisage a society in which human activity is largely limited to supervising a diversity of specialized machines. This sequence from agriculture to industry to services is not universal, however. As some societies develop, industrial employment remains rather low and stable, and the reduction in agricultural employment is absorbed by services. In some countries this results from a premodern heritage of commerce, which in modern times absorbs the surplus agrarian workers. In others, it is caused by the rapid expansion of government employment and other urban occupations. At the same time, it may reflect a failure to industrialize beyond a certain low level.

This shift in labor-force distribution reflects many other aspects of modernization, which are difficult to quantify in countries without adequate statistical services. It directly reflects agricultural improvement through greater use of machinery, chemical fertilizers, and irrigation; the growth in manufacturing, construction, and transportation; and the expansion of commerce and finance, and of central bureaucracies. Indirectly, these developments are also accompanied by improvements in health and education. More important, none of these developments is possible without a profound change in the values held by individuals as they come to accept the necessity of adapting their age-old traditional beliefs concerning the human condition to the rational approach that has evolved with the modern revolution in science and technology.

In the case of the Inner Asian societies, with the partial exception of Iran, which we are using as a benchmark, none of these aspects of economic and social change can be determined with any degree of accuracy. One must therefore do the best one can with the limited data available.

Economic Structure and Policies

Economic development in the societies of Inner Asia, with the limited exception of Iran, was at a very low level in the 1920s, and did not begin to evolve toward significant industrialization until 1945 or later. This was caused by a variety of circumstances. In Iran and Afghanistan the governments were primarily concerned in the earlier years with domestic security. Problems of territorial reorganization and the shock of the collectivization program delayed development in Central Asia. In Tibet the government showed no interest in economic development during the four decades it enjoyed virtual independence, and Sinkiang and Mongolia remained relatively undeveloped until China and the Soviet Union began to devote attention to them in the 1960s.

The simplest and least inaccurate indicator of economic development is the change in the employment of the labor force from agriculture to industry to services. More specifically, "agriculture" includes animal husbandry, fishing, and forestry; "industry" includes manufacturing, mining, and construction; and "services" include transportation, commerce, defense, and financial and personal services.

It is significant that, from a level of 80 percent or more of the labor force in agriculture in 1920, by 1980 only in Iran, the Kazakh SSR, and the Uzbek SSR had this share fallen below 50 percent. In the other Inner Asian societies, agricultural employment still absorbs from 60 to more than 80 percent of the labor force. It is clear from this pattern of development that Iran has benefited from its oil resources and the extensive participation of the West in its economy, and the Central Asian republics from the Soviet investment of vast resources in their economic growth and application of sustained developmental policies.

It is often said that only those less developed countries that enjoyed the benefits of colonialism have been able to develop, and Afghanistan and Tibet are good examples of the negative side of this generalization. But it is also true that colonialism is of no advantage if the colonizer is not interested in development. This was the case with Sinkiang and Mongolia until the recent decades.

Iran, among the political entities of Inner Asia, has been the most successful in using its resources to create a modern economic system. As the only country in Inner Asia that is not landlocked, Iran has benefited from being able to participate in global markets and trade directly through sea lanes. That Iran's best port facilities lie on the Persian Gulf rather than on the Gulf of Oman explains why Iran regards the Gulf as critical to its interests. In addition to its port facilities, Iran also has one of the world's largest reserves of petroleum, a resource that in the long-term economic perspective may have stunted the overall economic development of the country by making it possible to neglect other resources, industries, and incentives for economic infrastructure development. Thus, like cotton in the Uzbek and Tajik SSRs, petroleum exploitation in Iran has played such a critical role in producing revenue (and in perceived status) that agriculture, manufacturing, and development of the other resources have suffered. Commerce and trade, however, fueled by the spending of petroleum dollars, particularly after the formation of OPEC, have boomed. Although a certain amount of the benefit from oil exploitation trickled down through the economy, much of the profit remained in the hands of the Pahlavi-associated elites. High-ranking members of the military, a sector of government on which funds have been lavishly expended, also benefited from the oil profits. After an initial neglect, roads, railroads, and communications systems were developed, as were public health projects such as urban sewage and water systems.

Central economic planning side by side with traditional commercial activity mark the two poles of the Iranian economic structure during the modern period. These two poles are best represented by the government-owned central bank (Bank-e Markazi) and by the *sarraf* or moneylenders and changers of the bazaar. Both systems continue to operate today, with the *sarraf* serving as a quasi-legal black market under the Islamic Republic as well.

Given these two poles, which represent the traditional and modernizing structures, the trend since World War I has nevertheless been toward growth of the new economic structures, despite political change and periods of turmoil. Thus although the *sarraf* represents the tradition out of which support for the politically empowered leaders of the Islamic Republic of Iran came, the traditional economic structure is giving way before an increasingly centralized economy.

World War I capped a period in which Iran's economy remained without direction. This is especially marked in comparison with other Middle Eastern states of comparable population and history, such as Egypt and Turkey (E26, pp. 130–131). Steps toward restructuring the economy began with Reza Shah. The policies he instituted were multifaceted: financial restructuring, building a communications infrastructure, and encouraging private industry. Oil, the most exploited of Iran's mineral resources, accounted for only 13 percent of the gross national product during the period of Reza Shah; in the exceptionally high period of the early 1970s it rose to 70 percent.

The accomplishments of the 1920s and 1930s mark a conscious adoption of a modernization perspective following the Western model. Unlike the later period when Iran's development became closely tied to Western cooperation, personnel, and loans, however, this early period was marked by austere self-reliance. The effort was undertaken without foreign loans and with little foreign advice or personnel.

In building a communications network, the government launched a major effort to make roads passable for motorized vehicles and to build railroads, in particular rail lines connecting the fertile and populous central plateau and northwest with the Gulf coast on a north-south axis running through Tehran. Started in 1927 with German civil engineers and Iranian administrators and laborers, the railroad began running in 1936 but was not completed until after World War II. The project was financed with money raised from excise taxes on tea and sugar. The railroad has always been a symbol of the bootstrap effort at development and a source of pride in the accomplishments of the Reza Shah period.

Other efforts laid the groundwork for air and telephone communications, mainly between Tehran and other major cities. The establishment of the Agricultural and Industrial Bank in 1933 was indicative of the government's concern with encouraging private industry, especially that connected with basic consumer and export goods, such as refining (sugar from sugar beets) and processing (tea, silk, cotton, and other textiles). Financial restructuring became a cornerstone of the new economic thrust. Iran unilaterally canceled its commercial treaties (the Soviet Union under Lenin had already repudiated tsarist economic agreements), and worked to revise or better control its concessions, mainly petroleum. Its dispute with Britain over the oil concession went as far as the World Court and led to better terms and somewhat increased revenue from taxes and profits. Still, oil revenues, all of which were plowed into building up the military, accounted for only a fraction of income. The main development funds came from taxes and private industry.

Budgeting, control over expenditures, and a distinct movement toward government monopolies set the tone for later economic policy. The twenty-seven monopolies of the Reza Shah period covered many consumer goods such as sugar, tea, and tobacco.

Banking, previously controlled by the Imperial Bank (British), also came under government supervision with the establishment of the Bank-e Markazi which oversaw currency issue and the conversion of the money system to paper notes. Confidence in the banking system on the eve of World War II was reflected in the steady increase in deposits.

The decade between the abdication of Reza Shah (1941) and the adoption of the First National Development Plan (1951) witnessed economic disruptions caused by foreign interference and internal political upheaval. Trade and income fell while agitation for the nationalization of oil led to heavy dependence on this resource despite the recognition of the pitfalls of relying on a single resource. For example, the First National Development Plan was crippled by the drop in oil revenues resulting from a buyer boycott of Iranian oil following nationalization. From the period of oil-revenue stabilization (1954) on, Iran's economic policy has relied heavily on oil revenues and a planned central economy set forth in five-year development plans. The period between 1954 and 1978, roughly corresponding to the period of direct rule by Mohammed Reza Shah, saw the continuation of certain previous policies—heavy military expenditures, for example—but also greater attention to the relationship between economic and social development. This is reflected in the goals of the White Revolution, announced in 1963, which included land reform, the incorporation of rural economies into the fabric of the country, and the raising of social and economic standards through central planning and management. Iranian economic growth was unprecedented in the developing world during the 1960s and 1970s. Real gross national income rose by 13, 34, and 42 percent in the three years from 1972–1973 to 1974–1975. However, linked as Iran was to the world economy through its dependence on oil revenues, with the decline in income from oil, the country experienced a decline in the funds that fueled the national development plans.

In social terms the enormous economic development of Iran within the modern period has created a considerable amount of imbalance and dissatisfaction, particularly in the traditional sectors of society—agricultural and semiskilled workers. High expectations and an inability to meet those expectations, as well as a clash in values between tradition and modernity, led to social and political turmoil that sidetracked the economy. The political system did not develop apace with economic modernization. The basic trends in the economic system, however, have in principle been little affected by the Islamic revolution that replaced the monarchy. Central planning, reliance on oil revenues, and tight economic controls continue to form the basis for the economic future. The diversion of revenues into the war effort against Iraq (1981–1988) took a heavy toll on consumer goods and services and resulted in cost-of-living increases of unmatched proportions, increases that outpaced salaries in the public sector. The war also resulted in a sharp decline in investment. Because a large portion of the intelligentsia and general public was employed in the public sector, middle-class dissatisfaction with the economy ran deep. The restrictions on imports and luxury items necessitated by the decline in foreign reserves, which are needed to pay for military equipment, causes further dissatisfaction. Preferential treatment of members of traditional clerical elites and their extended families further exacerbates the situation. To compensate for revenues lost because of lower oil prices and a decreased capacity to produce and sell oil, the government resorted to prohibitive currency control (the rial to dollar exchange rate on the unofficial market had increased by 1,000 percent), excise and import duties, and the rationing of consumer goods and foodstuffs.

The war effort and politically unsettled conditions in the aftermath of sociopolitical change made economic goals seem less urgent. Rapid population growth and the accompanying demands for continued economic development, however, promise to force the government into renewed attention to the formulation of clear economic policies. Public funds will be needed for further development of resource diversification and exploitation (of copper, for example) and for basic socioeconomic development, and attention must also be paid to increasing agricultural and industrial output.

The Afghan economy in the 1920s, along with that of Tibet, was one of the least developed among the societies of Inner Asia. The social and political upheavals of the 1920s kept Afghanistan in an almost static economic state, and during this period the patterns that had evolved under Abdur Rahman continued. However, in the 1930s, the Afghans began their own economic development programs, centered around the activities of several energetic entrepreneurs.

After World War II, Afghanistan, which had remained neutral but had profited from the sale of agricultural products to the allied armies in India, attempted large-scale irrigation projects with foreign assistance: American in the southwest, Soviet in the southeast, Chinese north of Kabul. Problems precluded the predicted results, and led to huge debts for the Afghans. Other foreign-assisted programs simply increased the debts, so that by the time of the 1978 coup, Afghan exports were largely devoted to debt servicing.

However, as is discussed later, Daoud's second period witnessed great economic progress in every sector: the industrial components expanded; favorable export-import balances were achieved; hard currency and gold reserves rose perceptibly; agricultural production increased.

During the Cold War, both superpowers competed for the soul of Afghanistan. American projects were geared to assist; Soviet projects to exploit resources, which was only natural because the USSR and Afghanistan are next-door neighbors. Afghanistan's natural resources are considerable: natural gas (which flows through pipelines to the USSR and fills important energy requirements of Soviet Central Asia); oil (not yet developed); iron ore (one of the world's largest high-quality deposits is in the Hajigak area of central Afghanistan); uranium (much of which the Soviets have already removed); copper; and other minerals.

But agriculture and herding remain the mainstays of Afghanistan's economic structure, and plans for improvement and extension in the industrial sector have seldom figured in government policy, unless foreign governments prompted those in power.

Several partial (1950, 1955) and complete (1961–1963) economic slowdowns and blockades of the Afghan-Pakistan border threatened to force all Afghanistan's transit facilities to the north, but timely negotiations intervened. Each time, however, the Afghan economy became more dependent on the Soviet Union. By 1977, the Soviet Union and eastern bloc nations accounted for 40–50 percent of Afghanistan's import-export transactions, and the Soviet Union, which negotiated renewable five-year barter protocols, was Afghanistan's single most important trade and aid partner.

The 1961–1963 border closing caused a major shift in the annual migration of Afghan (Pushtun) seminomads. Previously, about 320,000 nomad-trader-laborers had crossed the Durand Line to winter in Pakistan. After the 1961 blockade, the number trickled to about 3,000 or so. Because enough foothill pasture lands were still available inside Afghanistan, the seminomads adjusted to the new conditions, but not without some altercations with neighboring villages.

In spite of the fact that Afghanistan received per capita one of the world's larger foreign assistance efforts, there was little improvement in the quality of life of the people in the countryside, the presumed target of all development efforts. The culture itself, as manifested by the individual's reactions in the society, was a great restraint to Western-style development.

The late 1960s and the 1970s witnessed two economic developments, both with positive and negative aspects. The first was the increase in the production of opium linked to the international drug market. Thousands of acres of opium poppies flourished along the main road from Jalalabad to the border. So many high officials benefited from this lucrative smuggling trade that the farmers grew this cash crop with impunity. Much of the acreage under food crops was turned into poppy fields because a farmer could make many times more growing poppies than wheat. And he could buy wheat in spite of inflated prices and still have what was to him a magnificent profit. This same pattern continued under the Soviet occupation, and has spread into the North-West Frontier Province of neighboring Pakistan.

The second development was the increase in migrant labor, which traveled to Iran, the Persian Gulf States, Saudi Arabia, and even Libya and Western Europe. In 1977, approximately three hundred thousand legal and illegal Afghans worked as migrant laborers and sent remittances home in hard currency. Before the 1978 coup, those who returned brought back instant wealth and poured part of it into the economy. They bought land and motor vehicles (including buses), and built new houses. They also returned laden down with radios, tape recorders, TV sets, and even refrigerators. The government, however, never did solve the dilemma of equitably taxing the income of migrant workers, most of which was usually deposited in Da Afghanistan Bank.

In 1988, few of the migrant workers returned home. Most went to Pakistan to seek out their families in the refugee camps, where they used their money to gain influence with the refugees and Pakistani officials. The 350-plus refugee camps in Pakistan have economic lives of their own. The government of Pakistan does not permit refugees to own land, for this would give the impression that the refugees (or, at least some of them) do not plan to return home when the war ends. However, Afghan males do work as laborers, for Pakistani contractors say they work better (and for lower wages) than the local population. Refugee Afghan buses and trucks are very competitive in Pakistan.

The World Bank and the UN High Commissioner are financing three types of projects to help restore the ecological damage done in Pakistan by the three and a half million refugees and their more than three million head of livestock: (1) reforestation; (2) repair and expansion of the road system; (3) repair and improvement of the water facilities. Fifty percent of the workers are theoretically Afghan refugees, 50 percent local people.

Urban Afghan merchants and shopkeepers have invested in the local Pakistani economies, often with Pakistani partners. These urbanites will return home, but will leave their investments behind, thus expanding their economic links with Pakistan.

By early 1988, ten years after the first refugees arrived in Pakistan, social, economic, and political stresses had surfaced, but were still largely under control. The refugee influx has not been totally negative on the Pakistani side. Foreign aid, particularly from the United States, has greatly increased, including both economic and military assistance. An urban building boom has exploded in such places as Peshawar, the North-West Frontier, and Baluchistan, to accommodate those urban refugees who do not wish to live in refugee camps. International and bilateral organizations have spent millions of dollars and other hard currencies on refugee needs, and have given many jobs to Pakistanis who might otherwise be unemployed. New Pakistani refugee-oriented businesses flourish.

More important, the refugees have been exposed, many for the first time, to educational opportunities, public health facilities, and medical treatment. No matter what shape a future free Afghanistan government may take, the returned refugees will demand such facilities as their right for collected taxes.

The Muslim societies of Soviet Central Asia have resembled Iran in the extent to which their economic development has been achieved with significant Russian and other European investment and assistance. The two cases differ significantly, however: in Central Asia the foreigners came as settlers and administrators, and in effect established a modern economy parallel to and distinct from the agricultural and herding economy of the indigenous peoples.

By the first decade of the twentieth century, the economy of Central Asia, which was under the domination of the Russians, was effectively divided into two segments: the traditional agricultural and nomadic realm which had essentially been left untouched in the hands of the indigenous Turkic and Iranian peoples, and the evolving urban industrial, manufacturing realm established and essentially manned by the incoming Russian colonists. Although the diversity of agricultural products was remarkable and local handicraft industries were well developed among the local populations, little was done to open trade beyond regional markets, and little or no attempt was made to accumulate surpluses for central investment and growth. At the onset of the revolution and the civil war in the tsarist empire, Central Asia remained in the main an agricultural and nomadic region, with farming, animal herding, and local trade as the primary economic activities. It was in these economic pursuits that the indigenous peoples found their basic employ.

Between 1926 and 1930, after several administrative reorganizations, Central

Asia was divided into five Soviet Socialist republics. The former General Government of the Steppe became the Kazakh SSR, with somewhat enlarged frontiers; and the Kirgiz, Tajik, Turkmen, and Uzbek SSRs were formed from the General Government of Turkestan. At the same time the continued influx of European settlers—Russians, Ukrainians, Byelorussians, and Volga Germans—changed the ethnic balance in this area. By the 1980s, non-Muslims outnumbered Muslims by a considerable margin in the Kazakh SSR, and formed a substantial minority in the Uzbek SSR. Since the non-Muslims were predominantly concerned with the industrial sector, the agrarian-industrial and rural-urban balances became increasingly synonymous with the ethnic balance between Muslim and non-Muslim.

As the European population moved into the cities and major centers of settlement, they brought with them—and dominated—new factories, industries, and industrial occupations. As might have been expected, not only did the cotton-milling and textile plants come under Russian control, but the critically important railway and telegraph systems they introduced served as the technological sinews of imperial rule.

This basic pattern did not change during the first decade of Soviet rule in the 1920s, and the Turkic and Iranian indigenes were not brought into the urban and industrial workplace in any significant way. As the communications and transport networks were consolidated and expanded, they remained the province of the European newcomers, as did the construction, mining, and energy industries. The basic division between the rural agricultural world of the Muslim peoples and the urban industrial world of the Slavs was preserved. Those Turkic and Iranian groups that did enter the urban arena did so in small numbers and in unskilled capacities, while the size of Slavic communities in the countryside was similarly unremarkable. The period of the New Economic Policy essentially left the old symbiotic economy of the nomadic, agricultural, and urban regions in place, and, other than consolidating the Slavic hold over the urban networks of Central Asia, did not disturb traditional prerevolutionary patterns.

The first major break from this benevolent neglect came with the initiation of the series of five-year plans beginning in 1928. Two dramatic departures were undertaken at that time: (1) the rapid industrialization of the urban sector of the Central Asian republics to correspond to the political emphasis and drive toward heavy industrial development throughout the Soviet system; and (2) the collectivization of agriculture and settlement of the nomadic peoples, a process that struck especially hard at the Kazakh clans of the northern steppes. The drive toward rapid industrialization, which marked the entire period until 1941, not only catalyzed an astonishing growth of industry in Soviet Central Asia—statistics made more intelligible and less dramatic by the virtual zero starting point of such growth—it also initiated the creation of a substantial indigenous labor force which began to move into the cities and master the industrial skills necessary in that new setting. Conversely, the price for this industrialization was paid in large part by the rural and steppe population which was forced into collective agricultural settlements and compelled to deliver its surplus product to the state to cover the investments in industry. The human, livestock, and material costs of collectivization were enormous. Although the expectation of war and the need to prepare the state for this emergency are often given as the rationale for this extraordinary episode, the available evidence would indicate that factional domestic politics and the tactical maneuvering associated with such factionalism also played a large role.

Such development and the very concept of the five-year plans were clearly government-designed and directed. The private sector, which had been preserved and even partially encouraged during the 1920s, was destroyed. The revolutionary state, which had come into being in 1917 with promises of land for the people and control to the workers, had in some sense come full circle, and instituted a centrally owned and directed strategy of state enterprise stressing radical industrial development. The social and political significance of this unique volte-face had more to do with Stalin and the bitter political infighting of the time than it had to do with Marx and his theories of economic development.

It has been calculated that the level of industrial output of the Central Asian republics in 1928 was still below that of 1913. The remarkable spurt that characterized industrial growth in the region thereafter included mining and railroad development; the intensified exploitation of mineral deposits; coal and nonferrous metals extraction; the construction of textile mills, agricultural machinery, factories, and food-processing plants. Much of the mining and railway development was carried out in the mineral-rich areas of the Kazakh and Kirgiz northern areas, whereas the textile and rural machinery plants were constructed in the cotton-rich and agriculturally southern regions of Uzbekistan. However low the starting point for such growth—to say nothing of the appalling human costs—the rapid growth of industrial development during the decade before the war was impressive.

This growth received an additional impetus during the war years when substantial segments of the industrial plant of the western European regions of the USSR around the major urban centers of Moscow, Leningrad, and Kiev were evacuated to the east to take them out of the reach of the advancing German armies. Whatever normal industrial expansion was previously planned for the Central Asian republics was substantially augmented by the emergency evacuation of factories from the European west. Tractor works, electrochemical plants, textile and agricultural machinery factories, glassworks, and other metallurgical installations all benefited from the transfer of such critical equipment. Both old and new plants in and around the major cities of Tashkent, Alma Ata, Ashkabad, Frunze, Ferghana, Samarkand, Aktiubinsk, and Chirchik were the beneficiaries of such tactical moves. Much of this was supplemented by investment in new war-related facilities, since the remoteness of Central Asia from the war zones made it relatively secure.

Although much of the transferred industrial plant was returned to European Russia and the western regions of the Soviet Union after the war, a good portion of it remained to enhance Central Asian capabilities. The war period served to strengthen substantially both the material basis for industrialization of the region and the technical skills and training of the indigenous population which had been pulled into the process.

Nevertheless, these patterns of investment in the Central Asian republics did not continue into the postwar period. Whatever the strategic reasons for curtailing diversification of industrial investment throughout the USSR as a whole may have been, Moscow's primary concern in these years was the reconstruction and rehabilitation of the badly damaged plants and facilities in the European and western regions of the Soviet Union. On the whole, the essential profile of the Central Asian economy continued to be agrarian and pastoral until the late 1950s. Until then, the rate of investment in industrial growth in Central Asia remained lower than the all-Union average.

It was only with the five-year plan of 1959 that this rate was projected at a level comparable to all-Union trends, and this rate was maintained subsequently. In spite of this intensification, and the impressive industrial growth produced, much of this buildup was supplementary to the plantation economy of the region, and was concentrated in such areas as agricultural machinery, hydroelectric power and energy, chemical fertilizers, and transportation. There had also been an important move of the population into areas of light industry and services. Throughout the early 1980s, there were increasingly urgent and articulate voices heard in these republics calling for a more complex and sophisticated diversification of the local economies as well as increased central investment in the region. Substantial advances had been made over the previous thirty years in economic diversification, and such successes seemed to have raised further expectations and demands.

One major issue around which many of these discussions revolved was the long-debated river-diversion project intended to turn the waters of the northern Siberian rivers toward the Central Asian south to irrigate new areas and thus enhance the economies of those republics. The decision on this gargantuan proposal was several times postponed, and seemed to have been finally shelved and canceled in the summer of 1987, but its debate may have catalyzed the emergence of an embryonic lobby in the region calling for more sophisticated development strategies for Central Asia in the future.

Sinkiang's economic development is poorly documented, in contrast to the record of economic growth in the Muslim republics of Soviet Central Asia. Population has grown substantially, though much of the increase has been the result of immigration by Chinese (Han), a policy promoted by both the Nationalist government in the 1940s, and the Communists thereafter. In 1949, the population of Sinkiang was roughly 4 million, and about 75 percent Uighur, 10 percent Kazakh, 6 percent Mongolian, and 5 percent Chinese (Han); the remaining 4 percent was divided among nine smaller groups. By 1982, there were about 13 million inhabitants altogether, of which Uighurs numbered 5,949,661 as against 5,186,533 Chinese (Han).

During roughly the same period the province developed quite substantially, with mining, oil production, and industry growing faster than agriculture. Many of China's rocket and nuclear-weapon facilities are also located in Sinkiang. Much of the work force in these new industries, however, would appear to consist of Chinese immigrants, and not local workers learning new tasks. Official figures state that compared to 1954, by 1984 the gross value of industrial and agricultural output had risen 10.02 times, agricultural output was up 5.94 times, grain output up 3.4 times, and cotton up 12.9 times. Sinkiang's overall contribution to the Chinese economy remains quite small, however, perhaps 1.4 percent of agriculture, 0.7 percent of industry.

Figures on the shares of consumption, investment, and government are unobtainable. However, there has been a large increase in the number of personnel in the state administration, and the Chinese press reported in the 1980s that administrative expenditures escalated alarmingly, rising 30 percent in 1984 and another 30 percent in the first half of 1985, although no base was given.

Similarly in Tibet, recent economic development after many decades of immobility has followed from the settlement of large numbers of Han Chinese civilian and military personnel. Estimates of the size of the Chinese settlements vary, but it appears that in the late 1980s they were roughly equal to the indigenous population.

The PRC guarantees special pay and benefits to Chinese who agree to spend a long period in Tibet. The transfer of Chinese workers to Tibet is officially referred to as a means to modernize Tibet's economy, though a direct effect of the transfer policy has been that thousands of Tibetans, especially in Lhasa, have lost their jobs. The PRC reports that the Chinese who are transferred to Tibet are technicians and skilled workers, though Western travelers in Tibet have observed Han Chinese unskilled laborers at work on projects. Government subsidies of Chinese immigrants' salaries in Tibet have served to add an economic dimension to the already existing polarization of cultures and politics of Tibetans and Chinese.

The Mongolian People's Republic, in contrast to Sinkiang and Tibet, has been protected from massive foreign settlements by its status as an independent country. For the same reason it has also lacked the stimulus for development that has accompanied foreign intervention in the neighboring territories.

In spite of the official MPR emphasis on developing industry, government statistics show a very modest growth in the number of workers employed in industry between 1960, 12.1 percent of all workers, and 1980, 15.2 percent of all workers (M45, p. 141). Although the number of workers employed in the agricultural sector dropped by one-third between 1960 (60.8 percent) and 1980 (40.2 percent), fields other than industry (such as public health, education, transport, and trade) seem to have absorbed those workers. In contrast to the MPR where twice as many workers are employed in the agricultural sector (which includes animal husbandry) as in industry, in the Inner Mongolian Autonomous Region the 1985 statistics show that well over three times as many workers were employed in industry as in farming and animal husbandry (D4, p. 95).

Nonetheless, the industrial sector of the MPR has grown steadily since 1950. In that year industry contributed only 9.8 percent of the MPR's gross national product. By 1983, that figure had increased to 32.2 percent (M39, p. 219). The comparable figure for industrial contribution to total output for the IMAR for 1984 was 43.7 percent (D4, p. 29).

Agriculture

The peoples of Inner Asia were predominantly engaged in agriculture and herding before the twentieth century. In view of the limited availability of water, these occupations produced little surplus in the form of taxes or profits that could be invested in manufacturing or social services. Forced collectivization in the territories controlled by the Soviet Union and China and in Mongolia sought to solve these problems. It met with such fierce resistance, however, that the ensuing destruction of lives and livestock significantly delayed the benefits that might have been derived from this reform.

During the period of Iran's impressive economic development, agriculture received limited attention. If in the category of agriculture we include animal husbandry, a relative decline in production can be seen. In the early part of the Pahlavi era, political struggle between the central government and tribal groups led to a policy of detribalization or at least settlement, which had the unintended effect of reducing sheep and other animal herds. The cumulative effect of this policy and rapid population growth has been to make Iran an importer of meat and poultry from Europe and Australia as well as neighboring areas such as Afghanistan when that option existed. As long as import capacity remained high, imported meats and poultry products sold at cheaper rates than locally grown equivalents, thus further reducing the incentive to increase or maintain production capacity. When lower oil prices and the diversion of money to the war effort made it harder to pay for imports, meat and poultry had to be rationed. Although there appears to be a trend toward repasturalization of some tribes, Iran's available pastures have been deemed incapable of maintaining the herd levels of 1975. Overgrazing would reduce available pastures to desert, thereby aggravating the problem. Thus, meat production will remain a difficult problem, even under stable political conditions.

Despite the low priority accorded to the agricultural sector in development planning and expenditure, several measures have been introduced to deal with agricultural problems. Most important have been the land-reform and water-management programs, and agribusiness, price support, and credit policies. In discussing these, however, the large-scale population shift from rural to urban areas should serve as a backdrop. The urban population is expected to reach 60 percent or more by the close of this century, up from 31 percent in 1956.

Land reform constituted the main part of the White Revolution announced by Mohammed Reza Shah in 1962–1963. Overall the plan aimed at decreasing large landholdings and making landowners out of tenant farmers and sharecroppers. The system of absentee landlords owning tens or hundreds of villages was to be converted to small resident-family-owned farms with the landlord receiving a set price for the land and the government supplying seed, water, and tools, and buying the harvest. Of the approximately fifty-five thousand villages in Iran 4 percent or about two thousand either belonged to the Pahlavi family or were public domain lands. The public lands were already distributed by the time the shah announced the "Revolution of the Shah and the People" in 1963 by which privately held lands would also undergo sale and distribution. Opposition by landowners and many among the clergy stalled the operation, but it was finally begun in 1963 and completed by 1975.

Among the many problems arising from the sale of land was that of providing for the resources offered by the landlord, such as seeds and tools. The government set up an elaborate bureaucracy to deal with credit and with the purchase of harvests, and invested in a plan for rural cooperative societies. A second problem was the resale of land and whether owners ought be given the right of sale. Landlord families also circumvented mandatory sale by reallocating villages among family members, thus taking advantage of the section of the law that allowed the landlord to retain "one village." Some of the problems were related to uneven planning: access roads from villages to the harvest sales centers were not improved as rapidly as necessary. Storage facilities did not keep up with need, resulting in spoiled crops. Another adverse factor was the shah's attempt, in the mid-1970s, to set up agribusinesses and to force farmers who had received land to surrender their holdings and join government-sponsored corporations. Nevertheless, the land reform has been accomplished in its essence, and so far has not been basically changed by the revolutionary government. But whether in the future it can lead to higher production to meet the needs of a fast-growing population remains in doubt, especially in the meat-production sector.

The government has also taken a strong interest in water-resource control and development and has experimented with agribusiness. Water control has been accomplished by two methods widely regarded as essential components of economic modernization: dams and wells. By 1972 dams on twelve rivers had created water reservoirs to supply mushrooming urban areas, hydroelectric power, and controlled water for agriculture and an increase in irrigated land. The increase in irrigated land promised from these dam projects has fallen short of goals by over half because of inadequate distribution systems. Displacement of rural valley populations has accompanied dam construction.

Wells and diesel pumps have also increased arable land and have come to supplement the traditional means of irrigation through underground channels.

The latter system, heavily reliant on communal cooperation (usually through a landlord) and the availability of cheap labor for maintenance, has undergone considerable deterioration as dams and pumps tap alternative sources of water: rivers and aquifers. These modern, technologically advanced techniques also carry with them long-term problems in agriculture that have plagued Western agriculture: depletion of aquifers, evaporation, and salinization. Increased use of chemical fertilizer, produced cheaply from the abundant natural gas of the oil industry, and pesticides threaten agricultural problems similar to those that remain unresolved in the modernized world. Chemical fertilizers have been subsidized by the government, putting the cost of both imported and local fertilizers below real costs of production and encouraging their widespread use. Farming with fertilizers is in the process of replacing integrated animal-land farming.

Technological advances in agriculture, widely espoused by the government and built into the five-year plans, may come to represent something short of the panacea touted by advocates of modernized agriculture as side effects of applied technology become felt. For example, a major project in Fars Province, begun under the shah but continued under the Islamic Republic, is developing citrus groves in dry areas through the use of wells and pumps and has begun to yield marketable produce. However, the aquifer on which the project relies may exhaust its capacity within a decade at the current rate of use. Such an event would not only disrupt the production of citrus but displace hundreds of families settled as part of the depastoralization of members of the Qashqa'i tribe. In recognition of the problems in applied modern technology, the Iranian government supported research projects that have led to the use of ever newer technological improvements in agriculture: new high-yield, disease-resistant seed, drainage systems, and experiments with drip-irrigation in orchards. Widespread adoption of new technologies from pesticides to proper seed use requires standards of educational and social organization that may lag behind technology adoption for years to come.

When the Democratic Republic of Afghanistan was established in 1978, about 85 percent of the population was engaged in agriculture, herding, or combinations of the two. Yet only 12 percent of the total area of Afghanistan was cultivable, and because of water shortages and inhospitable soil or terrain less than 6 percent was annually farmed. Nevertheless, before the 1950s Afghanistan was self-sufficient in foodstuffs and could export large quantities of agricultural produce, particularly fresh and dried fruits and nuts. The introduction of large-scale infrastructure projects, however, attracted many rural males away from the farms. As the rural population was lured away from the land, with the result that smaller crops were grown, Afghanistan began to import foodstuffs—mainly PL 480 wheat from the United States.

In the 1960s and 1970s, a slow reversal began. More young Afghans in agricultural engineering returned home and more foreign technicians helped in the process. By the mid-1970s Afghanistan had once again become self-sufficient in wheat, and exports of fruit, nuts, and meat increased. Land under cultivation rose from about 9,400,000 acres in 1966 to about 9,600,000 in 1978. Wheat yields increased from 772 to 1,007 pounds per acre. Rice jumped from 1,351 to 1,695 pounds; sugar beets from 12,460 pounds to 16,910 pounds; vegetables from 4,474 to 6,183 pounds. From 1975 to 1978, agricultural exports rose from $170.71 million to $221.61 million, and imports fell from $20.96 million to $18.30 million.

Grandiose irrigation and power projects undertaken by foreigners—the United States in the Hilmand-Arghandab valleys; the USSR in the Jalalabad area; and China in Kohistan north of Kabul—proved to be less than successful, and were partly destroyed in the fighting after 1978.

Land reforms decreed in 1978 by the Democratic Republic of Afghanistan failed for several reasons. First, the *mujahidin* controlled most of the country-side. Second, Islam respects private ownership of property, and even tenants objected to the state unilaterally seizing land to distribute it to landless peasants. Also, according to a 1963 survey, approximately 60 percent of all farmers in Afghanistan owned land; 20 percent were sharecroppers of one type or another; another 20 percent worked for wages.

The back-to-back 1971–1972 droughts in central Afghanistan illustrate the problems faced by land reform. Several thousand people died before the government (with US AID assistance) was able to bring foodstuffs to the affected areas on trucks pressed into duty on an involuntary basis. The afflicted region was very difficult to reach, and only through emergency organization and police power was a larger tragedy prevented. The government, however, had learned its lesson, and grain-storage bins were built around the country at strategic points.

An encouraging sign for agriculture began to appear by 1965. The number of tractors purchased by independent owners over a twelve-year period (1965–1977) reached almost two thousand. However, in the proposed seven-year plan (1976–1983) of the second Daoud period, private agribusiness was played down in favor of a collective-farm orientation, chiefly because none of the Afghan planners understood the agricultural scene. The April 1978 coup torpedoed any implementation of Daoud's plan.

Decree No. 6 of the DRA abolished all mortgage arrangements and loans made prior to 1973, and prorated those agreements entered into after 1973. The problem was that the decree struck at the heart of the reciprocal rights and obligations around which Afghan rural life was organized. Legal abolition of usury does not eliminate the small farmer's need for extra capital, and viable alternatives had not been established by the DRA before the decree was promulgated. Also, widespread insurrection and revolts and land reforms are incompatible ingredients, as the Americans discovered in Vietnam.

The escalation of the war brought about by the Soviet invasion in December 1979 exacerbated the problems, as Soviet tactics of "rubblization" of rural villages was followed by "migratory genocide." Over one-third of the prewar population of about fifteen million Afghans, mainly rural folk, fled the country, the majority to Pakistan (c. 3.5 million) and Iran (c. 2 million). At least another one million are internal refugees, having moved from their destroyed villages to nearby valleys or to urban centers. By January 1985 about twelve thousand of Afghanistan's twenty-two thousand villages had been destroyed and deserted, and approximately five thousand had been substantially damaged.

The Soviet and DRA aircraft have also attempted to wipe out livestock, thus denying the villagers and the *mujahidin* needed foodstuffs and transport animals (camels, horses, mules, donkeys). The commodities necessary for agricultural production were also blocked: seeds; fertilizer; chemicals to control weeds, insects, and diseases.

All twenty-nine provinces of Afghanistan were affected by this ecological devastation, and this can, if uncorrected, cause famine. In addition, the destruction of the irrigation systems, terraced vertically in the mountains, dug horizontally on the plains, or built as underground canals, also set the stage for potential famines. As much as 30 percent of the arable land was returned to weeds. These generations-old canals, built with available technology, cannot be rejuvenated quickly.

In Central Asia the Soviets inherited the traditional economic division between the Kazakh steppes and grasslands to the north and the southern desert and river valley areas of the Uzbek, Turkmen, Tajik, and Kirgiz regions of Turkestan. The nomadic pastoralism of the Kazakh tribes had long been the characteristic activity of that region, while the more diversified southern regions of Turkestan sustained agriculture, seminomadism, and substantial urban complexes. The appearance of the Russians here in the late eighteenth and nineteenth centuries had several major effects on these patterns.

The primary immediate effect in the north was to curtail gradually the amount and quality of land available to the nomadic clans and tribes because of the settlement patterns of the rural Russian and other European newcomers. In turn, this phenomenon brought pressure to bear on the Kazakhs themselves to settle and turn to agricultural pursuits. The process was actively encouraged by the tsarist authorities who attempted to resettle Kazakh groups that had lost some of their best pastures or had their traditional migration routes blocked by the new Slavic farmlands. In some ways, although there was little coercion and the process was marked by none of the extravagant violence that occurred in the later 1930s, this trend presaged the events of the great settlement and collectivization drive under Stalin. This partial adaptation to sedentarism had affected a substantial segment of the Kazakh populace by the time of the Russian revolution; some estimates indicate that as many as 80 percent depended in part on agriculture for their livelihood. This process was further intensified in the decade thereafter. Adoption of the scythe instead of the sickle allowed the Kazakhs to lay in greater supplies of winter fodder and actually expand their care and raising of cattle, though this process too impelled them toward new patterns of settlement.

However minor the role of the Kazakhs may have been in this process of agricultural settlement in this transitional period, the process was well underway and received new impetus in the postrevolutionary decade. It was the Slavs who had spearheaded the agricultural transformation of the grasslands. From the 1880s on, European migrants had moved into the northern plains area and slowly turned it into a grain-producing belt: wheat, oats, rye, barley, potatoes, corn, and other food crops. By the eve of the First World War, close to forty million acres of the Kazakh steppe lands had been sown and were in cultivation, almost 10 percent of the whole area, an impressive figure compared to the less than 3 percent under cultivation in the more traditional agricultural regions in the river valleys of the Uzbek south.

Tsarist policy since the late eighteenth century had encouraged the settlement of Russians and other Europeans in Kazakh lands, and had also sought to persuade the Kazakh nomads to settle and turn to agricultural pursuits. In the Uzbek regions to the south, the cutting off of cotton imports by the American Civil War led the Russians to encourage the intensification of cotton growing and the introduction of higher-grade American varieties of cotton. In the central Ferghana district alone, the areas allocated to cotton were expanded from 15 percent of the cultivated land in 1885 to almost 50 percent by the time of the revolution.

This central policy shift from grain to cotton came to have extremely negative consequences for the region during the difficult years of the civil war and its aftermath from 1918 to 1923. The longstanding concentration on cotton kept food production low, which crippled the populace in the face of serious grain shortfalls under war conditions. With Central Asia virtually cut off from grain supplies from the central Russian regions, a series of severe famines devastated the area and its indigenous population. The meager grain supplies that did exist locally were further depleted either through forced requisitions by Soviet authorities, or through raids by local bandits. Soviet estimates indicate that as many as 1,100,000 people may have died in Turkestan in 1919 alone. The numbers of famine victims in the Kazakh grasslands to the north were similarly high.

It was the New Economic Policy that reversed some of the worst features of War Communism, curtailing food requisitions in the area, and introducing limited opportunities for surplus accumulation and private sales. Growing policies were liberalized and free trade practices were encouraged to reestablish local markets, food supplies, and exchange. Soviet authorities paid renewed attention to reconstruction of irrigation systems which had fallen into disuse or been destroyed during the turmoil of the revolution and civil war, and special reclamation committees were formed to assist the peasantry in such rebuilding projects. Here again there were differences in such patterns between the Kazakh north and the regions of Turkestan to the south.

A decree of early 1924, which specified that lands earlier confiscated from rich peasants should be redistributed to newly sedentary nomads by the Kazakh Commissariat of Agriculture, resulted in very little actual land distribution, but at least established the principle of such use. The new atmosphere of permissiveness at a minimum allowed local authorities and communities the breathing space to rebuild patterns of viable economic life. In spite of tremendous earlier losses during the revolution and civil war, both herd sizes and the percentage of sown land in 1925 were back to two-thirds of their level in 1917.

Similarly, without any special prodding from Soviet authorities, the share of Kazakh labor in agricultural investment and output also rose by over 10 percent over the course of the decade. The very success of this pattern at local levels eventually was to lead to its curtailment by central authorities. By 1926–1927, the disparity between low government payments for agricultural foodstuffs and the high prices available to the Kazakh herder and agriculturalist on the private market had caused many producers to withhold their products from the state market, thus lowering supplies to the center and the cities. It was this crisis, compounded by intensified political factionalism within the Kremlin, that led to the decisions of the Fifteenth Party Congress in 1927 to end private ownership in the countryside, collectivize agriculture, and thereby produce a grain surplus and capital to drive a rapid industrialization campaign. Similar patterns pertained, with slightly different specific characteristics, in the regions of Turkestan.

Between the date of the territorial demarcation and 1927–1928, substantial investments were made by economic authorities in the southern republics, especially the Uzbek SSR, to reestablish the irrigation systems that had suffered so badly during the revolution and the civil war and expand agricultural production. The emphasis in this process was clearly on cotton acreage and output, with a series of special investments and taxes restricting grain growth to nonirrigated areas and irrigated lands being increasingly shifted to cotton production. By the end of 1927, such investments produced an area devoted to cotton larger than that in 1914, while the land in grain was less than two-thirds the 1914 level. Of the three and a half million irrigated acres under cultivation in Uzbekistan, almost 45 percent was still in grain, with just under 40 percent devoted to cotton. But, with the collectivization policies introduced by the central government in the next year, these ratios were to shift dramatically and quickly, so that even by 1932 the total irrigated acreage increased to four and a half million, with about 56 percent given over to cotton and the acreage in grain declining to 15 percent.

The policy of agricultural collectivization instituted by Stalin with the first five-year plan in 1928 was designed to subsidize the rapid industrialization the changing leadership perceived to be the only way out of its economic dilemma. With the NEP-sponsored pattern of rural production in the countryside, Moscow found it impossible to secure either the essential food supply for its growing urban complex or cheap agricultural surpluses to pay for industrial expansion. The establishment of collectives was designed to permit Moscow to control both the labor and the produce of the peasantry, and keep agricultural prices artificially low as a way of subsidizing what it felt to be critical industrial investment.

Excessive and callous pressures on the Uzbek and southern Central Asian peasantry to collectivize led to a pattern of resistance, slaughter of livestock, and an initial drop in agricultural production similar to that in European Russia. The authorities mixed tribal and clan groups indiscriminately in the formation of the early collectives, also mixing sedentary, nomadic, and other socioeconomic groups with little plan or sensitivity. Females from among the indigenous populations were often assigned work positions together with unrelated males, as little appreciation was shown for the specifically tribal or religious characteristics of these peoples. Resistance to such intrusiveness was stubborn and predictable. The slaughter of cattle, sheep, goats, and horses was carried out on a broad scale, and the drop in their numbers over the first five years from 1928 to 1932 was appalling, the herds being reduced from just under six million in Uzbekistan to somewhat more than three and a half million. There were corresponding declines in the adjacent republics.

The Kazakh experience was especially poignant. The central leadership under Stalin, as well as the Kazakh party headed largely by Russians, had taken the decision early in this process that collectivization was essentially to be equated with settlement. To break the power of the old social and political order, the traditional nomadic economy would have to be destroyed along with the dominance of the Kazakh clan elders. To do this, the nomads would have to be settled. The process was in effect a political, not an economic one. The ensuing spiral of coercion and counterforce wreaked havoc on the economy of the affected Kazakh regions. The pastoral nomadism of the Kazakh clans was effectively crushed by the end of the decade, with over half a million nomads settled in agricultural areas during that span. As many as another half-million emigrated from the northern steppes, either escaping to China and Afghanistan or attempting to move to other republics less hard hit. Reliable estimates indicate that one and a half million Kazakhs perished in the violence, armed raids and counterraids, migrations, and famine of the times. Even the collectives established were often an empty shell, lacking effective shelter for either their livestock or human members, and inadequately provisioned with critical agricultural machinery or equipment, seed, water, and food supplies.

The lack of planning and provision of necessary infrastructure resulted in immense losses, and made it clear that the primary purpose of the exercise was sheer settlement rather than agricultural collectivization as such. Only toward the end of the decade were more sophisticated approaches devised in the establishment of the network of collectives, approaches that displayed more respect and appreciation for the ethnic and cultural distinctiveness of the indigenous Turkic peoples. Collective farm complexes were increasingly formed on the basis of separate clan structures, and appropriately segregated work arrangements were designed for the male and female contingents within such establishments. Special financial and equipment incentives were also made available to make membership more attractive. In addition to having all former debts canceled upon joining the collective, members were offered machinery and essential farm tools at no cost, together with substantial credit and loan opportunities. At the very least, the protection afforded by such collectives against the vicissitudes of attempting to survive alone during the harsh and famine-plagued years of the 1930s became one of the more compelling attractions in consolidating this pattern by the eve of the Second World War.

The immense losses of territory, population, productive farmland, and livestock to the Germans in the early months of the conflict placed an enormous pressure on the surviving agricultural regions to feed and sustain the state in the war effort. A special burden fell in this respect on Kazakhstan and the other rural sectors of Central Asia. Throughout the critical years of the war, essential food crops were to be expanded and there was a corresponding decrease in the area allotted to cotton. Yet there were, from the very beginning, immense obstacles to the realization of such an adjustment. Nearly half a million Kazakh males were mobilized for service during the war, leaving the number of agricultural field workers extremely low. The supply of farm machinery, transport, and essential agricultural equipment was also badly limited, and Moscow was able to provide very little practical assistance to the republic in meeting the ambitious goals set by the center. Grain harvests actually dropped over the course of the war, and central authorities were moved to lash out at Central Asian "slacking" as the explanation for the shortfalls. Ideological rather than material reasons were found for these deficiencies, and there was little additional investment in grain cultivation in the region in the postwar period as Moscow was distracted by the task of reconstructing the western European zones which had been so badly devastated in the conflict. Such investment as was made in the area was intended for the redevelopment of the vitally important cotton economy. The brief and inefficient wartime shift to food crops and subsistence farming proved to be a temporary aberration, as the Stalinist regime resumed its traditional emphasis on Central Asia's role in the growing and production of cotton.

The traditional economic distinction between the northern steppe regions, devoted to animal husbandry and the large-scale development of agriculture, and the southern river valley zones, earmarked for the concentration of cotton production, was highlighted even further by Khrushchev's introduction of the Virgin Lands project in the Kazakh north. The program proclaimed in the spring of 1954 initiated the organization of over three hundred state farms throughout the republic which would convert almost nine million acres of grazing land into cereal crops. The *sovkhozy* were also to rationalize patterns of animal husbandry and expand the production of meat and milk.

It was an extraordinarily ambitious and complicated program from the very beginning, and met with mixed success. Production goals were constantly being revised and personnel shifted; some key appointees such as Brezhnev made their reputation with interim victories in the enterprise. The initiative was fundamentally marred by the inability of central authorities ever to provide the requisite farm machinery, technical personnel, or agrichemicals indispensable to its full realization. The sheer magnitude of the goals virtually precluded their implementation: more than fifty million new acres were plowed between 1954 and 1958, and the effort demanded a level of investment in machinery and expertise the center was unable to sustain. With endemic support and equipment deficiencies, the experiment became an economic and political morass, and its dismal record played a role in the decline and fall of Khrushchev in 1964.

Throughout the late 1960s and 1970s, there was a persistent tendency to attempt to solve the problems of agricultural shortfalls by extensive approaches, expanding the ploughed and cultivated area to be devoted to food crops, rather than through intensive approaches that would devote new equipment, expertise, and resources to the existing base. This continuing flirtation with giantism in many ways remains the heart of the problem, as the megacomplexes designed to bring ever-increasing areas under government control leave little room for rational individual skills, and provide little incentive for members of these collectives to put their best skills at the service of the enterprise. The decline of morale and the corresponding increase in corruption in this sector of the economy set the background for the extraordinary crackdown on the Kazakh party leadership at the end of 1986, when the long-time party head Dinmukhamed Kunaev was removed along with many of his cronies throughout the republic apparatus.

Moscow's heavy emphasis on cotton in the river valley regions of the Uzbek south has created a set of center-periphery tensions in that area. Such irrigated land as has existed has consistently and predominantly been given over by the tsarist and Soviet authorities to cotton production. Large-scale canal projects completed in the 1950s and 1960s underscored the continuity of that pattern. Construction of the five-hundred-mile Qara-Qum Canal from the Amu Darya to Ashkhabad; completion of the Mirzachol Sahra irrigation network, which resulted in two great transfers of land from Kazakhstan to Uzbekistan in 1956 (425,000 acres) and in 1963 (2.4 million acres for cotton, and almost 7 million acres for associated grazing land); together with the building of the Chu Canal in Kirgizia, and the Bahr-i Tajik reservoir serving Tajikistan from the mouth of the Ferghana valley—these and similar Soviet irrigation projects have by and large, though not exclusively, served the expansion of cotton culture. Here again, there has been some question whether these massive projects have served the purposes of the local populations together with the best interests of the Soviet economy as a whole, or whether they have misdirected resources that might better have been used in a broader and more economically sound diversification of Central Asian agriculture.

In the case of Sinkiang, the critical influences on its agricultural development have been political rather than economic: the collectivization which was completed in 1955, the creation of communes in 1958, and the de facto decollectivization some twenty years later of fields and herds. Little is known about the process. It is suggestive, however, that in 1962, in the catastrophic aftermath of the Great Leap Forward, some seventy thousand Kazakhs and

Uighurs fled into the USSR and that many people slaughtered their herds rather than permit their confiscation. A brief political respite ensued, followed as elsewhere by the appalling chaos of the Cultural Revolution, which saw, among other things, vicious internecine fighting, and a threat by the local party boss Wang Enmao to seize the nuclear-test facilities at Lop Nor.

Generally speaking, pressure on land is relatively low in Sinkiang, and production can be increased simply by opening new areas to cultivation. In 1985, about 8.3 million acres were under crops, with about three times that area said to be suitable for cultivation but undeveloped. The increase in cultivated area was about 60 percent over 1949. In some areas, considerable mechanization has been carried out. Water, however, appears to be a limiting factor, despite optimistic talk about the inexhaustible resources of mountain glaciers. Much farming is carried out by the army, through its Production and Construction Corps, which also serves as a conduit for subsidized immigration by Chinese (Han). The population of the farms run by the corps now numbers over two million. Its 169 farms and 729 industrial enterprises accounted for one-fourth (2.6 billion yuan) of the total regional product in 1984. Most of the corps's personnel are recruited from outside Sinkiang, and these officially sponsored immigrants have been given land, including some of the area's most fertile, that was taken from local inhabitants.

Grain output in 1981 was placed at over eleven billion pounds. Cotton output has also increased substantially. Livestock numbers are difficult to judge. Official figures show about 16 million in 1953, 22 million in 1958, and 24 million in 1965, with the slowdown in growth probably reflecting the disasters of 1959–1962. In 1978, when the area was recovering from the Cultural Revolution, the figure was unchanged at 24 million, though by 1985 it had increased to 36 million. This growth coincided with a return of flocks to private owners: according to the official Chinese news agency, in 1981, 8.3 million or 31 percent of Sinkiang's livestock were privately owned.

The failures of agriculture elicited considerable criticism in the late 1970s, and in 1978 a new set of policies gave families instead of collectives responsibility for production, and permitted private plots, orchards, and flocks. State farms, however, apparently continue to run deficits, while substantial subsidies from Peking are applied to a wide range of uses in Sinkiang.

In the Mongolian People's Republic, animal husbandry still accounts for about 70 percent of the gross agricultural product, a figure that has not fluctuated greatly since 1960. Animal husbandry in the MPR has recently been characterized by a Soviet specialist as "not intensive, but an extensive, traditional nomadic and seminomadic type" (M39, p. 222). Given the fact that the MPR is second only to New Zealand in number of livestock per capita, it is not surprising that animal husbandry still retains its central economic importance. The most obvious reason pastoral nomadism has not been subjected to any radical modernizing campaigns since collectivization in the 1950s, is, to use the words of a

Mongolian writer, that "the Mongolian traditional free-range horse-breeding is regarded as the cheapest way of rearing horses" (M62, p. 31).

Changes in livestock raising have of course occurred in the MPR. At present, about 80 percent of all livestock belongs to state and cooperative farms, and only 20 percent is owned privately. The MPR government has sought to improve animal husbandry by increasing the fodder base, making more water for livestock available by drilling more wells, building more animal enclosures and more veterinary stations staffed by trained veterinarians, and mechanizing work processes. The increased use of hay and fodder is a response to the continuing ecological disasters (heavy winter snowfalls and severe frosts) that periodically affect Mongolian livestock. Four farms have been set up in the MPR specifically to grow and store hay as state emergency fodder. Yet, even in 1986, only 1.4 percent of all fields devoted to agriculture and pasturage were specifically set aside for hayfields (M39, pp. 233–236). The raising of poultry and pigs has been added to the traditional Mongolian "five types of animals" (horses, sheep, camel, goats, and cattle).

Just as 80 percent of all livestock belongs to state and cooperative farms, so approximately 80 percent of all cultivated fields belongs to state farms in the MPR. The first large-scale Virgin Lands program in the MPR dates from the early 1940s. The emphasis has been on grain, which in 1983 was produced on 81.1 percent of all cultivated fields. By contrast, only 0.4 percent of cultivated fields are devoted to growing vegetables, a fact that presumably reflects both climatic realities and dietary preferences. Ever since apple trees were first introduced into the MPR from Siberia in the early 1940s, however, fruit and berry cultivation has been on the increase (M39, pp. 239–241).

Food shortages have plagued the Tibetan Autonomous Region ever since 1950, largely because of the influx of Chinese settlers. An observer sympathetic to PRC rule of Tibet notes that in the 1980s the availability of food for the average Tibetan had increased "only slightly" since 1950 (N14, pp. 168–172). Tibetan refugees of the 1960s, however, painted a grimmer picture of grains and foodstuffs being siphoned off from communes to government "reserves," leaving little for commune members to eat (N36, p. 119). In 1980 Tibet reportedly imported over thirty thousand tons of food (N1, p. 5).

Reforms since the Cultural Revolution have led to the disbanding of communes and the redistribution of land to individuals, at first on fifteen-year deeds, then in 1984 on thirty- to forty-year deeds. Livestock has similarly been redistributed. In spite of such reforms, the overall failure of PRC economic policies in Tibet is reflected in the fact that in 1986 state subsidies accounted for approximately 98 percent of Tibet's budget (N1, p. 5).

Manufacturing, Trade, and Services

Although the peoples of Inner Asia had a long tradition in the conduct of trade, which expanded substantially in the twentieth century, manufacturing and the exploitation of natural resources were slow to develop and were undertaken predominantly at the initiative of Europeans and, after 1950, the Chinese.

The Iranian government has played an important role in the development of the manufacturing, trade, and service sectors of the economy. Both in terms of rate of growth and meeting of set developmental goals, the success of these three sectors has outpaced that of most other developing countries, including neighbors in Inner Asia. Government participation in these sectors has been in the areas of licensing, finance and credit, protection of certain industries, and indirectly in education of skilled and professional personnel. Although much of the momentum of the 1960s and 1970s has been lost in the course of the establishment of the Islamic Republic of Iran and as a result of the Iran-Iraq war, the potential for rapid development may be seen in the events of the two decades prior to the revolution.

The main goal of the manufacturing sector has been to meet local needs, largely in the consumer or light industry area, rather than to produce for export. Despite a growth of exports in light industry, the main export items of Iran remain petroleum and petroleum products. Here too, however, the aggressive expansion into refining and the formation of Iranian companies that would administer well to (gas) pump operations on a global scale indicate the strength and potential of Iranian industry.

Manufacturing in the early part of the modern period was in such traditional areas as sugar, vegetable oils, and textiles but has now expanded to include assembly plants for cars, trucks, and tractors. Initially relying on imported parts that were then assembled in Iran, the automotive industry increasingly manufactured basic parts. Agreements for such "Iranian" vehicles were signed with European automobile manufacturers who supplied parts. The Iranian car Peykan, for example, is a version of the British Hillman. Iran even began the export of some vehicles such as buses and passenger cars to Eastern Europe and Afghanistan. Coupled with prohibitive duties on wholesale imports of foreign cars, local manufacturing encouraged consumer purchases of locally assembled vehicles.

At the same time, opportunities for corruption lay in the licensing, which as a matter of course required silent partnership with someone close to the sources of political power who would facilitate not only licensing but also credit through the many new financial institutions established to service industrial growth.

Heavy industry, aside from petroleum, was limited to mining (copper, coal, iron ore, lead, aluminum, and chromite), until the construction of the steel mill outside Isphahan during the mid-1960s. The establishment of a steel mill had been an elusive Iranian political goal for some decades. Although the natural resources necessary for the industry existed, the initial costs in infrastructure and equipment were very high, and the mill's costs of production were higher than the cost of steel on the world market. The mill, completed in 1965, resulted from a contract with the Soviet Union and marked a typical Soviet venture that carried greater political than economic weight. Soviet technicians lived in this complex outside Isphahan, isolated from the Iranian population. For Iran, the steel mill represented heavy industry, diversification, and status. For the Soviet Union, it provided the major access to the Iranian economy aside from the gas-purchase agreement.

As indicated by employment figures, the industrial sector of the Iranian economy grew by over 150 percent during the twenty years between 1956 and 1975. With the exception of the steel industry, Iranian manufacturing was run on all levels by trained Iranians, with occasional outside consultants. The bulk of the large influx of Americans working in Iran was employed within the military-related technological complex rather than private industry. In this same period, the trend in investment in industry was moving from roughly equal amounts from government and private funds toward a ratio of one to three with the major exception of oil. Public offerings of shares in industry lay as the goal for the future financing of industrial expansion.

Apace with the growth of industry, increases have occurred within the service sector as well. Banking, insurance, medicine, and education represent four areas of service growth. In all these areas the role of government has been critical. Semiprivate banks and private hospitals attracted not only Iranian money but also other Middle Eastern funds, especially from the Gulf. Iran's diverse and quickly expanding university and technical educational system attracted many from developing countries in addition to accommodating thousands of Iranians, many from recently rural backgrounds.

Another service area, transport, launched as a byproduct of the Allied occupation of Iran during World War II, when Iran served as a conduit for war materiel to the Soviet Union, grew rapidly as north-south trucking from ports on the Gulf met the demands for consumer products and industrial growth. Another land route from Europe through Turkey brought perishable goods, mainly imported foodstuffs such as eggs, cucumbers, and refrigerated materials from the West. The growth of the transport system in turn fed small service shops all along the main routes, transforming in one generation, in some dramatic cases, shepherds into mechanics.

With the boom in the Iranian economy, urbanization, and population growth came a rapid growth in housing, both multiple story and single family. Tehran, Isphahan, and Shiraz experienced urban sprawl that devoured agricultural lands and strained water and sanitation facilities. Pollution and other problems of modern urban centers await a solution here, as in other developed and developing areas. The infrastructure and mind-set to deal with the problems of modern societies may take many more years to develop in a period of political instability.

Much of this growth represents public confidence in the strength of the Iranian economy, but the strength of the economy, on the eve of the revolution, continued to rest on the financial success of the oil industry. During the early 1970s when there was a fourfold increase in the price of oil, confidence and expenditure on growth remained high. After the cresting of prices and the eventual decline, confidence in the economy began to waver, particularly in light of social and political upheaval. Nevertheless, the potential for growth, that is, manpower, natural resources, and considerable infrastructure, are all in place, allowing for future growth.

The economy of Afghanistan was greatly affected by the turbulent events following World War I. The end of the war and the Bolshevik conquest of Central Asia brought many refugees, mainly Turkmen, Uzbek, Tajik, and Kirgiz, into northern Afghanistan. The skills brought by these refugees made it possible for Afghan entrepreneurs to add two new export items, carpets and karakul skins (mistakenly referred to as "Persian lambskins"), to the traditional exports such as furs and embroidered sheepskin coats. In 1922 karakul skins were introduced to the London market, which until World War II took almost all the skins the Afghans could supply.

Also, the *basmachi* revolts of the 1920s devastated the Central Asian countryside, and cotton production fell to almost nil. Cotton and cotton cloth had been major exports in tsarist days. Since the ecologies of Afghan Turkestan and Soviet Turkestan are almost identical, Afghan entrepreneurs made deals with the Soviets to grow cotton which would be exported to the USSR. Payments would be half in gold (the "Nikolai" coin) and half in cotton cloth to be sold in Afghan urban bazaars.

The creation of the Sherkat-i-Sahami-Afghan (later known as the Bank-i-Melli, National Bank) as a stock company in 1932 launched the Afghans into a period of innovative capitalistic development. In 1934, the institution became an investment bank. The bank contributed greatly to pre–World War II small-scale industrial development in Kabul, Kunduz, and Pul-i-Khumri.

The *sherkat* system (government monopoly) dominated banking activities. Under this system the government controlled 40–50 percent of the stock in a company, although seldom investing that percentage of capital. The private sector owned 55–60 percent of the stock. The *sherkat* system came into being to control production and guarantee investment capital and profits to investors, as well as to provide the government with an easy source of extracted income. The *sherkats* also issued drafts payable at the government treasury and monopolized foreign currency, gold purchases, and most government imports.

Wealthy merchants borrowed capital from the bank to establish private joint-stock companies to export wool, karakul, animal hides and skins, and fresh and dried fruits and nuts. Entire factories were imported from the USSR, the United Kingdom, and Germany, and paid for by the Afghans. To this extent, economic development was not a post–World War II innovation of the West. Since many members of the royal family held large blocks of stock in various *sherkats*, government cooperation helped sustain high profits to stockholders.

Few Afghans believed in cotton as an investment, but Abdul Majid Zabuli, founder of the Bank-i-Melli, along with Abdul Aziz Londoni, purchased land cheaply in the north and underwrote part of the cost to open up new farms to cotton. Small-scale industries (factories purchased from abroad) sprang up, particularly in Kunduz: cotton gins and pressing mills, seed-pressing mills; soap and ceramic factories. Textile mills were built in an unsuccessful attempt to make Afghanistan self-sufficient in cotton cloth.

The Kunduz Cotton Company expanded its activities after the 1929 civil war, which exhausted the government treasury after a year of looting and corruption. To replenish the government larder, the new king, Mohammed Nadir Shah, forcefully encouraged many well-to-do landholders and merchants to purchase infertile land in the north. New settlers, encouraged and financed by the Cotton Company, drained the swamps, and the north developed through the joint processes of persuasion and coercion.

So thorough was the control of the Bank-i-Melli that between 1933 and 1946 it invested in more than fifty trading and industrial holding companies, which dominated over 80 percent of the import-export trade. Among the other companies controlled by the Bank-i-Melli were woolen textile mills, a sugar-beet factory (which also sold refined sugar), a match factory, a tannery, a canning plant, and a metal foundry. The bank literally had a monopoly on the private sector.

Da Afghanistan Bank (State Bank of Afghanistan) was incorporated in 1938 as fiscal agent of the Ministry of Finance in competition with the partly free enterprise Bank-i-Melli. Also, Da Afghanistan Bank supervised both Afghan currency (the afghani) and foreign exchange transactions.

Afghanistan remained neutral in World War II, just as it had in World War I. Most of the world's resources were geared to military needs, so Afghanistan could import very little. However, it was able to export most of its agricultural produce to the Allied armies in India and accumulated large sums of US dollars and British pounds sterling. At the end of the war, New York replaced London as the major buyer of karakul skins, and Paris and Moscow siphoned off some of the trade.

When Prime Minister Shah Mahmud came to power in 1946, economic development began to escalate over the protests of Zabuli (at that time Minister of National Economy) and others, who favored small projects for which the Afghans could pay cash. But large-scale development fever caught the imagination of the "developing world," and the United States and the USSR began to compete for friends through military pacts and economic assistance programs (grants and loans).

The Americans were on the scene first. In 1946, the Afghans contracted with an American engineering company to help build a large-scale irrigation, land-reclamation, and energy system in the Hilmand-Arghandab river valleys of southwest Afghanistan. The project was burdened with human, ecological, and engineering problems from the very beginning, problems that were just beginning to be solved when the April 1978 coup d'état occurred.

The Soviets entered the scene with economic aid in 1955, a $100 million, long-term development loan. And in 1956, the Afghans started the first in a series of five-year plans: First, 1957–1961; Second, 1962–1967; Third, 1968–1972; Fourth, 1973–1977. The plans were all overly ambitious with no legitimate statistical springboards from which the projects could be launched and adequately monitored.

The Ministry of National Economy was split into two distinct ministries (the Ministry of Planning and the Ministry of Commerce) in order to avoid confusion and duplication in planning and implementation. However, the move was less than successful. What really happened was that foreign economic assistance became a substitute for internal efforts, and led to a growth of foreign debts, the very things Zabuli had warned against. Foreign assistance had produced some spectacular achievements, especially in the infrastructure; roads, communications, airports, and river ports, and also in certain irrigation and electrification projects, public health, education, and the like. But as the services grew and improved, foreign debts continued to escalate.

Other nations entered the foreign assistance arena, the more important being West Germany, the People's Republic of China, and the East European countries. The United Nations also sponsored and implemented several programs.

Probably the most important attempt to bring Afghanistan into the world's economic mainstream occurred with the promulgation of the Foreign and Domestic Private Investment Law of 1967. The FDPIL had limited success, but it did lure in foreign investors, including Americans (motor vehicle agencies), Germans (medicinal drugs), Italians (a winery), Pakistanis (repair shops), Indians (textile investments), Iranians (general import-export), Swiss (general import-export), British (carpets); nevertheless 85 percent of all investors were Afghans. Bureaucratic constraints, however, remained constant, and bribes were necessary to get licenses.

An interesting development pattern emerged in the 1960s. US-USSR competition became de facto—if not de jure—cooperation at several levels. In the Ministry of Planning, experts from the United States, the USSR, West Germany, the United Nations, and others, helped make plans that included each other's grants and loans. Incidentally, most Soviet aid was in the form of loans; American aid was mainly grants.

The Soviets constructed roads from the north; the United States built roads from south to north. The roads had to come together somewhere and cooperation was necessary. The United States aerially mapped the southern two-thirds of Afghanistan; the Soviets, the northern one-third. Overlapping bench marks were placed on the ground by American-Soviet teams. In addition, the construction of the Kabul International airport required US-USSR cooperation because the Soviets constructed the airport facilities and runways, and the Americans installed the communications equipment. The Afghans were experts in getting various nationalities to cooperate (if grudgingly). American assistance, however, began to drop away in the early 1970s, and the Soviets stepped up their aid to the "economic Korea."

On July 17, 1973, a coup d'état overthrew the monarchy, and the Republic of Afghanistan, led by Mohammed Daoud, was founded. From 1973 to 1977 Afghanistan's favorable balance of payments and foreign reserves jumped phenomenally. The balance of payments surplus rose from $2.2 million to $70 million by 1978, and Afghanistan's convertible foreign exchange (hard currency) increased from $18 million to $130 million. But the republic still depended more on foreign assistance for development resources than on internal revenue. Under the republic's seven-year plan (1976–1982) internal revenue for development was to total $1,251.4 million compared to $2,533.2 million from foreign sources.

A new factor entered the development scene when the shah of Iran promised Afghanistan $1.141 billion in grants and loans, more than the total of all foreign development assistance since the mid-1950s. Only a small percentage of the promised Iranian aid reached Afghanistan, however, before the downfall of Daoud and the shah.

Since World War II a new economic class catering to the needs of foreigners has developed in Afghanistan, and new hotels, restaurants, and night clubs patronized by the emerging Afghan urban middle class have sprung up. Tourist agencies boomed until the Soviet invasion of December 1978. In addition, many Afghans, mainly from rural areas around Kabul, worked as cooks, bearers, gardeners, watchmen, and the like for the burgeoning community of foreign diplomats, technicians, and academicians.

With the Soviet invasion, economic development came to a virtual standstill, but trade, though greatly reduced, continued. Drivers of lorries paid bribes, not only to Afghan government officials and Soviet troops, but to *mujahidin* as well, because the resistance controlled many stretches of even the main roads. And smuggling, endemic in this part of the world, increased perceptibly.

In Central Asia economic life was transformed by the dramatic expansion of the rail network by the Russians in the latter half of the nineteenth century. It replaced the caravan trade, and reoriented commercial networks toward the Russian northwest. It built linkages not only with the Russian metropolitan complexes on the European fringe, but between the urban centers of Central Asia itself as the Russians established and consolidated their administrative and commercial presence there. As the Soviets expanded this network, the natural pattern of construction favored supply and trade lines between the emerging urban industrial centers dominated by the Russian technocrat and proletarian newcomers. Central Asian trade had long been oriented through Bukhara to India, but that pivot now swung decisively to the west with the building of the Russian railways.

Although the initial Soviet emphasis was on the restoration of the cotton industry of the region after the revolution and the civil war, attention was soon paid to the modest production in small plants of such immediate consumer items as clothing and footwear. Cotton-processing plants, agricultural-machinery factories, thermal-power stations, and essential hydroelectric plants expanded the productive capacities of southern Central Asia, although they did not diversify the economy to any substantial degree.

The basic division in the industrialization pattern in the region again fell between the northern Kazakh steppe lands and the river valley areas of the Central Asian south. With the first five-year plan of 1928, the Russians intensified the exploitation of mineral deposits with new mining of coal and nonferrous metals in Kazakhstan. The extension of new railway networks to link these emerging sites laid the basis for important later industrial development, began the shift of the economy of the region from food processing to mining, metals, and fuels, and consolidated the dominance of the Slavs in the urban industrial zones. Copper, lead, and zinc plants were established at Jezkazgan, Ridder, Ust-Kamenogorsk, and Balkhash, and fertilizer plants were put into operation at Aktiubinsk and other sites. Manganese, nickel, phosphorite, molybdenum, tungsten, and chromium were found and mined in Kazakhstan in the 1930s, and these deposits became one of the principal sources of such metals for the USSR during the difficult war years of the 1940s. The extraction of coal and oil from such sites as Karaganda and Emba also was accelerated, and important plants for the construction of heavy mining equipment were established in Karaganda.

The war years were an important developmental period for Kazakhstan. Almost 150 factories were evacuated from the European west and relocated here, many of them retooled to produce military equipment for the war effort. Coal and oil facilities were expanded, and electric power plants were put on line at such sites. These trends continued after the war as the Russians developed the Karaganda area into a major iron and steel center, using the available mineral resources of Kustanay and Ekibastuz. New oil fields were also opened on the Mangyshlak peninsula, and corresponding rail lines were built to move essential equipment and materials to the north. As the Virgin Lands program was initiated in the late 1950s, similar rail networks were constructed to transport the grain westward. Most of this development has been carried out in the Russian-settled and populated northern sections of Kazakhstan, and the indigenous Kazakh populations in the countryside and to the south have benefited less dramatically from this process than the statistics might suggest.

Although economic development in the southern republics of Central Asia was less diversified, focusing as it did on cotton, and the introduction of industries proceeded more slowly and cautiously, the relative exclusion of the indigenous nationalities from the process of industrialization was very similar, as Russians came to dominate the key managerial positions and technical occupations. Between the introduction of the first five-year plan in 1928 and the beginning of the Second World War, the industrial labor force of Uzbekistan, the most developed of the four southern republics, was 85 percent Russian. Nativization of the cultural, social, agricultural, and, to some extent, political apparatus proceeded apace, but key military, political, security, and industrial positions were retained in Russian hands. Certainly as far as the economy was concerned, the ethnic split was between the Slavic-dominated industrial sector and the Uzbek agricultural and rural world. The same holds true for Turkmenistan, Kirgizia, and Tajikistan.

To be sure, there has been an impressive development of industrial centers and urban complexes in these southern republics, as natural gas, metallurgical, and chemical industries and facilities have been opened. The production of agricultural machinery and cotton-textile processing have also increased. This process has naturally increased the absolute numbers of the indigenous populations involved in industry, but their relative numbers remain small, by comparison both with the Slavs involved in industry, and with the number of indigenes involved in nonindustrial sectors of the economy. At the beginning of the 1980s, the indigenous populations remained concentrated in the traditional agricultural and service spheres.

The significance of these trends for potential ethnic discontent is clear. There is some evidence that the Uzbeks and the other Turkic populations have until recently been relatively content with such patterns, remaining in the scientific, educational, and service occupations, while perhaps consciously shunning a more active and enlarged role in heavy industry and the technical professions. But as demographic growth and relative economic stagnation have lessened opportunities for career mobility, new pressures have been felt, and new voices among the Turkic elites have been heard calling for economic diversification and increased economic investment in the Central Asian republics. These pressures are exacerbated by the growing rural overpopulation in these republics. The unhappiness expressed by elites in the region with the recent cancellation of the river-diversion project, a cancellation that had substantial ethnic overtones, may generate further discontent. The economic and political choices Moscow faces in this situation are sometimes dramatically reduced and oversimplified to the false options of either attempting to move this surplus labor force to traditional industrial centers in the RSFSR (Russian Soviet Federated Socialist Republic) or moving industries and factories to the Turkic republics. The issue is far more complex, and, at the very least, will require the subtle and sophisticated redistribution of economic, social, and political roles within Central Asia among the Turkic and Slavic ethnic groups.

Sinkiang's economic development has benefited from the Chinese-Soviet rivalry in the region. Its oldest and best developed industry is petroleum. Known to exist since ancient times, Sinkiang oil first began to be extracted in 1897 at Dushanzi, and daily output by the 1940s was estimated at 150 tons. The Russians consistently took a great interest in Sinkiang's resources, though the joint companies they had formed with the Nationalists did not survive long into the People's Republic. The Urho field near Karamai in the western Jungar basin was completed in 1955, and is connected by a double pipeline to a refinery at Wusu and then to the railhead at Urumchi. A third field has been opened, and joint-venture negotiations for more exploration and for petrochemical manufacture are underway. By the 1980s Sinkiang produced more than four million metric tons of petroleum, though this was only about 4 percent of China's total. Coal and natural gas production is also developing.

Attempts have been made to develop other industries in Sinkiang, though it would appear that resources have been even less efficiently allocated here than elsewhere in the PRC, and that the new plants have been plagued by unusual problems of inefficiency and industrial accidents. Over one hundred million yuan were used to build the Hejing Iron and Steel Plant, which was found to be useless, while another two hundred million yuan were invested in an Urumchi oil refinery that was still not in operation several years after its completion. In 1984 a partially completed reservoir collapsed causing direct losses of several hundred million yuan and an unstated number of deaths. In the early 1980s, a program was announced to "straighten out" thirty-two of the region's seventy-four medium to large sized enterprises. In 1985 gross value of the province's industrial output exceeded ten billion yuan for the first time.

Lack of adequate transport is one of the factors that limits Sinkiang's growth most seriously. Only motor roads existed before the arrival of the Communists: in 1985 there were 13,798 miles of highways and seventy-thousand motor vehicles. The extension of the single-track railway from Lanzhou in Gansu to Urumchi was completed in 1962. Work was begun on a further extension to Wusu, and eventually to the Soviet line, which in 1988 terminated at Druzhba, near the Jungarian gate. Construction of the South Sinkiang Railway, begun in 1971, was resumed after the Cultural Revolution. It is designed to link the rich agricultural area of the Turfan Depression with valuable mining resources in the T'ien-shan. In 1985 Sinkiang had a total of 683 miles of railways.

Trade orientation has also shifted repeatedly, reflecting both politics and changes in transport patterns. In 1942, about 90 percent of Sinkiang's exports were estimated to go to the USSR, and Soviet presence was substantial everywhere. But with the Sino-Soviet split, tension rose and trade stopped. Only in the 1980s, apparently, did it begin to reopen: in 1983 it had reached over $600 million U.S.; two years later it had nearly tripled.

Sinkiang obtained steel, cement, chemical fertilizer, and motor vehicles from the Soviet Union and sent back cotton, hops, and garlic. Even as Soviet trade increases, however, efforts have been made to interest Americans in developing the area, while the reports of Japanese visitors continue to be among our best sources (this section draws on O1 and O2).

Similarly in Mongolia and Tibet, recent economic development has been predominantly the result of Soviet and Chinese economic and strategic concerns. Although the Mongolian People's Republic is by far the smallest contributor to the trade under the auspices of the Council for Mutual Economic Assistance (Comecon), in 1987 accounting for only 0.4 percent of all Comecon trade, virtually all of its international trade is with its Comecon partners. Only 1.5 percent of MPR import-export trade is with so-called capitalist countries. The USSR is the

MPR's basic trading partner, and it has also contributed enormously to the development of industry in the MPR.

The largest portion of capital investment in industry has been in the fuel and energy branch (53.9 percent in 1983). The emphasis on energy is understandable since more than 150 deposits of coal have been discovered on MPR territory. The seventh five-year plan (1981–1985) included the creation of a large coal-mining operation in Baga Nur (75 miles southeast of Ulan Bator), a high-voltage electric transmission line from Baga Nur to Choir, and a cement-lime complex in Khutul.

The two showcases of industrial progress—the cities of Erdenet (copper-molybdenum ore-dressing plant) and Darkhan (coal mining, cement plant, brickworks)—are both in the northern railway corridor linking the MPR with the USSR. Since the first railroad connecting the MPR and the USSR was built in 1939, railways have become the most important means of transport within the MPR, accounting for 69.2 percent of all transport of goods within the MPR, as well as 29.4 percent of all passenger transport. In addition, the eighth five-year plan calls for a 40 percent increase in the length of paved roads (M60, p. 110).

The importance of livestock breeding to the economy remains. Animal products account for more than 80 percent of MPR exports, including finished goods made from raw materials. Similarly, livestock breeding in the MPR provides the main source of food to the population. The MPR is the world's third greatest producer of meat per capita. It is thus likely that future efforts at modernizing the MPR economy will concentrate on preexisting strengths in the area of livestock (M71, M62, M39, M14).

In the 1960s the resources of the *Tibetan Autonomous Region* were concentrated on road and bridge building. During the Cultural Revolution, new industrial enterprises such as the opening of coal mines were undertaken. At present, wool and lumber are the TAR's major exports to China proper. Industrial enterprises include leather-tanning factories in Kham and a farm-equipment factory in Lhasa. Foreign tourists, thirty thousand of whom visited Lhasa in 1986, could be a continuing source of revenue, though the political hazards connected with allowing foreigners to witness Tibetans' hostility toward PRC rule may limit development in this area.

In terms of future economic development, the PRC undoubtedly has its eyes focused on Tibet's rich reserves of oil, uranium, gold, lead, chromium, and tungsten. Protests have already been raised concerning the devastation of Tibet's forests by clear cutting, and concerning the installation of allegedly a quarter of the PRC's nuclear-weapons force in Tibet and the disposal of nuclear waste there (N30; N1, pp. 16–19).

Conclusions and Comparisons

As one might have predicted from their record before the modern era, the native leaders of the Inner Asian societies played a relatively passive role in economic development in the twentieth century. It was the foreign governments and entrepreneurs who provided the engines of economic growth, motivated in part by profit but increasingly after World War II by considerations of national strategy.

The role of foreigners in the economic development of Inner Asia may be conceptualized in terms of three patterns: in Iran and Afghanistan there was a significant degree of cooperation between foreign and domestic initiatives; in Tibet, Sinkiang, and Mongolia interest in economic development came entirely from abroad, but the indigenous peoples were gradually drawn into enterprises established by foreigners; and in Soviet Central Asia the foreigners established industrial enterprises parallel to the native agrarian economies.

Iran represents the most balanced example of the interaction of foreign and domestic economic initiatives. The exploitation of its petroleum resources by a foreign company provided the initial basis for economic growth, and domestic government policies built on the availability of petroleum income. The nationalization of the petroleum industry in 1951 marked a turning point in domestic-foreign economic relations, although the Status of Forces Agreement concluded in 1964 reflected the limitations of Iranian control over foreign economic activities. Not until the 1978 revolution did the Iranian government gain full control over its economic policies.

Developments in Afghanistan were less dramatic, but the domestic-foreign relationship followed a pattern similar to that in Iran. The differences lay in the significantly lower availability of natural resources in Afghanistan, the poorer transport facilities, the more limited government initiative, and after World War II the aggressive efforts of the United States and the Soviet Union to gain influence through economic assistance.

This pattern of foreign-domestic relations in economic assistance resembles in a general way the comparable relationships in the Japanese, Russian, and Ottoman empires. The differences are greater, however, than the similarities. Japan and Russia, and to a lesser extent the Ottoman Empire, had a much greater ability to obtain foreign assistance without being dominated by it; and in all three countries foreign entrepreneurship had ceased to play a dominant role by the 1920s.

At the other end of the spectrum, the native leadership in Tibet, Sinkiang, and Mongolia expressed no interest in economic growth, and did not have the capacity to initiate agricultural improvement or industrial development. As a result, there was little modern economic activity until the Soviet Union and China undertook to promote economic development in their effort to secure their strategic interests in these areas after World War II. In due course the indigenous peoples were drawn into the modern economy first as workers and later as managers. This pattern resembles that in the oil-producing Arab states, and also in the African states following their achievement of independence in the 1960s and 1970s.

The third pattern is represented by the five Muslim Socialist Soviet republics in Central Asia. The distinguishing feature of these territories is that the Russians and other European settlers have moved in to establish modern agricultural and industrial activities without interacting significantly with the native peoples. This is particularly the case in Kazakhstan, where non-Muslims now outnumber Muslims, and are engaged in a wide variety of industrial activities. The Kazakhs have in the meantime continued to maintain their traditional agrarian and declining nomadic way of life. In Uzbekistan a somewhat similar situation prevails, with the difference that the Uzbeks are much more involved in political, cultural, and economic activities, and are less inclined to tolerate a dominant Slavic role. In the three smaller Muslim republics the Soviet economic role is more limited to producing textiles from locally grown cotton, without seeking to draw the indigenous peoples into the mainstream of Soviet life.

This pattern may be compared to other areas where Europeans have intruded into less-developed territories to establish separate and parallel economic and social systems in which the indigenous peoples play a very limited role. Colombia, Venezuela, Brazil, Peru, Bolivia, and the Central American republics fit this pattern, as did the North African countries before independence.

12

Social Integration

Introduction

The consequences of societal modernization are so diverse and affect so many different facets of human activity that it is difficult to find a more specific term than "social change" to describe them. Whereas consolidation is the main characteristic of political development and growth of economic, "integration" may be seen as the dominant theme in the social sphere. The various units of society—families, kinship groups, communities, ethnic groups, commercial organizations—become increasingly integrated within a single society.

Seen over the long term, and with many exceptions arising from local conditions, societal modernization is characterized by the evolution from relatively isolated and self-contained communities toward a world society that is slowly but inexorably being united by a network of common values and interests. This network is reinforced not only by agreement among a diversity of societies and cultures regarding the goals of social policy, but also by intellectual, political, and economic pressures that make it increasingly difficult for premodern institutions and values to remain unchanged. As is the case with all aspects of modernization, the way in which any given society adapts to these forces depends on the heritage of traditional institutions and values that form the starting point of change. For the Inner Asian societies this heritage has certain common characteristics that distinguish them from other groups of societies. We discuss these common characteristics, as well as significant differences, in terms of three categories: human resources, organizational contexts, and redistributive processes. In the premodern period these factors were relatively static. In the modernizing period of the 1920s to the 1980s they underwent increasingly rapid change. Modernization was advancing, but the tenacity of elements in the regional heritage exercised a restraining force.

The changes characteristic of human resources as societies come under modernizing influences include the rapid growth of the population as the demographic cycle moves from high birth and high death rates to high birth and reduced mortality rates. Marked changes also occur in per capita wealth, although a general increase is not distributed evenly among the population; and there is a steady increase in movement from the countryside to cities, with accompanying changes in occupation. Again, the usual course may be distorted by a state determined to centralize organizational formation or by religious or other barriers to new associations.

The most characteristic organizational features involve the change from relatively isolated communities and local institutions toward a greater social cohesion. This cohesion is reflected in the emergence of educational, professional, and political organizations seeking to increase the influence of their interests on policy makers.

Redistributive processes are concerned with changes in status resulting from social and occupational mobility. Migration, occupational changes from agrarian to manufacturing and services, and changes in rents, income, and taxes, are all aspects of this process. Disturbed by the consequences of these processes, however, powerful elites may intervene and set back the course of modernization.

Human Resources

The countries and territories of Inner Asia share two features that have shaped the character of their human resources in the twentieth century: the prevalence of nomadism, and the importance of the role of foreigners.

As noted in the opening pages (see ''The Problem: Inner Asia and Modernization''), the nomads have gradually been settled, but even in the 1980s they retained a degree of influence throughout the region and predominated in Kazakhstan and Mongolia. One must also take into account the role of foreign colonizers and immigrants. In all of these polities, although to a different degree in each one, we are dealing with dual societies: two populations that interact but remain distinct. Frequently, these populations differ greatly in their acquaintance with modern ways, as well as in their commitment to gradual means of adjusting national customs to new circumstances.

The population of Iran has grown at a rapid pace throughout the modern period, increasing from ten million in 1920 to thirty-four million in 1975 and forty-four million in 1987. In addition, increased urbanization has shifted the population to the cities in large numbers, further accelerating forces for social change. The trends are toward increased urban growth from the present roughly equal proportion of urban and rural population. Despite rapid urbanization, population growth has remained high, especially in rural areas where it has reached forty per thousand. This has placed an increasing burden on health-care, water, and other utility systems as well as on housing. Welcomed as a means of better mobilizing Iranians for modernization, urban growth brought with it the close proximity of population elements that contrasted in wealth, education, and general world views. Increased expectations of the newly urbanized for employment and social services became hard to meet in the cities, and underemployment of newly educated youths without special skills became widespread.

This burden was enhanced by the rising expectations of the elites. The early part of the twentieth century saw Iran heading for change through concerted efforts by three primary social elements: the intellectuals, the religious leaders, and middle-level merchants together with those associated with them, called loosely the bazaaris. Rural peasant elements were peripheral. The singularly important symbolic change resulting from this effort was adoption of a constitution that endeavored to limit the power of the monarchy. The Constitutional Revolution (1906) established the principles for social and political mobilization. It did not succeed, however, in establishing the institutions for ordering human resources toward a changing society. This task fell largely to the post–World War I period and the emergence of Reza Shah Pahlavi. For example, although the constitution accepted the principle of suffrage, universal suffrage came only later in the modern period. Likewise, the acceptance of the ideal of public education in the premodern period awaited implementation during the Pahlavi period when funds were allocated for schools and teacher-training institutions, and laws were passed making public education mandatory for girls as well as boys.

With the change in government attitudes toward the role of women in society following the supremacy of religious elements after 1980, women have been gradually discouraged from working outside the home. Coupled with an emphasis on population as a positive resource, this factor has led to even more rapid population growth than in prior years. Moreover, there is some indication that curtailed activities for women outside the home is resulting in larger families for working women as well.

Prerevolutionary government efforts at population control, or at least limiting births, met with virulent attack from traditional elements among whom the newly urbanized were a significant factor. Contraception was regarded as immoral from an Islamic perspective, and family-planning efforts succeeded only among professional sectors and in those families where the women were skilled employees. For a large portion of society, better health care and other social services, and an improving economy based in large part on oil revenues, meant better conditions in which to rear healthy children. Even the urban birth rate stood at a high twenty-four per thousand in 1975. The effort to place more women in the work force, a goal of both the Pahlavi monarchs at least since 1935, affected mainly the upper and middle classes.

The urge toward modernization as well as a wish to eliminate political challenges from tribal elements led Reza Shah not only to disarm the tribes but also to insist on their sedentarization. The forced settlement of tribes had the added advantage, from the government perspective, of weakening their social organization and reducing the political influence of their leaders. As a security measure, members of tribal families were settled in Tehran to ensure tribal cooperation. With the breakdown of the authority of the monarchy in 1979, tribal elements have attempted to reassert political power or to return to pasturalism. To eliminate the emerging political threat, the government executed leaders of the Qashqa'i during the formative years of the Islamic Republic.

Integrating society and breaking down old identity patterns, as seen in the case of the tribes, were reflected in other ways during the Pahlavi period. Symbolically important were the elimination of titles (1935), which had proliferated during the Qajar period, the introduction of last names, and the issuing of internal identity cards. All were intended to better organize society for social and economic change.

In the bid to create new identities that focused on a secular, Persian-based Iranianness, a clear conflict arose that strikes at the heart of the modernization dilemma in Iran, and possibly the rest of Inner Asia as well. This dilemma consists of two problems: that of building nationally oriented institutions and attitudes while remaining true to a past where identities either spanned modern international boundaries or were regionally based, and that of satisfying the cultural and political aspirations of a multi-ethnic and multi-confessional population.

The first problem led to regional tension, especially with Iraq over the Kurdish (and to a lesser extent Arab and Assyrian) shared populations and with the Soviet Union over the Azeri population. In large part because of their cross-border status, the Kurds have succeeded in rejecting a Persian-based Iranian identity. The second problem has never been successfully addressed in the modern period and remains potentially disruptive for political as well as social integration.

Modernizing reforms have clashed with ecclesiastical institutions in Iran for whom a secular state was a threat. In his authoritarian manner, Reza Shah, the monarch-initiator of modernization in Iran, dealt with the clerical establishment in two ways: first, he ensured the reorganization of institutions in a way that would eliminate the most fanatical and illiterate elements, and second, he attempted to forge a link between Islam as preached by the Prophet Muhammad and the necessity for modernization. As an outgrowth of these two steps, Reza Shah banned memorial processions during the Shi'ite month of mourning, Muharram, introduced the eventual compulsory unveiling of women (1936), and established a system of advancement by examination into the ecclesiastical hierarchy. At the same time, he stressed his personal public piety through ritual visits to Shi'ite shrines and preached the complementary nature of modernization and religion: in effect he said that there was no conflict between reform and modernization on the one hand, and religion and faith on the other. "If the Great Lawgiver of Islam were alive today to see the progress of the world," said Reza Shah, "he would confirm the complete harmony of his true teachings with the basis and institutions of the civilization of today."

Reza Shah's son, Muhammed Reza Shah, attempted to carry on a similar pattern of creating a compliant ecclesiastical body while he himself remained conspicuously pious. On the part of both father and son, however, an implicit assumption existed that a modernized Iran would of itself abandon arcane and hindering traditions associated with Islam. They further assumed that the institutionalization of the clergy within the central government structure would reduce its past political strength, leaving those outside the government structure impotent. Neither assumption proved valid. The traditional clergy retained strength, and many among the ostensibly modernized elements advocated radicalized Islamic customs.

Afghan statistics are notoriously unreliable, not unique but among the extreme examples in third-world nations. What statisticians often called ''intelligent estimates'' are no more than ''wild guesses based on inadequate data.'' The first semiserious attempts to estimate Afghan demographic data occurred during the early 1960s when Soviet specialists in the Afghan Ministry of Planning were literally forced to come up with a population growth figure. Drawing on their research in Soviet Central Asia, the demographers estimated a total of about eight million in 1962 with an estimated 2.5 percent annual growth.

These figures were accepted and each year the Royal Government of Afghanistan dutifully added 2.5 percent to the previous year's calculations. Somewhat more accurate figures were obtained in the late 1960s and early 1970s, when a team from the State University of New York (SUNY) at Buffalo, under a US AID contract, conducted a selective Knowledge-Attitudes-Practices survey, aimed primarily at birth control and attendant population issues. The population figure of about 15.5 million (or, according to some, 16 million) was accepted by the Republic of Afghanistan in 1975, and even by the Democratic Republic, which claimed to have undertaken an independent census in 1980. Under the existing wartime conditions, the attempt failed, but the DRA announced results amazingly similar to those of the SUNY team.

The post–World War II population patterns began to shift as Afghanistan became a focal point in the economic competition between east and west, mainly the United States and the USSR. Large-scale capital-intensive development projects, like the coal-mining operation in the Darra-i-Suf in northern Afghanistan, or the irrigation projects of the Hilmand-Arghandab valleys, Ningrahar, and Kohistan, offered new occupational opportunities to the underemployed countryside. The creation of a nationwide infrastructure (roads, airfields, telecommunication networks, river ports) brought forth hundreds of thousands of laborers, some of whom became skilled in the occupations needed for these multipurpose projects. Some would return to their villages; others would travel from job to job.

The slow—in the minds of many Afghans educated in the West, too slow—evolutionary economic (as well as political and social) development was shattered by the leftist coup d'état of April 1978. The leaders of the Democratic Republic of Afghanistan were initially cheered by many among the urban literati: the one-hundred-plus years of Mohammadzai Durrani Pushtun domination at the top had ended. But almost immediately the combined People's Democratic Party of Afghanistan, which initially included both Khalq and Parcham, began purges of potential "enemies of the state." Many of these enemies would have cooperated with the regime if asked for their cooperation to build a new Afghanistan. Many Afghans educated in the USSR or Eastern Europe were also purged. By late 1978, most provinces were in revolt, and with the Soviet invasion of December 24, 1979, fighting became one of the main occupations of the underemployed in the countryside.

Whereas only a small portion of the Afghans was fighting in December 1979, the bulk of the population began to resist after the Soviet invasion. Many refugees fled the country, and by 1988 over three and a half million lived in Pakistan—the world's largest single refugee population. Another two million had fled to Iran. Another one-half million or so lived scattered in other countries. About one million had been killed inside Afghanistan in the fighting. Out of the remaining eight and a half million, about one and a half million became "internal refugees," having fled their own devastated villages and settled temporarily either in neighboring rural areas untouched by the war or around the major towns and centers. The population of Kabul, the capital, had swollen from some six hundred thousand in 1978 to about two million. Many of these rural-urban migrants work either for the Republic of Afghanistan (formerly the Democratic Republic of Afghanistan) or the Soviet war machine, but also cooperate with the resistance. After the Soviet departure in February 1989, the war continued and scattered mines further slowed the return to villages.

In Soviet Central Asia, the dramatic demographic explosion among the Turkic and Muslim peoples over the last half-century has created a series of sensitive issues for policy makers in the Moscow center. Population growth rates for the Turkic peoples have been three to four times as high as those for the Russians. In the decade between the censuses of 1959 and 1970, the Muslim population of the USSR increased by almost half, and the following decade of the 1970s saw the indigenous peoples of the Central Asian republics grow by another third. By the beginning of the 1980s, the Soviet Union had the fifth largest Muslim population in the world, with close to forty-five million such citizens within its borders, more than thirty million of whom were in Central Asia. The population of the five Central Asian republics, including the non-Muslim inhabitants, is some forty-eight million.

As the decade of the 1980s began, only 1 percent of the Russian population was living in households with seven or more family members residing together. By contrast, well over 40 percent of the Uzbeks, Turkmen, and Tajiks in the Central Asian republics were residing in such households, with the Kirgiz and Kazakh populations not far behind. Trends in age differentials by nationality and associated demographic projections indicated that by the turn of the century the Muslim population would be seventy-five million within a total census of three hundred million, roughly one in four of the Soviet populace. The implications of these statistics are staggering.

The Moscow center was faced with urgent problems of social management: how to handle the implications of these demographic trends for military recruitment patterns and the profile of the armed forces; what to do about substantial labor surpluses in the Turkic rural areas at a time when the larger Union-wide economy was beginning to face critical labor shortages; how to resolve regional investment dilemmas as it decided whether to bring industry to the Turks or bring the Turks to major new industrial sites in Siberia and Russia; how to manage the sensitivities entailed by the location of these demographically growing Turkic republics all along the critical Chinese, Afghan, and Iranian borders; how to address the troubling phenomenon of a potentially hostile ''unofficial'' Islam in the region; and, finally, how to contain the extraordinary new cultural vitality among these Turkic and Iranian peoples in recent decades as they have begun an intense search for their ethnic roots and heritage. The earlier repression and destruction of traditional Turkic elites and cultural patterns in the 1920s and 1930s were clearly neither terminal nor irreversible.

The statistics on urban-rural trends are on the surface striking, but they may be misleading. Over the half-century between the mid-1920s and the mid-1970s, the urban population of Uzbekistan alone increased over fivefold, from approximately a million to more than five and a half million. While the urban populace rose from a quarter of the republic's total to almost 40 percent over that same period, the ethnic Uzbek share grew very little. By the 1970s the Uzbeks made up little more than 40 percent of all urban inhabitants, and no more than a quarter of all ethnic Uzbeks lived in cities. There was no doubt that the absolute number of Uzbeks residing in urban complexes had gone up, but the overwhelming majority of them continued to live in the countryside, and rural overpopulation was becoming a major problem for the Muscovite center. Although this latter trend was especially severe in Uzbekistan, similar patterns were at work in the other Central Asian republics. By the early 1980s, statistics showed that the share of the urban population in Kazakhstan was 54 percent, in Turkmenia 48 percent, in Kirgizia 39 percent, and in Tajikistan 35 percent, but in each case the titular nationalities of those republics comprised considerably less than half of those urban residents, with Russian and Slavic citizens still making up the core of such concentrations. Analysts are divided on the significance of such demographic trends. Some focus on the continuing importance of Slavic-dominated cities as a systemic control feature serving the Moscow center. Others properly note the striking increase in the absolute numbers of indigenous ethnic groups who have come to live and work in the expanding urban industrial complexes of Central Asia. These interpretations are of course not mutually exclusive but complementary, and serve to highlight two aspects of a complex, evolving phenomenon.

Whatever the continuing significance of urban networks as administrative centers serving the maintenance of an all-Union system, there can be no question regarding the important diversification of functions and occupations that has become available to the indigenous Turkic and Iranian peoples of the area, and of their having made extensive use of such networks to alter substantially the occupational patterns of their traditional social, economic, and cultural communities.

Likewise in Sinkiang the population has grown substantially over the past five decades (see "Economic Structure and Policies," chapter 11). Uighurs are the most numerous Turkic group: others are the Kazakhs, Kirgiz, Uzbeks, and small pockets of Tatars. Tatars tend to be found in cities, Uzbeks in rural areas.

Much of this increase reflects relentless Chinese immigration: in addition to the large PLA garrison, waves came in the 1940s, in the 1950s, and most recently during the Cultural Revolution, when young Chinese were sent down to Sinkiang; about two-thirds of them have stayed. The Turkic people of Sinkiang "are obsessed with fear of absorption by the Chinese, both physically and culturally" (O14, p. 249). Their sense of ethnic difference is reinforced by religious beliefs, such as the Muslim notion of "clean" and "unclean." There is considerable informal segregation (the two groups often take different long-distance buses), and tension is often high. The Turkic peoples do mix quite freely with the Tungan (or Hui), ethnic Chinese and long-term residents who are Muslims, and many of whom, unlike the newer arrivals from China, can speak Uighur.

In Mongolia the official policy of encouraging population growth has resulted in large gains: as of January 1, 1985, the MPR population stood at 1,866,300. The rate of growth from 1964 to 1984 was 2.8 percent, a rate that is expected to continue for the next two or three decades (M39, pp. 23–24). The birth of the two-millionth MPR citizen was celebrated in September 1987. Life expectancy, which in the period of Ch'ing sovereignty did not exceed 30 years, by the mid-1960s had reached 64.6 years for men and 66.5 years for women. The MPR population is young, with 45.5 percent under sixteen in 1981 (M39, p. 25).

In terms of urban-rural distribution, the statistics indicate that a majority of MPR citizens live in cities (though the definition of "city" is not always clear). In 1984, there were 937,700 inhabitants of cities (of which 470,500 lived in Ulan Bator alone), and 882,700 rural inhabitants (M39, p. 28).

Population statistics for Tibet differ according to the geographic definition of what constitutes Tibet and according to the source of information. The 1982 PRC census reported 1,892,393 residents of the Tibet Autonomous Region of whom 94.41 percent were ethnic Tibetans. The total ethnic Tibetan population of the PRC as a whole, according to the same census, is 3,870,068 (N14, pp. 218–219). A different source adds together 2.5 million ethnic Tibetans in Chinghai (Amdo), 2.0 million in Kham (eastern Tibet), and 1.7 million in the TAR to reach a total of 6.2 million for the traditionally accepted geographic entity known as Tibet (N40, pp. 12–13). Life expectancy in Tibet is approximately forty years as compared to sixty-five in the PRC as a whole (N1, p. 10).

Organizational Contexts

The evolution of the activity and identity of individuals from families, clans, and villages to more complex organizational forms in twentieth-century Inner Asia, took a variety of forms depending on local conditions. For example, in Central Asia and Afghanistan the Muslim establishment was organized on a local basis and not as a "church," and lacked a central direction in the preservation of its values, which permitted greater freedom for the clergy to adapt to the pressures of modernization and for the state to campaign against religion. In Iran under Ayatollah Khomeini, by contrast, the clergy came to play a dominant role in the central organization of society. Buddhism, by contrast, was a centrally organized religion, as reflected in the structure of Tibetan society and less rigidly in that of Mongolia.

Another factor in the organizational development of Inner Asia was the mixture of ethnic groups, which tended to remain distinct when they were not openly hostile. Although there was frequently a remarkable symbiosis of linguistic cultures, with Turkic employed in government and Persian in business, apart from the ethnic languages used at home, this urban linguistic sophistication did not necessarily lead to political cooperation. The sharpest cleavage was of course between the native inhabitants and the foreign intruders—Russians and other Europeans in Central Asia, and Han Chinese in Tibet, Sinkiang, and Mongolia. These two groups still remain essentially distinct, to the extent that—apart from Iran and Afghanistan—one must think in terms of two parallel organizational structures.

The diverse interest groups have expanded their organizational bases and sought through collective action to gain influence with the central authorities, who in turn have created organizations designed to control society—in particular the military and the police.

In Iran, the old urban and rural patterns broke down with improved communications, urbanization, education, and the formation of new employment patterns in the bureaucracy and in industry. The new developments highlighted the insufficiency of channels for new organizational relationships. The traditional social structure built around formalized but organizationally informal institutions such as the *dawrah* (cycle; E7, pp. 44–45) had met premodern needs for professional and interest-group interaction. In this informal system, a group meets periodically, usually rotating the meeting place among the membership. In contrast to formal organizations such as the Iranian Medical Association, a *dawrah* may not have a name but simply include those of similar interests whether the interests be professional (such as those of guild members), political (such as the *anjumans* so critical to the Constitutional Revolution), or family centered. The *dawrahs* have functioned in Iran much as private clubs have in England and the United States, with a similar exclusiveness toward outsiders. This pattern of organizational relationships allowed for decision making within a trusted and known circle that provided security from outside interference. Transforming such social organizations into inclusive, open, and integrative bodies has proven difficult on two levels: trusting total strangers who are unrecommended has been a barrier, and the efforts by central authority to break up the *dawrahs* in favor of national or regional organizations have been regarded as a means of controlling organizational action. Thus there already existed a formidable cultural barrier to successful, formally functioning organizations, even as the need for such organizations came into existence in the modern period.

The introduction of a Westernized view of organizations is symbolized by the figure of Reza Shah, a monarch who gained position through leadership in the most important new institution in Iran, the military. The need for an organized military resulted from nineteenth-century colonial pressures, and up into the contemporary period, the military and the paramilitary (including the intelligence services also organized to handle matters of national security) performed an important function in social integration. Because the military organization has had the capability to affect the political situation, it has received close attention and supervision from the central government. During the period of Mohammed Reza Shah the top military figures were appeased with modern weaponry and privileges, as well as promoted and demoted to prevent their acquiring too much political power. After 1980 the military organization gradually was superseded by the Revolutionary Guard of the Islamic Republic, whose loyalty to the Islamic Revolution appeared less compromised by past service to secular authority.

The military organization functions to promote social integration through conscription of broad segments of society, through limited skill and literacy training, and through some success in engendering levels of loyalty to national identity above regional or other loyalties. The military and associated national security organizations such as the Gendarmerie (provincial police), SAVAK, the Imperial Guard, military intelligence, military police, and town and city police steadily increased in size from 1921 on. The ground, naval, and air forces combined grew from eighty thousand men in the 1930s to three hundred thousand by the mid-1970s (E2, p. 435). The air force, the segment requiring the most sophisticated training, increased most rapidly. Most conscripts came from the rural and lower economic classes and served for two years. Those with advanced education served for a shorter period. All were liable for reserve duty until age forty-five.

The training of an officer corps at first took place abroad, beginning with groups sent to France and Germany in 1922. Later, officer-training schools were established in Iran itself. Loyalty to the government represented by the shah appeared strong among the officer class but less apparent among the conscripts, at least in the critical period of the riots and demonstrations preceding the Islamic revolution. Thus although Reza Shah had been able to use the embryonic

Iranian army to crush regional and ethnic revolt during the 1920s and 1930s, and his son had used the military effectively in Oman in 1975, the military did not serve to uphold the monarchy in 1979. The shah did not choose to unleash the technological potential of the armed forces, and conscripts would not fire on Iranian crowds.

Suspicion about the loyalty of the military to the person of the shah (and those representing his interests) led to a declining role for the regular military during the eight years of the Iran-Iraq war. Instead the Islamic Republic rulers relied on the Revolutionary Guard, from which a dedicated but ill-trained ground force emerged. These men came from the lower classes and radical religious groups. As partial successors to the regular military, they also served as integrative social forces. Functioning as quasi-political, quasi-police, as well as military forces, they have the potential to wield considerable organizational force that can be harnessed by leadership from the Islamic Republican party or from other sources.

The second organizational context providing for social integration comes from the civilian operations of the central government, that is the extensive bureaucracy and associated government organizations that provided the main source of employment for the newly educated youth. While private employment in the service-related professions offered some outlet for the educated, large numbers of technocrats and the intelligentsia found jobs in the educational field (nearly all dominated by government institutions), and in direct government service. The merchants, craftsmen, agriculturalists, pasturalists, and those engaged in the manufacture of consumer goods remained outside the government employment sphere.

With the transformation of the labor market in the wake of other changes in the country, the ground was laid after World War I for the emergence of new organizations that would facilitate channels for communication. Under the aegis of the Socialist and Communist parties, a wide assortment of workers, including teachers, textile and tobacco workers, oil workers, and telegraphers, became union members. It is significant, however, that this initial effort made headway only among Armenians and Azeris who had emigrated from Azerbaijan province (E2, p. 130). All these unions operated under the Central Council of Federated Trade Unions (CCFTU). When the Iranian Communist party turned sharply left in 1927, the government banned all trade unions and arrested labor organizers, including members of the Qazvin Educational Society. Of those who escaped Reza Shah to the Soviet Union, many died in the Stalinist purges.

With the abdication of Reza Shah, trade organizations reemerged, once more in association with the Tudeh, the Iranian Communist party. Many of the unions came together in 1942 to form the Council of United Workers which gained strength as it reduced its reluctance to strike. By 1944 it had transformed itself into the old CCFTU, led nearly forty strikes in 1944 alone, and increased membership in the countryside from one hundred thousand to two hundred thousand. Most strikers demanded higher wages.

In the climate of political upheaval that marked the 1940s, other political groups also attempted to emulate the Tudeh party and form counter labor unions or win over existing ones. Strikes in all industries and labor sectors were rampant, as was inflation. The labor unions, which were confined mainly to urban workers, continued to have a strong ethnic flavor. They maintained their association with the Tudeh, and by 1946, a major demand of the political coalition led by Tudeh was its insistence that the CCFTU be recognized "as the only legitimate organization of the Iranian working class."

With the downfall of the National Front and the restoration of the Mohammed Reza Shah in 1953, labor and political organization became an initiative of the central government, and attempts to form viable organizations from below all failed.

In Afghanistan, in contrast to Iran, a sense of national cohesion developed only after the Soviet invasion in 1979. Through the 1920s, 1930s, and World War II, rural Afghanistan remained largely outside the sphere of centralized national life. Provincial governors and other administrators, as they had in the past, dragooned labor for specific projects. The entrepreneurs contrived to expand their free enterprise activities in the import-export trade, and after the civil war in 1929 some were forced to invest in land to the north, especially in the Baghlan, Kunduz, and Taliqan areas. The treasury of King Mohammed Nadir was empty, and he "encouraged" wealthy landowners and merchants to invest in and move to that region. The migrants were mainly Pushtun, and this constituted the second Pushtun migration to the north, the first having occurred in the Abdur Rahman Khan period (see "Identity Patterns," chapter 2; and "Distribution of Political Power" and "Political Leadership and Participation," chapter 3). The new settlers drained the malaria-ridden swamps and cotton became a major cash crop.

The Soviet invasion of Afghanistan in 1979 triggered a pattern of "remigration." The descendants of those Pushtun sent to the north by Abdur Rahman have been returning to the homes of their ancestors in southern and southwestern Afghanistan. Those remigrating generally bring their families to refugee camps in Pakistan, and return to their ancestral homes to fight with the *mujahidin,* who are often distant kinsmen. It must be added that the non-Pushtun peoples of the north have actively "encouraged" the Pushtun to leave. Possibly some Pushtun who migrated north to the Kunduz area in the 1930s may return to the north, but they will constitute a minority.

In the course of the 1980s, most of the southern border villages and valleys of Afghanistan were devastated and their occupants fled to Pakistan. In spite of the fact that the Soviet military used firebombs to burn crops in the fields, some hardy Afghan farmers seasonally crossed the border to plant both cereals and vegetables, and periodically returned to try to reap the fruits of their labor. Also, since 1986, when the Stinger and Blowpipe shoulder-fired, ground-to-air missiles made the air uncomfortable for Soviet pilots, there has been an increase in productivity in some regions.

Islam remained important in the daily lives of the people. The Sufi orders were led by hereditary *pirs,* who gave spiritual guidance to their followers. Some were royalist and semisecular. Leadership in the main Sufi groups engaged in widespread commercial and entrepreneurial activities, and one was unfairly chided by Western media for having the Peugeot dealership in Kabul before the war.

The Sufi *pirs* played important roles in organizing early resistance against the PDPA. They (and others in the Seven-Party Alliance) became part of the conduit for arms and other assistance through Pakistan to the resistance. Some resistance commanders inside Afghanistan swore loyalty to the *pirs,* but most eventually became independent politically while following the spiritual guidance of the *pirs.* Sunni-Shi'a antagonism was manifested in the Soviet-Afghan war, and the groups sometimes fought each other. Also, some Shi'a groups—pro-Khomeini and anti-Khomeini—fought among themselves for regional power. The Sunni-Shi'a rivalry is still a part of the overall ethnolinguistic rivalries in Afghanistan.

Educational opportunities rapidly expanded in the post–World War II period to meet the personnel needs of government bureaucracies, the foreign-funded and often foreign-staffed development projects, and the slowly developing free enterprise sector. Yet, overall educational rates remained low (see chapter 13).

Political organizations beyond the kinship-oriented institutions rose and fell. The political parties functioned during two major periods: that of the Liberal Parliament (1949–1952), and that of the Constitutional Experiment (1963–1973). The former ended in disaster for several reasons. Opposition was directed at the monarchy and the Muslim establishment, neither of which was willing to share power; for many, in and out of government, a successful "liberal" parliament would have meant less corruption, and a better way of life. Massive nonliteracy prevented the "liberal" press from having an impact outside its own circles, and personal attacks on the royal family and the institution of Islam alienated many fence sitters. In fact, almost everyone in Afghanistan looked on opposition activities as preparation to overthrow the government, a common feeling among elites in power in the third world.

The Constitutional Experiment witnessed the rise of political parties, representing the full spectrum from right-wing secular and conservative religious to left-wing socialists, social democrats, and Marxists. Parties rose, split, and fell, but were mainly influential among the urban literati, especially those detribalized groups who moved either voluntarily or involuntarily into the main cities— Kabul, Kandahar, Herat, and Mazar-i-Sharif—during the nineteenth and twentieth centuries. Many parties were identified with a particular ethnic-religious background.

In Central Asia, as the Soviets secured their military and political control in the wake of the revolution and civil war, new republican structures were established that fragmented and divided the area, while also providing a remarkably comprehensive set of social organizations and bureaucracies through which the elites and masses of the region would come to channel and reshape their talents and energies. The complex tribal and clan structures that had long marked that extensive and far from homogeneous landscape were reshuffled in a series of legislative moves throughout the 1920s and early 1930s. The Kazakh steppe area to the north and its closely related Kirgiz uplands gradually yielded to the Kazakh and Kirgiz republics, while the old Turkestan administrative region was broken down into its relatively logical components of the Turkmen, Uzbek, and Tajik republics. The Soviet autonomous republics of Khorezm and Bukhara, which had been based on the earlier khanate of Khiva and the emirate of Bukhara respectively, were incorporated into the Uzbek republic.

These territorial divisions, perforce somewhat arbitrary and artificial, did bear a rough correspondence to the traditional ethnic, linguistic, and anthropological contours of this sprawling region. Critics could surely point to many flaws, forced associations, and omissions; nevertheless, this administrative demarcation had the advantages both of not doing undue violence to the broad historical and cultural patterns of the region and of creating a set of plausible subdivisions that would facilitate the social management of the region from the Moscow center.

At the same time, with the articulation of this sometimes arbitrary but functional structure of republics, the Soviet system developed an extensive network of new administrative and managerial bureaucracies to attract and engage the skills and ambitions of the local ethnic elites. A plethora of economic, agricultural, industrial, social, and cultural ministries and related organizations was established that occupied the energies of new generations of Uzbek, Kazakh, Kirgiz, Turkmen, and Tajik clerks, technical specialists, and other functionaries. These beneficiaries of the system acquired a stake in its maintenance since their career advancement and mobility came to depend on the continued existence and prosperity of the new regime and its bureaucracies. New social allegiances were formed which put a premium on the preservation of such opportunities.

None of this is to say that this transformation was carried out without violence to the traditional cultures or elites of Central Asia. On the contrary, the primary purpose of the central government in Moscow was to destroy the traditional institutions and structures of these societies, and thus destroy their ability to resist the intensive program of social engineering and modernization the Soviet system envisaged. Fragmented tribal and clan structures that continued to define the functions and identity of the individual as a member of a tight family hierarchy were anathema to the modernizing revolutionary regime that had come into power in Moscow. That regime was determined to make clear that the ultimate allegiances of the individual were not to his primordial clan structure, but to the modernizing state and its evolving social, economic, and political functions.

The territorial demarcation into distinct republics, together with the accompanying elaboration of an extended network of bureaucracies and ministries to engage the energies of sympathetic ethnic elites, was but the first step in a complex process. It should be remembered that there was a very strong *jadidist* reform element within these societies, especially in Uzbekistan, which saw the future of these polities best served in alliance with progressive Russian forces from Europe. In their eyes, it was the conservative Islamic religious establishments that were the true enemies of progress and prosperity for their communities. In their eyes, change and reform were best sought through cooperation with the Soviet regime and gradual modification of the more restrictive features of their traditional Islamic societies. As the Bolshevik forces had won their victories in Central Asia in part through the co-optation and contributions of local ethnic contingents, so the Soviet regime was to man its bureaucracies and build its cadres through the effective recruitment of these ethnic elites.

In assessing the degree of social integration and regime adherence in these Central Asian areas, it would be remiss to ignore specific coercive features of the Soviet system that served to condition and direct the social behavior of the indigenous peoples from the 1920s on. The structure of military and militia force in the region, marked by Slavic command and personnel, has clearly reinforced the interests and control of the Moscow center. That center has always made it clear that it was not hesitant to use those forces in maintaining allegiance to the state apparatus. Given the paranoia of the central leadership from the late 1920s to the early 1950s, the prominence of networks of secret police and informers is not surprising. Ubiquitous surveillance techniques and the constant monitoring of the citizens' movement and behavior contributed to habits of self-censorship and caution which heightened norms of regime adherence and shaped patterns of social integration. The effects of these coercive mechanisms served to internalize behavioral norms that both served the purposes of central control and helped destroy the institutions of the traditional society. The specific measures taken in the latter regard were to become more extreme in the late 1920s and 1930s. A variety of steps, some relatively benign, some entailing violence, attempted to destroy traditional patterns of social integration and reshape the society in conformity with perceptions of the Moscow center.

The territorial demarcation of Central Asia into distinct republics was paralleled by an energetic and extensive program of redefining and codifying languages and alphabets throughout the region, largely in harmony with the political boundaries of the republics. Prior to this time, the cultural scene in Central Asia was marked by the ubiquitous use of Arabic as the religious language, Persian both for administrative record keeping and as an important vehicle for literary expression, and Chagatai Turkish as a major literary language that provided a common Turkic form of expression in belles lettres uniting the disparate Turkic and Iranian peoples of the region (see "Identity Patterns," chapter 2). Although the vernaculars throughout the area had an extremely rich and active tradition of oral epics and balladry, they were largely unwritten, unstudied, and not standardized.

An army of linguists and grammarians was deployed to compose innovative descriptive grammars and dictionaries of Uzbek, Karakalpak, Kazakh, Kirgiz, Turkmen, and Tajik. Standard literary versions of these languages were elaborated for the first time, each roughly corresponding to the dominant vernacular of its respective eponymous republic, and becoming, together with Russian, one of the official languages of those republics for administrative, judicial, cultural, and educational purposes. This process was accompanied by a similar set of innovations in alphabet policy. Starting in 1925, the Latin alphabet was substituted for the Arabic script, but when Kemalist Turkey introduced a similar change in 1928, Soviet authorities, concerned about cultural influences that might emanate from the ethnically and linguistically similar Kemalist republic, switched tactics yet again and began to shift each of these languages to the Cyrillic alphabet over the course of the 1930s.

This linguistic standardization and canonization of the vernaculars, reinforced by tactical shifts in alphabet usage, had two immediate and dramatic effects. On the one hand, the changes initiated a crucial cutoff of these peoples from their common literary heritage, ensuring their segmentation and development along separate social and cultural lines. On the other hand, they opened up striking new career opportunities in local republican bureaucracies and social structures. These territorial and linguistic measures not only served to redefine the immediate social universe within which these peoples would function, they also established the institutional mechanisms and media through which the local elites would acquire and pursue new goals, advance their careers, and eventually seek to reshape their own societies in the long term.

For most of the first four decades of the Soviet period, the construction of these new bureaucratic mechanisms of social integration was paralleled by a series of continuing attacks on the older institutions of the traditional societies. Immediately after the civil war, the Soviet government began to move against the Muslim mosques, clergy, schools, law courts, and religious foundations. Attacks on the courts of religious law, to which the local peoples had long turned for social and theological justice according to the *adat* and the *shari'at,* were initiated during the revolution itself and continued throughout the 1920s and 1930s. Their functions were systematically transferred to new state and people's courts. Religious schools and seminaries came under special attack starting in 1923, as the local Soviets and government organs used different means to cut their funding, close them, and transfer educational responsibilities to new state schools.

Local organizations of atheist zealots, the Allahsizlar ("those without Allah") and the Dinsizler ("those without religion"), following institutional models established and dictated by the Moscow center, moved against the mosques and mullahs in an intensive campaign that began in 1925. Usually accusing the traditional clergy of various crimes and corruption, or bringing charges of social parasitism, these groups succeeded in closing, confiscating, or destroying the vast majority of such establishments by the beginning of the Second World War. Many mosques were torn down and destroyed as a political gesture, but the vast majority were converted into clubs, movie houses, or libraries. On the eve of the First World War there were almost twenty-seven thousand mosques in the territory of the tsarist empire. At the onset of the Second World War, this number had declined to just over one thousand.

Between 1925 and 1930, the Soviet government similarly confiscated the enormous landholdings of the *wakfs*. The revenues from these holdings had gone to support the work of the mullahs, religious schools, and voluntary hospital work. At the beginning of the 1920s, these holdings comprised close to 10 percent of all cultivated lands. Covering this process with calls for distribution of these confiscated lands to the poor peasantry, the government was able, with very little resistance, to eradicate the *wakf* establishment by 1930.

The Soviet regime was able to make a similar set of inroads in breaking the hold of other traditional institutions. Primary targets were the patriarchal family and the subservient position of women in that structure. Identifying Muslim women as the weak link, or what some have called "the surrogate proletariat," in traditional Central Asian society, Communist party and government organizations and cadres initiated an intensive program in the late 1920s to draw women out of seclusion and into open roles in the world of public and social affairs, as well as the work place. Using the symbolic issue of discarding the facial or body veil, party and government organs sought to liberate the female, and simultaneously break the power of the traditional Muslim patriarchal family. This campaign was accompanied by considerable violence, inflicted by both its conservative opponents and the reformers themselves. Given its goals and purposes, it was a mixed success, indeed bringing substantial female talent and energies into the mainstream of the modernization process in the republics, but failing ultimately to destroy the strength and resilience of the patriarchal Muslim family itself.

As early as the spring of 1923 the Soviet government passed a decree vesting water control in the hands of the state, taking this central feature of social and community organization out of the hands of the traditional village elders and councils with whom it had resided. Parallel decrees at that time also took questions of crop control and prices away from local village communities, transferring them to new state committees. These early moves to strip the traditional agricultural sector of its control over irrigation and planting policy, along with the right to estimate and determine equitable prices, presaged the later moves toward collectivization and total subordination of the rural economy to the state's purposes of rapid industrialization.

The collectivization and settlement of nomadic communities took on especially destructive forms in the Kazakh steppe lands to the north, where the number of deaths through state violence and starvation was especially high, but the costs of the initial disruption caused by the campaign were felt throughout the Central Asian republics. The primary purpose of the new state collectives that came into being was the mechanization and rationalization of agriculture, both to produce an agricultural surplus and to free excess rural labor to drive the engines of industrialization. Nevertheless, the destructive effects of the campaign were very high, and did not produce either the desired crop yields or an efficient management structure (see "Agriculture," chapter 11).

The campaign did, however, succeed in subordinating traditional rural and steppe communities to state and party bureaucracies, and set the pattern for similar "storming" techniques used by the state in later decades: the establishment of the intensive cotton economy in Uzbekistan, the gigantic Virgin Lands program in Kazakhstan, and the massive inputs of agricultural machinery, all within the context of large state and collective farm management and control. Local communities had little or no say in these processes, and in effect became one of the objects of state planning. These approaches produced an essentially passive rural populace, which merely responded to the strictures of central state planning units.

The system did not produce the desired economic results, as inept management, poor use of machinery and fertilizers, a lack of proper incentives, an unbalanced economy, and poor weather took their toll. Agricultural management and production remain even today the Achilles heel of the Soviet economy, and the skewed concentration on certain crops such as cotton and the lack of diversity within the Central Asian economy are the subject of increasing dissatisfaction and criticism among local Turkic elites. Such dissatisfaction and criticism in the 1930s earned its exponents persecution, prison, and often execution at the hands of the Stalinist state apparatus. The more receptive attitude toward reform initiatives and restructuring of the mid-1980s permitted a more open and frank reconsideration of these social and economic control structures, the process of collectivization itself was being subjected to intense criticism, and new approaches to social organization and integration were under review. It remains to be seen how these debates will play out both in Central Asia and in the Soviet system as a whole.

Sinkiang's organizational development resulted from Chinese policy, driven by strategic concerns, and one must be cautious about interpreting developments as if they were economically driven. The entire province is heavily subsidized by Peking, and military expenditures in particular are not disbursed locally.

Industrialization and urbanization have been considerable. Uighurs from north of the T'ien-shan and the Ili valley, who tend to be somewhat Western in their education and secular in their orientation, emigrate to Urumchi more easily than do those from southern Sinkiang, who focus on Kashgar. The city of Urumchi, which now has about 800,000 inhabitants, is mostly Chinese. The older and more traditional Kashgar, with a population of 120,000, remains 90 percent Uighur. This reflects the fact that most of the workers in new industries are not rural Uighurs moving to the city, but already urbanized Chinese moving from China to Sinkiang. Many of the cities they go to are also new, so that ethnic separation is being continued even in the presence of the kind of economic development that is supposed to undermine it. It appears that "a new formula . . . [is] taking shape whereby the Chinese immigrants are being segregated from the Uighurs (and other natives). In this formula, new industry is located away from the older towns and the Chinese workers make their homes near the new industries thereby creating new embryonic 'Chinese only' towns'' (O14, p. 253). Within small towns, family organization is paramount. Religious organizations are also important: Muslim education is flourishing, and young people are actively recruited into Islamic organizations.

Participation by local people in government is difficult to assess, if one distinguishes the reality from the appearance of power. The administration numbers more than four hundred thousand, with 44 percent or so from the native population. Competition exists not only between Uighurs and Chinese, but also between the Uighurs and the Kazakhs who have sometimes allied with them, and sometimes (as in the 1930s, when they feared Uighur domination) cooperated with the Chinese.

In the Mongolian People's Republic, state-sponsored organizations and activities have attempted to fill the vacuum left by the suppression of the Buddhist religion. Following the Soviet model, the MPR set up trade unions in the 1920s. By 1982, approximately 425,000 people belonged to trade unions. A Mongolian Revolutionary Youth Union, founded in 1921, had over 200,000 members between the ages of fifteen and twenty-eight by the mid-1980s. Similarly modeled on the Soviet pattern, a Suke Bator Pioneer Movement had about 300,000 pioneers aged ten to fifteen in the early 1980s. Separate political organizations for women also exist in the MPR. In 1981, women constituted 27 percent of MPRP membership, and in 1982 about 80 percent of all women were employed (M39, pp. 199–201).

In more remote pastoral settings, the MPR government has made great efforts to reach out to herdsmen and their families by setting up social and cultural gathering points in the form of "houses of culture" and small libraries. A small reading room might be located in a structure in the brigade center of a state farm, for instance. Nearly every family in the countryside owns a radio. In as sparsely populated a country as the MPR, the radio and newspaper serve to integrate what would otherwise have remained a highly fragmented, localistic society (M13, pp. 164–166).

The importance of the clan as a socially unifying force among the Mongols has been greatly diminished. Generally speaking, however, Mongols in both the MPR and Inner Mongolia know their own clan name and genealogy, and clan reunions, attended by dozens or even hundreds of kinsmen, are not unheard of.

In Tibet, in contrast to the MPR where the state has managed to supplant the monastery with other sorts of socioeconomic and professional organizations, the monastery, or, where it is physically no longer in existence, belief in Buddhism, serves as the only society-wide integrating force. The landed estates of earlier times disappeared with the institution of communes which in turn were disbanded after the Cultural Revolution. The popularity of the fourteenth Dalai

Lama and the hope that he will some day return to live in Tibet undoubtedly serve as a unifying point for the majority of Tibetans in the PRC today. Local units of the Chinese Communist party, the state government, and the army extend into the countryside, as do such mass organizations as the Communist Youth League, but the extent of popular participation on the local level is unclear.

Redistributive Processes

The political, economic, and social changes that one associates with modernization possess the capacity to provide an equitable distribution of goods and services to all strata of society. The record of the advanced industrial societies, which varies considerably from one country to another, tends to show that the opposite has been the case. As compared with Mongolia or the Kazakh territories at the beginning of the nineteenth century, the advanced societies have greater disparities among social groups.

In the United States in the 1980s, for example, the most affluent fifth of the population receives some 46 percent of the household income, the poorest fifth receives no more than 5 percent, and 21 percent of the population is classified as poor. The records of most other advanced societies are better, but are attributable to determined governmental efforts to alter the otherwise uncontrolled effects of modernizing forces, not to the forces themselves.

Although the social changes characteristic of modernization may not result in a more equitable distribution of resources, in the case of Inner Asia, the redistributive factors that one would normally consider—mobility, migration, and changes in political authority, taxes, and rents—are all influenced not only by the colonial and semicolonial state of these territories, but also by an immigration of foreigners so extensive that they may represent the majority of the population.

In the case of Iran, recognition of the need to implement social, political, and economic redistributive policies dawned only in the wake of the political agitation that culminated in the near establishment of democratic institutions under the National Front in 1953. Land reform had been a goal of the trade union movement and the Tudeh party in the 1940s. It continued to be an objective of the foreign pressure on Iran once the internal voices of opposition were silenced.

Orderly redistribution and the creation of channels to continue the process, however, have not come about despite recognition of the problems and sporadic efforts to redistribute, if not to establish channels for sustained effort. Despite several significant changes in government—from Qajar to Pahlavi, from Pahlavi to National Front, from National Front back to Pahlavi, from Pahlavi to Islamic Republic—only the National Front has been willing to relinquish control of the redistributive processes to government institutions. For this reason, since 1953 no independent political parties that can claim grass-roots support have been granted legal status in Iran. Political parties instead have been created to carry forth a process of election demanded by the constitution (and Western pressure) without allowing dissent a party voice. Thus Iran has vacillated between periods of two-party elections and one-party elections, neither of which represented a real democratic process.

The redistribution of political power came largely as a result of dissent based on two factors: first, the social and political integration of newly educated intelligentsia into secular, underground organizations; and second, the technological integration of traditional and religious social sectors which allowed these two elements to join forces and bring about political change.

A group formed as a result of the first factor gained power in the early 1950s. With Dr. Mohammed Mossaddegh as prime minister, reforms were attempted on many fronts: feudal dues and forced labor were abolished, government land in Tehran could be sold in small plots to those needing housing, the landowners' share of the agricultural product was reduced by 20 percent with half the difference going to the farmer and the rest into new local development funds. Provisions were made for drinking water, pest control, education, assistance to the elderly, loans to needy farmers, and construction and maintenance of public facilities. A Social Security Organization obliged employers to help defray the costs of workers' insurance for unemployment and other benefits. These trends indicated the government's willingness to redistribute wealth sufficiently to begin improving the position of the underclasses, in both urban and rural settings.

With the reestablishment of the shah in 1953, most of the achievements were canceled or, when a "White Revolution of the Shah and the People" was announced ten years later, at best partially implemented. The twelve points of the "revolution" were designed to gain for the shah the support of the peasants as well as the good will of dissident intelligentsia. Recruitment into the establishment from the latter group was an especially important program in the early 1960s. On another plane, the White Revolution represented a partial step toward a program that, if fully implemented, would have engendered social integration on a national scale, integration based on both redistribution of land and political and economic institutional expansion. Land reform, the linchpin of the program, involved only tenant farmers and not agricultural laborers who were the poorest of the rural sector. This factor, added to faulty implementation of the land reform, has meant that continued redistribution remains a necessity.

Another important point in the White Revolution was the enfranchisement of women. This step came as the culmination of several decades of struggle to allow Iranian women personal and social freedom. The shah's sister, starting in 1958, headed a High Council of Women's Organizations that oversaw public activities. Part of the attack on the shah that followed stemmed from what were viewed as his secular and irreligious policies, as symbolized by his government's steps with regard to women. General acceptance of education for women or their personal freedoms has been slow. Thus when the Islamic Republic retracted secular divorce laws, the protest from much of the population was limited. Moreover, the Islamic Republic and those of like mind have launched an extended response, based on religious grounds, arguing among other things that women's emancipation is a Western trick to divert third-world minds from real issues of freedom and to sell cosmetics and related paraphernalia.

Iran in the modern period has experienced autocratic rule under two monarchs, one of whom did not recognize the need for social integration and a second who did. Yet the first monarch, Reza Shah, built an institution, the standing army, that resulted in an organizational context that allowed the integration of many diverse elements. The second monarch, Mohammed Reza Shah, recognized the need for social integration but out of fear that he himself and the establishment he protected would lose authority, lacked the political will to implement it. Thus Iran remains a country on the threshold of the major leap into a modernized society. It has developed certain of the values needed, it has available the skills and manpower resources, but it lacks the institutions that would allow the sustained transformation a modern society requires.

In Afghanistan, several types of mobility evolved from the 1920s through the 1980s. Major migration into Afghanistan from Central Asia occurred during the Basmachi revolts of the 1920s and continued into the 1930s; the last groups crossed over during World War II. These non-Pushtun peoples augmented the refugees from tsarist oppression. The Pushtun sent north by Abdur Rahman and Nadir Shah have already been discussed (see the previous section). Large numbers of Safi Pushtun from the Jalalabad area were shifted to Mazar-i-Sharif province after the Safi revolts of 1948–1949.

Post–World War II development projects opened many new job opportunities. Men would leave farms to work on projects. Some would return, using their savings to purchase land, acquire brides, open shops, or buy lorries or buses to compete in the transport trade. Even those who did not return maintained their rural roots, horizontal links from the city to the vertical kinship structure in the countryside.

The Panjsheri Tajiks, for example, operated a virtual monopoly of the servant population for foreigners. A Mafia-like structure developed, and only after more foreigners arrived than the Panjsheri could handle were non-Panjsheri permitted to work.

After Amir Abdur Rahman's conquest (1891–1893), the Hazara became virtual slaves of the Pushtun. Thousands were transplanted to Kabul and other major cities. Gradually freedom came, but the urban Hazara continued to live in special quarters in Kabul. An industrious people, they dominated several bazaar sections and internal trade. Saving their earnings, the urban Hazara began to buy back the traditional lands seized from their forefathers by the Pushtun. The Hazara then had agricultural links back in their home territory and maintained their commercial links in the cities.

A migration pattern developed in the late 1960s and early 1970s. Iran, the Persian Gulf states, Saudi Arabia, and other West Asian countries needed labor for their massive oil-financed development projects, and Afghanistan (and Pakistan) furnished a large portion of the laborers. The remittances of these migrant workers became very important as hard currency reserves.

Also, when the workers came home they brought along much electronic gadgetry from the developed world, including television sets, radios, air conditioners, and refrigerators. The returnees could also enhance their status (and that of their families) by building guest houses, and mosques complete with loudspeakers.

One of the more important episodes in modern Afghan history occurred in 1959. Prime Minister Mohammed Daoud wished to strike at certain key Afghan customs that wore a mantle of religious sanction, although no formal religious justification existed. His chief legal advisers, young religious leaders trained in both Islamic and Western law, carefully examined each modernization step, to ensure that Islamic tenets were not violated.

One of the first customs to be challenged was purdah, the isolation of women. Having determined that purdah and the wearing of the veil could not be unqualifiedly justified in Islam, the king, prime minister, top-ranking civilian officials, and military officers appeared on the reviewing stand during the 1959 Jeshn (Independence Day parade in August) with their unveiled wives and daughters.

Leading religious leaders protested, but Daoud insisted the move was voluntary. Women became integrated into the ministries, and others served as cabinet members or were elected to parliament. In spite of this, many families held their women back. Over the years, however, the number of women in public offices and private work places increased.

Therefore, the claims of the PDPA to have been the originators of "women's rights" are false. In fact, the position of women has lost ground since 1978. Families have kept girls out of school to prevent their being indoctrinated in Communist doctrines, and many refugee families (especially urban ones) fled the country to prevent their daughters from being subjected to Communist ideas.

Four major categories of external refugees can be identified. Those in refugee camps in Pakistan (c. 3.5 million) and Iran (c. 2 million) are primarily from rural areas, and in all probability well over 90 percent will return to their home villages. This runs counter to the "mythology" of the refugees as expounded by several groups in Pakistan and echoed by some Westerners. The theory is that the Afghans in refugee camps "have never had it so good," and do not want to return. Such reasoning ignores the basic fact that three-fourths of the residents in refugee camps are women, children, and old people. Most of the adult males are across the border fighting or have gone elsewhere to work. Also, the refugees cannot legally own land in Pakistan, and the women do not have the freedom of movement they had in their home villages. Nor can the women contribute to the family's social and economic welfare while cooped up in camps. So, the overwhelming majority of the rurally oriented refugees want to return home to resume productive lives.

The second category consists of shopkeepers and entrepreneurs. Many in the urban category have brought capital to Pakistan and either alone or with Pakistani partners have entered the business community. Some may remain in Pakistan, but most will probably return to the towns and cities from which they fled. However, a majority will probably leave their investments behind in Pakistan, so that they will have an economic foot in both countries.

Professionals, intellectuals, and technocrats make up the third category. In Pakistan, Iran, India, the Gulf states, and other Asian nations there are also *mujahidin,* although they collect money and wield pens instead of weapons. Many of these individuals want to return home. Some, however, have settled their families in Western Europe or North America and will be torn by two forces in the postwithdrawal period: family pressures to stay in the West; patriotic loyalty to help reconstruct Afghanistan.

The above equation is compounded by assassinations by KHAD (the Afghan security services) of several leading intellectuals in Pakistan over the past few years. It is quite possible that KHAD is no longer under the control of the Soviets, and that Dr. Najib (general secretary of the PDPA) is trying to frighten the refugee professional class from returning to Afghanistan, or trying to drive the professionals out of Pakistan. If the professionals return, they will be able to establish a functioning government without the participation of the PDPA. Najib may still believe a coalition government with the PDPA dominant is possible, but those who believe this are in the distinct minority.

Actually, the assassinations have hardened the resolve of refugee professionals to remain in Pakistan. Many who had been planning to emigrate to the West have postponed their departure.

Few refugees of the fourth category—professionals educated in Western Europe, North America, the USSR, and Eastern Europe who now live in Europe or North America with their families—will return. Many have been out of Afghanistan for ten years, with children growing up or being born in exile. Whole families have been integrated into Western societies.

However, some teachers, doctors, engineers, agricultural specialists, and the like have indicated that they will sign one-, two-, or three-year contracts to help their devastated country through its reconstruction period.

A special category of the refugees is the disabled, those wounded badly and with missing limbs, including both sexes of all ages. Little has been done for their rehabilitation in the refugee camps, but, in most cases their minds are active and they have some motor ability. Untold thousands exist, and they should be integrated into a free Afghanistan as useful citizens.

In the case of Soviet Central Asia, in spite of the historical and structural shortcomings noted here in the development of the social structure of the rural sector of society, one should not underestimate the significance of the new bureaucratic and organizational structures which the Soviet state made available through the establishment of the formal network of the republics. The advantages and attraction of career mobility and advancement, management training and skills, and occupational diversification and sophistication were recognized by the

Turkic and Iranian elites in these republics, and there is ample evidence that they have made substantial use of these opportunities.

In addition to populating the official governmental and party bureaucracies, these elites have been adept at filling the ranks of the cultural, scientific, and artistic professions. Nevertheless, imbalances persist, and few Central Asians can be found in key positions in defense, military, or heavy industrial enterprises. These tend to be dominated by European Slavic populations who cluster in urban settings in proximity to essential raw materials and the required heavy industrial base. The continuing rural orientation of the indigenous populations conditions the concentration of their career choices, and they remain lightly represented in professions having to do with the military, with high technology, with engineering, or with positions at the Moscow political center.

The indigenous Central Asian peoples not working in agriculture or the urban administrative, scientific, cultural, and artistic professions indicated above, tend to be found in light industry, in food processing, in services, and in those areas of the economy where they have access to goods and resources they have been able to manipulate to their advantage. Although the incomes of Slavic workers in heavy industrial sectors in the region seem to be higher on paper, closer analysis shows that the diversion of goods and resources by the indigenous peoples to semilegal and illegal sectors of the "second economy" has given the latter substantial supplementary sources of income and a quite tolerable standard of living. Such private activity in the local economies is considerable, and neither apparent shortages of food and consumer goods nor official statistics on disparities in the wages of Slavic and Turkic workers give a true picture of comparative living standards. Traditional Muslim family networks have been preserved, and traditional patterns of self-interest in these networks have tended to bend available social resources to their advantage. Recent sociological studies have shown that the Turkic peoples in these areas have preserved a critical set of their older features: a sense of belonging to an extended family; shared social and cultural values; an aversion to external state interference; strong intergenerational respect; rare outmigration; stability of traditional neighborhoods; strong attachments to family and place.

The occupational distribution associated with such patterns, and the concomitant Turkic control over food resources and consumer goods, have led both to reasonably comfortable standards of living and to genial patterns of corruption at their base. In the mid-1980s, in the midst of a remarkable reform movement at the Moscow center itself, these patterns put the indigenous populations of the Central Asian republics on the horns of a dilemma. It was obvious that in the fervor of the internationalist and rationalist atmosphere that pervaded this Union-wide reform phenomenon, such patterns of genial corruption would no longer be tolerated. The permissiveness of the Brezhnevite period, which spawned the lax habits of the second economy, would now be curtailed. The vigorous crackdown on Central Asian crime and corruption undertaken by the Gorbachev regime violated the tacit social contract these peoples had felt was implicit in their relations with the Brezhnevite center since 1964 (see "Identity Patterns," chapter 9).

Under these circumstances, the occupational and professional profile of these peoples would put them at a serious disadvantage. For much of the previous two to three decades, they had shaped their lives in the expectation that this social contract would hold. With the ascent of Gorbachev, new internationalist and rationalist themes at the center, and the resulting crackdown on local corruption, the imbalances of their existing demographic and occupational profile were highlighted.

For at least twenty years there were those among the Turkic elites who had argued for economic diversification in Central Asia, for new investments by the Moscow center in industrial development in the Turkic republics. The abrupt cancellation of the river-diversion project by Moscow in 1987, and the parallel decision of central planning authorities in that year not to allocate additional funds for investment in further industrial development in Central Asia, came as something of a shock to the Turkic elites (see "Economic Structure and Policies," chapter 11).

Since the early 1960s, these elites have shown an impressive ability to master the administrative techniques and bureaucratic intricacies of the Soviet system and turn them to their own advantage. They survived the crushing blows of the state apparatus in the 1920s and 1930s, and have demonstrated their intention to use the very instruments of that apparatus to shape their own social, cultural, and economic identity. The mid-1980s found them with a firm social and cultural sense of that identity, but at a critical turning point in their mastery of the economic and political levers of the system, with the end product of that process unpredictable. In this dilemma, they shared the insecurity and uncertainties of the rest of their fellow Soviet citizens, Slavic and non-Slavic alike. But the peculiar pressures on the minority peoples of Central Asia, and their positioning at a sensitive transformational stage in their own national developments, made these insecurities especially poignant.

Sinkiang differs from the other political entities in Inner Asia in that it has no national identity but is rather a borderland where central policies are determined by Chinese strategic needs. Mobility is limited by the difficulties of traveling in Sinkiang. Unless a Uighur has relatives living in a town other than his own, the chances of visiting that town are remote. Traditionally, such mobility as there was came from religion. Religious networks continue to be more closely knit than the secular ones: perhaps as a result of the existence of Sufi brotherhoods, religious leaders in small towns seem better informed about other places than are secular leaders. Young people continue to learn Arabic and make the pilgrimage to Mecca. The development of modern higher education has also provided some stimulus to change. Technical training schools and universities have been established in Urumchi, and many young Uighurs are leaving home to study there, living in sex-segregated dormitories for several years. Many of these newly educated people will remain in urban areas where they will work and marry.

Perhaps the most actively changing group of Uighurs are those adults roughly under the age of forty-five. These, because they have had Chinese educations, are fully able to compete with the Chinese for positions in the Sinkiang bureaucracy, and are likely to be highly distressed when Chinese are imported to fill posts. There is a high percentage of women in this group. One interesting subgroup consists of Uighurs educated at the National Minorities Institute in Peking after the Cultural Revolution. Five years together in an alien environment appears to have solidified ties within this group that can overcome their differing origins. People from Sinkiang also travel all over the People's Republic of China (rather as Georgians do in the USSR), selling local fruit, trading, and dealing in currency.

Contacts with the outside world are being restored. In recent years, substantial numbers of Uighurs from the Soviet Union have visited relatives in Sinkiang, while some Sinkiang Uighurs have been allowed to travel abroad with goodwill missions to overseas Chinese. The opening of the Karakoram highway has restored some contact with Pakistan (where quite a few Sinkiang residents have relatives). Some Sinkiang residents have served in the Peking foreign service, particularly in Turkic countries. Several have defected, however, which should indicate if not the superficiality, at least the perhaps unexpected consequences, of the educational and administrative opportunities created by Chinese colonial policy.

In the Mongolian People's Republic, undoubtedly the single most important prerequisite to upward career mobility is proficiency in the Russian language, since so much of the economic, political, and cultural life of the nation is tied to the USSR. Knowledge of Chinese is of the same importance for Mongols of the IMAR. In the MPR, the Russian language is taught in all schools, and in Ulan Bator there are even two special schools where Mongolian schoolchildren take all their classes in Russian (M36, p. 43). Higher degrees earned from Soviet universities and institutes ensure advancement in academic, technological, and other fields in the MPR. It is not clear what range of career possibilities exist for children of herdsmen, although the example of the first Mongolian cosmonaut, Zhugderdemidiina Gurragchi, who was born into a family of herdsmen in the MPR, offers hope to the younger generation.

Upward career mobility for Tibetans today almost certainly is connected to membership in the Chinese Communist party. It is unclear to what degree careers in the military are open to Tibetans.

Conclusions and Comparisons

If one thinks of integration as involving a whole society, then this process in Central Asia, Sinkiang, and Tibet should involve integration between the indigenous population and the foreign settlers. This has not taken place, and instead one should think in terms of separate and parallel processes of change. Even in

Iran and Afghanistan, the divisions among tribes and religious and ethnic groups have not been significantly closed. In the five Central Asian republics, for example, urbanization has affected primarily the Russian and other European settlers, while the indigenous peoples have remained primarily rural.

Of the institutions that have tended to foster integration in the earlier-modernizing societies, the formation of national armies has had the most significant integrative effect. To a more limited extent the educational system has also served this purpose, but only at the more advanced level. Except in Iran, primary and secondary education still tends to be in the languages of the separate ethnic groups. Intermarriage among ethnic groups is also relatively rare, as ethnicity is a value most of the peoples of this region still seek to preserve. By comparison with European Russia and with the West, Inner Asia is still in the early nineteenth century in these respects.

Modernization is not at an advanced level in any Inner Asian society. To the extent that it has progressed, external centralization and trade played a predominant role. Iran's oil, Soviet central planning and control, and Chinese mobilization have obliged local populations to respond to powerful intruding forces. Such responses are inevitably partial, leaving substantial pockets of resistance to modernization. For example, demographic variables, including average household size and birth rates, are slow to change, and migration to cities and to nonagricultural jobs away from one's home community is limited.

For a time, many indicators of modernization advance rapidly as the external forces make an impact. The gaps between them and other indicators widen. Only as the coercive or one-sided economic factors are relaxed can we judge whether other social conditions are ripe for continued modernization. The Inner Asian societies face a crossroads where domestic, well rounded development must become the engine of modernization. This crossroads is also faced to some extent in the Soviet Union and China, but a more extreme transition will be required in Inner Asia itself.

In most of these respects the Inner Asian societies resemble other later-modernizing countries that have come under colonial rule. The difference lies in the much more rigid controls, combined in most cases with a large influx of foreign settlers, that are characteristic of Soviet and Chinese policies. This reflects the distinction between territorial and overseas empires. Territorial empires generally favor the integration of the subject peoples into the mainstream of society. In the case of overseas empires, the subject peoples retain a much greater degree of freedom for autonomous development.

13

Advancement of Knowledge

Introduction

The ultimate contest between tradition and modernity takes place in the realm of knowledge—the acceptance of a rational approach to human affairs and the establishment of institutions of education and scholarship designed to disseminate this outlook. Unlike many aspects of social change, where premodern ways of doing things evolve gradually into modern ways over many decades, this is one area in which the traditional and the modern clash head-on.

In the premodern period the demand for the acceptance of modern knowledge came chiefly from elites who had been exposed to the West. In the twentieth century, the initiative came from governments. This initiative took several patterns. In Iran, where the government could draw on its growing political authority, supported by its oil revenues, the Western world view and related educational institutions could be imposed on the country despite the resistance of the clergy. In Afghanistan, the central government also took the initiative, but was too weak until the end of the century to exercise control outside of a few cities. In the rest of Inner Asia, the initiative came chiefly from the foreign colonizers, who imposed their values and institutions on the indigenous population. The exception once again is Tibet where the government has been the chief obstacle to change and the Chinese colonizers have not yet come to dominate the scene.

Throughout the twentieth century opposition to this aspect of modernization came from the religious establishment. The key to this opposition was not religion itself, but rather the particular outlook of the clergy. In the case of the Muslim faith, the clergy was often challenged by members of the Sufi orders, who stressed the historic role of Islam in the realm of science and other forms of innovation. Likewise in the areas where Buddhists predominated, as was the case in Tibet, the monks who controlled the political establishment resisted the occasional efforts of the Dalai Lama to introduce reforms. Only in the late twentieth century did a younger generation of Tibetans, brought up in exile, come to question the failure of their fathers to bring Tibet into the modern world.

World Views: Between Tradition and Modernity

In Iran, the impetus for shifting the paradigms of society that began to emerge at the beginning of the century has taken several turns in the modern period. Although the contours of the road ahead remain unclear, the general direction of the future appears to have been clarified as a result of the Iranian revolution. The headlong leap into the adoption of the values of a secular, Westernized society has been checked by the mass-supported Iranian revolution, the basis of Iranian society in Islam has been reaffirmed, and the future of Iranian society appears to remain rooted in the twin traditions of Persian culture and Shi'ite religion. Moreover, this turn in direction appears to reflect a general popular inclination rather than the single-minded goal of political elites. However the original path of the revolution becomes modified, Iranians are less likely to measure their values against New York and Paris than against Ankara, Riyadh, and Kabul.

The immediate question that the rerouting of values raises is why another political upheaval will not alter radically the apparent norms promulgated since 1979. The answer lies in the continuity and development of the world view of Iranians throughout this century, the alienation of old elites from the bulk of the population, and the foreignness of the world view that was being pressed onto Iran in a top-down fashion by highly Westernized elites.

Iranian intellectuals and even some among the technocrats of change recognized the danger of alienation, of the emergence of two separate societies. But they offered few answers for the problems of painful change: the repudiation of Shi'ism for an uncertain value system, and the emergence of individual materialism devoid of ethics and aesthetics. The shifting values emerging in society were not accommodated or guided in any way. The goals of the educational system turned on two pivots: technical and scientific training, and Iranian nationalism. No mechanism for dialogue and compromise existed in the political or social system. Thus education continued to mean what literacy a century before had implied: a bureaucratic enterprise.

The secular world view promoted by the highly centralized government emerged out of the chaos following the demise of the Qajar monarchy and the institution of the Pahlavi period in 1925. The initial desire to modernize became blurred gradually with a wish to acquire Western material goods, and the entertainment and the social customs that were perceived to accompany them. Thus modernization, the term under which all change was justified, came to imply a radical world view at constant conflict with the values that typified traditional Iranian world views. Not only was religion cast into the ash heap, but traditional family loyalty, honor, and modesty, among other social values, came to be regarded as outdated and old-fashioned. This trend spread throughout urban areas, particularly after oil wealth made possible vastly improved opportunities for communications and travel abroad. These trends accelerated after World War II. The lack of opportunity for legitimate political expression and dissent created a split within the potentially modernizing elite between those who cooperated with the government and those who regarded the suppression of democratic trends after 1953 as having made it impossible to pursue any position other than that of dissent. This dissent frequently took the form of anti-Westernization, since the evil of Iranian society to dissidents was not modernization but its perversion into Western imitation. Thus anti-Westernism became a political stand of an essentially modernizing elite. The influence of this anti-Western elite was considerable, especially in the arts, letters, and education. This elite, however, found itself alienated not only from the co-opted elites and from the religious elite, but also from the poor urban and rural Iranians. Setting aside for the moment the different ethnic and religious minority groups in Iran, the major rift in world view remained between the masses of traditionally oriented Iranians and the urban elites. The Shi'ite leadership remained attuned to the traditional masses not only because it functioned on the ward and quarter *(mahalah)* level, but also because it came to embody an important Iranian tradition that resisted government-decreed changes. An example from the mid-1970s illustrates this point.

Following her coronation in 1966, the empress of Iran, Shahbanu Farah, instituted the annual Shiraz Arts Festival at which avant-garde events in music and drama would be performed by international figures together with stagings of Iranian cultural events. Very popular for foreign visitors and Westernized Iranians alike were staged performances of the *ta'ziyah* (see "Popular Education and Literature," chapter 6). These performances were done by professional actors imitating the amateur actors who traditionally play these roles. To recapture the flavor of the original performances, the plays were staged in simulated village commons or at Hussainiyeh, the religious structures intended for non-worship religious activities that wealthy towns boasted. Because the arts festivals were scheduled for the summer, the performances did not coincide with the dates on the lunar calendar (Ashura, the first ten days of Muharram, the month of mourning) when similar performances actually were organized by the *mahalah* in commemorations of palpably real religious significance. The contrast in the audiences, participants, and general atmosphere of the events marks the vast contrast in Iranian society that had emerged on the eve of the Islamic revolution: the first audience had moved so far from its past traditions that it viewed the performances as exotic entertainment; the second audience continued the living tradition of the original religious occasion.

The secular perspective that emerged in Iran during the Pahlavi period, although onerous to pious Shi'ite clergy and laity, served well the purposes of the non-Muslim minorities. In this period they advanced through education in the public system or were allowed their own schools on the principle that indigenous language schools for religious minorities allowed the teaching of religiously necessary languages. In the secular atmosphere of Tehran and other large cosmopolitan urban areas, as long as minorities adhered to the slogans of Iranian nationalism, a concept devoid of religious overtones, they could progress along many career paths or at least be subject only to the same restrictions as other secularized Iranians.

The emphasis on Iranian nationalism, embodied more and more in the monarchy, bred several issues that set Iran apart theoretically from its neighbors. The Aryan background of Iranians, as extracted from pre-Islamic historical monuments, allowed members of the Iranian elite to regard themselves not only as different from their Semitic neighbors, the Arabs, but also to feel themselves more akin to Europeans. In an earlier extreme form, in the 1940s, this issue had led to the formation of Iranian fascism. Thus whereas most of their countrymen prided themselves on being good Muslims and as religiously linked to the Arab world, Iranian elites developed an affinity toward Europe that was based on a vague sense of common historical origin. This atmosphere furthered the propensity to blame Islam for the backwardness of Iranian society and suggest, among certain elites, that progressive Bahaism or even benign Zoroastrianism would be religions better suited to a modernizing Iran.

Many of these attitudes came to be expressed among youth as they were exposed to the elite world view through the centralized education system. Resistance to secular nationalism, and to the material advantages of the Westernized elites led in two directions: political dissent and religious entrenchment. A yearning for answers to the modernization dilemma that would allow for the retention of the integrity of traditional values strengthened the popularity of charismatic preachers such as Ali Shari'ati, Ayatollah Mahmud Taleghani, and most important, the exiled Ayatollah Rohullah Khomeini.

The world view of rural Afghans usually encompassed their village valleys, and nearby town bazaars. The nonsedentary segments of the population knew their winter and summer pasture lands and their routes of migration from one to the other. But, with the dispatch of several hundred Afghans abroad for advanced education in the 1930s the intelligentsia broadened its horizons. Students went to France, the United Kingdom, British India, Germany, Italy, Japan, and the United States. Thousands were also sent to the USSR and Eastern Europe in the 1960s, 1970s, and 1980s.

While abroad and after their return, these foreign-educated Afghans maintained and emphasized a fierce pride in their culture and history. They also developed a defensive guilt complex concerning their repressive monarchy, as they saw it, the superstitious-ridden religion of the masses encouraged by a semiliterate class of mullahs, and their technological inferiority as compared to their neighbors. And being landlocked did not help their feeling of isolation.

King Amanullah and his European-oriented reform programs challenged both the established clergy and hardened local religious practices and customs, many of which were pre-Islamic survivals, but believed to be Islamic by the rural population. The territorial, tribal bases of power also felt threatened by the "democratic" ideas of the king. Anarchy resulted and Amanullah was overthrown.

During the nine-month-long Habibullah II interregnum, civil war prevailed until Mohammed Nadir Khan overthrew Habibullah and was proclaimed Mohammed Nadir Shah. The new king brought the mainstream, conservative religious elements back to serve as arbiters of social behavior and political right thinking—in other words, promonarchy. The religious leaders held their own during the slow movement toward modernization during the Avuncular Period (1933–1953). After the assassination of Nadir Shah, the uncles of Nadir's son and successor, Mohammed Zahir Shah (1933–1973), dominated the political scene.

The first administration of Prime Minister Mohammed Daoud, first cousin and brother-in-law of Zahir Shah, put a damper on the conservative clergy, and witnessed a rise in importance of a new generation of "modernist" religious leaders, led by Mohammed Musa Shafiq, whose father was a leading figure in the old order. The new religious leaders were trained in local *madrasas,* the great center of Islamic learning at al-Azhar in Egypt, and often in one or another European or American law school.

Daoud used these young religious leaders as spearhead troops, and introduced voluntary abolition of purdah and removal of the veil, thereby creating a potential 100 percent increase in the labor force, a major revolutionary move. He also encouraged land reform through tacit pressures at local levels, and laid the intellectual groundwork for a new, relatively secular constitution, promulgated in 1964 (Daoud had resigned as prime minister in 1963).

The advent of the cheap transistor radio and tape recorder in the 1960s created a communications explosion in Afghanistan and much of the third world. Few villages, even the remotest, lacked at least one transistor radio and all town bazaars had several in teahouses. An American student demonstration or French workers' strike was common knowledge to Afghan villagers within hours. Even nomads, traveling with their herds, had transistor radios clasped against their ears.

The outer world was rapidly making itself known in the Afghan rural world. The inward-looking society began to look out through the windows of the world. Television represented the last frontier, and the Japanese helped install a government-controlled TV network in the early 1970s.

Daoud's republic was replaced by the Democratic Republic of Afghanistan in April 1978. The regime dropped the word "democratic" in 1987, and reverted to the Republic of Afghanistan. The DRA, as had all previous governments with the capability, used radio, TV, and the press as vehicles of propaganda, but also showed outdated American and European movies and programs pirated from sources abroad. In this and other ways, the traditional values were challenged by a rather chaotic image of the Western world.

The study and analysis of Central Asia in the modern period have been strongly colored by internal and external political circumstances. For this reason, politics has been largely perceived to determine the world view of Soviet Central Asians in both a negative and a positive way. That is, because of the absolute control of cultural and educational institutions as well as economic ones by the all-Soviet and local Communist parties, both Moscow and outside observers had expected that the entire world view of Central Asians would in short order become a reflection of the ideals of the Russian-dominated Soviet state.

The challenge to this expectation arose in the wake of the observed persistence of tradition and more recently in young Central Asians' renewed concern with their local values. The trend toward russification, so pronounced and apparently overwhelming in the first two decades of the Soviet state, has gradually given way to the resolidification of Central Asian identities and perspectives. Moreover, just as political patterns are proving ephemeral in all of Inner Asia, so too in Soviet Central Asia the restructuring of the Soviet state will result in uncertain political relationships in Central Asia. This political uncertainty makes it even clearer that the Central Asian world view in the modern period is shaped by factors other than politics. These factors reflect the traditional premodern Central Asian world view as well as the complexities faced by it and other Inner Asian societies undergoing change. Therefore, the issue of secular versus religiously based world views, nomad versus urban circumstances, Western (read Russian in this case) versus traditional values, has provided the basis for a confusion of world views.

Soviet political control of Central Asia occurred in a period of deep internal turmoil bred from the conflict in the premodern period between two groups of Central Asian elites: the modernizers (Jadidists) and the traditionalists (Kadimists). Out of this basic conflict in world views arose political polarization that facilitated Soviet division of Central Asian society and its control.

Initially, many among the Jadidists came to regard the Russian revolution as a harbinger of modernity and new political relationships that would engender societal revival for Central Asia, just as the 1920s did for Afghanistan, Iran, and Turkey, the three countries with which Central Asia shared culture. Yet within a decade of the Soviet conquest of Bukhara, the Jadidists gradually fell before sweeping changes wrought by the Stalinist Soviet state. By 1938, the main active modernists of Central Asia had been killed after show trials (Faizullah Khojaev, d. 1938) or internal exile (Abdur Rauof Fitrat, d. 1932?, Abdullah Qadiri [Jolqonboy], d. 1938). The first phase in the cultural transition of Central Asia toward modernity ended in tragedy.

In the meantime, traditionalists suffered a different means to a similar end: some fled directly to Afghanistan, Sinkiang, or British India, many among them eventually finding themselves in Turkey together with remnants of *jadidist* refugees. Others waged primitive guerrilla warfare against the Soviet state through bands of Basmachis, the last of which were eliminated by 1932. The fate of those who remained appears unclear except that, because of the class background of the traditional leadership, evidently for at least one, perhaps two generations, entire families were excluded from institutions that would allow them access to positions in the formal state hierarchy or to advanced education. Some families disguised their nonproletarian backgrounds to gain access to education and advancement, and joined the Communist party. For some, these efforts proved successful.

As a result of such political circumstances, a vacuum in leadership of indigenous culture and values emerged. To give credence to the ideal of self-rule in the nascent Soviet republics of Central Asia, figurehead Central Asians of little education or natural leadership position were inducted into office to rubber-stamp implementation of Soviet policy. Designed to integrate Central Asians into a Soviet Russian mold, these policies, covering issues from language acquisition to education and culture, served to eliminate traditional culture from the official agenda. In its place, the world view promoted became that of the Soviet state, Islam was portrayed as a collection of superstitions, secularism became integrated into Soviet socialism, and traditional lifestyles, nomadic and sedentary, were by degrees and by various means forced into new patterns. The expectation was that the new patterns would serve as transitional phases to the emergence of a new Soviet man steeped in Russian culture.

Instead, seventy-some years into the Soviet period, Central Asians are emerging as a complex group who prize their heritage, retain their indigenous languages, and cling to their homeland. Although they are integrated into the Soviet system on some levels, their world view, personal values, and habits appear as a hybrid of tradition and modernity. They enjoy a high literacy rate, born of a well-organized educational system, and a good communications system, particularly through the indigenous print medium. At the same time, rural habitation patterns persist, religious customs are defended as part of the national heritage, and a sense of identity separate from the Russian has emerged together with a new interest in Islam.

The world view of Central Asians has shifted considerably in the modern period. Of all the peoples of Inner Asia, the elites of Central Asia have been most influenced by the outside world. This shift has also permeated by degrees to the rest of the community. As with their coreligionists in East Turkestan, however, the overall literacy and educational improvements belie the absolute shift toward a modernizing philosophy among Central Asians. For example, the reluctance to engage in industrial work, the relatively low level of women's participation in the work force, the predominance of Central Asians in the humanities and social sciences rather than in the applied and pure sciences, all indicate the persistence of traditional perspectives. Therefore although the world view of Central Asians has become oriented toward modernization in the fields of knowledge and education and is probably irreversible, the penetration of that change to other aspects of society remains to be made.

In Sinkiang, description and analysis of the world view of the indigenous inhabitants are complicated by the fact that the demographic situation in the modern period, which drastically affects the area as an integral part of Inner Asia, has undergone a rapid transformation within two generations. Like northern Soviet Kazakhstan, Sinkiang has been subjected to mass immigration, in this case by the Chinese. Although there was a nominal administrative and merchant Chinese presence during the premodern period, the effect on the patterns of knowledge and education among local inhabitants had been minimal. In the period after the Chinese revolution of 1911, Chinese administration in Sinkiang assumed a new, and repressive, attitude that was also accompanied by a greater influx of Chinese immigrants and the establishment of Chinese-based institutions, particularly in the field of education. Whereas before 1928 Western missionaries and local Jadidists were the sources of modern values, more recently Sinkiang has come under diverse influences. These include Soviet-inspired Chinese, Chinese Communists, and Red Guards, and in the 1980s Turks, Muslims, and other outsiders.

No clear pattern that would indicate a lasting trend in modern world views is as yet discernible. Nevertheless, social, economic, and political shifts may be identified that affect the world view of elites and that may have some influence on popular world views as well.

The modernizing stimuli for Sinkiang have always been filtered in the modern period through neighboring areas, two of which, Soviet Central Asia and China, have been the most important. Whereas earlier in this century *jadidist,* then Soviet influence, appeared dominant, by mid-century a shift toward a Chinese medium of modernization appeared to have overcome the influence from the West. Despite the centuries of close cultural and commercial ties between West and East Turkestan and shared ethnicity and religion, for the decades between 1960 and 1979 the Sino-Soviet border appeared to have become an effective barrier to influence. Increasingly, urban inhabitants of Sinkiang turned toward the study of the Chinese language and toward study in eastern China. This redirection of political and educational orientation by itself, however, would not have affected attitudes and values without the presence of large numbers of Chinese in Sinkiang. Unlike Russian and other outsider immigration to Central Asia, Chinese immigrants occupied not only cities but villages.

The agents for changed values among local people in rural areas were limited by the extent to which educational systems permeated into the countryside. Otherwise traditional values associated with regional ties, with Islamic practice, and with ethnic patterns of behavior continued to dominate people's world view. Organization of rural agriculture into collectives and the repression of religious expression, including the destruction of mosques, shrines, and cemeteries, drove traditional values underground. But as the resurgence of religious instruction of the young, private agricultural production, and the rebuilding of mosques and shrines since 1980 indicates, local values remained strong among local inhabitants. In other words, the effects of secularism, Communist ideology, and sinification appear to have been negligible in the agricultural countryside, especially in the predominantly Uighur-inhabited areas of the Tarim basin.

A distinction must be made in Sinkiang between the Kazakhs north of the T'ien-shan and the Uighurs who reside in the area south of Urumchi. The lifestyle and world view of Kazakhs at every level have been influenced by developments in the modern period. Flight to the Soviet Union has divided many Kazakh families and to a lesser extent Uighur, Uzbek, and Kirgiz ones on the one hand, while Sino-Soviet vigilance in guarding the international border from mutual influences damped family contacts until the 1980s. Direct mail and bus service between Alma Ata and Urumchi have once again opened the indigenous people of Sinkiang to influence from a westerly direction with probably considerable consequences for the Kazakhs on both sides.

Over the years since 1970, a new Kazakh elite has emerged that claims for itself humbler roots than those of traditional leaders such as Osman Khan, the Kazakh nationalist hanged in 1951. The departure of Kazakh traditional elites to Turkey through Pakistan in 1949; purges during the 1950s of such leading Kazakhs as Abduraim Arsa, the head of the Ili Kazakh Autonomous Chou; the flight of Kazakh herdsmen to the Soviet Union in 1963—all depleted the ranks of traditional elites allowing the rise to power of men from lower ranks. These new recruits know some Chinese, and although from rural origins, form the first generation of urbanized Kazakhs. Their orientation is toward Peking, but they maintain ties to both the émigré Turkestani community in Turkey and interested Muslim communities in the Arab world, at the same time retaining an active interest in Kazakh affairs in Alma Ata.

Among Uighurs the situation is somewhat different in that Uighurs have been the demographically dominant indigenous population and both the spearhead of resistance to Chinese pressure and victims of this pressure. Unlike the Kazakh community, that of the Uighurs consisted of a traditional urban elite that was considerably affected by modernizing trends around it. Merchant and religious classes formed the traditional elites and it was from this group that leadership initially emerged in the modern period. The world view of this group of Uighurs was shaped by traditional Islamic perspective, Turkic solidarity, *jadidism,* and Soviet Central Asian events to a far greater degree than by Chinese culture. Augmented by Volga Tatars also living in Urumchi and Kulja, the urban Uighurs have pressed for modernization of educational, cultural, and economic conditions while struggling to retain Uighur identity for Sinkiang in the face of the expanding Chinese presence.

By far the largest body of Uighurs resides in the area south of Urumchi in what has been called Kashgaria, Altishahr, and East Turkestan proper. A veritable cul-de-sac, this area forms the bastion of Uighur conservatism dominated by Islamic traditions, shrines, and places of learning. Superseded by Urumchi in power and wealth, Kashgar has been little affected by the Chinese immigrant presence, in part because of poor transportation. When it, like Urumchi and Turfan, becomes a rail head in the expanding railroad network, it too may face expanded immigration. Kashgar witnessed an important indigenous rebellion in the 1930s that was at once nationalist and Muslim. It continues to serve as the center of Uighur traditional culture. On the direct land route from Pakistan, Kashgar and its surrounding towns and villages appear more receptive to the emerging Islamic world view as manifested in Pakistan.

The Mongolian People's Republic has likewise been exposed to a diversity of outside influences that have led to considerable confusion as its elites have sought to adapt their Buddhist heritage to a variety of modern outlooks. After the 1921 revolution, the government realized the value of developing educational contacts with the West, and thus in May 1926, the MPR Minister of Education accompanied thirty-five Mongolian children, aged thirteen to seventeen, to Germany to be placed in German and French schools for a general education and technical training (see M75). Selected from among the best students in Ulan Bator's only secondary school, these children remained in Germany and France for three years during which some of them apprenticed in cartographic and printing firms, in a tannery school, in a brick-manufacturing operation, and in a textile school. Several members of this educational experiment went on to achieve prominence in academic, literary, artistic, and technical fields in the MPR. Indeed, Mongolia's most celebrated national poet and writer, D. Natsagdorj (1906–1937), was one of those who studied at a German boarding school in the 1920s.

In spite of these early contacts with the West, the majority of Mongols in the MPR today look to the Soviet Union and Eastern Europe as the only window to the West. Statistics on scholarly and work-related trips abroad bear out this generalization. Since the 1920s over twenty-seven thousand Mongolian students have studied in the USSR and Eastern Europe (M36, p. 42). Since 1961, more than six hundred Mongolian researchers affiliated with the MPR Academy of Sciences have traveled to the USSR to conduct research at Soviet academic institutions (M39, p. 363).

In Tibet, the pattern has been different. For those Tibetans who have remained in Tibet, contact with China proper offers virtually the only introduction to a comparatively more technologically advanced society. This contact has occurred mainly through the immigration into Tibet of Chinese government, party, and military personnel, and, more recently, of Chinese workers. A report issued in 1987, however, states that seventeen thousand Tibetan schoolchildren have been sent to schools in nine of China's provinces to receive a Chinese education. Education abroad is an unattainable goal for most Tibetans; in 1987 only three of the approximately seventeen thousand PRC students studying at American universities were Tibetan (N1, pp. 10–11).

The Chinese have not been successful in eradicating Buddhism from its central place in the Tibetan world view, in spite of the fact that all but a dozen monasteries throughout Tibet were physically destroyed between 1959 and 1979 (N21, p. 63). Given the highly restricted possibilities for Buddhist scholarship and schooling in Tibet today, the tenacity of the Buddhist world view can be explained mainly in terms of its connection with Tibetan nationalism. Buddhism, so deeply a part of Tibetan cultural identity, is not likely to be replaced by a more secular world view.

Elite Education, Research, and Publishing

In Iran, the main educational question for secularized elites was not whether to receive higher education in Iran or abroad but whether that education should be sought in Europe or the United States. Although Tehran University and twelve other universities or colleges sprang into being between 1928 and 1978, elite education, undergraduate and graduate, held more value when the student matriculated abroad. The question of whether that student would return, and whether on return he or she would fit into the Iranian work place and home mores, loomed large as during the 1960s many highly trained Iranians refused to return. Their reasons were either that Iran did not have laboratories, hospitals, and engineering posts advanced enough to suit their skills or that the political climate hampered their freedom of work and expression. It is estimated that between 1960 and 1975, one hundred thousand Iranians went abroad for study and never returned.

By the early 1970s the number of Iranian students in Europe and the United States had increased dramatically as small colleges and state universities recruited large numbers of Iranian students whose education was funded through the Iranian government. When the government stepped into the funding picture on a massive scale, foreign education was removed from the area of elite education. Although elites and would-be elites continued to fund their children's education privately at European and American preparatory schools in anticipation of entry to an elite institution, the aura surrounding foreign education diminished and foreign education no longer guaranteed high placement in the bureaucratic ladder.

Iranian-government funding of education in the United States, especially for bright students with particular aptitude in the technical sciences, had a secondary effect. It allowed students from the middle and even the lower middle classes to rise through merit into a position where they could expect substantial financial rewards. Yet, after their exposure to Western society and its positive and negative sides, these students returned to Iran to find that because they did not belong to the elites, their educational credentials at nonelite American institutions did not secure the good jobs they had anticipated. With the drop in oil income after 1977, meeting the employment needs of such trained persons in a stagnant economy became difficult for the government. Dissatisfaction multiplied.

Other inequities also arose in higher education and employment. For example, different status was informally accorded those educated in Iran and those educated abroad, with the latter receiving preferential treatment. Part of the differential came from the fact that Iranian education did not usually include foreign languages. As the growing influence of the United States led to an increase in the use of English, the government redesigned one of its leading universities to promote instruction and research in English only. Shiraz University, renamed Pahlavi University, served as a source of employment for foreign-educated Ph.D.s and a place where students would be expected to compete with those educated overseas not only in subject matter but also in the use of English. With a relatively good medical, engineering, and agricultural school, this university attracted a significant number of foreign students, especially Ismailis from East Africa, Pakistanis, and even some Americans. Nonetheless resistance to an English-language curriculum remained high among students who frequently received inadequate preparation for study in English. Moreover, since university assignment was based more on placement-test results than on student choice, many students who wished to study at Tehran University were sent to Pahlavi instead. Their poor English-language skills depressed their grades. One of the first policy decisions taken after the Islamic revolution was to return Persian as the language of instruction and to change the name of Pahlavi back to Shiraz University.

Elite religious instruction functioned separately from secular education. Confining itself to its own enclave in the holy city of Qom, fifty miles south of Tehran, the *madrasah* system produced generation after generation of teachers and religious leaders. Funded through the religious endowments *(wakf),* the *madrasah* and special lectures and seminars held by master teachers there influenced Iranian elite education in a way different from the universities, although students from the universities did come under the influence of Qom through the mandatory mosque on every campus. On the other hand, some *madrasah* graduates, such as Mohammad Beheshti and Mohammad-Javad Bohonar, went on to earn degrees from the Faculty of Theology at Tehran University (E8, p. 41).

In the field of research and publishing, the main step taken was to recognize the need for research institutions and for quality research publications. Heavy censorship of printed material limited the expansion of publishing. Several universities issued journals in various fields, either in Persian or in bilingual Persian and English formats. In addition, several distinguished literary journals were established during the thaw of the late 1940s, and some continued to publish regularly until the revolution. Political journals had shorter life spans.

Many Iranians conducting research in the natural or social sciences found that greater prestige accrued from foreign publication than publication in an Iranian journal. Since all universities were government funded, all research was by necessity government funded. Since the government was more interested in technical application than theoretical work, the equipment and funding for basic research were lacking. Some funds were allotted to fields such as ''regional development'' as part of an effort to improve economic and social development in rural areas. Generally, however, the government placed less value on innovation than adoption. In this manner, the minds that might promote the conditions for continued change remained abroad while room was made for those who were satisfied to adopt and adapt. Recognition of this loss to Iran from the effect of the brain drain came late on the eve of the revolution. Plans for research institutions never materialized as the revolution swept such dreams away. Thus the only effective research institutions dealt with the promotion of the Persian language and history.

Popular magazines, paid for by advertising revenues, subscription, and newsstand sales flourished as the middle-class appetite for fashions, recipes, and gossip about celebrities spread. The ministries also published several good journals, not the least of which, *Farhang-O Honar* (Arts and Culture), a richly illustrated magazine with articles on ethnography, history, and literature, was issued by the Ministry of Arts and Culture. The government published other materials through the various ministries, as well as census and census-related materials. There were no news magazines except for weekend supplements to newspapers.

Book publishing flourished. Schoolbooks were all published by the Ministry of Education; other ministries published other books. Private book publishing entailed specific arrangements between the bookseller, the author, and the printer. A well-known bookstore, Danish, for example, published a journal by the same name. Because there was no national distribution system, the number of copies of each volume remained small, rarely rising above five thousand. Translation series were popular among booksellers, and scientific texts as well as imaginative literature were widely translated. Reference and teaching materials translated into Persian in Tehran served advanced students in Afghanistan as well, especially during the 1970s when expanded relations made such sharing less cumbersome.

Newspapers, though widely available, were more heavily censored under the Pahlavis than were other print media. Depending on the political party or parties allowed, organs of these institutions published regularly. Television and radio were part of the government bureaucracy and heavily censored. Although considerable time was devoted to news broadcasts, foreign affairs received wider coverage than internal affairs. During the period of the revolution, the print media expanded and for a few months were free of censorship. After the first year, however, the pattern reverted to that of the period of the shah, with censorship and strict controls, in particular over television and radio. The Iran-Iraq war allowed the government to justify such actions.

In Afghanistan, there was a significant expansion of secondary-school education in the 1920s, and of the development of higher education in the 1930s. The first high school, an English-language school, was established by Habibullah I, and in 1923 it was renamed Habibia by his son Amanullah. The teachers were Indians until World War II, when they were replaced by Americans, but in the

1960s Indians were gradually brought back. Other high schools established in the 1920s included Istiqlal (French, 1923), Nejat (German, 1924), and Ghazi (English, 1928). After 1978, Soviets replaced all other foreign teachers.

Kabul University, the goal of all literate young Afghans who failed to go abroad for their higher education, began in 1932 as a faculty of medicine affiliated with the University of Lyons, France. As other faculties were added, each was affiliated with a foreign institution to provide models and advice. Thus the faculties of agriculture, education, and engineering had American affiliates; science and economics had a German affiliate; law and political science had a French affiliate; and the Polytechnic Institute had a Soviet affiliate. The faculty of theology was affiliated with Al-Azhar University in Cairo. Other countries with contractual relations with Kabul University included Italy, China, Japan, India, and Iran. In 1964, when all the faculties were moved to a single campus, the student body became coeducational.

After 1978, these affiliations were discontinued, and only Soviet and East European institutions now have links with the various faculties. The structure and curriculum of the university have been changed to meet the ideological predispositions of the new regime. For example, all deans of faculties were replaced by Communist party loyalists; and the concept of *jihad* (struggle) has been dropped from the courses in theology and emphasis has been placed on the compatibility of Islam and communism. Out of the total of 750 faculty members before 1978, 276 have become refugees, 36 have been executed, 6 jailed, and 2 have been killed in the fighting.

In 1965 Ningrahar Medical College was established in Jalalabad in response to demands for an institution of higher education in a predominantly Pushtun area. It was affiliated under a USIA contract with Loma Linda Medical School in the United States, but was closed because of the war.

During the 1980s, some twenty thousand Afghan students were sent to the Soviet Union and Eastern Europe in an attempt to create a cadre loyal to the republic. Both males and females, ranging in age from six to the early twenties, have gone. Every summer some twelve hundred are also sent to Pioneer camps in the USSR, some without their parents' permission. These efforts at indoctrination have largely failed, however, and instances of violence by Soviet citizens against Afghan students have been reported.

The press has also flourished in the course of the twentieth century, although its freedom from government censorship has fluctuated with changing regimes. Two important newspapers existed during the first two decades of this century. *Seraj ul- akhbar-e afghaniyah* was an independent paper edited by the Afghan nationalist and reformer Mahmud Tarzi. The British finally banned it because it was anti-imperialist and popular among both Muslim and Hindu nationalists. Tarzi entered Amanullah's government in 1919, and the new editor, Abdul Hadi Dawi, changed the name to *Aman-i-Afghan* (Afghan Peace), and it became an official organ of the state.

The next period of the free press was during the Liberal Parliament. Overnight several newspapers sprang up, each with a circulation of approximately fifteen hundred. They were all opposition papers, criticizing both the government and the royal family, and attacking religious fanaticism as the major institution holding back Afghan progress. The jibes and double-entendres directed at powerful religious leaders—some articles and speeches approaching obscenity—drove many fence-sitters away from the "liberal" camp. The government finally closed down the free press. A final period of press freedom was permitted between 1966 and 1973, but most of the papers were weeklies.

After the revolution in April 1978 the media were limited to propaganda, although Islamic elements were introduced to mollify the religious feelings of the population. The republic also published several newspapers in Baluchi, Turkmen, Uzbek, and Nuristani, emphasizing the uniqueness of each minority group but also insisting that all ethnolinguistic groups belonged to the single nation of Afghanistan (see A27). The refugee groups in Pakistan now support extensive publications in native languages and in English, designed to inform the world of developments within Afghanistan and also to sustain the morale of the *mujahidin.*

In Soviet Central Asia, where the old elites, whether modernizing or traditional, were regarded with suspicion by the Soviets, the entire issue of elite education held a special place in the building of a new society from the 1920s on. Despite the emphasis on literacy as a necessity for reading the Koran, a good education previously had been largely the privilege of the elite, even in sedentary oases where religiously endowed schools were many. The emphasis on education in the Soviet period therefore was directed at the masses rather than the elites. Compulsory universal education gradually was extended from four to seven years. As in other areas of Central Asia, among the Kazakhs the government mobilized all those who were literate in a campaign against illiteracy. (Note the early date of this campaign—1922—in contrast to a similar literacy corps in Iran formed in 1963.) Although early efforts with campaigns and organizations (the Red Yurt directed toward women, for example) failed in part because of insufficient reliable personnel, the steady pattern of growth of primary and secondary schools ensured literacy in the native language. Moreover, education for most Central Asians became available in the vernacular chosen for their nationality group, thus overcoming a basic hurdle to literacy in the past. On the other hand, the shift in alphabets within the first two Soviet decades hampered not only education for all Central Asians but publishing as well. For many people the shift from an Arabic-based to a Roman-based alphabet and finally (in 1940) to alphabets based on Cyrillic meant that they received their education in an outdated alphabet. Leading transitional figures, such as Sadriddin Aini, continued to write in the Arabic alphabet but were published in Cyrillic.

The change to Cyrillic writing systems cut Central Asians off from their written heritage and reduced the influence of past elites, as well as influences from other parts of Inner Asia. The separate alphabets developed for each of the recognized nationalities led to a linguistically unjustified barrier to inter-Turkic communication that blatantly served the sole purpose of political division. Beginning in the 1960s, indigenous scholars have protested this artificial separation of written Turkic languages, but it is only in the contemporary period that the cause has engaged the attention of cultural figures who have popularized it.

Closely tied to the organization of basic school systems was the need for teacher-training schools. The early varieties, technicums for elementary teachers and institutes for secondary school teachers, proved of uneven quality, especially the institutes. Improvements in the teacher-training schools were followed shortly by the establishment of a system of higher education on various levels. Prominent in this system is Tashkent Lenin State University, established in 1920 as the Central Asian University, a place that attracts many Central Asians who are not Uzbeks as well as third-world students. Uzbekistan has a second university, the Samarkand Alisher Navai State University (1933), and each of the other republics of Central Asia subsequently established its own institutions: the Kirov Kazakh State University (1934), the Lenin Tajik State University (1948), the Gorky Turkmen State University (1950), the Kirgiz State University (1951).

Education of Central Asian elites frequently takes place outside this system, often in the RSFSR as well as the Ukraine. Russian has become the language of higher education although certain faculties in the humanities, for example, use the local language as the medium of instruction. In addition to the university system within Central Asia, a system of higher education in technical fields exists. For example, during 1983–1984 in the Uzbek SSR alone there were forty-two schools of higher education (G1, p. 280).

As in the field of education, a transformation in the area of research has occurred in the modern period that promises a long-term impact on the society. Research establishments are organized mainly through the Academy of Sciences within each republic. These academies in turn are composed of institutes that parallel university faculties but have no pedagogical function. The academies publish the main body of research conducted in Central Asia. The issue of language (native or Russian) has been controversial in the work of the academies as in all fields of knowledge. Additionally, the participation of nonindigenous inhabitants of Central Asia (mainly Russians) in higher education and research has resulted in tension. As within the directly political establishments such as the Communist party, the practice has been to staff the leadership position with a member of the titular elite.

Research in important fields of Central Asian archaeology, literature, and history has shifted gradually from Moscow and Leningrad to Central Asia. Increasingly, although the research is conducted by indigenous scholars, the results appear in Russian to allow for broad readership. There is also a growing tendency to publish in English.

General publishing in the languages of Central Asia has greatly expanded in volume in the Soviet period. All publishing appears to be official, with the exception of clandestine religious publication, which has recently come to light. Newspapers and schoolbooks, published in the language of the titular nationality and in Russian, on occasion also appear in the languages of other minorities if the numbers and political pressures dictate. Therefore, in the Tajik SSR, Uzbek-language publications appear in order to reach the approximately 23 percent Uzbek population of Tajikistan. Karakalpak, Crimean Tatar, and Greek publishing takes place in Uzbekistan while in Kazakhstan Uzbek, Uighur, and German are published. With the exception of items intended for use in other parts of Inner Asia (which appears in the appropriate Arabic alphabet), all local language publishing in Central Asia appears in the Cyrillic alphabet.

In Sinkiang the education of elites in the modern period has been subject to a diversity of influences. This factor means that today there is no group of indigenous elites in senior capacity with a common educational experience. This factor alone hampers the ability of existing elites to form a coherent body that may actively seek to promote local interests. Because local elites are divided not only ethnically but in educational experience, Chinese influence in elite positions becomes that much more pervasive.

To illustrate this problem, we may examine the educational experience of a sixty-year-old urban Uighur in a high- to middle-level post. He will have begun his education at a religious or secular elementary school studying Uighur in the Arabic alphabet. His knowledge of Chinese will be rudimentary, especially on a written level. His secondary school experience has allowed him some Chinese language lessons in Urumchi during the 1940s, but in the absence of secular higher educational institutions in Sinkiang itself during the 1940s, his family, if wealthy, will have sent him away to educational centers outside the region. As late as the 1940s, Uighurs still went to Istanbul to acquire an education. Tashkent became an increasingly attractive alternative during the 1950s, and for some Nanjing provided a reasonable alternative. Returning to Urumchi, this young man will have entered the burgeoning educational institutions or the bureaucracy rather than industry and commerce. In part this is a result of the nontechnical training (except medical) that he might have acquired and in part a result of the small scale of local industry.

The typical members of elites now in senior positions have had such a diversity of educational experiences that they personally use several alphabets to write their own language although most publications since the 1970s appear in a modified Arabic alphabet. Moreover, except for those educated in Chinese institutions to the east, their command of Chinese is poor. For some, a stay in the USSR, often in Central Asia, together with close association with Russians and other Soviets in Sinkiang through 1960, has enforced their Russian-language skills as well as a certain latent pro-Soviet (or pro-Central Asian) attitude that the Chinese regard with suspicion.

Combined with long-term imprisonment (and execution) of politically inclined elites who sought independence or autonomy, the educational pattern of local elites has led to ineffective leadership. The decline in the use of Uighur and Kazakh for government or educational purposes (except symbolically) is directly attributable to the fact that local elites themselves did not have the ability to use their language in modern situations. Many of those who did spent a decade or more of their potentially most productive years in prison.

Local elites educated after 1949 show far greater potential to seek and acquire leadership positions within the region. As an Autonomous Region, Sinkiang enjoys symbolic cultural freedom which in the case of education has come to be translated into a substantial number of schools at all levels. Aside from compulsory elementary education, required to sixth grade, students may be channeled into technical schools or college preparatory secondary schools. In urban areas Chinese language acquisition dominates the curriculum, and some subjects are taught in Chinese. In addition, as in Soviet Central Asia, some local elites choose to send their children to Chinese schools, thus limiting their local language ability to what is acquired through family conversation. The perceived advantage of Chinese schools is that they provide a better overall education and offer the opportunity to learn English.

As the Iran experience has illustrated, however, elites are not only secular. Traditional elites educated in the extensive *madrasah* system, especially those from Kashgar (particularly at Artush), Khotan, Kulja, and Turpan, dominated leadership positions prior to the modern period. During the 1930s, merchants and those exposed to the modernizing philosophy of the Jadidists encouraged the private funding of elementary and some secondary schools, especially around Kashgar. These schools admitted girls as well as boys and were viewed neutrally by Chinese authorities. The opportunity for traditional education faded gradually, although a tutorial relationship continued to produce a limited number of men who were able to read the classical texts, versify in Turki (Uighur) and in Persian, and understand Koranic Arabic. Only in 1987 did the Chinese government allow the official opening of an institution in Urumchi to continue the tradition of classical Islamic training and manuscript study. In several Muslim communities of Sinkiang, particularly among the Chinghai Hui, Arabic and Koranic study, including law, takes place within the mosque from a diversity of books in Arabic. This practice has been much expanded since the political relaxation of the 1980s.

Schools of higher education in Sinkiang include Sinkiang University (established as Sinkiang Institute in 1935, it became Sinkiang University in 1960) and the Sinkiang August First Agricultural College (established in 1970), as well as universities in Kulja and teaching colleges elsewhere. Students from all ethnic groups come to these schools, but only the Uighur literature program in Urumchi and the Kazakh literature program in Kulja use local languages for instructional purposes. Chinese is the dominant language of instruction above the secondary school level. The same pattern holds true at the several teacher-training colleges in the region.

Aside from the educational institutions, where a limited amount of research is conducted into such culturally relevant subjects as history, linguistics, and literature, the several museums and the Academy of Social Sciences assume the major task of research into cultural topics. The institutes of the academy, symbolically headed by Uighurs and other local people, have undertaken important projects such as histories of particular ethnic groups in the region—Nigmat Minjani's Kazakh history for example—and linguistic projects including a computer program to translate Uighur into Chinese. Applied and pure science projects are conducted at the Academy of Sciences and its institutes, in particular in the field of petroleum and mineral retrieval. This endeavor has tended to be dominated by Chinese.

Publishing as a field has had a varied history very much formed by political events. As many visitors during the 1920s noted, the Chinese authorities prohibited both publication and receipt of published materials, especially newspapers, from the outside for indigenous and Chinese people alike. By the 1930s newspapers in Uighur began to appear, first from Kashgar. These were followed by government-sponsored publications from Urumchi and then from more remote places such as Tarbaghatai, Ili, and Altai. This flourishing of publications subsided after World War II diverted Soviet attention from Sinkiang, but reemerged during the East Turkestan Republic and under the subsequent coalition government until 1949. During the 1950s when the Soviet presence in Sinkiang again increased, Uzbek- and Kazakh-language publications from Soviet Central Asia were widely available in Sinkiang to the extent that Uzbek schoolbooks entered the urban school system. After the rupture with Peking in 1960, political turmoil, rebellion, and the Cultural Revolution interrupted both education and publishing. The official arts and literature journals *Tarim* and *Shinjan Adabiyat San'ati* (Sinkiang Literature and Art, 1961) appeared after Soviet departure to fill the gap. The 1980s have seen the flourishing of the Uighur periodical press as well as considerable book publishing in Kazakh. Much of the periodical press consists of journals such as *Turpan,* which exist uneasily alongside the many approved publications. All publications appear in the modified Arabic alphabet.

In the Mongolian People's Republic, with the closing of most Buddhist monasteries in the 1930s, elite education was reoriented toward secular institutions of learning based on the Soviet model. As early as 1921, the Buriat scholar Jamtsarano had founded the Mongolian Scientific Committee, which consisted of thirteen staff members and a state library of about two thousand volumes (M55, p. 133). In 1961, the committee became the MPR Academy of Sciences. In 1982, approximately 900 researchers were affiliated with the MPR Academy of Sciences; among the 900 were 30 Ph.D.s and more than 120 "candidates" (a degree somewhat higher than, though comparable to, an M.A.) (M39, pp. 361–362).

The Mongolian State University, founded in 1942 in Ulan Bator, consisted, by 1983, of about seventy departments in which more than ten thousand students were enrolled. The university employs more than seven hundred faculty members. Institutes affiliated with the university include the State Pedagogic Institute, founded in 1951–1952; the Medical Institute, founded in 1961–1962; and the Polytechnic Institute and Pedagogic Institute of the Russian Language, both founded in 1982–1983. There is also an Agricultural Institute, founded in 1958 (M39, pp. 352–353).

Virtually all publications issued since the early 1940s in the MPR have been printed in the Cyrillic alphabet. The MPR was spared the brief experiment with Latinization the Buriat Mongolian Autonomous Republic (and other republics in the USSR) passed through in the 1930s (D8, pp. 35–36). Until recent curriculum reforms in MPR schools, which now teach the old script to students from the seventh grade up, the ability to read old Mongolian script among the younger generations was limited to trained literary specialists.

In Tibet, where elite education was synonymous with monastic education, the gutting of the traditional monastic education system since 1959 has created a vacuum. In spite of the relaxation of some restraints on the surviving monasteries after 1979, the lack of trained scholar-teachers has reduced the old system to a shadow of its former self. Between 1985 and 1988 sixteen hundred monks left Tibet and went to India to pursue their studies; many of the older teachers who remain in Tibet are survivors of twenty-year prison sentences (N20, pp. 63–64).

The Chinese have opened up a few new avenues for Tibetans who wish to pursue secular education. By 1985, twenty-two technical schools and four colleges (the Tibet Institute for Nationalities, Tibet University, Tibet Medical College, and Tibet Institute for Agriculture and Animal Husbandry) had been established (N14, p. 173). Who attends these institutions of higher learning is another question. By one estimate, in 1984, two-thirds of the two thousand students enrolled in Tibet's three colleges were Chinese, not Tibetans (N1, p. 11). At the new Tibet University established in 1985, however, twice as many Tibetans are enrolled as Chinese, although there is some question as to whether Tibetan students have equal access to such popular courses as English-language instruction (N1, p. 11).

Popular Education and Literature

In Iran, the foundations laid for a comprehensive educational system have been steadily expanded since the beginning of the Pahlavi period. Although emphasis on education has shifted with nationalistic, then religious interpretation dominating in textbooks, the principle of universal education for boys and girls has not been questioned. By 1934 public education had begun to ease out the private schools, which had dominated before and served the needs of elites. Thousands of public schools have been opened in the years since, and private schools (foreign and religious minority schools) have been restructured to emphasize Iranian content. By the mid-1970s about nineteen thousand primary schools existed serving 3.5 million boys and girls in a ratio of two to one. In addition the

Literacy Corps, established in 1964, served the needs of one-half million adults (E14, p. 46). In roughly the same period there were 1.3 million secondary school students.

Statistics, however, convey only a part of the story. In addition to the regular curriculum that would prepare students to enter college, Iran has technical schools at various levels intended to train for industrial skills. During the 1970s some 133,000 students attended these schools. In addition the *madrasahs* continued to function although they begin after compulsory public education is completed.

Public education has been reorganized several times in this century to meet the more sophisticated labor needs of a modernizing society. From an original division of six years in primary and six years in secondary school, a shift to a middle school after five years of elementary education has come about, during which students are "guided" toward the kind of education they will pursue. Students take qualifying examinations for the university and are placed according to rank.

Gender separation has been practiced at the adolescent level throughout the history of public education, although in the elementary and college levels, classes have been coeducational. Teachers at all levels can theoretically be of either gender, although at the high school level there is a tendency to separate teachers by gender into boys' and girls' schools.

Compulsory education and the Literacy Corps have combined to raise the level of literacy dramatically in Iran, albeit at an uneven rate between rural and urban areas and between males and females. Female literacy runs at 48 and 30 percent for urban and rural respectively; male literacy has climbed to 77 and 56 percent. These rates tripled between the 1960s and the 1980s.

It is important to note that literacy means the ability to read Persian. Instruction in the student's native language is officially frowned on unless the language is needed for religious instruction. Thus Kurdish, Turkmen, and Azeri children, to name a few, can be literate in Persian under the government program. Despite leniency in this regard during special periods of internal or external stress, such as during the early years of the revolution, the principle of education in Persian, the national language of Iran, remains in place.

Widespread literacy has, as much as any other factor, stimulated the expansion of imaginative literature by providing a large potential readership. Many factors account for the shift away from the classical tradition of creative writing which was almost entirely devoted to poetry. In contemporary Iran, the novel and the short story have gained in popularity and status while poetry has changed from a solidly classical base toward greater variety in form and content.

The development of modern literature in Iran is traceable to the publication of Jamalzadeh's story "Yaki bud yaki nabud. . ." (Once upon a time. . .) and Nima Yushij's free verse poem "Afsanah," both appearing in 1921. These publications set the trend toward experimentation with new forms and the presentation of themes stated in a personal and direct manner. Persian literature in the modern period contains great variety of expression, but it is also marked by a certain starkness and spareness, a compression that owes much to poetry. This is especially true for such prose writers of the 1930s to the 1960s as Sadegh Hedayat, Bozorg Alavi, Sadegh Chubak, and Ghulam Reza Sa'idi. These writers of short stories and novellas portrayed the Iranian life of back alleys, loneliness, alienation, and injustice. The most famous work has been Hedayat's *The Blind Owl* (which has appeared in Western translation as well), a work steeped in Persian folk materials and historical allusion that is at the same time dark and pessimistic. Chubak, Alavi, and Sa'idi also write of the contrasts in human behavior, the coarse in contrast to the delicate, the power of the mind, and superstition.

The longer novel, although written since the 1930s, did not gain maturity and weight until the 1970s when two novelists of depth and promise emerged. Both set their stories in rural traditional Iran and explore relationships across generations and gender and of man and the environment. Mahmud Dowlatabadi's *Kelidar* (a mountain near Nishapur) appeared in ten volumes between 1974 and 1984. M. A. Afghani's *Showhar-e Ahu Khanum* (The Husband of Ahu Khanum) was published in 1961.

Persian literature, like the rest of Iranian society and culture, has undergone a period of internationalization in which it has shed tradition and convention and adopted new forms. As the modern literature emerges from a period of experimentation and finds its own style, voice, and subject, it is becoming more satisfying and indigenous than it was in the 1950s. This confidence in the literature means that other experimentation may be undertaken without abandoning the achievements of the rich traditional and contemporary literature. Perhaps the maturing of modern Persian literature may serve as an allegory for the ability of Persian society and culture to ingest and adapt to a modernizing world view without abandoning the grace and beauty of the culture.

In the Republic of Afghanistan, despite grandiose claims, literacy remained low in 1988, probably no higher than 10 percent. Also, the *mujahidin* lacked one important weapon in their struggle against the Kabul regime. All successful revolutionary movements since World War II have had educational components, teachers who gave the tool of literacy to the resistance fighters and used this tool to preach a specific ideology. Afghan *mujahidin* groups usually lived in groups of twenty to thirty men, natural schoolroom sizes. However, few attempts were made to teach the *mujahidin* reading and writing in their spare time, and spare time they had in abundance. In guerrilla wars, more time is spent in leisure than in fighting, and during the quiet periods, classes could have been held. But this did not occur during the Afghan *jihad.*

One interesting educational pattern evolved during the war. The *mujahidin* often taped their fire fights on cassettes and brought them back to play to families and friends in the refugee camps. Out of these tapes, folk tales were born, and heroes among the *mujahidin* were lauded in song and poem, often somewhat exaggerated as are many war stories regardless of place, time, and the people involved. But the folk tales will blend into history when the war ends.

In Pakistan, on the other hand, the three and a half million refugees were exposed to education, public health, and other social services. Initially, the conservative Jamaat Islami Pakistan established camp schools with at least tacit approval of the government of Pakistan. To counter these, the Afghan parties initiated schools in many camps, and even girls' schools came into being, though rarely. They also opened schools in Peshawar, Quetta, and elsewhere, teaching not only basic subjects, but their own brands of Islam. Because of this exposure to education, not necessarily qualitative, Afghans will demand a continuance of these services when they return home. Any postwar Afghan government will have to satisfy these new demands.

Several volunteer relief organizations established schools to train Afghan refugees in skills that would be needed when they returned home—as well as basic literacy when it was needed, a common occurrence. Also, volunteer agencies established and staffed schools inside Afghanistan, and Afghan *mujahidin* groups themselves founded schools in their areas of control. In spite of all these efforts, possibly a generation of young Afghans has been lost to education. The young males preferred to fight in the *jihad* rather than attend schools.

The depth of this problem will only become apparent, and crucial, when the Afghans try to staff government ministries, schools, and hospitals in the postwar period. The massive exodus of Western-trained, Western-oriented, Western-reacting Afghans, now located mainly in Western Europe and North America, will be a great handicap when peace is restored. Probably few of these individuals and their families will return, creating a great gap in administrative and technological expertise.

In spite of all the problems that face the returning Afghan refugees, several important positive factors do exist. The war has shattered the inward-looking aspects of Afghan society. Those who fled the country were exposed to many institutions heretofore unknown to them, such as education and public health. Those inside were exposed to the outside world through the horrors of war, and realized that change can occur, albeit violently—and they became ready for postwithdrawal peaceful change.

Although Islam is important and may initially dominate in postwar Afghanistan, religious leaders will lose power in the political arena as the dust and smoke of warfare settle down, and the Afghans return to the serious business of nation building. All wars bring about quantum jumps in technological advancement and major sociopolitical changes. Afghan society will never be the same, but the patterns that evolve will be recognizable as Afghan.

In Soviet Central Asia, with the introduction and establishment of compulsory universal education, the role of informal education has been curtailed, although popular education continues to serve as the basis for the distinctness of successive generations of Central Asians and their continued limited incorporation into

Soviet life. Because popular education has not been studied much by Soviet or Western scholars, the channels for popular education appear less clear in the modern than in the premodern period. The role of women as transmitters of culture has been widely recognized, as has the part played by elders within the traditional extended family. Since religious instruction was formally banned after 1928, the persistence of religious belief and knowledge may be attributed in large part to the family. In addition, the underground existence of Sufi brotherhoods and shrines points to the continued role as informal educators that Sufi leadership may continue to play. Clearly, popular education remains a divisive factor in Central Asia in that it sets Central Asians apart from outsiders. For this reason, the content of popular education and the details of its transmission are important. How popular education takes place also is significant in the study of the retention of an Islamic perspective within the formal atheistic Soviet Central Asian culture.

The effects of popular education may be observed in modern literature, particularly that from the 1980s when party controls became more relaxed. Today's writers suffer less from the self-censorship that the terror of the past engendered. Therefore, through literature may be observed the allegories of the Central Asian heritage, popular versions of epics as well as memories of the recent past transmitted communally, if not within the family. The literature also reveals the conflicting levels of Central Asian identity that overlap or are superimposed on formal political identities. Since modern literature appears chiefly in indigenous languages, it can speak directly to the group addressed by the author. This factor, in addition to the latitude of expression that interpretation allows, results in far greater expressiveness of attitudes and perceptions in literature than in formal historical writing.

. Nonetheless, the field of literature has become highly institutionalized within the Soviet period. Dictates by Moscow through all-Union writers' organizations have periodically worked to shape the content of literature. High on the list of suitable content for all forms of literature has been the theme of "friendship of peoples," which usually has been specifically interpreted to mean the friendship of indigenous people with Russians and as a corollary, the portrayal of Russians as benevolent older brothers and sisters. Classical literature, the epics, and early Soviet literature that deviated from this rule appeared in later editions in suitably purged form. The strict observance of this rule from the 1930s through the 1950s especially, has meant that Russian characters have always appeared as benevolent whether pro-Soviet or not.

A second content directive has been the glorification of workers and the proletariat, a subject alien to Central Asian literary traditions. This directive has resulted in protagonists who are lifeless and pathetic rather than real and heroic. Particularly in the literature of the 1920s and 1930s, the intrusion of this kind of protagonist led to writers attempting to describe lifestyles and feelings unfamiliar to them. Sadriddin Aini, long regarded as the father of Uzbek prose and modern

Tajik literature, in the 1930s specialized in this mode of expression and attempted to enliven his characters by inserting folk proverbs into their speech at every chance. Schoolteachers as protagonists were also acceptable and have served as more believable characters, being closer to the psychological landscape known to writers.

History as the subject of literature has presented considerable problems because of the frequent accusation that Central Asians used such content to glorify a decadent past. Therefore, the classical heritage has served more often as the subject of opera and ballet, where specificity of character is not required, than of novels, plays, or poems. On the other hand, the recent past, especially the transition into the Soviet period, has provided several authors with successfully executed content. At first treated as starkly contrasting periods—before the revolution and after—early Soviet studies in the form of novels and short stories have gradually emerged. The most prominent writer in this vein has been Chinghis Aitmatov, beginning with his collections from the early 1960s. Aitmatov's personalization of the early Soviet period through such devices as the relationship of a Kirgiz horse breeder to his horse (*Farewell Gulsary*, 1963) and more recently the recollections of the Stalinist era by a railroad worker (*The Day Can Last More Than a Hundred Years*, 1981) have allowed him to escape criticism for statements that have clear political implications. A recent Uzbek novel dealing with the same early Soviet period did not escape censorship, however. The author was instructed to make revisions before further publication.

An important tendency emerging in Central Asian literature that may have significant implications for the future is the increased publication of creative literature in Russian. This change is more apparent in the Kazakh and Kirgiz areas than in the southern Central Asian republics, possibly because urban Kazakh and Kirgiz areas are more heavily influenced by Russians and the indigenous literary heritage has been weaker than in the south. Aitmatov, a Kirgiz, and Oljas Sulaimanov, a Kazakh and another leading Central Asian writer, publish in Russian although they are both fluent speakers of their mother tongues.

Although most Central Asian writers publish in their mother languages, increasingly they appear to come from urban settings. Many of the younger writers have served in the Komsomol and are party members. Most belong to the writers' union of their republic although this is not a requirement for publication. The privileges that membership in formal unions offers in housing, research trips, and salaries, as well as prizes, make membership in such groups, and conformity to their rules and criticism, tempting for many writers.

In Sinkiang popular education has expanded with local-language schools available in most communities, although only the major groups (Chinese, Uighur, Kazakh) have adequate indigenous-language materials. The level of literacy, which in the immediate premodern period was comparable to that of Afghanistan in the same period, in the 1980s expanded to roughly 40 percent of the population. The low figure represents the relatively late introduction of schools into rural areas, the lack of teaching materials, and finally the change in alphabets that has made several generations effectively illiterate.

Using another measure of popular education, however, it is apparent that the strong family structure of the indigenous community makes cultural transmission the chief means of popular education. Moreover, older men trained in the traditional manner in Turkic and Muslim culture continue to educate small-town youth privately and unofficially. After the relaxation in control during the 1980s, Arabic-language books from Pakistan and elsewhere in the Middle East became available for this kind of mosque-associated education of children. In the same manner, Islamic prayer and ritual books became available in private kiosks in Urumchi and Kashgar; some of these arrive from abroad and others are undated lithograph publications from Kucha(r) and elsewhere in Uighur Sinkiang.

Literature, like other aspects of knowledge and education, has changed in part out of indigenous aspirations but mainly in response to political pressure. Poetry, the main genre of traditional literature, began to carry nontraditional messages during the 1930s. Periodical publications from this period devoted a section to politically inspired poetry. Heavy censorship, assassination of "nationalists," and turmoil have prevented the preservation of such materials. However, orally transmitted poems from that period have begun to reappear in journals and books as they were preserved among illiterate people. For example, the poetry of Abid'ul Khaliq Uighur, killed in the 1930s, has been collected from just such sources.

Following the period of Soviet influence, prose literature emerged among local people, and the first novels and short stories made their appearance. Translations of Soviet Central Asian writers are frequently published, especially in the translation series *Gulistan*, where, among others, Aitmatov's works have appeared.

A special effort to preserve the oral and popular literature and culture of local people has resulted in several book series devoted to anecdotes, riddles, and proverbs from the Uighur tradition. Related to this are historical novels and a respectable collection of specialized dictionaries and glossaries to aid in the reading and understanding of the traditional culture. The pirating of Soviet research aids (such as dictionaries) is not unknown. Among Kazakhs who form a relatively small community in Sinkiang, publication in the modified Arabic alphabet of especially important Soviet Kazakh works is widespread. A good example is the two-volume *Abai* appearing in 1981 from Urumchi. This is the Chinese Kazakh version of Mukhtar Auezov (Avezoli's) novelistic biography of the famous Kazakh poet and epic composer.

Although the oral epic literary tradition has nearly disappeared, the only living *Manas* poet, a Kirgiz, has received much honor in Sinkiang. Likewise a *Manas* cycle has been published. In the effort to preserve their disappearing cultural heritage, the Uighurs have also begun to issue editions of classical Turki works, such as Mahmud al-Kashgari's *Divan-e Lughat-e Turk* (The Compendium of the Turkish Language), and even more significant politically, histories from the eighteenth and nineteenth centuries recording local resistance to Chinese rule.

For prerevolutionary Outer Mongolia statistics on literacy differ widely. Soviet and MPR sources generally put literacy rates in this period as low as 1 percent or 3–4 (M39, p. 342; M36, p. 42). The distinguished MPR scholar B. Rinchen, however, estimated that about 35 percent were literate before 1921, and he has described the rationale behind the claim of many Mongols living under Ch'ing rule that they were illiterate while in fact they were avid readers: they were attempting to avoid being held liable for clerical service in the government (M61, p. 60; M4, pp. 247–248).

The issue of literacy is closely tied to the issue of political legitimation; the accomplishments of prerevolutionary Mongolian culture are played down so as to legitimate the revolution and its costs. It is thus difficult to accept unquestioningly modern-day claims of near-total literacy in the MPR. One MPR scholar describes Mongolia today as a nation of readers: on average, each MPR family subscribes to four or five periodicals. Each year the twenty or so MPR publishing houses put out almost six hundred titles, printing in total six million books (M36, p. 43).

The number of elementary schools has grown dramatically since 1921, when the first such school was established in Urga (Ulan Bator) with one hundred students. In 1983 there were altogether 888 grade schools in the MPR; those in towns and in *aimak* (provincial) centers have ten grades, while many in rural areas have only eight grades. The Ministry of Education hopes that by 1990 all schools will offer ten compulsory grades. In 1984, 77.8 percent of all students in rural areas lived in state-financed boarding schools. Even though the trend is for pastoral herders to adopt a more settled way of life, the government still targets as a priority the expansion of the network of state boarding schools to accommodate more children of herders. One can only wonder how the traditionally close-knit Mongolian family unit has been affected by the removal of children for much of the year to boarding schools (M39, pp. 342–347; M76, p. 8).

In Tibet, the issue of literacy is as politically charged as in Mongolia. While those who stress the positive aspects of Chinese rule in Tibet dismiss traditional Tibetan monastic education as amounting to the mere recitation of texts from memory (N14, p. 16), others estimate a pre-1950 literacy rate of 50 percent or more (N22, p. 139). There is no doubt that a large number of schools have been built in Tibet since the 1940s; there are more than six thousand primary schools and approximately seventy middle schools (see N14, p. 173; N1, p. 10; and N35, p. 72 for differing statistics). In rural areas, though, only 30 percent of the children attend school, and the shortage of middle schools means that many children receive only a primary education (N14, pp. 172, 174). One writer estimates that literacy today in Tibet stands at only 30 percent (N1, p. 10). Instruction in the Tibetan language was the practice in TAR schools in the 1950s and early 1960s; during the Cultural Revolution, however, instruction in Tibetan was dropped. Tibetan has recently been revived as a second language in the schools (N1, p. 11).

Conclusions and Comparisons

To a greater extent than in most developing countries in Asia, the various dimensions of change in the Inner Asian societies have been affected by ethnic diversity and by multiple outside influences. The ethnic identities of the various linguistic and religious groups within each society, with the limited exception of Tibet, were severely handicapped in the twentieth century by the wide range of diverse and conflicting influences.

The world views of the Inner Asian societies reflected this chaotic situation. In Iran within one generation, for example, West European, American, Iranian nationalist, Soviet, and Shi'ite world views were alternately and together imposed on the thinking public. In Afghanistan, tribal, Sunni, Shi'ite, Western, and Soviet world views competed for influence. In Central Asia the situation was simpler, because of the predominance of the Soviet outlook during most of the twentieth century. By the 1980s, however, the Soviet world view was disintegrating into uncertainty, and the Islamic peoples of the region were seeking to regain historical values. Sinkiang was subjected to both Soviet and Chinese influences, and was further divided by the differences between Uighur and Kazakh outlooks. Mongolia resembled the Central Asian republics in the predominance of Soviet influence and the resurgence of ethnic identity in the 1980s. Even Tibet, which for so long has faced the world with a united front, was confronted by a Chinese world view that was vacillating uncertainly between Communist and Western values, and by a generational conflict among Tibetans in exile between supporters of the status quo and of change.

Elite education was confronted by similar conflicting influences. In Iran and Afghanistan, students who went abroad brought back differing technical cultures ranging from Soviet to American. In Afghanistan, even within the country, specialized training programs were affiliated with a variety of foreign institutions, and teaching staffs were alternately American, Indian, and Soviet. The societies under more direct Soviet or Chinese influence benefited from educational programs that were more consistent and generally of higher quality, although by the 1980s both Soviet and Chinese leaders were questioning their own educational philosophies.

In literature there has been a greater assertion of ethnic values, although in the societies under Soviet and Chinese influence these values have had to interact with guidelines set by political authorities. The relatively low literacy in these societies has enhanced the role of oral literature, which adheres to traditional themes and models. To the extent that written literature is available, it is handicapped by changes in orthography. Just as much of the Turkish literary heritage was lost when the Latin alphabet was introduced, in some Inner Asian societies the official shift from Arabic or Persian to Latin and later to Slavic alphabets has blunted the ethnic heritages.

By the 1980s, the various elements of values and knowledge were in a process of transition in which outside influences were losing their predominant position and ethnic values were gaining greater freedom of expression. The formation of distinctive Inner Asian world views is nevertheless still at an early stage of development.

III

Patterns and Prospects

Inner Asia and the World

14

Patterns of Modernization

In the course of the twentieth century the societies of Inner Asia evolved in a manner that was in many ways similar to that of other developing countries, but they differed in important particulars. In the 1920s and 1930s the foreign influences predominated and the traditional structures were bypassed or superseded. Then gradually after the Second World War—in part because of the distraction of outside influences caused by the war—the indigenous political cultures began to reassert themselves. By the 1980s, the indigenous peoples were seeking to appropriate the political and economic institutions introduced by the foreigners and to assert their desire for greater autonomy as a framework for policies more consonant with their cultures and interests.

In chapters 9–13, which are concerned with the period of the 1920s to the 1980s, we have directed our attention to the roles of the earlier-modernizing European countries in introducing modern institutions and values. To what extent and in what manner the indigenous premodern heritages have been able to adapt to the requirements of modern societies has been our focus in these chapters. It has been a common assumption among the early-modernizing societies that the natural way for latecomers to modernize was to reject their cultural heritages and to adopt those that have been developed by the "West." It is only recently that the Westerners have come to realize how much of their own premodern heritage survives today, and how little of it interferes with modernity.

As in the case of other later-developing regions, foreign intervention has played an essential role in the modern transformation of the Inner Asian societies. Beyond this rather obvious generalization, however, it is clear that no two cases have followed the same mode of interaction between the institutional heritages of the later-modernizing societies and the aims and capabilities of the more developed societies that have become involved with them.

Among the societies of Inner Asia, we find two patterns in the adaptation of premodern institutions to modern functions. In Iran, and to a lesser extent in

Afghanistan, the premodern political institutions were sufficiently developed that they could respond in both political and economic terms to the initiatives of the foreigners, and by the end of the century could sustain governmental functions and developmental programs without predominant foreign assistance. The second pattern is exemplified by the remaining Inner Asian societies, which depended almost entirely on foreign settlers and influences to introduce modern institutions.

In Iran the foreign institutions that accompanied the economic and social programs of the Pahlavi rulers were widely regarded as alien to Islamic culture, and the Islamic state established after the fall of the shah in 1979 may be interpreted as a reaction of the indigenous peoples to foreign influence. Defeats in several wars and military occupation during both world wars did not diminish Iran's capacity for self-government and self-development. Despite the marked differences in the policies of the shah and the ayatollah, and the different alliances of interest groups that have supported their administrations, Iran has survived as a country where a majority of the labor force is engaged in manufacturing and services rather than in agriculture.

The case of Afghanistan is different in that the reforming efforts of Amanullah, and later Daoud, and the Marxist republic established in 1978, have sought to establish modernizing institutions that did not relate adequately to traditional customs and practices. Political authority still resides mainly in the hands of local and regional leaders without whose cooperation the central government has little authority. One is reminded of the fate of human organ transplants, when the tissues of the recipients are of a different type from those of the donor, and hence reject the new organ. The receptivity of local Afghan leaders to modern reforms has been tested several times, and one of the principal challenges in the postoccupation era will be to obtain a consensus among the local Afghan leaders and interest groups as to an appropriate program of modernization.

In the other Inner Asian societies, legitimacy and bureaucracy were provided by the authority of the foreign occupying forces. In the Central Asian Union republics, for example, the Communist party and the Soviet government, following the precedent of the imperial system, provided the initiative for the development of modern functions. Rather than seeking to transform native institutions concerned with policy making and economic initiatives, they established parallel foreign institutions into which the indigenous peoples were only partially absorbed over the long run.

There are significant differences, however, among these five societies. In Kazakhstan, with a majority of the population non-Muslim, and the Muslim population including eleven national ethnic groups, there is only a weak basis for a Kazakh identity, despite the sophistication of the native elite. In Uzbekistan, by contrast, there is a strong basis for a distinctive Uzbek identity. The Uzbeks are in a majority in their republic, where Muslims outnumber non-Muslims by a ratio of five to one. The foreigners have played a less dominant role than in

Kazakhstan, although they have effectively run the cotton industry. The Uzbeks are foremost among the Muslim peoples of this region in pressing for their own policies and in taking advantage of the Soviet-imposed institutions to pursue their goals. The Kirgiz and Turkmen republics are predominantly Muslim, but are less developed than the Uzbeks and lack the basis for asserting independent policies. In Tajikistan the Muslims form 85 percent of the population but have not pressed actively for an autonomous modern society.

In the contrasting case of Outer Mongolia, there was an indigenous national administration with which the Soviet government could deal. In the prevailing revolutionary context, however, the premodern Mongolian officials were swept away and a new government was established in the Soviet mold. Even after five or six decades, the foreign-native balance in influence and initiative did not approach that of Iran or Afghanistan, and Mongolia in the 1990s was only beginning to emerge from what was in effect colonial status.

Turning to the areas of Chinese predominance, in Tibet the Chinese claim to have exercised Chinese suzerainty since the eighteenth century, and the Dalai Lama in his statement of June 1988 appeared not wholly to reject this definition of the relationship. Tibet remains torn between a Buddhist clergy, which still dominates domestic policy to the extent possible under Chinese occupation, and the Tibetans in exile, who tend to be divided along generational lines. Tibet is the one society in Inner Asia where the indigenous peoples are concerned more with reacting to foreign, that is Chinese, influence than with developing a program of modernization consonant with their traditional culture.

In Sinkiang the continuing flow of Chinese immigration is leading to a situation in which the Chinese will predominate in population as well as in political authority. At the same time, Chinese policy appears to be more sensitive than Soviet policy in Kazakhstan, for example, to the needs of the indigenous peoples. The traditional cultures of the Uighurs and the Kazakhs, which the Red Guards sought to obliterate, are now being cautiously encouraged within the limits of Chinese security interests.

Despite these differences among the Inner Asian societies, they have in common the relation of the indigenous people to foreign influences. Their political, economic, and social institutions were so weakly developed at the start of the twentieth century, with the limited exception of Iran, that they did not have the capacity to resist foreign discrimination.

The political and bureaucratic apparatus of administrative and social institutions introduced in the 1920s was long regarded by the indigenous peoples as an instrument of oppression. They participated in these institutions unwillingly, and sought to preserve their own institutional heritage to the extent possible. Now, however, the societies in the Soviet and Chinese orbits have begun to breathe nationalist life into the foreign political structures and are using them to challenge the authority of the outsiders.

This is a common phenomenon among colonial peoples. The programs of the leaders of the independence movements in India and Africa, for example, were all based on the teachings of the colonizers. More often than not, the efforts of the colonizers to introduce modern institutions and values were at first resisted by the indigenous peoples and then appropriated and turned against them. Indeed, the first generation of nationalist leaders was often too ''Western'' in its approach to societal transformation, and it took several subsequent revolutions, led by younger generations of nationalists, before the indigenous peoples learned to borrow more selectively from the West and to adapt their own institutional heritages to modern functions.

Perhaps the closest analogies to the situation in which the peoples in the Soviet and Chinese orbits find themselves are those Latin American countries— Bolivia, Paraguay, Colombia, Ecuador, Peru, in particular—where minorities of European extraction rule over the majority of Indian and mestizo inhabitants. In these cases, the Europeans are reluctant to share political authority with the native populations, and the whole process of national development has been delayed. At the same time, the Muslim people of Central Asia have a greater capacity than the Indians in Latin America to press their claims for autonomy.

The profound upheavals underway in the Soviet Union and China made the 1980s a critical testing time for the relations between the native peoples and the foreigners in Inner Asia. The resolution of these uncertainties will be a critical factor in the prospects for the indigenous peoples under Soviet and Chinese rule.

15

Inner Asia and World Politics

Introduction

Our study has been concerned not with the role of Inner Asia in world politics, but with the ways in which the heritages of institutions and values of this region have been adapted in the twentieth century to the challenges of modernity. Our conclusions about these processes, and how they compare with those in other regions of the world, have been presented in chapter 14. Yet Inner Asia should not be seen simply as a laboratory of political, economic, and social processes. It is also a frontier of Soviet and other West European, Chinese, Japanese, and American security interests. The contemporary competition for influence in Inner Asia is as much a competition of policies of modernization as it is a competition of political and military power.

Much of the twentieth-century history of Inner Asia has little to do with local factors: it can best be understood by looking to Moscow or Peking, London or Washington. In some areas, state structures implanted by conquerors have provided frameworks conducive to the development of the attributes of modern nation-statehood. Thus vague nomadic identities, arbitrarily fixed by Soviet officials, have provided the kernels for strengthening senses of protonational affiliation in the Central Asian republics. Furthermore, attempts at enforced cultural assimilation in such regions, particularly when accompanied by a vocabulary of nationhood and self-determination, seem to create a cultural reaction against the would-be enforcer.

The workings of these two processes suggest that if and when the tides of Soviet or Chinese conquest recede from Inner Asia, they will leave behind far more substantial and stable polities than did earlier Inner Asian conquerors. Uzbekistan, for example, was endowed by its Soviet creators with sham forms of nationality, which may now take increasing life, driven (like similar development of national feeling in Tibet and Sinkiang) by reaction to alien conquest.

329

Until recently, however, the possibility that such conquest would recede seemed remote. Soviet control over Central Asia, like Chinese over Tibet and Sinkiang, seemed unshakable. Ironically, however, both the Soviet and Chinese polities, in their Communist forms at least, are entering a phase of crisis. Like the old nomadic empires, they are losing their military edge internationally, as well as their ability to coerce internally. Economically they are abandoning autarky, and depending more and more on international economic relations. Perhaps most important, they have lost faith in the ideology that once gave them cohesion. The situation today resembles that at the turn of the century, when the great powers discontinued their policies of confrontation in Inner Asia and concluded a series of treaties that compromised their interests. At that time their priorities were determined by their greater concern for the German threat in Europe. Today, the domestic problems of China, the Soviet Union, and the United States lead them to avoid confrontation in Inner Asia.

States lacking the firm underpinnings of identity provided by a common agricultural heritage are still volatile, as Pakistan and Afghanistan demonstrate. But today's Pakistan is more secure than was the immediate postpartition state: institutional development, years of facing a common military threat, and the coming of age of a nationally educated population have seen to that. Afghanistan too, even while divided by bitter political rivalries, has emerged from Soviet occupation with a stronger common sense of Afghan identity than before. Inner Asian polities, by comparison with France, say, or even Egypt, are still fragile. But they are gaining strength.

Enduring Influence of Political Culture

The following long-term characteristics of the political cultures of Inner Asia should be taken into account in considering the prospects for those countries and peoples.

Iran

The conservative or "fundamentalist" political system established by the Ayatollah Khomeini has deep roots in Iranian culture, and it is likely to survive in some modified form. There is already evidence that among some of his clerical followers there exists a more pragmatic view of the world. The Salman Rushdie affair notwithstanding, an overall trend toward decreasing confrontational policies in international relations in favor of compromise may be seen in Iran's grudging acquiescence to working within the region (as in OPEC) and building ties to select Western European countries. With the passing of Khomeini, no person of the moral stature to dictate strict interpretations of Islamic doctrine remained. Even if a doctrinaire successor were to take power in Iran, he would lack the stature to continue the confrontation over issues that has brought about Iran's current isolation in international affairs.

Moreover, because of its technological defeat in the Iran-Iraq war, Iran has come to recognize the importance of interconnections with the world community, especially the ultimate continued dependence of developing societies on technologically advanced ones. This lesson has certain similarities to the lesson learned in 1953: Iran could not survive in economic isolation faced with the Anglo-American oil boycott. In the same way, Iran could not continue to face the threat of a Western and Soviet-armed enemy, Iraq, in 1988. Therefore, from 1953 to the early 1970s Iran turned toward inner reconstruction, and in the process worked to eliminate its dependence on a single-buyer oil market. As a result of the Iran-Iraq war, it is not unlikely that Iran could turn to developing means of arming itself without reliance on outside suppliers. Common sense and international agreements affecting the entire region may prevent the emergence of chemically armed states, a fact that now seems probable in the Middle East with which Iran is so intimately connected.

On the other hand, during the later years of the Pahlavi regime, a greater concern with its role within the region allowed Iranian attention to turn eastward toward its Inner Asian neighbors, a direction it had ceased looking in since the termination of its dispute with Afghanistan over Herat in 1857. Khomeini's Iran continued the concern with Inner Asia partially in response to the Soviet forces in Afghanistan and partially as a result of its own quickened awareness of Muslims in neighboring areas of the USSR and China. This interest in Inner Asia will probably continue, if only as long as the form and stability of government in Kabul remain uncertain.

Afghanistan

In this war-torn country, the key long-term factor is the strength of a regional elite based on local and tribal loyalties. It is these regional solidarities that permitted the *mujahidin* to resist the Soviet occupation forces and the army of the republic for a decade. They have been represented abroad by the seven-party alliance, which has its headquarters in Peshawar pending a return to Afghanistan.

Despite the great destruction wrought by the Soviet occupation and the accompanying civil strife, two results of the struggle will have an effect on the long-term modernization of Afghanistan. First, the struggle has led to the cooperation of the regional leaders who had traditionally spent much of their time fighting each other. They have now virtually for the first time begun to give Afghanistan as a nation priority over regional interests, and to recognize the need for joint action if they are to secure the future independence of their country. Second, the three and a half million refugees in Pakistan have become familiar with standards of sanitation, health care, education, and organizational activity beyond any they were familiar with at home. When they return to Afghanistan, they will not wish to give up these attributes of modernity and will insist on a higher standard of living.

The structure most consonant with Afghan political culture would be an Islamic federated republic providing for some degree of autonomy for six to ten regions or provinces. The boundaries of these provinces would be determined by: (1) the distribution of ethnolinguistic groups; (2) river patterns; (3) lines of communication and commerce between cities; and (4) natural resources and regional potential for development. The leadership of this new political structure would be collective, based on the traditional pattern in Afghan villages and nomadic camps of councils led by family or lineage heads.

A fundamental feature of the postwithdrawal era will be the firm determination of Afghan leaders to decide on the destiny of their country without outside interference. Outside assistance for reconstruction will be necessary and an effort will be made to acquire it within the framework of a nonaligned foreign policy. At the same time, the Afghan leaders recognize the very extensive investments made by the Soviets over the years in the natural gas, coal, copper, iron ore, fertilizer, cement, gold, uranium, and emeralds in the mountainous north. The Soviet economic role in the development of northern Afghanistan will continue to be important, but it is not likely to lead to significant political influence. The Tajik, Uzbek, Turkmen, and Karakalpak minorities who inhabit this region are vehemently anti-Russian, and Soviet political or military interference would mean continued warfare.

More generally, a postwithdrawal outcome along the above lines based on Afghan political culture would mean that alternative outcomes that have been the subject of speculation are not likely to be feasible. For example, the regional leaders would not accept the cooperation of Najibullah or other members of the Parcham branch of the Communist party in a coalition government. The influence of the Khalq branch in some elements of the army is not strong enough to stem the large number of recruits defecting to the *mujahidin*. It is also not likely that the former King Mohammed Zahir would be called back from his exile in Italy, or would exert much influence if he returned. Finally, the determination of the regional Afghan leaders to guide their own destiny ensures that they would not accept any foreign interference in their domestic affairs. In particular, efforts of Pakistan to influence the postwithdrawal settlement are likely to be rejected, despite the role played by that country as the host of the refugees, as a conduit for American and other weapons to the *mujahidin*, and as a bulwark against Soviet influence south of its present borders.

Soviet Central Asia

Ethnicity has not been an organizing political force in this region. It has always been subordinate to broader patterns of empire in the geopolitical structure of the area. Extreme tribal and clan fragmentation has marked the political life of the region for the last two millennia. There has been little or no overarching political vision or unity based on ethnic identification. Similarly, religion has not been a unifying political factor in the region. The differing and often competitive forms of Islam in the several subregions of Central Asia have served to fragment rather than unite the numerous tribes and clans.

Empire within Inner Asia has historically been based in multi-ethnicity, with social patterns in urban areas largely interactive and cooperative.

The various Turkic and Iranian peoples of this fragmented political landscape were unable or unwilling to unite against the external Slavic intruder at the end of the nineteenth century. The Russians were able to manipulate this diverse set of peoples to their advantage through a policy of *divide et impera,* as many of these groups collaborated with the advancing tsarist forces in the search for temporary parochial benefit against their ethnic and religious kinsmen.

Nothing resembling cohesive political nationalism has yet materialized in the region, as modern forms of sociopolitical identity have only recently begun to emerge on the basis of the once presumed artificial territorial division of the Union republics. These patterns of political nationalism based on republican identity are embryonic. They remain effectively contained by in-system incentives offered by the Moscow center, which is also reasonably confident of the ultimate political allegiances of the Central Asian republics.

Nevertheless, the years since World War II have witnessed the emergence of increasingly accomplished and confident indigenous elites who have developed aspirations for local social, cultural, and economic control. Not only have they shown strong new interests in the literary, historical, and cultural roots of their identity, they have begun to formulate developmental and modernizing priorities of their own. During the 1980s these elites began to make new requests for increased central investments, industrial diversification, agricultural development, and the initiation of major Siberian river-diversion projects which would benefit the region. Decisions taken at the Twenty-seventh Party Congress in Moscow in 1987 rejected most of these critical requests, setting the stage for potential center-periphery confrontations.

The reinvigorated internationalism of the Gorbachev leadership, one of the hallmarks of the center's new policy, has threatened to encroach upon some of the hard-won prerogatives these republics had secured over the previous two decades, as Moscow has initiated a major drive against corruption and localism in Central Asia. In the perception of these local elites, that drive against corruption may be virtually indistinguishable from the reassertion of Great Russian or central dominance. That perception, coupled with the center's recent rejection of republic requests for increased investments in economic diversification, makes for a new volatility in the nationalities sector. It is ironic that the very base for this potential challenge, the emergence of newly skilled managerial elites among the Central Asian peoples, had been designed and developed by the Moscow center itself.

The stability of this sector will be affected by several important shifts in external policy on the immediate Soviet periphery: (1) the success of first steps toward an important political and economic accommodation with China; (2) the final Soviet withdrawal from the long and bloody war in Afghanistan; (3) the reduction of Soviet forces in Mongolia; and (4) the unpredictable evolution of Iranian politics in the post-Khomeini period. Perhaps more important, the stability of this sector will be affected by the course of the evolving Gorbachev experiment, and the extent to which internationalist and nationalist themes continue to come into conflict as the Moscow center attempts to resolve the intricate dilemmas of its political economy.

Sinkiang

In traditional times Sinkiang lacked any distinct regional identity: what structure it has was given by Chinese conquerors. Little has happened to change this fact. In the south, it is true, the Uighur sense of identity is growing stronger, as is witnessed both by local anti-Chinese unrest and by the defections of Uighur diplomats and athletes to Turkey. But in northern Sinkiang, Chinese immigration has turned the demographic balance against the Uighurs. So Sinkiang can in no way be compared to Tibet, a proto-nation-state under foreign control. Nevertheless, change is underway in Sinkiang, and will probably continue.

The most important factor leading to change in Sinkiang is the larger crisis of communism in China. Attempts to create a new society and with it a new set of identities reached their climax in the Cultural Revolution, whose impact in Sinkiang was powerful. Its aftermath, however, has seen a strong reassertion of local Turkic identity in language, literature, and religion, as well as of earlier social and economic patterns.

Toward the revival of Uighur identity, Peking's policy has been one of appeasement or co-optation. Thus the central government is financing the reconstruction of mosques ruined by Red Guards. But this policy has not been entirely successful, and while the rest of China has been opening up, most of the Tarim basin has remained closed, at least in part because of ethnic tensions there.

The need to deal with economic ruin has similarly inclined Peking to allow events in Sinkiang to take their own course. Little attempt is made any longer to control economic developments, and Sinkiang residents are active traders and black marketeers, the Georgians of China. Perhaps more significantly, overland trade with the USSR has begun again, and an intention to complete the railway linking Urumchi to Alma Ata has been announced. This is a particularly bold step, given the high degree of economic influence the USSR once exercised in Sinkiang.

The strategic position of Sinkiang, however, will impose certain limits on this process. It is a key border area, and under no circumstances will Peking allow it to come under foreign influence. This is true not least because Sinkiang is the base for China's nuclear-weapons program. Uranium mining is carried out in the western part of the province, while nuclear bombs are tested at the vast military reservation near Lop Nor.

But exercising this control will become more difficult in the years ahead. Increasing contacts with neighboring countries will bring new sources of wealth and new ideas into Sinkiang, feeding both local dissent and the ambitions of Chinese stationed there. Without some centrally defined orthodoxy, regionalism will become stronger. Islamic revival and Uighur national feeling may lead to outbreaks of terrorism and sabotage, though it seems unlikely that these will reach such a level as to threaten fundamental Chinese interests.

The challenge for China's rulers, as for those of the USSR, will be to find a set of new institutions that, while replacing centrally planned societies, will avoid plunging the state into chaos. It is significant that the two countries are facing crisis at the same time. Otherwise one would be tempted to meddle in the other's affairs. But under these circumstances, it seems likely that the two capitals will cooperate to keep the peace in their borderlands.

Mongolia

As the Mongolian People's Republic enters the 1990s, it may at last look forward to destalinization. The gigantic statue of Stalin that stands in front of the Academy of Sciences in Ulan Bator as a vivid symbol of the more oppressive aspects of the political and cultural life of the MPR is slated for removal. The stifling economic policies of the Brezhnev-Tsedenbal era will undoubtedly give way to attempts at reform under Batmonh (general secretary of the MPR since 1984) and Gorbachev.

The MPR will still for the foreseeable future remain within the Soviet economic orbit. With approximately 80 percent of its current trade with the USSR and another 15 percent with other Comecon nations, it seems unlikely that economic ties with non-Comecon countries will be developed rapidly. Normalization of relations with the PRC, a slow process that remains one step behind USSR-PRC normalization, may, however, open new markets for MPR exports.

Contact with Western nations has focused mainly on cultural and academic exchanges, rather than economic trade or assistance. One of the earliest results of the opening of MPR-US diplomatic relations in 1987 has been the establishment of a US-MPR research exchange program. The exchange of scholars between the two countries will undoubtedly generate a more favorable atmosphere, and will at the very least lead to more accurate perceptions of one another.

Tibet

Because of the PRC stance that Tibet is an integral part of China, it is difficult to visualize Peking allowing Tibet to turn to non-Chinese sources for aid in modernizing. Tibet's strategic position along a disputed border coupled with the probability of continued displays of Tibetan dissatisfaction with China's heavy-handed policies will make Peking hesitant to give Tibetans more autonomy in most realms. Although Gorbachev promises to remove the majority of Soviet troops from the MPR's border with the PRC, one hears nothing about removal of Chinese troops from either Tibet's borders or interior regions.

The Dalai Lama's concession of Tibet's foreign policy to the PRC in his speech of June 15, 1988, at the European Parliament in Strasbourg has produced division in the ranks of Tibetan émigrés, many of whom still call for Tibet's independence. The trial in January 1989 of twenty-seven Tibetan pro-independence demonstrators, resulting in harsh punishments, reflects the PRC's stance on the issue of Tibetan independence. Yet the fact that some Tibetans still demonstrate publicly, and occasionally violently, while undoubtedly knowing that their actions will be severely punished, is evidence that the independence issue has not been fully put to rest by the Dalai Lama's conciliatory speech of June 1988.

The death in January 1989 of the Panchen Lama removed an important link between Peking and the Tibetan public. How Peking handles the replacement of the Panchen Lama will tell us much about future policy directions.

Observers sympathetic toward PRC efforts to modernize Tibet recognize the mutual animosity between Communist cadres, both Tibetan and Chinese, and the general population of Tibet. If party cadres continue to ridicule openly the practice of Buddhism, as they reportedly do, it is unclear how the party will manage to win over the needed support of the Tibetan population in the drive toward modernization. Certainly, without broader support among the indigenous Tibetan population, the PRC leadership will face a long and difficult path in the process of bringing Tibet even up to current PRC standards of modernity. If the PRC allows more cultural (that is, religious) freedom throughout Tibet, it may soften the resistance to Chinese-initiated reforms. Yet, religion in Tibet continues to be a political force, as reflected in the participation of monks in anti-Chinese demonstrations.

The Prospects for Inner Asia

The prospects for further political development, economic growth, social integration, and intellectual advancement in Inner Asia depend on a delicate balance between indigenous initiatives and foreign influences. Both elements were in a state of flux in the late 1980s.

The capacity for initiatives varies greatly among the peoples of Inner Asia, from the well-established political system in Iran and the vigorous assertion of the Uzbeks for self-expression to the relatively weak political organization of the Kirgiz, Turkmen, and Tajiks, and the Tibetans and the Uighurs and Kazakhs in Sinkiang. It remains to be seen to what extent the Muslims and Buddhists of Inner Asia can work together or separately toward the achievement of national programs of modernization, as the other peoples of Asia have succeeded in doing, should circumstances change sufficiently to permit such a possibility.

These circumstances, in turn, depend on developments in the Soviet Union and China. The restructuring they are undergoing is of a profound and controversial character, which will take a decade or two to work itself out. It seems unlikely that either the Soviets or the Chinese will simply abandon their empires as the British did theirs. The influence of Moscow and Peking on their borderlands, however, seems almost certain to diminish and local autonomy to increase. In some cases this will lead to conflict, as we are already seeing in the Caucasus and elsewhere in the USSR, and in Tibet. But the possibility exists that the state structures put in place by the Soviet Union and China may end up functioning, like the British legacy on the Indian subcontinent, as the framework for a pattern of future relations.

Comparative Chronology
of Inner Asia

The following chronology of events in Inner Asia from the sixteenth century to 1989 is offered as a quick reference for the reader of the narrative section of the book. Events within Inner Asia have been interconnected by the different subareas' shared cultural, economic, and political patterns. The chronology gives tangible shape to the concept that Inner Asian subareas were frequently affected in a domino manner by change along the area's borders with settled and powerful states, as, for example, when Iran adopted Shi'ism or Yellow Hat Buddhism triumphed in Mongolia. The expansion of the Russian state from the sixteenth through the twentieth century and the effect its pressure on Inner Asia had on internal and external developments are readily illustrated in the chronology.

Critical periods of change have been given more space than more static ones. Underlying the choice of materials included is the assumption that the chronology of events for neighboring areas of China and Russia is relatively well known and more readily available than that for Inner Asia.

Iran

16th century

1501	Safavid rule established
	Shi'ism becomes state religion
1510	Iranian-Uzbek wars for domination of Khurasan
1514	Ottoman-Iranian wars for domination of the Caucasus, Anatolia, and Mesopotamia
1561	English Moscovy Company, Shirley Brothers, and Portuguese all visit and set up trade relations
1587	Shah Abbas the Great, greatest of Safavid rulers, begins reign

17th century

Formation of Shahsevens as crown supporters in opposition
  to tribal chiefs
Flourishing of Persian art and architecture
1629   End of Abbas's reign
1664   Russian mission to Iran
Cossack raids in Caucasian territory
Attention to town improvement, especially Isphahan, Meshhed,
  and Tabriz

18th century

Decline of Safavids
1722   Afghan invasion and overthrow of Safavid power
1724   Russian and Turkish states agree to dismember Iran
1730   Rise of Nadir Shah (Afshar) and roll back of Russian and Turkish
  armies from Caucasus and Mesopotamia
Invasion of India, Bukhara, and Khiva
1747   Assassination of Nadir Shah at Kandahar
1750   Rise of Karim Khan Zand with capital in Shiraz
1794   Rise of Agha Mohammed (Qajar) with base in Tehran
1798   British induce Iran to attack Afghanistan over Herat to distract
  Afghans from Indian territory and guard overland trade routes

19th century

Qajar dynasty rule
1800   East India Company concludes commercial and political agreement
  to deny Afghan or French chance to interfere with India overland
  trade of British
1804   War with Russia over Caucasus and Caspian territories
1806   Napoleon attempts to counter British and Russians
  in Iran with military aid
1808–10   British attempt to replace French officers in Iranian army and
  promise subsidy
1813   Treaty of Gulistan forces Iran to give up Caucasian lands after
  military losses to Russia
1814   Mutual aid treaty with Britain and subsidy promise
1825–28   Russia takes more territory south to Tabriz. British give no support
  despite treaty
1828   Treaty of Turkmanchai through which Iran loses Azerbaijan to Aras
  River; forced to pay huge indemnity

1834	First American missionaries arrive in northern Iran
1850	Execution of the Bab, leader of a sect that led to Bahaism
	First newspapers in Iran, from minority Christian communities under European missionary influence
1851	Dar ul-Funun, first secular educational institution of higher learning, established in Tehran
1856	Iran attempts to retrieve Herat area but fails as British aid Afghans. Boundary established in 1872 with Helmand River issue still to be settled
1864, 1870	Telegraph lines connect Iran to Baghdad and Odessa
1872	Beginning of concessions to British and Russian commercial interests for control of Iranian resources
1878	Cossack Brigade established under Russian officers
1882	Iran loses rights to Transcaspia following Russian conquest
1889	British-backed Imperial Bank of Persia lends to royal family
1890	Exiled reformer Malkom Khan publishes antiregime journal *Qanun* from London
1891	Forced cancellation of Tobacco Regie through clerical and nationalist pressure encouraged by Said Jamalludin al-Afghan

20th century

1900	Russian-British competition for influence increases
1901	Oil concession granted to D'Arcy, a British subject
1905–6	Constitutional Revolution
	Attempt by reformers to create constitutional monarchy
1907	Anglo-Russian convention to divide Iran into three spheres to ward off German interests and secure economic concessions
1908	Oil strike in Kurdish area
1909	Anglo-Persian oil company established
	Law for public education adopted
1909–11	Russians attack northern Iran and bombard shrine at Meshhed
1911	Morgan Shuster, American invited to reform Iran's tax system, opposed by Russians and British. Dismissed on Russian ultimatum
1914	Iran declares neutrality in WWI. Disregarded by all sides
1919	At Paris peace conference Iran attempts to regain 19th-century territorial losses but British block seating of delegation
1920	Soviet troops attempt to set up the Soviet Republic of Gilan in Iran
1921	Coup d'etat of Reza Khan
	First modern Iranian prose fiction published in Berlin
1925	Reza Khan declared shah
1926	Iranian-Turkish-Afghan Treaty of mutual security
1928	Iran declares foreign concessions canceled

Traditional ethnic clothing outlawed

Faculty of medicine established

1933 New oil treaty signed with British

1934 Universal compulsory public education begun

Tehran University formed from various faculties

1937 Arrest of leading intellectuals on charges of propagating Communist views: these "53" form nucleus of the Tudeh, pro-Moscow Communist party of Iran

1939 Trans-Iranian Railway opened

1941 Reza Shah forced to abdicate in favor of son Mohammed Reza Shah as Allies use Iran as supply route for USSR

1946 Democratic party of Azerbaijan formed by Pishavari and supported by the Tudeh. Soviet occupation army in Azerbaijan prevents Tehran from taking any action against ethnic demands of this group based in Tabriz

Kurds form Democratic Party of Kurdistan in Mahabad with Soviet backing

Mossadegh becomes prime minister as head of coalition trying to nationalize petroleum

Shah flees Iran

1953 CIA-assisted military coup brings back shah

1955 Oil consortium agreement doubles Iran's oil profits

1957 SAVAK, secret police, established with US help

1961 Ayatollah Ruhollah Khomeini begins anti-shah campaign

1963 Three days of antiregime riots lead to many deaths; Khomeini exiled

Dam-building projects begun

1965 Tudeh splits in wake of Sino-Soviet dispute

1967 Mohammed Reza Shah crowned Shahenshah (emperor)

1971 Celebration of 2,500 years of Iranian monarchy

Siakal incident sparks leftist religious and secular antiregime guerrilla fighting

1973 Inflation begins to erode middle-class gains

1975 Creation of single political party

Algerian mediation of Shattul Arab dispute between Iran and Iraq

1977 Shah relaxes police activity and protests mount

Writers' Association allowed to revive

Street demonstrations begin when police break up large crowd at poetry readings sponsored by Writers' Association

1978 Anti-Khomeini newspaper article outrages religious elements and leads to riots in Qum

From this follow "40th day" mourning demonstrations

Strikes cripple economy

1979 Shah leaves Iran

Khomeini returns to Iran
American embassy in Tehran occupied and 44 held hostage
Shah dies in Bahaman exile
1980   Iraq attacks Iranian areas in southwest in hopes of capturing oil
            fields and raising anti-Iranian movement among Arab subjects
1981   American hostages released
1988   Iran accepts truce ending Iran-Iraq war
1989   Khomeini dies

Afghanistan

16th century

1504   Babur invades Afghan area, sets up capital in Kabul
1558   Safavids occupy Kandahar
1584   Uzbeks take Badakhshan
1594   Moghuls take Kandahar

17th century

1622   Safavids take Kandahar
1638   Moghuls retake city
1647   Moghuls abandon northern Afghanistan to Uzbeks
1648   Safavids retake Kandahar and Pushtuns prevent Moghul
            reemergence through rebellion
1698   Series of Georgian governors rules Kandahar on behalf of Safavids

18th century

1703   Baluch rebellion against Kandahar governor
1706   Rise of Ghilzai tribal confederacy in Kandahar replacing Abdalis
1709   Ghilzai rise under Mir Wais (vakil, d. 1715) and kill hated Georgian
            governors
1711   Ghilzai defeat combined Iranian and Abdali attack
1717   Abdalis declare independence from Safavids in Herat
1719   Ghilzai attack Iran
1722   Ghilzai take Isphahan and displace Safavids
1736   Nadir Khan (Afshar) takes Kandahar aided by Abdalis
1747   Ahmad Khan (Abdali) takes power after assassination of Nadir Shah
            and sets up rule from Kandahar
1757   Territorial zenith of Durrani empire; Afghan control extends to Delhi
1773   Capital moved to Kabul; loss of Indian territories
1799   Punjab lost to Sikhs, dynastic conflict among Sadozai Durranis

19th century

1809	First agreement with British
1819	Loss of Kashmir to Sikhs
1834	Loss of Peshawar to Sikhs
1838	Tripartite treaty (British, Sikhs, Shah Shuja) to secure throne for Shuja
1839–42	First Anglo-Afghan War
1855	Anglo-Afghan Treaty of Peshawar to prevent Persian and Russian territorial incursions
1878–79	Second Anglo-Afghan War
1880	Amir Abdur Rahman gains throne, receives British subsidy, and pacifies country, laying basis for contemporary Afghanistan
1885	Panjdeh incident; Russian troops annex area claimed by Afghans
1893	Durand agreement settling Afghan border from Baluchistan to Chitral. Validity of agreement disputed by Afghans
1895	Pamir boundary settlement, with Wakhan given to Afghanistan for payment
	Amir Abdur Rahman pacifies Kafiristan; renames it Nuristan after bringing about conversion to Islam

20th century

1903	Mahmud Tarzi returns to Afghanistan from exile to head modernization movement of intellectual and public life
1911	First important Afghan newspaper, *Seraj ul- akhbar-e afghaniyah*, begins publication
1919	Third Anglo-Afghan War results in Afghan control over foreign affairs
1921	Treaty of friendship with Soviet Russia
1923	Promulgation of Fundamental Law or Constitution
1925	Afghani replaces rupee as medium of exchange
1928	Outbreak of revolts against fast-paced reforms of King Amanullah
1929	Dynasty ends with accession of Tajik, Habibullah II. Major role played by leader of Mujaddidi Sufi branch, Hazrat-e Shor Bazar
	Habibullah Ghazi (II) overthrown by another branch of Pushtun royal family
	Nadir Shah closes northern borders to Basmachi, ending use of Afghan territory for continued resistance to Soviet rule in Central Asia
1932	New constitution calling for bicameral legislature
	First Afghan joint-stock company set up by Abdul Majid Zabuli

	Faculty of medicine marks start of Kabul University
1934	Sherkat-i sahami-ye Afghan becomes Bank-i Melli (national bank)
1937	Afghanistan, Iran, Iraq, and Turkey join in Sa'adatabad Treaty of Non-Aggression and Friendship to guard against pressure from all European powers
1938	Pushtu declared national language of Afghanistan, its study made mandatory
1940	Afghanistan declares neutrality in WWII
1946	Helmand River valley irrigation and power project begun as first U.S. development project in Afghanistan (funded by Afghans)
1947	Pushtunistan issue emerges as strain in Afghan-Pakistani relationship as subcontinent divided following British withdrawal
1950	Partially in response to U.S. support of Pakistan, Afghanistan turns to Soviet Union and signs barter trade agreement, oil-exploration agreement that replaces Swedes in northern Afghanistan, and agreement for free transit of Afghan goods through Soviet Union
1949–52	Experiment with democratic elections and debate
1955	New and expanded trade and loan program with USSR calling for road construction, dams, airport improvement, and other building of infrastructure
1956	Kabul turns to eastern bloc for arms after two refusals by U.S.
1959	Women officially appear unveiled in Kabul
1961	Afghanistan and Pakistan cut diplomatic ties over Pushtunistan issue. Afghan trade airlifted by Soviet and Afghan craft
1963	Mohammed Daoud steps down as prime minister, ending border impasse with Pakistan
	Elected governments succeed for ten years
1964	New constitution drafted but political-parties law not signed
	People's Democratic party of Afghanistan (PDPA), known as Khalq (people), comes into being under leadership of Nur Mohammed Taraki, passionately pro-Soviet Pushtun
1965	Press law results in mushrooming of press activity and informal political parties
	Killing of students during political demonstration leads to annual anniversary political activity
1968	Parcham (banner) forms as urban-intellectual rival branch of PDPA; Babrak Karmal at head
1971	Two-year drought taxes government effort to provide for relief and weakens government
1973	Mohammed Daoud displaces government, establishes republic by exiling his cousin the king. Parcham faction of PDPA enters government

1975	Daoud draws Afghanistan closer to Iran and Middle Eastern states and farther from Moscow
1977	New constitution promulgated
	Khalq and Parcham wings of PDPA effect unified front under Soviet sponsorship
1978	Bloody coup by PDPA replaces government with Communist regime bent on social change. Leaders come from foreign-educated Ghilzai intellectuals
	Heavy presence of Russian advisers; Soviet experts installed in all ministries
	Social change by decree arouses resistance
	Parcham faction eased from partnership and forced into diplomatic exile
	Series of friendship and trade treaties, containing secret clauses, signed with USSR
1979	Resistance swells in countryside and engages government troops from Pakistani territory
	Refugee population begins flight to Pakistan, Iran, and elsewhere
	Taraki killed in confrontation with Hafizullah Amin who becomes head of government after September 15
	Soviet rapid deployment troops airlifted into Kabul December 24, followed by ground troops after December 26. They kill Amin, place Parcham head, Babrak Karmal, in power
	Parcham-Khalq feud deepens
1980	Resistance grows; Afghans become largest refugee population in world by 1982
	Soviets withdraw Central Asian reservists
	PDPA retracts Khalq's most offensive changes and attempts to recapture religious authority from Mujahidin with little success
	Afghan youth and children in large numbers sent to Soviet Union, especially Soviet Central Asia, for organized holidays, study, and training
1983	East Germans help train Afghan secret police (KHAD) headed by Najibullah
1985	Soviet troops, 100,000 strong, regularly harassed by Afghan resistance
	Karmal resigns; replaced by Najibullah
1987	Americans begin supply of anti-aircraft weapons forcing Soviet Union to change its war patterns. Soviet losses increase
1988	Afghan resistance attempts another unity organization
	Exiles and refugees create provisional government, but it is strife ridden
1989	February 15, Soviets withdraw troops leaving behind many experts to aid Najibullah government
	Civil war

Central Asia

16th century

	Uzbeks under Mohammed Shaybani Khan emerge as political force in Transoxiana, clash with Safavid Iran in Transcaspia
1552	Kazan falls to Russian forces
1554	Fall of Astrakhan to Russian forces cuts Central Asia from western Turkic areas
1599	Shaybanid line ends; Astrakhan heirs of Chinggissids exiled in Bukhara become khans. Dynasty called Janid or Astrakhanid. Minor Shaybanid line continues rule in Khwarazm

17th century

	Russians move into Kazakh areas
1613	Kalmyks invade Khwarazm
	Shift in Amu River forces change from Urgench to Khiva
1650s	Abu'l Ghazi Bahadur Khan of Khiva writes *Shajareh-ye Turk* (Origins of the Turks) in Chagatai language, one of first "histories" in Turkic
1645–47	Mughuls attempt recovery of former Timurid areas but only reach Balkh
1640–1702	Considerable construction of educational institutions (madrasas) in Bukhara and Samarkand

18th century

	Issues of freedom of Russian slaves and trade dominate diplomatic contact between Bukhara, Khiva
	Russia intent on spying routes to India
	Kazakh relations with Russia dominated by Kalmyk (Mongol) pressures
1700	Independent khanates form at Kokand and Balkh, the latter nominally accepting Bukhara rule
1716–19	Kazakhs appeal to tsar for protection
1730	Small and Middle Horde Kazakhs seek Russian protection from Mongolian expansion
1731	Abul Khayr Khan of Little Horde takes oath of allegiance to Russia
1740	Nadir Shah invasions disrupt political patterns
1743	Karakalpaks seek Russian protection from Kalmyks
1747	Astrakhanids forced to accept Amu River as southern boundary Khiva asserts itself after Nadir Shah dies

1773	Kazakhs aid in Pugachev rebellion
1785	Rise of Manghit dynasty in Bukhara
	Kokand Khanate forms into a rival
	First Russian attempt to attack Khiva

19th century

1801	Inner Horde formed, accepted by Russians, and moves into former Kalmyk lands
1809	Kokand extends power to Tashkent
	Bukharan power expands in wars with Kokand
	Russian advance
1822–45	Russia abolishes position of Kazakh khans
	Kazakhs try to resist peasant encroachment
1865	Tashkent falls to Russian army
	Defeat of Bukhara and formation as protectorate
1867	Imperial decree forms governor-generalship of Turkestan with capital at Tashkent
1871	Turkestan government annexes Ili valley
1873	Khiva submits to Russia as protectorate
	Railroads extended
1876	Kokand annexed by Russia
1881	Gok Tepe, last major Turkmen resistance
1883	American cotton seed and machinery introduced into Turkestan
1884	Russia gives up most of Ili valley
	Bilingual Russian-native schools opened in Turkestan
1885	Merv oasis annexed in Panjdeh incident
	Rebellion of Khan Tore in Ferghana valley
1887	Anglo-Russian accord on Afghan-Bukharan frontier
1892	Tashkent cholera epidemic; riots in Kokand and Tashkent
1896	Russian Resettlement Administration and Trans-Siberian railroad bring close to million settlers to Kazakh lands by 1908
1898	Andijan rebellion
1899	Russian peasants armed and given lands of displaced rebels in Ferghana

20th century

	Rise of Jadidists
1906	Central Asians participate in 3d all-Muslim congress; Kazakhs send representatives to first Duma
	Taraqqi, one of first in series of Central Asian newspapers seeking political reform and equality for Muslims
1908	Jadid (new, reform) schools authorized in Bukhara
1910	Shi'a-Sunni clash in Bukhara, Jadidists driven underground

1911	Tashkent decrees teachers and students must be of same ethnic group, driving wedge between Tatars and local people
1912	First Bukharan newspaper
1914	Bukhara closes all Jadid schools
1916	Great Central Asian revolt triggered by mobilization of Central Asians into worker battalions
1917	Russian revolution
	Union of Muslim Workers
	Series of Central Asian Muslim conferences
	Kokand declares independence
	Alash Orda attempts alliance with White forces but is rebuffed
	Alash Orda tries same with Bolsheviks
1918	Tashkent military attacks Kokand
1919	Frunze Commission set up
1920	Red Army pacifies Central Asia; a few pockets of resistance near Afghan border
	Bukharan People's Consular Republic established
	Khwarazmian People's Consular Republic established
	Government of Transcaspia Region declared in Ashkhabad; British promise help
	Red Army wipes out Turkmen government at Ashkhabad
1921	Kazakhs pass laws to take back from Russians territory on Kazakh plains
	Bukharan Peoples' Consular Republic requests Afghan help against Russian treaty violation
	Turkmen Republic
1922	Enver Pasha killed; important phase of Basmachi ends
1923	Arrest of Sultan Galiev
1925	Uzbek SSR established
1926	Kirgiz Autonomous Republic
1927	Alash Orda members eliminated from public life
1928	Alphabet for Central Asian languages changed to Latin
	Power of religious establishment curtailed
	First five-year plan devastates herds
1929	Tajik SSR established with capital in village of Dushanbe
1932	Karakalpak ASSR
	Major purge of Central Asian intellectuals removes important Jadids
	Fitrat disappears
1933	Purge of Tajik leaders begins
1936	Kazakh SSR, Kirgiz SSR
1938	Show trials and purges
1939	Turkmen president, representing last of nationalist leaders, executed
1940	Cyrillic replaces Latin alphabet

1943	Official institution of Muslim religious directorates revives controlled form of Muslim religious structure
1944	Crimean Tatars exiled to Central Asia
1950s	Contention over acceptability of Turkic epics such as *Manas* and *Alpamish*
1956	Slow start to rehabilitation process
1963	Hungry Steppe transferred from Kazakhs to Uzbekistan
1968	*Muslims of the Soviet East* begins publication in Tashkent Tashkent emerges as representative of Soviet Muslims
1975	Russian-language instruction stressed at expense of local languages
1976	Nurek hydroelectric dam on line in Tajikistan
1985	Purges of Central Asians on charges of corruption upset political picture
1986	Replacement of Kazakh political figures with Slavs leads to Alma Ata riots
1988	Local "nationalist" groups form to promote local languages as official languages on equal or superior footing with Russian Ecological issues (Aral Sea dessication, polluted drinking water, nuclear pollution) mix with nationalist tendencies

Sinkiang

16th century

1503	Shaybani Khan captures Ahmad and Mahmud, brother rulers of Mughulistan, Aqsu, and Tashkent respectively
1514	Said Khan, son of Ahmad, attacks Kashgar, destroys Dughlat family power Said and brothers conquer other Tarim towns to revive old Mughulistan
1533	Said attacks Baltistan and Tibet in *jihad* but falls short of Lhasa
1540	Hazrat-e Makhtum-e Azam (itinerant Bukharan missionary) favored by Chagataids, dies in Kashgar Rival sons of Makhtum-e Azam attach themselves to rival Kirgiz tribes, Aqtaghliq and Qarataghliq
1555–56	Abdur Rashid, son of Said Khan dies; pressure from Kazakhs, Kirgiz, and Uzbeks together with internal strife breaks down Chagataid empire

17th century

	Oirots gain control over Urumchi under leadership of Khotokhtsin (or Khungtayji Batur)

1653	Khotokhtsin enters into diplomatic relations with Russia; acquires firearms
1673	Galdan Khan, son of Khotokhtsin, comes to power
1677	Galdan Khan gains control of Khoshut Mongols near Tibet; some seek Chinese protection
1678	Galdan Khan invades Kashgaria, Oirot governor at Yarkand
	Khojas under Hidayatullah establish theocracy in Kashgaria under Oirot suzerainty
1679	Hami and Turfan come under Oirot dominion, Oirots seek Chinese recognition of empire
1688	Oirots fight in Khalkha wars, pose threat to Ch'ing
1690	Chinese army defeats Galdan Khan
1696	Decisive defeat of Galdan Khan near Urga

18th century

	Khojas pay little heed to Oirot overlords after Galdan Khan's death in 1697
1702	Kirgiz from Yenesei transferred by Oirots into T'ien-shan region
1716	Oirots reemerge as political power and reorganize Kashgaria
	Oirot power expands westward to Lake Balkhash and Lake Zaysan
1717	Oirots under Tsevan-Rabtan attack Khoshot-ruled Tibet, marching to Lhasa from Kashgar
1720	Chinese army retrieves Tibet
1750	Rebellious Oirot faction creates opportunity for Chinese attack on Jungaria
	Chinese set up own Jungar candidate, Amursana
1756	Chinese army reenters as Amursana rebels
1757–58	General Chao-hui undertakes defeat of Oirots and pacification of Jungaria; envoy sent to bring *khojas* under Chinese suzerainty killed
1759	Chao-hui defeats Yarkand and Kashgar, pursues *khojas* into Ferghana, bringing it into Chinese tribute system
	Ambans set up in Urumchi and Yarkand
	Resettlement of Kashgar natives into Ili valley from which Oirots not killed had been driven out
	Other groups resettled on former Oirot areas in Jungaria
1760	Kazakh nomads begin to migrate into Tarbaghatai region despite Peking objection
1771	Ablay Khan of Middle Horde forced to swear allegiance to Manchus
1799	Imperial decree forbids Kazakh allegiance in effort to reduce entry into Jungaria

19th century

1825–31	Jehangir Khoja invades from Kokand to reestablish power in Kashgar
1846	*Khoja* rebellion
1861	Freeing of Russia's serfs leads to peasant settlers on Kazakh lands and forces many toward Jungaria
1862	Tungan rebellion in Kansu spreads to Jungaria
1864	Chinese lose control of Kashgar
	Protocol of Tarbaghatai establishes Chinese border in northwest Jungaria, placing Middle Horde under Chinese suzerainty
1866	Independence declared by Yakub Beg
1867	Yakub Beg removes *khoja* overlord and takes power, setting up capital in Kashgar
1871	Russians occupy Ili valley
	Yakub Beg signs commercial treaty with Russia
1873	Douglas Forsyth signs commercial treaty in Kashgar on behalf of British India
1875–77	Tso Tsung-t'ang army crushes rebellions, joins north and south into new territory, Sinkiang
1876	Yakub Beg dies under suspicious circumstances
1881	Treaty of St. Petersburg negotiates Russian withdrawal from most of Ili and passes in return for money
	Regarded by Chinese as "unequal treaty" in which Chinese lost rightful territory
1883	Kazakhs move further east within Jungaria after second treaty of Tarbaghatai
1884	Imperial decree announces creation of Sinkiang ("New Territory") with the capital at Ti-hua (Urumchi)
	General administration taken over by Chinese rather than Manchus
1890	British set up consulate in Kashgar
	Russian-Asiatic Bank finances cart road from Kashgar to Russian border
1892	Swedish Free Church missionaries arrive to set up medical and educational facilities in Kashgar, Yarkand, and Yangi Hissar
1895	Anglo-Russian agreement gives Russia much territory in Pamirs claimed by Chinese
1899	Russians establish post at Tashgurghan in continued eastward movement

20th century

1911–12	Yuan To-hua, Manchu governor in Ti-hua, resigns in favor of Yang

	Tseng-hsin, a Yunnanese who brings many others into administration of Sinkiang
	Mongols from Outer Mongolia attack Altai area
	Komul seeks independence
	Ili rebels
1913	Russians help Yang secure Mongolian withdrawal from Altai
1916	Yang disposes of Yunnanese plotting against him
	More than 300,000 Kazakhs flee to Sinkiang to avoid Russian labor conscription. Most forced back, a few remain with fellow Kazakhs
1919	Japanese propose dispatching troops to Ili and Chuguchak as part of post-WWI Allied rescue effort of Czechs and Slovaks
1920	Commercial treaty between Yang and Bolsheviks
1921	Last Japanese, operating out of Urumchi, leave Sinkiang
1922	Sinkiang mission to Kabul followed by Afghan mission which develops close following in Yarkand
	British opposition thwarts Afghan attempt to get consular agreement
1924–25	Five Soviet consulates open in Sinkiang, including Khulja and Kashgar, unstaffed since 1918
1926	Germany establishes consulate in Urumchi; it fails
1927	Kuomintang breaks diplomatic relations with USSR but Sinkiang continues relationship
1928	Yang accepts Kuomintang flag for Sinkiang
	Yang assassinated in coup
	Chin Shu-jen becomes governor
1930	Series of Tungan raids led by troops of Ma Chung-ying
1931	Komul Khanate abolished by Chin, sparking rebellion by native Muslims, later joined by Kansu Hue
1932	Turkic Muslim rebellion in Khotan
1933	Sheng Shih-ts'ai replaces Chin
	Newspapers permitted for local populations
	Islamic Republic of Eastern Turkestan established with Khoja Niyaz as president
1934	Ma Chung-ying leaves Sinkiang for USSR
1935–36	Six Great Policies enunciated by Sheng; include anti-British, anti-Japanese, pro-Soviet stances
1937	Soviet economic development model adopted
1938	Sheng invites CCP activists to join government. Among these is Mao Tse-min, brother of Mao Tse-tung who, with others in the CCP, is later accused of anti-Sheng plot and executed
1941	Soviet aid ceases as Germany attacks USSR

	Sheng turns to Kuomintang
1943	Russians withdraw technical personnel and equipment
	Kuomintang insists on direct control of Sinkiang
	Sheng leaves for minor post in Kuomintang
1944	Kazakh rebellion in Ili
	East Turkestan Republic declared in Khulja
	Mainstay of ETR is Kazakh cavalry led by Osman Batur
1946	Khulja group enters Urumchi government; reform promised
1947	Masud Sabri, an Uighur, placed as governor
1948	Sabri, opposed by Ahmedjan Qasim and Khulja group, replaced by Burhan Shahidi
1949	Khulja Group, on way to Peking to negotiate relationship with PRC, dies in suspicious airplane accident
	Provisional People's Government established in December
1950	Sino-Soviet agreement negotiated; jurisdiction over Kazakh areas remains unsettled until 1953
	Chinese troops use Sinkiang area to attack Tibet from west, staging troop movements from Khotan
1951	Osman Batur executed
1953	Pacification and reeducation campaign conducted by CCP
1954	Peking announces that Turkic languages to be written in Cyrillic instead of Arabic alphabet
	Ili Kazakh Autonomous Chou is created
	Ti-hua (the suppressed) dropped officially in favor of Urumchi
1955	Sinkiang-Uighur Autonomous Region created
1956	"Hundred Flowers" liberal period demonstrates continued Uighur and Kazakh desire for independence from China and preference for USSR
1957	Purge of leading Kazakh and Uighur intellectual and political figures
	Chinese make Aksai Chin invasion route a motor road provoking Indian dispute
1958	"Great Leap Forward" curtails minorities' traditional rights, creates large communes that change economic structure of Kazakhs pasturalists in particular
	Use of Latin alphabet announced for Turkic languages
1958–59	Small-scale rebellions following famine resulting from economic dislocation
1960	All Soviet technicians withdraw from Sinkiang
	Peking adopts Latin alphabet for Uighur, Kazakh, and Kirgiz
1962	Peking allows emigration from Sinkiang to USSR and Hong Kong, then attempts to curb this. Riots and massacre by CCP in Khulja lead to more disruption. Soviet consulates issue false passports to émigrés

	Chinese troops in Sinkiang clash with Indian troops
1963	Sino-Pakistani border agreement demarcates border of Sinkiang with Hunza; Chinese give up claims to this area
1964	Soviets beam radio programs to Sinkiang in Uighur, Kazakh, and Kirgiz
1967	Fighting between Uighur separatists and PLA
1969	Sino-Soviet military clash
1979	Policy decision to promote more Turkic minorities to high positions
	Economic liberalization in policy toward livestock and land use
1980	Shanghai youth forcibly working in Sinkiang demonstrate and fast to return home
	Anti-Han Uighur riots in Aksu
1982	Announced reintroduction of Arabic alphabet
1987	Riots in Urumchi protesting nuclear testing and Han presence

Mongolia

16th century

	Revival of Eastern Mongols under Dayan Khan
	Revival of Mongolian culture under Altan Khan
1578	Altan Khan meets Tibetan patriarch of the Yellow Hat at Koko Nor; gives him title of Dalai Lama and accepts his spiritual authority over Mongols, settling Red Hat–Yellow Hat controversy in favor of latter
1586	Erdeni Juu, monastery near Karakorum, and many others built in succeeding years

17th century

1632	50,000 Torgut Mongol families migrate to lower Volga
1634	Legdan Khan, ruler of Chahar Mongols, and resister of Manchu hegemony, dies
1642	Gushri Khan, a Khoshut Mongol, invited to invade Tibet and establish power of Yellow Hat.
	Descendants rule Tibet to 1720
1688	Galdan Khan attacks Khalkha Mongols
1691	Manchus defend Khalkhas from Galdan Khan and incorporate Khalkha Mongols into Manchu state
1696	Death of Galdan Khan

18th century

1756–57	Amursana of Jungar Mongols rebels against the Manchus
	Annihilation of Jungars

1757	Following death of second Jebtsundamba Khutughtu, discovery of incarnations among Mongol princes forbidden; subsequent discoveries from Tibet
1770–71	Torgut Mongol remnants reach Ili valley after century of immigration to lower Volga. Russians demand their return; China does not comply

19th century

1860	Sino-Russian convention regulating limited Russian commercial activity in Outer and Inner Mongolia
	Chinese migration into Mongolian steppe legalized
	First Russian consulate opened in Urga
1881	Treaty of St. Petersburg allows Russia further trade and consular rights in Mongolia
1895	Jebtsundamba Khutughtu seeks Russian aid against Chinese

20th century

1902	Prince Gungsangnorbu establishes in Inner Mongolia first of series of modern schools for Mongols, with Japanese instructors
1909	First Outer Mongolian newspaper
	Chinese railroad reaches Kalgan in Inner Mongolia spurring large influx of colonists
1911	Khalkha Mongols take advantage of Manchu fall to sever allegiance to China
	Khalkhas seek Russian protection
	Urianghai declares independence but Russian troops squelch movement
	China takes steps to avoid similar independence in Inner Mongolia
1912	Schools established in Urga run by russified Buriats
1914	Urianghai area set up as Russian protectorate
1915	Tripartite Treaty of Kyakhta sets boundaries of present MPR
1919	Chinese army marches into Urga; abrogates independence of Outer Mongolia
1921	White Russian army of Baron von Ungern-Sternberg takes Outer Mongolia
	Red Army pursues and wins
1921–24	Dual (secular-religious) government in Outer Mongolia
1923	Chinese railroad reaches Paotow and Suiyuan, making transportation of Chinese colonists and agricultural goods commercially viable
1924	People's Republic of Tannu-Tuva established
	Death of eighth and last Jebtsundamba Khutughtu, head of Outer Mongolian Buddhist church

	Mongolian People's Republic proclaimed
	First MRP constitution adopted
1928	Inner Mongolia divided into four administrative units
1929	MPR government edict forbidding all reincarnations of lamas
1930s	Prince Demchugdungrub (Teh Wang) establishes PIMAPC in Jehol and western areas to promote Mongolian autonomy
	MPR government persecutes Buddhists and closes monasteries
1934	Pro-Chinese princes found Suiyuan Inner Mongolian Autonomous Political Council as rival to PIMAPC
1939	MPR-USSR railroad link completed
1941	Adoption of Cyrillic alphabet for MPR
1944	Tannu-Tuva becomes the Tuvinian Autonomous Oblast of RSFSR
1945	Plebiscite establishes complete independence for Outer Mongolia
1946	China recognizes independence
1947	Inner Mongolian Autonomous Region established by CCP
1955	Chinese laborers brought to MPR
1961	MPR joins United Nations
1962	Chinese workers expelled from MPR in wake of deteriorating Sino-Soviet relations
1972–73	New emphasis on publication in Mongolian in Inner Mongolia
1983	Trainloads of resident Chinese expelled from Ulan Bator; go to PRC
1984	Slow thawing of MPR-PRC relations; border treaty signed
1987	U.S. establishes diplomatic ties with MPR

Tibet

16th century

| 1582 | Dalai Lama founds school for scriptural studies at Kumbum, one of Tibet's largest monasteries |

17th century

| 1642 | Dalai Lama becomes spiritual head of Tibet after Mongols eliminate opposing sects |
| 1650s | Panchen Lama established by Dalai Lama; position comes to be used to rival authority of Dalai Lama |

18th century

1705	Ch'ing attempt to enthrone own candidate as Dalai Lama
1714	Tibetans appeal to Jungars for help against Ch'ing
1717	Jungars seize Lhasa
1720	Ch'ing establish rule with help of popular Dalai Lama; Jungars flee Lhasa

1728	Ch'ing military expedition to Lhasa
1750	Ch'ing military expedition to Lhasa
1792	Ch'ing military expedition to Lhasa
	Tibetan-Nepalese war results in Nepalese troops in Lhasa

19th century

1804	Ch'ing propose "golden urn" lottery for Dalai Lama selection following death of 8th Dalai Lama; Lhasa continually resists this and all subsequent Peking pressure to adopt lottery process
1888	British troops defeat Tibetans in traditional feudatory of Sikkim
1893	Sikkim-Tibet Convention between Britain and China

20th century

1904	Francis Younghusband representing British interests defeats Tibetans and marches into Lhasa
1907	With Anglo-Russian convention two parties agree to recognize Chinese suzerainty over Tibet
1908–10	Chinese invade Tibet; Dalai Lama flees to India
1913	Last Chinese troops leave by way of Calcutta
	Dalai Lama returns to Lhasa
1924	Telegraph lines, small English school for boys, gendarmerie, small modern army created by Dalai Lama; army allowed to deteriorate in 1920s
1928	Chinghai formed into a separate province of China with Sining as its center
1933	Death of 13th Dalai Lama
	Chinese presence again increases; Kuomintang uses Panchen Lama as political tool against Lhasa
1940	Fourteenth Dalai Lama enthroned
1944	Tenth Panchen Lama enthroned in China and a rival in Lhasa
1949	Kuomintang recognizes Panchen Lama candidate in Sining (Chinghai); Lhasa forced to concur in de facto selection in 1951 agreement with CCP
	Lhasa government expels Kuomintang representative
	Tibet declares independence
1950	Chinese Communists attack Tibet
	Tibet appeals to United Nations for relief
1951	Sino-Tibetan agreement by which Tibet incorporated into China but given regional autonomy with promise of no Chinese interference with traditions and government
1954	Military road to Lhasa from China completed

1956	Taxation, secular education, Chinese farmer settlements lead to guerrilla movement
1959	Dalai Lama flees to India; mass exodus of Tibetan refugees
	Chinese military dictatorship imposed
	Lamas persecuted, monasteries closed in attempt to suppress religion as societal force
	Increased Chinese settlers and urban workers
1965	Formal establishment of the Tibet Autonomous Region
1966–76	Monasteries largely destroyed during Cultural Revolution
1972	Modern printing house set up to print Tibetan-language books
1984	Dismantling of communes
1988	Speech by Dalai Lama at European Parliament in Strasbourg; concession of Tibet's foreign policy to PRC in return for Tibetan independence internally
1989	Fourteenth Dalai Lama receives Nobel Peace Prize

Glossary

Adat   Local customary Muslim law in Islamic Persian society.

Aksakal   "White beard"; village elder selected by peers in Central Asia.

Aliahsizlar   "Those without Allah"; atheist zealots in Central Asia.

Amban   Title of Chinese imperial representative in Tibet (and elsewhere in Chinese imperial domains).

Amir   A nobleman, independent chieftain, or native ruler in the Muslim world.

Anjumans   Iranian societies, some secret, formed in the early twentieth century to promote liberal political action.

Arad   Mongolian commoners or herdsmen.

Argal   Dung, used for fuel in Mongolia.

Ashura   The tenth day of the holy month of Muharram, on which Shi'ites mourn the killing of Husayn and his family.

Aul   A grouping of two to eight nomadic families in Central Asia.

Ayimagh (aimak)   "Tribe"; in Ch'ing times, a geographic-administrative division imposed on the Mongols; a province in MPR.

Azalis   Members of the Babi movement who retained the teachings of the Bab after the split of Babism in 1863.

Bab   "Gate"; title traditionally designated for the spokesman of the twelfth and last imam, leader of the Shi'ites, said to be alive and in hiding since the ninth century; assumed by Muslim spiritual leader Sayyid Ali Muhammad of Iran in 1844.

Babism   An obscurantist metaphysical popular movement in Iran formed of the followers of the Bab, influential in the mid-nineteenth century, split into Bahais and Azalis.

Bahaism   A widespread religion, an offshoot of Babism, founded in the nineteenth century by Baha'ullah, a Persian prophet, that strives toward the unification of humankind.

Banak   Long-term loans to craftsmen by wealthy sponsors.

Banner   see *Khoshighun.*

Biy (Beg)   Provincial governor or honorific title in Turkic cultural areas.

Bon   A pre-Buddhist shamanist religion in Tibet.

Buddhism, Tibetan   see *Lamaism.*

Caravansary   Caravan hostel.

Chagatai   The premodern Turkic literary language of Central Asia, also called Turki.

Cham   Tibetan and Mongolian masked dances.

Charkh   A primitive spinning wheel used in Central Asian cities.

Chighulghan   League or group of *Khoshighun;* see *Khoshighun.*

Chishtiya   A Sufi order popular on the subcontinent of India and in Afghanistan.

Darbar   "Council"; Afghanistan.

Dawrah   "Circle"; informal interest groups in Iran.

Dinsizlar   "Those without religion"; atheist zealots in Central Asia.

Farsi   Local Iranian name for the Persian language.

Firman Decree, issued by ruler.

Genbo Village elder, in Tibet.

Ger Nomadic dwelling.

Haji One who has made the pilgrimage to Mecca.

Hamsaya Afghan client groups receiving support or protection.

Hazara Persian-speaking ethnic group living chiefly in the central mountains of Afghanistan.

Ishan Title of the Sufi leader in parts of Inner Asia.

Islam "Submission"; the religion taught by the prophet Mohammad, with two principal sects: the Sunni adhered to by about four-fifths of the believers, and the Shi'a.

Isma'ilis A splinter branch of Shi'ism, important in the Pamir regions of Inner Asia; a large portion is headed by the Aga Khan.

Jadid "New"; movement founded by Tatar Muslims to modernize methods and values of nineteenth-century Muslim society, prevalent in Central Asia.

Jalan "Regiment"; (politics) two or more *Sumun,* see *Khoshighun.*

Jasak Appointed head of a *Khoshighun,* Mongolia; see *Khoshighun.*

Jebtsundamba Khutughtu Title of Supreme Lama, Outer Mongolia.

Jihad "Struggle"; usually translated as "holy war" of Muslims against opponents.

Jirgah Pushtun village council, southern Afghanistan.

Kadim "Old"; Muslim leaders who opposed reforms advocated by Jadidists.

Kadkhoda Village leader in Iran.

Kalantar Mayor in Afghanistan; term used occasionally for informal leaders.

Ketmen Long-handled hoe used in Central Asia.

Khadak   Silk Buddhist prayer scarves, once the main unit of currency in Urga, Outer Mongolia.

Khal'fa   Apprentice, the second stage in the three-stage Central Asian guilds.

Khan   Title given to various dignitaries in Central Asia, Iran, and Aghanistan. Also the title of Uzbek monarchs of Khiva, Bukhara, and Kokand in the premodern period.

Khanate   The jurisdiction of a khan.

Khoshighun   "Banner"; an administrative unit superimposed on the Mongols by the Manchus in Ch'ing times.

Khubilghan   Reincarnation, in Mongolian Buddhism.

Khural   "Council"; Mongolia's Supreme Soviet.

Kibitka   Household, basic social unit of Central Asian nomads.

Kilim   A pileless tapestry-woven rug, used in marriage contracts in Inner Asian Muslim societies.

Kopek   Russian coin, worth one one-hundredth of a ruble.

Korenizatsiia   Soviet policy of recruiting native personnel into the administrative system, "nativization."

Lamaism   The Tibetan form of Buddhism.

Liang   Chinese silver currency.

Machine Khana   Nineteenth-century industrial park in Afghanistan.

Madrasa   Religiously organized seminaries or universities established to educate Muslims in religious law, theology, and other disciplines.

Mahallah   Administrative ward or quarter of a town in a Persian-speaking area.

Mahdi   Religious leader in Muslim societies.

Mai Mai Ch'eng   (Mai mai khota in Mongolian) Main Chinese market in Urga (Ulan Bator), Outer Mongolia.

Majlis   Broad Persian term for gathering, parliament, northern Afghanistan; name of the Iranian legislature.

Maktab   Traditionally Islamic religious primary schools; schools in general.

Muharram   The Holy month, the first month of the Islamic lunar year.

Mujahidin   Those who fight in the jihad; applied especially to resistance fighters in Afghanistan.

Mujtahid   Highly trained Shi'a interpreters of the Koran; related religious texts.

Mulk   Property, land, in Islamic law.

Mulki-khurri-khalis   Lands free from taxes and administrative jurisdiction, in Islamic law.

Murid   Student in the Sufi order.

Murshid   Title of Sufi leader in parts of Inner Asia.

Naadam   A Mongolian national holiday.

Naqshbandiyya   A principal Sufi order with origins in Central Asia.

Nestorian   An eastern Christian sect which emphasizes the human side of Christ, found in Iran, Iraq, and Syria. At one time spread through Central Asia, Mongolia, China, and Siberia.

Nikolai   Russian gold coin.

Nomenklatura   The highest Soviet administrative officers, appointed directly by the Communist party.

Oblast   Province, in Russian administration of Central Asia.

Omach   Wooden plow used in Central Asia.

Pashmina   Fine wool made from undercoat of sheep or goats.

Pir   ''Elder''; title of Sufi leader in parts of Inner Asia.

Qadiriyya   A Sufi order widely followed throughout the Sunni world; especially important in Afghanistan.

Qanat   (Arabic for Persian and Pashto *Kharez*) Elaborate system of underground tunnels for irrigation.

Qazi   Judges in Islamic societies.

Rowshanfikran   "The Enlightened"; modernizing educated elite in Iran.

Ru-Howzi   Farcical, improvisational drama in Iran.

Safi Ali Shahi   A Shi'ite Sufi order in Iran.

Sain Noyon Khan   (title) A lay prince in Mongolia.

Samoprialka   Russian word for *charkh*.

Sardar   Title of prince, Afghanistan.

Sarraf   Bazaar moneylender.

Sarts   Until the sixteenth century Iranian merchants and craftsmen; later, urbanized, Persian-speaking, Central Asian Turkic people as well.

Shabi   Serfs attached to monastic estates, Mongolia.

Shagird   "Student"; first stage in three-stage Central Asian guilds.

Shah   King, prince in Iran.

Shaman   Priest or priest-doctor among northern tribes of Asia.

Shamanism   A religion of the peoples of Mongolia and parts of Central Asia characterized by belief in gods and spirits responsive to shamans.

Shari'at   Islamic law.

Shaykh (Sheik)   A nobleman; (title) a Sufi leader.

Sherkat   Government monopolies in Afghanistan.

Shura-i Islamiyah   Council of Reformists, Tashkent.

Sufism   A movement in Islam, outside of the mainstream of formal traditional Islamic law, which seeks to achieve direct union between individuals and reality *(haqiqa),* or God. This movement evolved under the leadership of masters, whose orders encompassed a variety of paths leading to the mystical union. The different paths, or rules of life, include rhythmic breathing, dancing, whirling, and incantations.

Sumun   "Arrow"; (politics) subdivision of *Khoshighun;* see *Khoshighun.*

Tariqa   "Path"; any of various sets of Sufi practices designed to ascertain *haqiqa* ("reality"; the respective natures of man and God) manifested in orders, or Brotherhoods.

Tayiji   Mongolian nobles.

Ta'ziyah   Shi'ite passion plays based on the martyrdom of the family of the Caliph Ali and especially his son Husayn.

Tekiya   Sufi hostel.

Uezd   County, subdivision of a province in Russian administration of Central Asia.

Ulema   Muslim scholar of theology.

Ulema Jamiyeti   Conservative clerical assembly in Tashkent.

Ustad   "Master"; (guilds) a master craftsman; (title) a Sufi leader.

Vereteno   Russian term for simple, portable loom used by nomads in Central Asia.

Volost   District, formed by groups of villages; subdivision of *uezd* in Russian administration of Central Asia.

Wakf   An endowment used to support a pious foundation such as a *madrasa, maktab,* or mosque.

Wakf avlad   Hereditary *wakfs.*

Wali   "Political leader"; (title) a Sufi leader.

Yasawiyya   A Sufi path originating in Central Asia, see *Islam, Sufism.*

Yerlik   "Local"; used by Turkic-speaking sedentary peoples of southern Sinkiang.

Bibliography

This introductory bibliography of predominantly English-language titles is designed for nonspecialists who wish to pursue further the topics treated in this book. It includes the works cited in the text.

Many of these works draw on the extensive scholarship in French, German, Italian, Russian, Chinese, Japanese, and the languages of the Inner Asian peoples.

I. Special Topics

    A. *International Context*
    B. *Nomadism*
    C. *Modernization Studies*

II. Regions, Countries, Territories

    D. *Inner Asia*
    E. *Iran*
    F. *Afghanistan*
    G. *Central Asia, Russian and Soviet*
    H. *Kazakhstan*
    I. *Kirgizia*
    J. *Tajikistan*
    K. *Turkmenia*
    L. *Uzbekistan*
    M. *Mongolia*
    N. *Tibet*
    O. *Sinkiang*

I. Special Topics

A. International Context

A1 Ahmad, Zahirudden. *Sino-Tibetan Relations in the Seventeenth Century.* Rome: Instituto Italiano per il Medio ed Estremo Oriente, 1970.

A2 Alder, G. J. *British India's Northern Frontier, 1865–95: A Study in Imperial Policy.* Royal Commonwealth Society, Imperial Studies 25. London: Longmans, 1963.

A3 Bradsher, Henry S. *Afghanistan and the Soviet Union.* Durham, N.C.: Duke University Press, 1983.

A4 Braker, Hans. *Die islamischen Türkvölker Zentralasiens und die sowjetischchinesischen Beziehungen.* Cologne: Bundesinstitut für Ostwissenschaftliche und Internationale Studien, 1984.

A5 Clubb, O. Edmund. *China and Russia: The "Great Game."* New York: Columbia University Press, 1971.

A6 Doolin, Dennis J. *Territorial Claims in the Sino-Soviet Conflict.* Stanford: Stanford University, 1965.

A7 Ewing, Thomas E. *Between the Hammer and the Anvil? Chinese and Russian Policies in Outer Mongolia 1911–1921.* Bloomington: Indiana University Uralic and Altaic Series 138, 1980.

A8 Fay, Sidney B. *The Origins of the World War.* 2d ed., rev.; 2 vols. in 1. New York: Macmillan, 1934.

A9 Fletcher, Joseph. "China and Central Asia, 1368–1884." In John K. Fairbank, ed., *The Chinese World Order.* Cambridge, Mass.: Harvard University Press, 1970.

A10 ———. "Ch'ing Inner Asia c. 1800." In John K. Fairbank, ed., *The Cambridge History of China, X, Late Ch'ing, 1800- 1911, Part I.* Cambridge: Cambridge University Press, 1978.

A11 ———. "The Heyday of the Ch'ing Order in Mongolia, Sinkiang and Tibet." In John K. Fairbank, ed., *The Cambridge History of China, X, Late Ch'ing, 1800–1911, Part I.* Cambridge: Cambridge University Press, 1978.

A12 ———. "Sino-Russian Relations, 1800–1862." In John K. Fairbank, ed., *The Cambridge History of China, X, Late Ch'ing, 1800–1911, Part I.* Cambridge: Cambridge University Press, 1978.

A13 Fromkin, David. "The Great Game in Asia." *Foreign Affairs* 58 (Spring 1980): 936–951.

A14 Garthoff, Raymond L., ed. *Sino-Soviet Military Relations.* New York: Praeger, 1966.

A15 Ginsburgs, George, and Michael Matheos. *Communist China and Tibet: The First Dozen Years.* The Hague: M. Nijhoff, 1964.

A16 Hasiotis, Arthur C. *Soviet Political, Economic and Military Involvement in Sinkiang from 1928–1949.* New York: Garland Press, 1987.

A17 Hsu, I. C. Y. *The Ili Crisis: A Study of Sino-Russian Diplomacy, 1878–1881.* Oxford: Clarendon Press, 1965.

A18 Jackson, W. A. Douglas. *The Russo-Chinese Borderlands: Zone of Peaceful Contact or Potential Conflict?* 2d ed. Princeton: Van Nostrand, 1962.

A19 Karamisheff, W. *Mongolia and Western China: Social and Economic Study.* Tientsin: La Librairie Francaise, 1925.

A20 Khalilzad, Zalmay. *The Return of the Great Game: Superpower Rivalry and Domestic Turmoil in Afghanistan, Pakistan, Iran, and Turkey.* Santa Monica: California Seminar on International Security and Foreign Policy, 1980.

A21 Klass, Rosanne, ed. *Afghanistan: The Great Game Revisited*. New York: Freedom House, 1988.

A22 Lattimore, Owen. *Inner Asian Frontiers of China*. New York: American Geographical Society, 1940; rpt. Boston: Beacon Press, 1962.

A23 McCagg, W. O., and Brian S. Silver, eds. *Soviet-Asian Ethnic Frontiers*. New York: Pergamon Press, 1979.

A24 Mancall, Mark. *Russia and China, Their Diplomatic Relations to 1728*. Cambridge, Mass.: Harvard University Press, 1971.

A25 Morgan, Gerald. *Anglo-Russian Rivalry in Central Asia, 1810–1895*. London: Cass, 1981.

A26 Moseley, George. *A Sino-Soviet Cultural Frontier: The Ili Kazakh Autonomous Chou*. Cambridge, Mass.: Harvard University Press, 1966.

A27 Naby, Eden. "The Ethnic Factor in Soviet Afghan Relations." *Asian Survey* 20 (1980): 237–256.

A28 ———. "The Iranian Frontier Nationalities: The Kurds, the Assyrians, the Baluchis, and the Turkmens." In William O. McCagg and Brian S. Silver, eds., *Soviet Asian Ethnic Frontiers*. New York: Pergamon Press, 1979.

A29 Nyman, Lars-Erik. *Great Britain and Chinese, Russian and Japanese Interests in Sinkiang, 1918–1934*. Lund Studies in International History. Stockholm: Esselte Studium, 1977.

A30 Pavlovsky, Michel N. *Chinese-Russian Relations*. New York, 1949; rpt. Westport: Hyperion Press, 1981.

A31 Petech, Luciano. *China and Tibet in the Early 18th Century: History of the Establishment of Chinese Protectorate in Tibet*. Leiden, 1950; rpt. Westport: Hyperion Press, 1973.

A32 Price, Ernest B. *The Russo-Japanese Treaties of 1907–1916 Concerning Manchuria and Mongolia*. Baltimore: Johns Hopkins University Press, 1933.

A33 Rossabi, Morris. *China and Inner Asia from 1368 to the Present Day*. London: Thames and Hudson, 1975.

A34 Sinor, Denis. *Inner Asia and Its Contacts with Medieval Europe*. London: Variorum Reprints, 1977.

A35 Skrine, C. P., and Pamela Nightingale. *Macartney and Kashgar: New Light on British, Chinese and Russian Activities in Sinkiang, 1870–1918*. London: Methuen, 1973.

A36 Vernadsky, G. *The Mongols and Russia*. New Haven: Yale University Press, 1953.

A37 Waldron, Arthur N. *The Great Wall of China: From History to Myth*. New York: Cambridge University Press, 1990.

B. Nomadism

B1 Barfield, Thomas J. *The Central Asia Arabs of Afghanistan: Pastoral Nomadism in Transition*. Austin: University of Texas Press, 1981.

B2 Barth, Fredrik. *Nomads of South Persia: The Basseri Tribe of the Khamseh Confederacy*. London: George Allen and Unwin, 1961.

B3 Eberhard, Wolfram. *Conquerors and Rulers: Social Forces in Medieval China*. 2d rev. ed. Leiden: Brill, 1979.

B4 Graivoronskii, V. V. *Ot Kochevogo Obraza Zhizni k Osedlosti (Na Opyte MNR)* (From the Nomadic Way of Life to Sedentarism [The Case of the MPR]). Moscow: Nauka, 1979.

B5 Jagchid, Sechin. "Patterns of Trade and Conflict between China and the Nomads of Mongolia." *Zentralasiatische Studien* 11 (1972): 177–204.

B6 Khazanov, A. M. *"The Monarchs of Central Asia."*
B7 ———. *Nomads and the Outside World.* Trans. Julia Crookenden. Cambridge: Cambridge University Press, 1984.
B8 Kwanten, Luc. *Imperial Nomads: A History of Central Asia, 500–1500.* Philadelphia: University of Pennsylvania Press, 1979.
B9 Lattimore, Owen. *Nomads and Commissars: Mongolia Revisited.* New York: Oxford University Press, 1962.
B10 Lindner, Rudi Paul. *Nomads and Ottomans in Medieval Anatolia.* Bloomington: Research Institute for Inner Asian Studies, Indiana University, 1983.
B11 *Pastoral Production and Society.* Proceedings of the International Meeting on Nomadic Pastoralism, Paris 1976. New York: Cambridge University Press, 1979.
B12 Salzman, Philip Carl, ed., and Edward Sadala. *When Nomads Settle: Processes of Sedentarization as Adaptation and Response.* New York: Praeger, 1980.
B13 Vladimirtsov, B. *Le régime social des Mongols: Le feodalisme nomade.* Trans. into French by Michel Carsaw. Paris: Librairie d'Amerique et d'Orient, 1948.
B14 Waldron, Arthur N. "Nomadism." In Ainslie T. Embree, ed., *Encyclopedia of Asian History.* 4 vols. New York: Scribners, 1988.

C. Modernization Studies

C1 Appleby, Joyce. "Modernization Theory and the Formation of Modern Social Theories in England and America." *Comparative Studies in Society and History* 10 (March 1978): 259–285.
C2 Apter, David E. *The Politics of Modernization.* Chicago: University of Chicago Press, 1965.
C3 Attir, Mustafa O., et al., eds. *Directions of Change: Modernization Theory, Research and Realities.* Boulder, Colo.: Westview Press, 1981.
C4 Avinieri, Shlomo. "Marx and Modernization." *Review of Politics* 31 (April 1969): 172–188.
C5 Binder, Leonard, James S. Coleman, Joseph LaPalombara, Lucian W. Pye, Sidney Verba, and Myron Weiner. *Crises and Sequences in Political Development.* Princeton: Princeton University Press, 1971.
C6 Black, Cyril E., ed. *Comparative Modernization: A Reader.* New York: Free Press, 1976.
C7 ———. *The Dynamics of Modernization: A Study in Comparative History.* New York: Harper & Row, 1966.
C8 ———. "Marxism and Modernization." *Slavic Review* 29 (June 1970): 182–186.
C9 ———, ed. *The Transformation of Russian Society: Aspects of Social Change since 1861.* Cambridge, Mass.: Harvard University Press, 1960.
C10 Black, Cyril E., Marius B. Jansen, Herbert S. Levine, Marion J. Levy, Jr., Henry Rosovsky, Gilbert Rozman, Henry D. Smith II, and S. Frederick Starr. *The Modernization of Japan and Russia: A Comparative Study.* New York: Free Press, 1975.
C11 Brown, L. Carl, ed. "The Modernization of the Middle East: Ottoman Afro-Asia and Its Successor States." Forthcoming.
C12 Chirot, Daniel. "Changing Fashions in the Study of the Social Causes of Economic and Political Change." In James F. Short, Jr., ed., *The State of Sociology.* Beverly Hills, Calif.: Sage, 1981.
C13 Desai, A. R., ed. *Essays on Modernization of Underdeveloped Societies.* 2 vols. New York: Humanities Press, 1971.
C14 Eisenstadt, S. N. *Modernization: Protest and Change.* Englewood Cliffs, N.J.: Prentice-Hall, 1966.

C15 ———, ed. *Patterns of Modernity*. 2 vols. New York: New York University Press, 1987.

C16 ———. *The Political System of Empires: The Rise and Fall of Historical Bureaucratic Societies*. New York: Free Press, 1963.

C17 Flora, Peter. *Modernisierungsforschung: Zur empirischen Analyse der gesellschaftlichen Entwicklung*. Opladen: Westdeutscher Verlag, 1974.

C18 Gaenslen, Fritz. "Culture and Decision Making in China, Japan, Russia, and the United States." *World Politics* 39 (October 1986): 78–103.

C19 Gumbrecht, Hans Ulrich. "Modern, Modernitat, Moderne." In Otto Brunner, Werner Conze, and Reinhart Koselleck, eds., *Geschichtliche Grundbegriffe: Historisches Lexikon zur Politisch-sozialen Sprache in Deutschland*. 6 vols. Stuttgart: E. Klett, 1972–1987.

C20 Gvishiani, D. M., and S. N. Mikulinskii. "Nauchno-tekhnicheskaia revoliutsiia" (The Scientific-Technical Revolution). *Bolshaia Sovetskaia Entsiklopediia*. 3d ed. 1974.

C21 Inkeles, Alex, and David H. Smith. *Becoming Modern: Individual Change in Six Developing Countries*. Cambridge, Mass.: Harvard University Press, 1974.

C22 Jones, E. L. *The European Miracle: Environments, Economies and Geopolitics in the History of Europe and Asia*. Cambridge: Cambridge University Press, 1981.

C23 Kautsky, John H. *The Political Consequences of Modernization*. New York: Wiley, 1972.

C24 Kim, G. F., ed. *Evoliutsiia Vostochnykh Stran: Sintez Traditsionnogo i Sovremennogo* (The Evolution of Eastern Societies: The Synthesis of Tradition and Modernity). Moscow: Glavnaia Redaktsiia Vostochnoi Literatury, 1984.

C25 Kuusinen, O. V., ed. *Fundamentals of Marxism-Leninism*. 2d rev. ed. Trans. Clemens Dutt. Moscow: Foreign Languages Publishing House, 1963.

C26 Lefebvre, Henri. *Introduction à la modernite*. Paris: Minuit, 1962.

C27 Levy, Marion J., Jr. *Modernization and the Structure of Society: A Setting for International Affairs*. 2 vols. Princeton: Princeton University Press, 1966.

C28 ———. *Modernization: Latecomers and Survivors*. New York: Basic Books, 1972.

C29 Matthes, Joachim, ed. *Theorienvergleich in den Sozialwissenschaften*. Darmstadt: Neuwied Luchterhand, 1978.

C30 "Modernization, Modernity." In Harry Ritter, ed., *Dictionary of Concepts in History*. Westport, Conn.: Greenwood Press, 1986.

C31 Moore, W. E. *World Modernization: The Limits of Convergence*. New York: Elsevier, 1979.

C32 O'Connell, James. "The Concept of Modernization." *South Atlantic Quarterly* 64 (1965): 549–564.

C33 Poggie, John J., Jr., and Robert N. Lynch, eds. *Rethinking Modernization: Anthropological Perspectives*. Westport, Conn.: Greenwood Press, 1974.

C34 Richta, Radovan, ed. *Civilization at the Crossroads: Social and Human Implications of the Scientific and Technological Revolution*. Trans. Marian Slingova. New York: International Arts and Sciences Press, 1968.

C35 Rozman, Gilbert, ed. *The Modernization of China*. New York: Free Press, 1981.

C36 Rudolph, Lloyd I., and Susanne Hoeber Rudolph. *The Modernity of Tradition: Political Development in India*. Chicago: University of Chicago Press, 1967.

C37 Salamon, Lester M. "Comparative History and the Theory of Modernization." *World Politics* 23 (1970): 83–103.

C38 Sinai, I. Robert. *The Challenge of Modernization: The West's Impact on the Non-Western World*. New York: Norton, 1964.

C39 ———. *In Search of the Modern World*. New York: New American Library, 1967.

C40 Wehler, Hans-Ulrich. *Modernisierungstheorie und Geschichte*. Göttingen: Vandenhoech & Ruprecht. 1975.
C41 Wisede, Gunter, and Thomas Kutsch. "Sozialer Wandel als 'Modernisierung'—Problematik eines Konzepts." In Joachim Matthes, ed., *Sozialer Wandel in Westeuropa*. 1979.
C42 Zapf, Wolfgang, ed. *Probleme der Modernisierungs-politik*. Meisenheim am Glan: Hain, 1977.
C43 ———. *Theorien des Sozialen Wandels*. 4th ed. Königstein: Atheneum, 1979.

II. Regions, Countries, Territories

D. Inner Asia

D1 Allworth, Edward. *Nationalities of the Soviet East: Publications and Writing Systems*. New York: Columbia University Press, 1971.
D2 ———. *Soviet Asia, Bibliographies: A Compilation of Social Science and Humanities Sources on the Iranian, Mongolian, and Turkic Nationalities, with an Essay on the Soviet-Asian Controversy*. New York: Praeger, 1975.
D3 Boulnois, L. *The Silk Road*. London: George Allen & Unwin, 1966.
D4 China, State Statistical Bureau. *Statistical Yearbook of China 1986*. New York: Oxford University Press, 1986.
D5 Dabbs, J. S. *History of the Discovery and Exploration of Chinese Turkestan*. The Hague: Mouton, 1963.
D6 Dreyer, June T. *China's Forty Millions: Minority Nationalities and National Integration in the People's Republic of China*. Cambridge, Mass.: Harvard University Press, 1976.
D7 Hedin, Sven Anders. *The Silk Road*. Trans. F. H. Lyon. New York; E. P. Dutton & Co., 1938.
D8 Henze, Paul B. "Politics and Alphabets in Inner Asia." *Royal Central Asian Journal* 42 (January 1956): 29–51.
D9 Huc, E. R. *Travels in Tartary, Tibet, and China during the Years 1844–5–6*. Trans. W. Hazlitt. 2 vols. London: National Illustrated Library, 1852.
D10 Myrdal, J., and G. Kessle. *The Silk Road*. London: Gollancz, 1980.
D11 Sinor, Denis. *Inner Asia: History, Civilization, Languages*. Bloomington: Indiana University Press, 1969.

E. Iran

E1 Abrahamian, Ervand. *Iran between Two Revolutions*. Princeton: Princeton University Press, 1987.
E2 Adamec, Ludwig W., ed. *Historical Gazeteer of Iran*. Graz: Akademische Druck Verlagsanstalt, 1976.
E3 Ahmad, Jalal al-e. *Gharbzadegi (Weststruckness)*. Trans. John Green and Ahmad Alizadeh. Lexington, Ky.: Mazda Publishers; original Persian appeared in Tehran in 1962.
E4 Algar, H. *Religion and the State in Iran: 1785–1906*. Berkeley: University of California Press, 1969.
E5 Arjomand, S. A. *The Shadow of God and the Hidden Imam: Religion, Political Order and Societal Change in Shi'ite Iran from the Beginning of 1890*. Chicago: University of Chicago Press, 1984.
E6 ———. *The Turban for the Crown: The Islamic Revolution in Iran*. New York: Oxford University Press, 1988.

E7 Bakhash, Shaul. *Iran: Monarchy, Bureaucracy and Reform under the Qajars, 1858–1896.* London: Ithaca Press, 1978.

E8 ———. *The Religion of the Ayatollahs: Iran and the Islamic Revolution.* New York: Basic Books, 1984.

E9 Banani, A. *The Modernization of Iran: 1921–1941.* Stanford: Stanford University Press, 1961.

E10 Bartsch, William H. *The Economy of Iran, 1940–1970.* Durham: University of Durham, 1971.

E11 Beck, Lois. *The Qashqa'i of Iran.* New Haven: Yale University Press, 1986.

E12 Bharier, J. *Economic Development of Iran 1900–1970.* Oxford: Oxford University Press, 1971.

E13 Bill, J. A. *The Eagle and the Lion: The Tragedy of American-Iranian Relations.* New Haven: Yale University Press, 1988.

E14 ———. *The Politics of Iran. Groups, Classes and Modernization.* Columbus, Ohio: Merrill, 1972.

E15 Brown, Edward G. *Literary History of Persia, Vol. IV, Modern Times, 1500–1924.* Cambridge: Cambridge University Press, 1924.

E16 Browne, E. G. *The Persian Revolution 1905–1909.* Cambridge: Cambridge University Press, 1910.

E17 Curzon, G. N. *Persia and the Persian Question.* 2 vols. London: Longmans, Green and Co., 1892.

E18 Elwell-Sutton, L. P., ed., *Bibliographical Guide to Iran.* Brighton: Harvester Press, 1983.

E19 Fasa'i, Hasan. *History of Persia under Qajar Rule.* Ed. and trans. H. Busse. New York: Columbia University Press, 1972.

E20 Fischer, Michael M. *Iran: From Religious Dispute to Revolution.* Cambridge, Mass.: Harvard University Press, 1980.

E21 Frye, Richard. *The Golden Age of Persia.* London: Weidenfeld and Nicholson, 1975; 2d ed. 1988.

E22 ———. *The Heritage of Persia.* London: Weidenfeld and Nicholson, 1962; 2d ed., 1976.

E23 Ganji, Manouchehr, and Abbas Milani. "Iran: Development during the Last 50 Years." In Jane W. Jaqcz, ed., *Iran: Past, Present and Future.* New York: Aspen Institute, 1976.

E24 Ghani, Cyrus. *Iran and the West: A Critical Bibliography.* London: Routledge U.K., 1987.

E25 Issawi, Charles Philip. *The Economic History of Iran 1800–1914.* Chicago: University of Chicago Press, 1971.

E26 ———. "The Iranian Economy 1925–1975: Fifty Years of Economic Development." In George Lenczowski, ed., *Iran under the Pahlavis.* Stanford: Hoover Institution Press, 1978.

E27 Jamalzadeh, Mohammad Ali. *Yeki Bud Yeki Nabud* (Once upon a Time). Trans. Heshmat Moayyad and Paul Sprachman. New York: Bibliotheca Persica, 1985.

E28 Jaqcz, Jane W., ed. *Iran: Past, Present and Future.* New York: Aspen Institute, 1976.

E29 Katouzian, Homa. *The Political Economy of Modern Iran: Despotism and Pseudo-Modernism, 1926–1979.* New York: New York University Press, 1981.

E30 Kazemi, F. *Poverty and Revolution in Iran.* New York: New York University Press, 1980.

E31 Keddie, Nikki R. *Roots of Revolution: An Interpretive History of Modern Iran.* New Haven: Yale University Press, 1981.

E32 Kedourie, Elie, and Sylvia G. Haim, eds. *Towards a Modern Iran: Studies in Thought, Politics and Society.* London: Cass, 1980.

E33 Khalilzad, Zalmay, and Cheryl Benard. *"The Government of God": Iran's Islamic Republic.* New York: Columbia University Press, 1984.

E34 Khatib-Semnani, M. A. *Peripherer Kapitalismus, der Fall Iran.* Frankfurt: Haag Herchen, 1982.

E35 Khomeini, Sayyed Ruhollah. *Islam and Revolution: Writings and Declarations of Imam Khomeini.* Trans. and annot. H. Algar. Berkeley: Mizan Press, 1981.

E36 Lambton, A. K. S. *Landlord and Peasant in Persia.* New York: Oxford University Press, 1953.

E37 Library of Congress, General Reference and Bibliography Division. *Iran: A Selected and Annotated Bibliography.* New York: Greenwood Press, 1968.

E38 Looney, R. E. *Economic Origins of the Iranian Revolution.* New York: Pergamon Press, 1982.

E39 McDaniel, R. A. *The Shuster Mission and the Persian Constitutional Revolution.* Minneapolis: Bibliotheca Islamica, 1974.

E40 Miroshnikov, L. *Iran in World War I.* Moscow: Nauka, 1964.

E41 Nashat, Guity. *The Origins of Modern Reform in Iran.* Urbana: University of Illinois Press, 1982.

E42 Oberling, P. *The Qashqa'i Nomads of Fars.* Paris: Mouton, 1974.

E43 Pahlavi, M. R. *Answer to History.* New York: Stein and Day, 1980.

E44 Parsons, A. *The Pride and the Fall: Iran 1974–1979.* London: Jonathan Cape, 1984.

E45 Razavi, H., and Vakil, F. *The Political Environment of Economic Planning in Iran: 1971–1983.* Boulder, Colo.: Westview Press, 1984.

E46 Savory, R. *Iran under the Safavids.* New York: Cambridge University Press, 1980.

E47 Shuster, W. Morgan. *The Strangling of Persia.* New York: Century, 1912; rpt. Washington, D.C.: Mage, 1987.

E48 Sick, G. *All Fall Down: America's Tragic Encounter with Iran.* New York: Random House, 1985.

E49 Stempel, J. D. *Inside the Iranian Revolution.* Bloomington: Indiana University Press, 1981.

E50 Tsukanov, V. P. *Neravnomernost' regionalnogo razvitiia Irana* (The Unevenness of Regional Development in Iran). Moscow: Nauka, 1984.

E51 Utas, Bo. *Women in Islamic Societies: Social Attitudes and Historical Perspectives.* Atlantic Highlands, N.J.: Humanities Press, 1983.

E52 Zabih, S. *Iran since the Revolution.* Baltimore: Johns Hopkins University Press, 1982.

F. Afghanistan

F1 Adamec, Ludwig W. *Afghanistan 1900–1923: A Diplomatic History.* Berkeley: University of California Press, 1967.

F2 ———, ed. *Historical and Political Gazetteer of Afghanistan.* 2 vols. Graz: Akademische Druck Verlagsanstalt, 1976.

F3 American University, Foreign Area Studies. *Afghanistan: A Country Study.* Washington, D.C.: U. S. Government Printing Office, 1973.

F4 Buck, Alfred, et al. *Health and Disease in Rural Afghanistan.* Baltimore: York Press, 1972.

F5 Canfield, Robert L. *Faction and Conversion in a Plural Society: Religious Alignments in the Hindu Kush.* Ann Arbor: University of Michigan Press, 1973.

F6 Dupree, Louis. *Afghanistan.* Princeton: Princeton University Press, 1973.

F7 Dupree, Louis, and L. Albert, eds. *Afghanistan in the 1970s.* New York: Praeger, 1974.

F8 Dupree, Nancy Hatch. *An Historical Guide to Afghanistan.* Kabul: Afghan Air Authority, Afghan Tourist Organization, 1977.

F9 Fry, M. J. *The Afghan Economy.* Leiden: E.J. Brill, 1985.

F10 Gregorian, Vartan. *The Emergence of Modern Afghanistan.* Stanford: Stanford University Press, 1969.

F11 Hall, Lesley. *A Brief Guide to Sources for the Study of Afghanistan in the India Office Records.* London: India Office Library and Records, 1981.

F12 Hammond, Thomas T. *Red Flag over Afghanistan: The Communist Coup, the Soviet Invasion, and the Consequences.* Boulder, Colo.: Westview Press, 1984.

F13 Hanifi, M. Jamil. *Annotated Bibliography of Afghanistan.* New Haven: HRAF Press, 1982.

F14 Kakar, Hasan. *Government and Society in Afghanistan: The Reign of 'Abd al-Rahman Khan.* Austin: University of Texas Press, 1979.

F15 Kamrany, Nake M. *Afghanistan Research Materials Survey.* Los Angeles: Modeling Research Group, University of Southern California, 1985.

F16 Klass, Rosanne, ed. *Afghanistan—The Great Game Revisited.* New York: Freedom House, 1988.

F17 Knabe, Erika. *Frauenemanzipation in Afghanistan.* Meisenheim am Glan: Hain, 1977.

F18 MacGregor, Charles. *Central Asia, Part II: A Contribution toward Better Knowledge of the Topography, Ethnology, Resources and History of Afghanistan.* Calcutta: Government of British India Publication, 1871.

F19 Michel, Aloys Arthur. *The Kabul, Kundez and Helmand Valleys and the National Economy of Afghanistan.* Washington, D.C.: National Academy of Sciences, 1939.

F20 *Military Report on Afghanistan.* Calcutta: Government of British India Publication, 1906.

F21 Poullada, Leon S. *Reform and Rebellion in Afghanistan, 1919–1929: King Amanullah's Failure to Modernize a Tribal Society.* Ithaca, N.Y.: Cornell University Press, 1973.

F22 Roy, Oliver. *Islam and Resistance in Afghanistan.* Cambridge: Cambridge University Press, 1986.

F23 Schinasi, May. *Afghanistan at the Beginning of the Twentieth Century.* Naples: Istituto Universitario Orientale, 1979.

F24 Shahrani, M. Nazif, and Robert L. Canfield, eds. *Revolutions and Rebellions in Afghanistan: Anthropological Perspectives.* Berkeley: Institute of International Studies, University of California, 1984.

F25 Sykes, Percy M. *A History of Afghanistan.* 2 vols. London: Macmillan, 1940; rpt. New York: AMS Press, 1975.

F26 United Nations. *Statistical Profile on Mothers and Children in Afghanistan.* New York: Statistical Office of the United Nations, 1978.

F27 ———. *Vital Health Statistics on Afghanistan.* New York: Statistical Office of the United Nations, 1977.

F28 Wilbur, D. N., ed. *Afghanistan.* New Haven: Human Relations Area Files, 1956.

G. Central Asia, Russian and Soviet

G1 Akiner, Shirin, *Islamic Peoples of the Soviet Union.* London: Kegan Paul International, 1983.

G2 Ali, Agha Shankat. *Modernization of Soviet Central Asia.* Lahore, 1964.

G3 Allworth, Edward, ed. *Central Asia: A Century of Russian Rule.* New York: Columbia University Press, 1967.

G4 ———. *Central Asian Publishing and the Rise of Nationalism: An Essay and a List of Publications in the New York Public Library*. New York: New York Public Library, 1965.

G5 ———, ed. *The Nationality Question in Soviet Central Asia*. New York: Praeger, 1973.

G6 American University. *Handbook of Central Asia*. New Haven: Human Relations Area Files, 1956.

G7 Bacon, Elizabeth. *Central Asians under Russian Rule: A Study in Culture Change*. Ithaca, N.Y.: Cornell University Press, 1966.

G8 Bartold, Vasilii Vladimirovich. *Histoire des Turcs d'Asie Centrale*. Paris: Adrien-Maisonneuve, 1945.

G9 ———. *Istoriia Kul'turnoi Zhizni Turkestan* (History of the Cultural Life of Turkestana). Leningrad: Akademia Nauk SSSR, 1927.

G10 ———. *Turkestan down to the Mongol Invasion*. London: Luzag & Co., 1928; rpt. 1968.

G11 Becker, Seymour. *Russia's Protectorates in Central Asia: Bukhara and Khiva, 1865–1924*. Cambridge, Mass.: Harvard University Press, 1968.

G12 Bennigsen, Alexandre, and Chantal Lemercier-Quelquejay. *Islam in the Soviet Union*. London: Pall Mall Press, 1967.

G13 Bennigsen, Alexandre, and S. Enders Wimbush. *Muslim National Communism in the Soviet Union: A Revolutionary Strategy for the Colonial World*. Chicago: University of Chicago Press, 1979.

G14 Carrere d'Encausse, Helene. *Decline of an Empire: The Soviet Socialist Republics in Revolt*. Trans. Martin Sokolinsky and Henry A. La Farge. New York: Newsweek Books, 1979.

G15 ———. *Islam and the Russian Empire: Reform and Revolution in Central Asia*. Trans. Quintin Hoare. Berkeley: University of California Press, 1989.

G16 ———. *Reforme et revolution chez les Musulmans de l'empire russe, Bukhara 1867–1927*. Paris: A. Colin, 1966.

G17 Chadwick, Nora K., and Victor Zhirmunsky. *Oral Epic of Central Asia*. Cambridge: Cambridge University Press, 1969.

G18 Demidov, S. M. *Sufizm v Turkmenii (Evoliutsiia i Perezhitki)* (Sufism in Turkmenistan: Evolution and Continuity). Ashkabad: Ylym, 1978.

G19 Devletshin, T. *Cultural Life in the Tatar Autonomous Republic*. New York: Research Program on the U.S.S.R., 1953.

G20 Fisher, Alan W. *The Crimean Tatars*. Stanford: Hoover Institution Press, 1978.

G21 Foust, Clifford M. *Muscovite and Mandarin: Russia's Trade with China and Its Setting, 1727–1805*. Chapel Hill: University of North Carolina Press, 1969.

G22 Gleason, Gregory. "Migration and Agricultural Development in Soviet Central Asia." Washington, D.C.: Kennan Institute, Occasional Papers 218, 1986.

G23 Grousset, René. *The Empire of the Steppes: A History of Central Asia*. Trans. Naomi Walford. New Brunswick: Rutgers University Press, 1970.

G24 Hambly, Gavin, ed. *Central Asia*. London: Weidenfeld and Nicholson, 1969.

G25 Haydar, Mirza Muhammad. *The Tarikh-i-Rashidi of Mirza Muhammad Haidar, Dughlat: A History of the Moghuls of Central Asia*. Trans. E. Denison Ross, ed. N. Elias. New York: Praeger, 1970.

G26 Hayit, Baymirza. *Some Problems of Modern Turkestan History*. Dusseldorf: East European Research Institute, 1963.

G27 Holdsworth, Mary. *Turkestan in the Nineteenth Century: A Brief History of the Khanates of Bukhara, Kokand and Khiva*. London: St. Anthony's College, 1959.

G28 Hopkirk, Peter. *Foreign Devils on the Silk Road: The Search for the Lost Cities and*

Treasures of Chinese Central Asia. Amherst: University of Massachusetts Press, 1984.

G29 Ivanov, P. P. *Ocherki po Istorii Srednei Azii (XVI-Seredina XIX v)* (Essays on the History of Central Asia, 16th to the Middle of the 19th Century). Moscow: Akademiia Nauk SSR, Institut Vostokovedeniia, 1958.

G30 Jansen, Godfrey H. *Militant Islam*. New York: Harper & Row, 1979.

G31 Joffe, Muriel. "The Cotton Manufacturers in the Central Industrial Region, 1880s–1914: Merchants, Economics and Politics." Ph.D. diss., University of Pennsylvania, 1981.

G32 Krader, Lawrence. *Peoples of Central Asia*. Bloomington: Indiana University Press, 1966.

G33 Lamb, Alastair. *Asian Frontiers: Studies in a Continuing Problem*. London: Pall Mall, 1968.

G34 ———. *Britain and Chinese Central Asia: The Road to Lhasa 1767 to 1905*. London: Routledge & Kegan Paul, 1960.

G35 Mandel, William. *The Soviet Far East and Central Asia*. New York: Dial Press, 1944.

G36 Massell, Gregory J. *The Surrogate Proletariat: Muslim Women and Revolutionary Strategies in Soviet Central Asia, 1919–1929*. Princeton: Princeton University Press, 1974.

G37 Matuszewski, Daniel C. "Development in Context: Inner Asian Trends (The Last Thirty Years)." *Conference on the Study of Central Asia*. Washington, D.C.: Wilson Center, 1983.

G38 ———. "Empire, Nationalities, and Borders: Soviet Assets and Liabilities." In S. Enders Wimbush, ed., *Soviet Nationalities in Strategic Perspective*. London: Croom-Helm, 1985.

G39 ———. "The Turkic Past in the Soviet Future." *Problems of Communism* 31 (July–August 1982): 76–82.

G40 Murzaev, E. M. *Sredniaia Aziia* (Central Asia). Moscow: Akademiia Nauk SSSR, Institut Geografii, 1968.

G41 Naby, Eden. "Central Asian Literature in Transition: Tajik and Uzbek Prose Fiction, 1909–1932." Ph.D. diss., Columbia University, 1975.

G42 Paksoy, H. B. "Central Asia's New Dastans." *Central Asian Survey* 6 (1987): 75–92.

G43 Park, Alexander G. *Bolshevism in Turkestan, 1917–1927*. New York: Columbia University Press, 1957.

G44 Petrash, Iu. G., and R. N. Khamitova. "Kharakteristiki protsessa modernizatsii sovremennogo Islama v SSSR" (Characteristics of the Modernization of Contemporary Islam in the USSR). *Voprosy nauchnovo ateizma* (Problems of Scientific Atheism) 4 (1967).

G45 Pierce, Richard A. *Russian Central Asia, 1867–1917: A Study of Colonial Rule*. Berkeley: University of California Press, 1966.

G46 ———. *Soviet Central Asia: A Bibliography, 1558–1966*. 3 pts. Berkeley: Center for Slavic and East European Studies, University of California, 1966.

G47 Pipes, Richard A. *The Formation of the Soviet Union: Communism and Nationalism, 1917–1923*. Cambridge, Mass.: Harvard University Press, 1954; rev., 1964.

G48 Quested, R. K. I. *The Expansion of Russia in East Asia 1857–1860*. New York: Oxford University Press, 1968.

G49 Rakowska-Harmstone, Teresa. *Russia and Nationalism in Central Asia: The Case of Tadzhikistan*. Baltimore: Johns Hopkins University Press, 1970.

G50 Rorlich, Azade-Ayse. *The Volga Tatars*. Stanford: Hoover Institution Press, 1986.

G51 Rumer, Boris. *Soviet Central Asia: "A Tragic Experiment."* London: Unwin Hyman, 1989.

G52 Rywkin, Michael. *Moscow's Muslim Challenge: Soviet Central Asia.* Armonk, N.Y.: Sharpe, 1982.

G53 Schuyler, Eugene. *Turkistan: Notes of a Journey in Russian Turkistan, Khokand, Bukhara, and Kuldja.* 2 vols. New York: Scribner, Armstrong & Co. 1877.

G54 Sinor, Denis, ed. *Cambridge History of Central Asia,* vol. 1. New York: Cambridge University Press, 1989.

G55 Skrine, F. H. *The Expansion of Russia.* 3d ed. Cambridge: Cambridge University Press, 1915.

G56 Sokol, Edward D. *The Revolt of 1916 in Russian Central Asia.* Baltimore: Johns Hopkins University Press, 1954.

G57 Treadgold, Donald W. *The Great Siberian Migration: Government and Peasant in Resettlement from Emancipation to the First World War.* Princeton: Princeton University Press, 1957; rpt. Westport, Conn.: Greenwood Press, 1976.

G58 Trimingham, J. S. *The Sufi Orders in Islam.* Oxford: Oxford University Press, 1971.

G59 Vambery, Armin. *Western Culture in Eastern Lands: A Comparison of the Methods Adopted by England and Russia in the Middle East.* London: J. Murray, 1906.

G60 Vitkind, N. Ia. *Bibliografiia po Srednei Asii* (Bibliography of Central Asia). Moscow: Kommunisticheskii Universitet Trudiashchikhsia Vostoka, Nauchnoissledovatelskaia Assotsiatsiia, 1972.

G61 Wheeler, Geoffrey. *The Modern History of Soviet Central Asia.* New York: Praeger, 1964; rpt. Westport, Conn.: Greenwood Press, 1975.

G62 ———. *The Peoples of Soviet Central Asia.* London: Bodley Head, 1966.

G63 ———. *Racial Problems in Soviet Muslim Asia.* London: Oxford University Press, 1967.

G64 Wimbush, S. Enders. "The Politics of Identity Change in Soviet Central Asia." *Central Asian Survey* 3 (July 1984): 69–79.

G65 ———, ed. *Soviet Nationalities in Strategic Perspective.* London: Croom-Helm, 1985.

G66 Zenkovsky, S. A. *Pan-Turkism and Islam in Russia.* Cambridge, Mass.: Harvard University Press, 1960.

H. Kazakhstan

H1 Demko, George J. *The Russian Colonization of Kazakhstan, 1896–1916.* Bloomington: Indiana University Press, 1969.

H2 Inoiatov, Khamid Sharapovich. *Central Asia and Kazakhstan before and after the October Revolution.* Moscow: Progress Publishers, 1966.

H3 Krader, Lawrence. *The Kazakhs.* Washington, D.C.: George Washington University, Human Resources Research Office, 1955.

H4 Olcott, Martha Brill. *The Kazakhs.* Stanford: Hoover Institution Press, 1987.

H5 Suleimanov, B. S., ed. *Kazakhstan v XV-XVIII vekakh (Voprosy sotsial'no-politicheskoi istorii)* (Kazakhstan from the 15th to the 18th Century: Problems in Sociopolitical History). Alma Ata: Akademia Nauka KazSSR, 1969.

H6 Winner, T. G. *The Oral Art and Literature of the Kazakhs of Central Asia.* Durham, N.C.: Duke University Press, 1958.

I. Kirgizia

I1 Dor, Remy. *Die Kirghisen des afghaniischen Pamir.* Graz: Akademische Druck— Universitäts Verlag, 1978.

I2 ———. *Chants du toit du monde: Textes d'origine Kirghiz suivis d'un lexique Kirghiz-Français*. Paris: Maisonneuve, 1982.

I3 Dor, Remy, and Guy Imart. *Le chardon d'echequete: Etre Kirghiz au XXe siecle: Le nomade et le commissaire*. Aix-en-Provence: Université de Provence, Service des publications, 1982.

I4 Hatto, A. T. *The Memorial Feast for Kokotoy-Khan: A Kirghiz Epic Poem*. London: Oxford University Press, 1977.

I5 Imart, Guy. *Kirghiz (Turk d'Asie central sovietique): Description d'une langue de litterisation recente avec une étude sur le dialecte Kirghiz du Pamir afgàn par Remy Dor*. Aix-en-Provence: Universite de Provence, Service des publications, 1981.

I6 Shahrani, M. Nazif Mohib. *The Kirghiz and Wakhi of Afghanistan: Adaptation to Closed Frontiers*. Seattle: University of Washington Press, 1979.

I7 Sherstobitov, Victor P. *Soviet Historiography of Kirghizia*. Moscow, 1970.

J. Tajikistan

J1 Atkin, Muriel. *The Subtlest Battle: Islam in Soviet Tajikistan*. Philadelphia: Foreign Policy Research Institute, 1989.

J2 Gafurov, Bobodzhan Gafurovich. *Istoriia Tadzhikskogo Naroda* (History of the Tajik Peoples). Moscow: Gos izd-vo polit. lit-ry, 1955.

K. Turkmenia

K1 Alladatova, D. A., ed. *Natsional'nyi dokhod Turkmenskoi SSR i faktory ego rosta* (National Income of the Turkmen SSR and Factors of Its Growth.). Ashkhabad, 1979.

K2 Annanepesov, M., ed. *Ocherk etnografii iuzhnogo Turkmenistana (XIX - nach.XX v.)* (A Study of the Ethnography of Southern Turkmenistan [XIX—Beginning of the XX centuries]). Ashkhabad, 1979.

K3 Chekushin, B. S. et al., eds. *Istoriia industriializatsii Turkmenskoi SSR. (Sbornik dokumentov)* (History of the Industrialization of the Turkmen SSR [A Collection of Documents]). Ashkhabad, 1978.

K4 Chokai-ogly, Mustafa. *Turkestan pod vlastiu sovetov* (Turkestan under the Rule of the Soviets). Oxford: Society for Central Asian Studies, 1986.

K5 Durdyev, B. D., ed. *Ocherki istorii gosudarstva i prava sovetskogo Turkmenistana* (Studies of the History of State and Law of Soviet Turkmenistan). Ashkhabad, 1975.

K6 Galuzo, P. G. *Turkestan—koloniia: ocherk istorii Turkestana ot zavoevaniia russkimi do revoliutsii 1917 goda* (Turkestan—A Colony: Study of the History of Turkestan from Its Conquest by the Russians to the Revolution of 1917). Oxford: Society for Central Asian Studies, 1986.

K7 Gapurov, M. G. *Sovetskii Turkmenistan* (Soviet Turkmenistan). Moscow, 1978.

K8 Iazkuliev, B. *Turkmenia*. Moscow, 1987.

K9 Irons, William. *The Yamut Turkmen: A Study of Social Organization among a Central Asian Turkic-Speaking Population*. Ann Arbor, 1973.

K10 Karryev, A., ed. *Istoria kul'tury sovetskogo Turkmenistana: 1917–1970* (History of the Culture of Soviet Turkmenistan). Ashkhabad, 1975.

K11 Osmanova, Z. G., and G. A. Kulieva, eds. *Ocherk istorii Turkmenskoi sovetskoi literatury* (A Study of the History of Turkmen Soviet Literature). Moscow, 1980.

K12 Redzhepov, Ata Redzhepovich. *Ot feodal'noi razdroblennosti k sotsialisticheskoi gosudarstvennosti: partiinoe rukovodstvo stroitel'stvom Turkmenskoi sovetskoi natsional'noi gosudarstvennosti v 1917–1937 gg* (From Feudal Fragmentation to Socialist Statehood: Party Management of the Construction of Turkmen Soviet National Statehood from 1917 to 1937). Ashkabad, 1980.

K13 Tashliev, Sh., ed. *Istoriia sel' skogo khoziaistva i daikhanstva sovetskogo Turkmenistana* (History of Agriculture and the Peasantry of Soviet Turkmenistan). Ashkhabad, 1979–80.

K14 *Turkmenistanda beiik oktiabr sotsialistik revoliutsiiasy ve grazhdanlyk urshy: bibliografik gorkezizhi* (The Great October Socialist Revolution and the Civil War in Turkmenistan: A Bibliography of Sources). Ashgabat, 1968.

K15 *Turkmen Sovet Entsiklopediiasy.* (Turkmen Soviet Encyclopedia). Ashgabat, 1974– .

L. Uzbekistan

L1 Allworth, Edward. *Uzbek Literary Politics.* The Hague: Mouton, 1964.

L2 Aminova, R. Kh., ed. *Istoriia Uzbekskoi SSR* (History of the Uzbek SSR). 4 vols. Tashkent: Akademiia Nauk Uzbekskoi SSR, 1967–1968.

L3 Khanazarov, K. Kh. *Intelligentsiia Uzbekistana: Mesto i Rol' v Obshchestve* (The Intelligentsia of Uzbekistan: Its Place and Role in Society). Tashkent: Fan, 1987.

L4 Medlin, William K., William M. Cave, and Finley Carpenter. *Education and Development in Central Asia: A Case Study of Social Change in Uzbekistan.* Leiden: Brill, 1971.

L5 Muminov, Ibragim Muminovich. *Istoriia Uzbekskoi SSR: S drevneishikh vremen do nashikh dnei* (History of the Uzbek SSR: From the Earliest Times to the Present Day). Tashkent: Fan, 1974.

L6 Tolstov, S. P., ed. *Istoriia Uzbekskoi SSR* (History of the Uzbek SSR). 2d ed. Tashkent: Akademiia Nauk Uzbekskoi SSR, 1955.

L7 Vambery, Armin. *History of Bokhara from the Earliest Period down to the Present, Composed for the First Time after Oriental Known and Unknown Historical Manuscripts.* 2d ed. London: H. S. King and Co., 1873; New York: Arno Press, 1973.

M. Mongolia

M1 Allsen, Thomas T. *Mongol Imperialism: The Policies of the Grand Qan Mongke in China, Russia and the Islamic Lands, 1251–1259.* Berkeley: University of California Press, 1987.

M2 Alonso, M. E., ed. *China's Inner Asian Frontier.* Cambridge, Mass.: Harvard University Press, 1979.

M3 Baddeley, J. F. *Russia, Mongolia, China.* 2 vols. London: Macmillan, 1919; rpt. New York: Franklin, 1963.

M4 Bawden, Charles R. *The Modern History of Mongolia.* New York: Praeger, 1968.

M5 Brown, William A., and Urgunge Onon, trans. and annots. *History of the Mongolian People's Republic.* Cambridge, Mass.: East Asian Research Center, Harvard University, 1976.

M6 *China's Minority Nationalities.* Peking: China Reconstructs, 1984.

M7 Endicott-West, Elizabeth. *Mongolian Rule in China: Local Administration in the Yuan Dynasty.* Harvard-Yenching Institute Monograph Series 29. Cambridge, Mass.: Harvard University Press, 1989.

M8 Fedorov-Davydov, G. A. *The Culture of the Golden Horde Cities.* Oxford: B.A.R., 1984.

M9 Friters, Gerard M. *Outer Mongolia and Its International Position.* Baltimore: Johns Hopkins University Press, 1949.

M10 Gerasimovich, Liudmilla K. *History of Modern Mongolian Literature, 1921–1964*. Trans. John R. Krueger, et al. Bloomington: Mongolia Society, 1970.

M11 Ginsburgs, George. "Local Government in the Mongolian People's Republic, 1940–1960." *Journal of Asian Studies* 20 (August 1961): 489–508.

M12 ————. "Mongolia's 'Socialist' Constitution." *Pacific Affairs* 34 (Summer 1961): 141–156.

M13 Graivoronskii, V. V. *Kooperirovannoe aratstvo MNR: izmeneniia v urovne zhizni 1960–1980* (Herdsmen's Cooperatives in the MPR: Changes in the Standard of Living, 1960–1980). Moscow: Nauka, 1982.

M14 Gungaadash, B. *Ekonomicheskaia Geografiia Mongolii* (Economic Geography of Mongolia). Moscow: Progress, 1984.

M15 Hangin, John Gombojab. "Cyrillic Script Introduced in the Inner Mongolian Autonomous Region in the People's Republic of China." *Mongolia Society Newsletter* n.s. 3 (February 1987): 11.

M16 ————. *Koke Sudur (The Blue Chronicle): A Study of the First Mongolian Historical Novel by Injannasi*. Wiesbaden: Harrassowitz, 1973.

M17 ————. "Traditional Mongolian Vertical Script Is To Be Taught in Public Schools in the Mongolian People's Republic." *Mongolia Society Newsletter* n.s. 3 (February 1987): 12.

M18 Hedin, Sven Anders. *Across the Gobi Desert*. New York: E. P. Dutton & Co., 1933; Westport, Conn.: Greenwood Press, 1968.

M19 ————. *Riddles of the Gobi Desert*. New York: E.P. Dutton & Co., 1933.

M20 Heissig, Walther. *A Lost Civilization: The Mongols Rediscovered*. Trans. D. J. S. Thomson. New York: Basic Books, 1966.

M21 ————. *The Religions of Mongolia*. Trans. Geoffrey Samuel. Berkeley: University of California Press, 1980.

M22 Hyer, Paul. "The Reevaluation of Chinggis Khan: Its Role in the Sino-Soviet Dispute." *Asian Survey* 6 (December 1966): 696–705.

M23 ————. "Ulanfu and Inner Mongolian Autonomy under the Chinese People's Republic." *Mongolia Society Bulletin* 8 (1969): 24–62.

M24 Hyer, Paul, and Sechin Jagchid. *A Mongolian Living Buddha: Biography of the Kanjurwa Khutughtu*. Albany: State University of New York Press, 1983.

M25 *Istoriia Mongol'skoi Narodnoi Respubliki* (History of the Mongolian People's Republic). 2d ed. Moscow: Nauka, 1967.

M26 Jagchid, Sechin, and Paul Hyer. "The Inner Mongolian Response to the Chinese Republic, 1911–1917." In Henry G. Schwarz, ed., *Studies on Mongolia*. Bellingham: Western Washington University, 1979.

M27 ————. *Mongolia's Culture and Society*. Boulder, Colo.: Westview Press, 1979.

M28 ————. "Prince Gungsangnorbu: Forerunner of Inner Mongolian Modernization." *Zentralasiatische Studien* 12 (1978): 147–158.

M29 Karamisheff, W. *Mongolia and Western China: Social and Economic Study*. Tientsin: Librarie Française, 1925.

M30 Lattimore, Owen. *Nationalism and Revolution in Mongolia*. New York: Oxford University Press, 1955.

M31 ————. *Nomads and Commissars*. New York: Oxford University Press, 1962.

M32 ————. "Religion and Revolution in Mongolia: A Review Article." *Modern Asian Studies* 1 (January 1967): 81–94.

M33 Lattimore, Owen, and Fujiko Isono, eds. *The Diluv Khutagt: Memoirs and Autobiography of a Mongol Buddhist Reincarnation in Religion and Revolution*. Wiesbaden: Harrassowitz, 1982.

M34 Legrand, Jacques. *L'Administration dans la domination Sino-Mandchoue en*

Mongolie Qalq-a. Paris: Collège de France, Memoires de l'Institut des Hautes Etudes Chinoises 2, 1976.

M35 Maidar, D. *Arkhitektura i gradostroitel'stvo Mongolii: Ocherki po istorii* (Architecture and Urban Construction in Mongolia: Historical Essays). Moscow: Stroiizdat, 1971.

M36 Maidar, D., and P. Turchin. *Raznolikaia Mongoliia: Etnograficheskii Ocherk* (Multi-faceted Mongolia: An Ethnographic Essay). Moscow: Mysl, 1984.

M37 Maiskii, I. M. *Mongoliia nakanune Revoliutsii* (Mongolia on the Eve of the Revolution). Moscow, 1955.

M38 ———. *Sovremennaia Mongoliia* (Contemporary Mongolia). Irkutsk, 1921.

M39 Matveeva, G. S., et al., eds. *Mongolskaia Narodnaia Respublika: Spravochnik* (The Mongolian People's Republic: A Guide). Moscow: Nauka, 1986.

M40 Mikhailov, G. I. *Literaturnoe nasledstvo mongolov* (The Mongols' Literary Legacy). Moscow: Nauka, 1969.

M41 Miller, Robert James. *Monasteries and Culture Change in Inner Mongolia*. Wiesbaden: Harrassowitz, 1959.

M42 Moses, L. W. *The Political Role of Mongol Buddhism*. Bloomington: Indiana University Press, 1977.

M43 Murphy, George C. S. *Soviet Mongolia: A Study of the Oldest Satellite*. Berkeley: University of California Press, 1966.

M44 Nachukdorji, Sh. *The Life of Sukebatur*. Trans. Owen Lattimore and Urgunge Onon. In *Nationalism and Revolution in Mongolia*. New York: Oxford University Press, 1955.

M45 *Narodnoe Khoziaistvo MNR za 60 let (1921–1981 gg.)* (The National Economy of the Mongolian People's Republic: 1921–1981). Ulan Bator: Central Statistical Board, 1981.

M46 Natsagdorj, Sh. "The Economic Basis of Feudalism in Mongolia." Trans. Owen Lattimore. *Modern Asian Studies* 1 (1967): 265–281.

M47 Ovdiyenko, Ivan. *Economic-Geographical Sketch of the Mongolian People's Republic*. Trans. members of the Mongolia Society. Bloomington: Mongolia Society, 1965.

M48 Pelliot, Paul. *Les Mongols et la papauté*. Paris: A. Picard, 1923.

M49 Pozdneev, Aleksei Matveevich. *Mongolia and the Mongols*. Trans. John R. Shaw and Dale Plank, ed. Fred Adelman and John R. Krueger. Bloomington: Indiana University, 1971.

M50 ———. *Religion and Ritual in Society: Lamaist Buddhism in Late 19th-Century Mongolia*. Ed. John R. Krueger, trans. Alo Raun and Linda Raun. Bloomington: Mongolia Society Occasional Paper 10, 1978.

M51 Ramstedt, Gustav J. *Seven Journeys Eastward, 1898–1912*. Trans. John R. Krueger. Bloomington: Mongolia Society, 1978.

M52 Riasanovsky, Valentin A. *Fundamental Principles of Mongol Law*. Indiana University Publications, Uralic and Altaic Series 43. Tientsin, 1937; Bloomington: Indiana University, 1965.

M53 Ross, Jeffrey A. "The Mongolian People's Republic as a Prototypical Case for the Development of a Comparative Politics of Communist Systems." *Canada-Mongolia Review* 4 (April 1978): 1–15.

M54 Rossabi, Morris. *Khubilai Khan*. Berkeley: University of California Press, 1988.

M55 Rupen, Robert A. "Cyben Zamcaranovic Zamcarano (1880–?1940)." *Harvard Journal of Asiatic Studies* 19 (June 1956): 126–145.

M56 ———. *How Mongolia Is Really Ruled: A Political History of the Mongolian People's Republic, 1900–1978*. Stanford: Hoover Institution Press, 1979.

M57 ———. *The Mongolian People's Republic*. Stanford: Stanford University, 1966.

M58 ———. *Mongols of the Twentieth Century*. 2 vols. Bloomington: Indiana University Press, 1964.

M59 Sanders, Alan J. K. *Mongolia: Politics, Economics and Society.* Boulder, Colo.: Lynne Rienner, 1987.

M60 ———. "Mongolia's Modernisations." *Far Eastern Economic Review* (May 29, 1986): 109–110.

M61 ———. *The People's Republic of Mongolia: A General Reference Guide.* New York: Oxford University Press, 1968.

M62 Sanjaa, B. "Mongolia's Five Treasures." *News from Mongolia* 20 (October 1986). In *Mongolian Society News Letter,* n.s. 3 (February 1987): 31.

M63 Sanjdorj, M. *Manchu Chinese Colonial Rule in Northern Mongolia.* New York: St. Martin's Press, 1980.

M64 Schwartz, Harry. *Tsars, Mandarins, and Commissars: A History of Chinese-Russian Relations.* Garden City, N.Y.: Anchor Books, 1973.

M65 Schwarz, Henry G. *The Minorities of Northern China. A Survey.* Bellingham: Western Washington Center for East Asian Studies, 1984.

M66 Sebes, Joseph, S. J. *The Jesuits and the Sino-Russian Treaty of the Nerchinsk (1689).* Rome: Institutum Historicum SI, 1961.

M67 Serruys, Henry. "Names of Mongol Tribes and Clans in the Early Sixteenth Century." Zentralasiatische Studien 17 (1984): 63–75.

M68 ———. "Smallpox in Mongolia during the Ming and Ch'ing Dynasties." *Zentralasiatische Studien* 14 (1980): 41–63.

M69 Skrine, C. P. *Chinese Central Asia.* London: Methuen, 1926; rpt. New York: Barnes & Noble, 1971.

M70 Tang, Sheng-hao. *Russian and Soviet Policy in Manchuria and Outer Mongolia, 1911–1931.* Durham, N.C.: Duke University Press, 1959.

M71 Tsevegjav, D. "Some Statistics on Mongolian Stockbreeding." *Mongolia* 1 (1986): 16.

M72 U. S. Government. *Area Handbook for Mongolia.* Washington, D.C.: U.S. Government Printing Office, 1974.

M73 Vladimirtsov, B. Ya. *Le Régime social des Mongols: le feodalisme nomade.* Trans. into French by Michel Carsow. Paris: Librairie d'Amerique et d'Orient, 1948.

M74 Vreeland, H. H. III. *Mongol Community and Kinship Structure: A Comparative Analysis of Social Change.* New Haven: Human Relations Area Files, 1953; rpt. Westport, Conn.: Greenwood Press, 1973.

M75 Wiens, Herold. "Geographical Limitations to Food Production in the Mongolian People's Republic." *Annals of the Association of American Geographers* 41 (December 1951): 348–369.

M76 "Within Everybody's Reach." *Mongolia* 5 (1986): 8.

M77 Wolff, Serge M. "Mongolian Educational Venture in Western Europe (1926–1929)." *Mongolia Society Bulletin* 9 (December 1970): 40–100.

N. Tibet

N1 Avedon, John F. *Tibet Today: Current Conditions and Prospects.* New York: U.S. Tibet Committee, 1987.

N2 Aziz, Barbara Nimri. *Tibetan Frontier Families: Reflections of Three Generations from D'ing-ri.* Durham, N.C.: Carolina Academic Press, 1978.

N3 Beckwith, Christopher I. *The Tibetan Empire in Central Asia: A History of the Struggle for Great Power among Tibetans, Turks, and Chinese during the Early Middle Ages.* Princeton: Princeton University Press, 1987.

N4 Bell, Charles A. *The Religion of Tibet.* Oxford: Clarendon Press, 1931; rpt. New York: Gordon Press, 1981.

N5 ———. *Tibet, Past and Present*. Oxford: Clarendon Press, 1924; rpt. New Delhi: Sterling, 1982.

N6 Cammann, Schuyler. *Trade through the Himalayas: The Early British Attempts to Open Tibet*. Princeton: Princeton University Press, 1951.

N7 Carrasco, Pedro. *Land and Polity in Tibet*. Seattle: University of Washington Press, 1959.

N8 Cheng Te-K'un. *An Introduction to Tibetan Culture*. Chengtu: West China Union University Museum Series 6, 1945.

N9 Ekvall, R. B. *Cultural Relations on the Kansu-Tibetan Cultural Frontier*. Chicago: University of Chicago Press, 1939.

N10 Goldstein, Melvyn C. *A History of Modern Tibet, 1913–1951: The Demise of the Lamaist State*. Berkeley: University of California Press, 1989.

N11 ———. "Serfdom and Mobility: An Examination of the Institution of 'Human Lease' in Traditional Tibetan Society." *Journal of Asian Studies* 30 (May 1971): 521–534.

N12 ———. "Taxation and the Structure of a Tibetan Village." *Central Asiatic Journal* 15 (1971): 2–27.

N13 Goodman, Michael Harris. *The Last Dalai Lama: A Biography*. Boston: Shambala, 1987.

N14 Grunfeld, A. Tom. *The Making of Modern Tibet*. Armonk, N.Y.: Sharpe, 1986.

N15 Hopkirk, Peter. *Trespassers on the Roof of the World: The Race for Lhasa*. London: J. Murray, 1982.

N16 International Commission of Jurists. *The Question of Tibet and the Rule of Law*. Geneva, 1959.

N17 ———. *Tibet and the People's Republic of China*. Geneva, 1960.

N18 Kolmas, Josef. *Tibet and Imperial China*. Canberra: Australian National University, 1967.

N19 Landon, Perceval. *Lhasa: An Account of the Country and People of Central Tibet and of the Progress of the Mission Sent There by the English Government in the Year 1903–4*. London: Hurst and Blackett, 1905.

N20 Lopez, Donald S., Jr. "The Monastery as a Medium of Tibetan Culture." *Cultural Survival Quarterly* 12 (1988): 61–64.

N21 MacDonald, David. *The Land of the Lama*. London: Seeley, Service and Co., 1929.

N22 Michael, Franz. *Rule by Incarnation: Tibetan Buddhism and Its Role in Society and State*. Boulder, Colo.: Westview Press, 1982.

N23 Rahul, Ram. *The Government and Politics of Tibet*. Delhi: Vikas Publications, 1969.

N24 Rhodes, M. G. "The Development of Currency in Tibet." In Michael Aris and Aung San Suu Kyi, eds., *Tibetan Studies in Honour of Hugh Richardson*. Warminister: Aris and Phillips, 1979.

N25 Richardson, Hugh E. *Tibet and Its History*. London, 1962; Boston: Shambala, 1984.

N26 Rockhill, W. W. "The Dalai Lamas of Lhasa and Their Relations with the Manchu Emperors of China, 1644–1908." *T'oung pao 11* (1910): 1–104.

N27 Schulemann, Gunther. *Geschichte der Dalai-Lamas*. Leipzig: Harrassowitz, 1958.

N28 Shakabpa, W. D. *Tibet: A Political History*. New Haven: Yale University Press, 1967.

N29 Snellgrove, David L., and Hugh Richardson. *A Cultural History of Tibet*. New York: Praeger, 1968.

N30 "Statement of His Holiness the Dalai Lama." *News Tibet* 22:2 (January–April 1988): 4–5.

N31 Stein, R. A. *Tibetan Civilization*. Trans. J. E. Stapleton Driver. Stanford: Stanford University Press, 1972.

N32 Thurman, Robert A. F. "Lamaism." *Encyclopedia of Asian History* 2, pp. 390–391.

N33 ———. "An Outline of Tibetan Culture." *Cultural Survival Quarterly* 12 (1988): 65–66.

N34 ———. "Tibet." *Encyclopedia of Asian History* 4, pp. 95–97.

N35 Thurston, Anne F. "The Chinese View of Tibet—Is Dialogue Possible?" *Cultural Survival Quarterly* 12 (1988): 70–73.

N36 *Tibet under Chinese Communist Rule.* Dharamsala, India: Information Office of His Holiness the Dalai Lama, 1976.

N37 Tucci, Guiseppe. *The Religions of Tibet.* Trans. Geoffrey Samuel. Berkeley: University of California Press, 1980.

N38 ———. *Tibet.* London: P. Elek, 1973.

N39 ———. *Tibet: Land of Snows.* Trans. J. E. Stapleton Driver. New York: Stein and Day, 1967.

N40 van Walt van Praag, Michael C. *Population Transfer and the Survival of the Tibetan Identity.* New York: U.S. Tibet Committee, 1986.

N41 ———. *The Status of Tibet: History, Rights and Prospects in International Law.* Boulder, Colo.: Westview Press, 1985.

N42 Waddell, L. Austine. *Lhasa and Its Mysteries: With a Record of the Expedition of 1903–1904.* London: Murray, 1905; rpt. Taipei: Ch'eng Wen Publishing Co., 1972.

N43 Younghusband, Sir Francis Edward. *India and Tibet; A History of the Relations which Have Subsisted between the Two Countries from the Time of Warren Hastings to 1910, with a Particular Account of the Mission to Lhasa of 1904.* London: J. Murray, 1910; Delhi: Oriental Publishers, 1971.

O. Sinkiang

O1 Bellew, H. W. *Kashmir and Kashgar: A Narrative of the Journey of the Embassy to Kashgar in 1873–74.* London: Trubner & Co., 1875.

O2 Bennett, Gordon. "The Xinjiang-Uygur Autonomous Region at Thirty." 1986.

O3 Benson, Linda, and Ingvar Svanberg, eds. *The Kazakhs of China.* London University, 1988.

O4 Dreyer, June Tempel. "The Xinjiang Uygur Autonomous Region at Thirty: A Report Card." *Asia Survey* 31 (July 1986): 721–744.

O5 Forbes, Andrew D. W. *Warlords and Muslims in Chinese Central Asia: A Political History of Republican Sinkiang, 1911–1949.* Cambridge: Cambridge University Press, 1986.

O6 Hoppe, Thomas, with the assistance of Ingvar Svanberg, Mark Oppermann, Peter Turpin, and Imke Mees. *Xinjiang—Provisional Bibliography 2: Xinjiang Uighur Autonomous Region, China, Natural Conditions, History, Ethnic Groups, Land Use.* Wiesbaden, 1987.

O7 Jarring, Gunnar. *Literary Texts from Kashgar Edited and Translated with Notes and Glossary.* Acta Regiae Societatis Humaniorum Litterarum Lundensis 74. Lund: Berlings, 1980.

O8 Kiernan, V. "Kashgar and the Politics of Central Asia, 1868–1878." *Cambridge Historical Journal* 2 (1955): 317–402.

O9 Kuropatkin, A. N. *Kashgaria: Eastern or Chinese Turkistan: Historical and Geographical Sketch of the Country, Its Military Strength, Industries and Trade.* Trans. Walter E. Gowan. Calcutta: Thacker, Spink and Co., 1882.

O10 Kuznetsov, V. S. *Economicheskaia politika Tsinskogo pravitel'stva v Sin'tsziane v pervoi polovine XIX veka* (Economic Policy of the Ch'ing Government in Sinkiang in the First Half of the Nineteenth Century). Moscow: An SSSR, Institut Dal'nego Vostoka, 1973.

O11 ———. "Tsin Administration in Sinkiang in the First Half of the Nineteenth Century." *Central Asian Review* 10 (1962): 271–284.

O12 Lattimore, Owen. *Pivot of Asia: Sinkiang and the Inner Asian Frontier of China and Russia*. Boston: Little, Brown & Co., 1950; rpt. New York: AMS Press, 1975.

O13 McMillan, Donald H. *Chinese Communist Power and Policy in Xinjiang 1947–1977*. Boulder, Colo.: Westview Press, 1979.

O14 ———. "Xinjiang and Wang Enmao: New Directions in Power, Policy, and Integration?" *China Quarterly* 99 (September 1984): 569–593.

O15 Naby, Eden, ed. Special issue on Sinkiang. *American Asian Review* 5.2 (Summer 1987).

O16 ———. "Uighur Elites in Xinjiang." *Central Asian Survey* 5 (1986): 241–254.

O17 Norins, M. R. *Gateway to Asia: Sinkiang, Frontier of the Chinese Far West*. New York: John Day Co., 1944.

O18 Whiting, Allen S., and Sheng Shih-ts'ai. *Sinkiang: Pawn or Pivot?* East Lansing, Mich.: State University Press, 1958.

Index

129783